Grammar
Form and Function 3

Second Edition

Milada Broukal

Lawrence J. Zwier
Contributing Writer

Grammar Form and Function 3, Second Edition

Published by McGraw-Hill ESL/ELT, a business unit of The McGraw-Hill Companies, Inc., 1221 Avenue of the Americas, New York, NY 10020. Copyright © 2010 by The McGraw-Hill Companies, Inc. All rights reserved.
1 2 3 4 5 6 7 8 9 10 11 12 QPD 08
ISBN   0-07-719223-0 (Student Book)

Developmental Editor: Amy Lawler
Contributing Writer: Diana Renn
Project Manager: Jenny Hopkins
Publishing Management: Hyphen – Engineering Education
Cover Design: Page2, LLC
Interior Design: Hyphen – Engineering Education

The credits section for this book begins on page 463 and is considered an extension of the copyright page.
Cover photo: Road through Monument Valley (Utah): ©Jeremy Woodhouse/Getty Images.

www.esl.mcgraw-hill.com

The **McGraw-Hill** Companies

Acknowledgements

The publisher and author would like to thank the following educational professionals whose comments, reviews, and assistance were instrumental in the development of the Grammar Form and Function series.

- Mary Ahlman, *Coastline Community College,* Fountain Valley, CA
- Tony Albert, *Jewish Vocational Services,* San Francisco, CA
- Carlos Alcazar, *Newport Mesa Adult School,* Costa Mesa, CA
- Ted Andersen, *INTRAX International Institute,* San Francisco, CA
- Leslie A. Biaggi, *Miami-Dade Community College,* Miami, FL
- Sharon Bidaure, *INTRAX International Institute,* San Francisco, CA
- Grace Low Bishop, *Houston Community College,* Houston, TX
- Taylor Blakely, *Newport Mesa Adult School,* Costa Mesa, CA
- Gerry Boyd, *Northern Virginia Community College,* Annandale, VA
- Marcia Captan, *Miami-Dade Community College,* Miami, FL
- Sue Chase, *Coastline Community College,* Fountain Valley, CA
- Yongjae Paul Choe, *Dongguk University,* Seoul, Korea
- Mei Cooley, *INTRAX International Institute,* San Francisco, CA
- Laurie Donovan, *Houston Baptist University,* Houston, TX
- Elinore Eaton, *INTRAX International Institute,* San Francisco, CA
- Emma Fuentes, *INTRAX International Institute,* San Francisco, CA
- Sally Gearhart, *Santa Rosa Junior College,* Santa Rosa, CA
- Betty Gilfillan, *Houston Community College,* Houston, TX
- Frank Grandits, *City College of San Francisco,* San Francisco, CA
- Mary Gross, *Miramar College, San Diego,* CA
- Martin Guerin, *Miami-Dade Community College,* Miami, FL
- Earl Hayes, *City College of San Francisco,* San Francisco, CA
- Patty Heiser, *University of Washington,* Seattle, WA
- Lillian Johnston, *Houston Baptist University,* Houston, TX
- Susan Kasten, *University of North Texas,* Denton, TX
- Sarah Kegley, *Georgia State University,* Atlanta, GA
- Kelly Kennedy-Isern, *Miami-Dade Community College,* Miami, FL
- Elisabeth Lindgren, *INTRAX International Institute,* San Francisco, CA
- Wayne Loshusan, *INTRAX International Institute,* San Francisco, CA
- Irene Maksymjuk, *Boston University,* Boston, MA
- Linda Maynard, *Coastline College,* Garden Grove, CA
- Gisele Medina, *Houston Community College,* Houston, TX
- Christina Michaud, *Bunker Hill Community College,* Boston, MA
- Mike Missiaen, *INTRAX International Institute,* San Francisco, CA
- Cristi Mitchell, *Miami-Dade Community College-Kendall Campus,* Miami, FL
- Ilene Mountain, *Newport Mesa Adult School,* Costa Mesa, CA
- Susan Niemeyer, *Los Angeles City College,* Los Angeles, CA
- Carol Piñeiro, *Boston University,* Boston, MA
- Michelle Remaud, *Roxbury Community College,* Boston, MA
- Diana Renn, *Wentworth Institute of Technology,* Boston, MA
- Corinne Rennie, *Newport Mesa Adult School,* Costa Mesa, CA
- Jane Rinaldi, *Cal Poly English Language Institute,* Pomona, CA
- Alice Savage, *North Harris College,* Houston, TX
- Sharon Seymour, *City College of San Francisco,* San Francisco, CA
- Larry Sims, *University of California-Irvine,* Irvine, CA
- Karen Stanley, *Central Piedmont Community College,* Charlotte, NC
- Roberta Steinberg, *Mt. Ida College,* Newton, MA
- Margo Trevino, *Houston Baptist University,* Houston, TX
- Duane Wong, *Newport Mesa Adult School,* Costa Mesa, CA

Contents

WELCOME TO

GRAMMAR FORM AND FUNCTION, SECOND EDITION!

Memorable photos bring grammar to life.

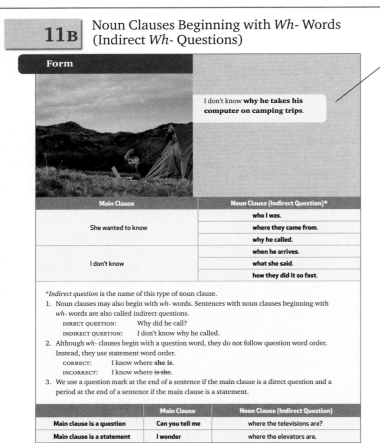

11B Noun Clauses Beginning with *Wh-* Words (Indirect *Wh-* Questions)

Form

I don't know **why he takes his computer on camping trips**.

Main Clause	Noun Clause (Indirect Question)*
She wanted to know	who I was.
	where they came from.
	why he called.
I don't know	when he arrives.
	what she said.
	how they did it so fast.

*Indirect question is the name of this type of noun clause.

1. Noun clauses may also begin with *wh-* words. Sentences with noun clauses beginning with *wh-* words are also called indirect questions.
   DIRECT QUESTION: Why did he call?
   INDIRECT QUESTION: I don't know why he called.
2. Although *wh-* clauses begin with a question word, they do not follow question word order. Instead, they use statement word order.
   CORRECT: I know where **she is**.
   INCORRECT: I know where ~~is she~~.
3. We use a question mark at the end of a sentence if the main clause is a direct question and a period at the end of a sentence if the main clause is a statement.

	Main Clause	Noun Clause (Indirect Question)
Main clause is a question	**Can you tell me**	where the televisions are?
Main clause is a statement	**I wonder**	where the elevators are.

e-Workbook 11B   Noun Clauses and Reported Speech **331**

FORM presentations teach grammar structures through clear comprehensive charts, each of which is accompanied by **a full-color photo** that facilitates students' recall of the target grammar structure.

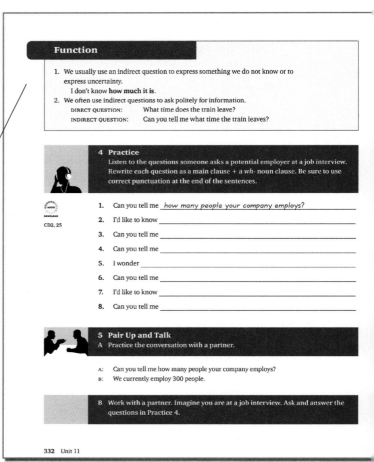

Function

1. We usually use an indirect question to express something we do not know or to express uncertainty.
   I don't know **how much it is**.
2. We often use indirect questions to ask politely for information.
   DIRECT QUESTION: What time does the train leave?
   INDIRECT QUESTION: Can you tell me what time the train leaves?

4 Practice
Listen to the questions someone asks a potential employer at a job interview. Rewrite each question as a main clause + a *wh-* noun clause. Be sure to use correct punctuation at the end of the sentences.

DOWNLOAD
CD2, 25

1. Can you tell me *how many people your company employs?*
2. I'd like to know _____
3. Can you tell me _____
4. Can you tell me _____
5. I wonder _____
6. Can you tell me _____
7. I'd like to know _____
8. Can you tell me _____

5 Pair Up and Talk
A Practice the conversation with a partner.

A: Can you tell me how many people your company employs?
B: We currently employ 300 people.

B Work with a partner. Imagine you are at a job interview. Ask and answer the questions in Practice 4.

332 Unit 11

FUNCTION explanations clarify how and when to use grammar structures.

PRACTICE activities guide students from accurate production to fluent use of the grammar.

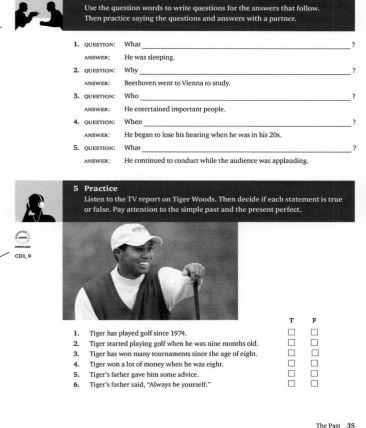

4 Practice

Use the question words to write questions for the answers that follow. Then practice saying the questions and answers with a partner.

1. QUESTION: What _____ ?
   ANSWER: He was sleeping.
2. QUESTION: Why _____ ?
   ANSWER: Beethoven went to Vienna to study.
3. QUESTION: Who _____ ?
   ANSWER: He entertained important people.
4. QUESTION: When _____ ?
   ANSWER: He began to lose his hearing when he was in his 20s.
5. QUESTION: What _____ ?
   ANSWER: He continued to conduct while the audience was applauding.

5 Practice

Listen to the TV report on Tiger Woods. Then decide if each statement is true or false. Pay attention to the simple past and the present perfect.

CD1, 9

		T	F
1.	Tiger has played golf since 1974.	☐	☐
2.	Tiger started playing golf when he was nine months old.	☐	☐
3.	Tiger has won many tournaments since the age of eight.	☐	☐
4.	Tiger won a lot of money when he was eight.	☐	☐
5.	Tiger's father gave him some advice.	☐	☐
6.	Tiger's father said, "Always be yourself."	☐	☐

NEW! LISTENING activities highlight the aural/oral dimension of grammar, further increasing students' ability to use and understand spoken English.

Writing: Write an Essay that Describes a Process

A process is a series of steps that leads to an end, for example, a set of instructions on how to set up a computer. Steps usually occur one after the other, but sometimes they happen at the same time. The order of the steps must be clear. If not, the process cannot be followed accurately. We can use time markers such as *first, then,* and *next* for the main steps.

STEP 1 Discuss these process topics with a partner. Take notes on the important steps.
  a. How courtship works in your country.   c. How you prepare for a New Year's celebration.
  b. How you prepare for a wedding.   d. How you prepare for a religious holiday.

STEP 2 Choose one of the topics from Step 1, or use your own.

STEP 3 Write your essay.
  1. Choose three or four of the main steps for your topic. Write a paragraph for each step. Give details and use some adjective clauses in your paragraphs. Look at the example in the box:
  2. Write an introduction to the essay. Include a thesis statement stating the number of steps and briefly summarize them.
  3. Write a conclusion. Your conclusion can summarize the information in the body and state why this process is important.
  4. Write a title for your essay.

  > Next, we prepare special food for this celebration. Dishes that are from an old tradition are prepared in a special way. For example, we always have a fish dish. The fish, which must be fresh, is boiled …

STEP 4 Evaluate your essay.
  Checklist
  _____ Did you write an introduction, a paragraph for each step, and a conclusion?
  _____ Did you write a title and put it in the right place?
  _____ Did you present the order of the steps correctly and clearly?
  _____ Would a reader who does not know the process understand it from your essay?

STEP 5 Edit your essay with a partner or a teacher. Check spelling, vocabulary, and grammar.

STEP 6 Write your final copy.

WRITING assignments guide students to develop writing and composition skills through step-by-step tasks.

ALL-NEW TECHNOLOGY ENHANCEMENTS!

NEW! e-WORKBOOK frees teachers from homework correction and provides students with a wealth of interactive practice anytime—anywhere.

Add instructional hours to the course, provide homework and additional standardized test-taking exercises, and help learners practice the form and function of each grammar point. Audio segments, photos, and video clips enhance many activities. To purchase e-Workbooks online, visit: **http://books.quia.com/books**.

NEW! AUDIO DOWNLOAD CENTER offers students the ability to access DOWNLOAD and download MP3 files for all of the listening activities in the Student Book. All Audio Download Center content can be found by visiting **www.esl.mcgraw-hill.com/audio**. To navigate the MP3 files, search for your: Unit Number>Page Number>Activity.

NEW! EZ ® Test CD-ROM Test Generator enables instructors to access a wealth of grammar items that they can use and customize to create tests for each unit. Assessment content is also available at **www.eztestonline.com**.

All-new Internet Activity Worksheets in the Teacher's Manual encourage students to access the Internet to read, research, and analyze information, developing necessary academic skills.

NEW SPECIAL FEATURES

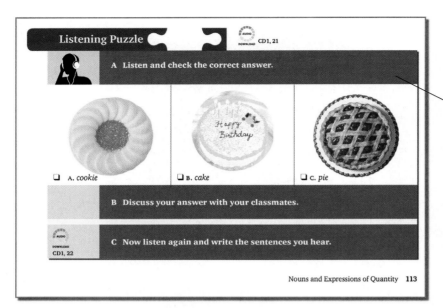

NEW! Listening Puzzles provide audio-based challenges for students to practice new grammar concepts.

NEW! Academic Reading Challenges recycle key vocabulary and grammar in longer contexts, prompting students to integrate their language and critical thinking skill development.

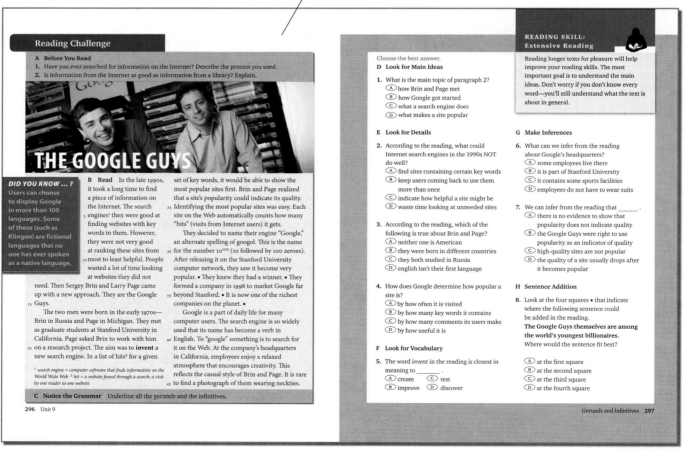

To the Instructor

Series Overview

Form is the structure of a grammar point and what it looks like. Practice of the form builds students' accuracy and helps them recognize the grammar point in authentic situations, so they are better prepared to understand what they are reading or what other people are saying.

Function is when and how we use a grammar point. Practice of the function builds students' fluency and helps them apply the grammar point in their real lives.

Mastery of grammar relies on students knowing the rules of English (form) and correctly understanding how to apply them (function). Providing abundant practice in both form and function is key to student success.

Grammar Form and Function, Second Edition is a three-level, communicative grammar series that helps students successfully learn the rules of essential English grammar (form) and when to apply them and what they mean (function). This new full-color edition ensures academic success and a greater ability to comprehend and communicate with ease through the addition of a robust listening program, new academic readings, new communicative activities, and more opportunities for practice with the e-Workbook.

Components and Unit Organization

Each level of Grammar Form and Function, Second Edition includes:

a **Student Book** with 14 units to present and reinforce the grammar. For each grammar point, the Grammar Form and Function, Second Edition Student Book follows a consistent format:

- **Presentation of Form**. The Student Book presents the complete form, or formal rule, along with several examples for students to clearly see the model. There are also relevant, full-color photos to help illustrate the grammar point.
- **Presentation of Function**. The text explains the function of the grammar point, or how it is used, along with additional examples for reinforcement.
- **Practice**. Diverse exercises practice the form and function together.
- **Application**. Students apply the grammar point in open-ended, communicative activities that integrate all language skills.

- All-new **Listening** and **Listening Puzzle** activities provide students with numerous opportunities to develop their oral/aural and discrimination skills.

- **Pair Up and Talk** encourages students to practice conversation and grammar structures with a partner.
- **Your Turn** invites students to personalize the grammar and language.

- **Read** and **Reading Challenge** activities develop reading and thinking skills.
- **Self-Test**. Students take a quiz to see what they learned and what they still need to work on and practice.

an **e-Workbook** that extends learning, practice, and testing opportunities.

a **Complete Audio CD Program** for teachers that contains all of the listening activities. Each listening activity will include an audio icon with CD and tracking information. The complete audio files are also available for students as **MP3 downloads**.

an **EZ Test ®CD-ROM Test Generator** that includes 560 additional testing items that teachers can use and customize to create tests.

a **Teacher's Manual** to make preparation quick. Each unit of this Teacher's Manual includes:
- an overview of each unit to summarize the contents
- **Notes on the Photos** to describe the photos in the Form and Function sections and give background and cultural information
- **Warm-Up Activities** to engage students in the topic and activate the target grammar
- useful teaching tips and techniques for both new and experienced instructors to provide students with the information they need
- multiple expansion ideas, games, and writing activities to extend and personalize learning
- **Notes on Culture, Notes on Usage, and Notes on Vocabulary** to help instructors clarify, explain, and present the information with ease
- answers to **Frequently Asked Questions** (FAQs) to provide the instructor and students with a deeper understanding of the structure
- answer keys for the exercises and Self-Tests
- **Unit Tests** in a standardized test format and test answer keys to assess understanding and mastery of the unit
- new reproducible **Internet Activity Worksheets** with Internet Activity Procedures to encourage students to expand their online learning and research skills
- new **EZ Test ®CD-ROM Test Generator**
- the **Complete Audio CD Program**

Teaching with Grammar Form and Function, Second Edition

Leveling and Use

While classes and instructors differ, the Grammar Form and Function, Second Edition Student Books are designed to be used in the following levels:

Grammar Form and Function 1, Second Edition: beginning

Grammar Form and Function 2, Second Edition: intermediate

Grammar Form and Function 3, Second Edition: high-intermediate to advanced

Grammar Form and Function, Second Edition is a flexible series, and instructional hours can vary depending on the needs of the learners. Instructors can greatly expand their instruction and increase their students' exposure to and practice with the language by using all of the activities in the Student Book, in the e-Workbook, and the additional suggestions and resources provided in the Teacher's Manual.

Assessment

Students and instructors of the Grammar Form and Function, Second Edition have numerous opportunities to assess progress. There are two **Self-Tests** for each unit – one at the end of each Student Book unit and another at the end of each e-Workbook unit. The Self-Tests build student confidence, encourage student independence as learners, and increase student competence in following standardized test formats.

The Teacher's Manual also includes comprehensive **Tests**. They serve as important tools for the teacher in measuring student mastery of grammar structures. In addition, Grammar Form and Function, Second Edition includes the **EZ Test® CD-ROM Test Generator**. This tool enables instructors to access a wealth of grammar items that they can use and customize to create tests for each unit.

Technology Resources

Grammar Form and Function, Second Edition includes an all-new e-**Workbook**. The e-Workbook can be used to add instructional hours to the course, to provide homework practice and additional standardized testing practice, and to help learners practice the form and function of each grammar point. Color photos, audio segments, and video clips enhance many activities. Students can access the e-Workbook at **http://books.quia.com/ books**.

Grammar Form and Function, Second Edition includes reproducible Internet Activity Worksheets that will help students expand their online learning and research skills.

Grammar Form and Function, Second Edition has a wealth of listening activities to encourage communicative competence. The audio icon in the Student book indicates when audio activities are available and the CD or MP3 tracking number. All of the listening activities are available for the instructors on the Complete Audio CD Program that is packaged with the Teacher's Manual. Students can also access and download the **MP3 files** for these activities at the Grammar Form and Function **Audio Download Center**: Go to **www.esl.mcgraw-hill.com/audio**. Select *Grammar Form and Function, 2nd Edition, Level 3*, and download the audio files.

Unit 1

The Present

Have you ever **seen** a volcano?

1A The Simple Present and the Present Progressive

Form

The king of animals is very lazy and **sleeps** a lot. He **sleeps** 20 hours a day. In this photo, he **isn't sleeping**.

THE SIMPLE PRESENT

1. We form affirmative statements in the simple present with a subject + a base verb or a base verb + -s or -es. We form negative statements with a subject + do not/don't or does not/doesn't + a base verb.

   I **like** football.
   Tom **likes** football.
   We **don't like** tennis.
   Tom **doesn't like** baseball.

2. We form *yes/no* questions in the simple present with *do* or *does* + a subject + a base verb. In short answers, we use a pronoun subject + *do/don't* or *does/doesn't*.

   A: **Do** you **like** soccer?
   B: Yes, I **do**./No, I **don't**.
   A: **Does** Sue **like** tennis?
   B: Yes, she **does**./No, she **doesn't**.

3. We use the *wh-* words what, where, when, how, which, why, who, and *whom* to form *wh-* questions in the simple present. We form these questions in two ways.

   a. If the *wh-* word is the subject of the questions, we do not use the auxiliary verbs *do* or *does*, and we do not change the word order of the subject and the verb.

   Who wants to play basketball?

   b. If the *wh-* word is not the subject of the question, we use the *wh-* word + *do* or *does* + the subject + the base verb.

Why do you **like** basketball?

What does the catcher **do** in baseball?

THE PRESENT PROGRESSIVE

4. We form affirmative statements in the present progressive with a subject + the present of *be* + a base verb + *-ing*. We form negative statements with the present of *be* + *not* + a base verb + *-ing*.

    The players **are trying** to score.

    They **aren't succeeding**.

5. We form *yes/no* questions with the present of *be* + a subject + a base verb + *-ing*. In affirmative short answers, we use a pronoun subject + the present of *be*. In negative short answers, we use a pronoun subject + the present of *be* + *not*. We usually contract negative short answers.

    A: **Is** our team **winning**?

    B: Yes, it **is**./No, it **isn't**.

    A: **Are** you **enjoying** the game?

    B: Yes, I **am**./No, I'm **not**.

    Note: There is no contraction for *am* + *not*.

    CORRECT: No, I'm~~ not~~.

    INCORRECT: No, I ~~amn't~~.

6. We form *wh-* questions in the present progressive in the same two ways as in the simple present, but we use present progressive verb forms.

    Who is winning?

    Why is that player **running** now?

    In speech and in informal writing, we often contract *is* with the *wh-* word. In speech, we also contract *are* with the *wh-* word, but we do not usually write this form.

    Who**'s** speaking?   CORRECT: What **are** you doing today?

    Where**'s** he going?   INCORRECT: ~~What're~~ you doing today?

    How**'s** your car running?

Function

1. Here are the uses of the simple present and the present progressive when we are referring to present time.

The Simple Present	The Present Progressive

a. To describe repeated actions or habits.
    I **get up** at seven every morning.
	a. To talk about something which is in progress at the moment of speaking.
	    It **is raining** right now.

The Simple Present	The Present Progressive
b. To talk about things that are always or generally true. The sun **sets** in the west. It **snows** a lot here.	b. To talk about something which is in progress around the present, but not exactly at the time of speaking. Tony **is looking** for a new job these days.
c. To describe a permanent situation or a condition with no definite start or finish and that is true now. They **live** in Mexico City.	c. To talk about situations which are changing, developing, or are temporary. Computers **are becoming** more and more important in our lives.
d. With adverbs of frequency such as *always, usually, often, sometimes, seldom, rarely,* and *never* to say how often we do something. If the verb is *be*, we put the adverb after the verb. If the verb is not *be*, we put the adverb before the verb. They are **seldom** late. She **often** studies in the library.	d. With adverbs such as *always* or *constantly* to express complaints or annoyance. He is **always** calling me late at night.
e. With time expressions that express habit such as *every day/week/year, in the morning/afternoon/ evening,* and *at night*. We can put these time expressions at the beginning or the end of the sentence. I go to the store **once a week**. **On weekends**, we have dinner at seven.	e. With time expressions such as *now, at the moment, at present, these days, nowadays,* and *today*. We can put these time expressions at the beginning or the end of a sentence. I'm writing an email message **right now**. **These days**, I'm using email to keep in touch with my friends.

2. We also use the simple present and the present progressive to refer to future time. See p. 66 (Section 3c) for information on these meanings.

See p. 66 (Section 3c) for information on these meanings.

1 Practice

Complete the sentences with the simple present or the present progressive. Use the words in parentheses.

I have a guest at my house. She is a friend, and she (stay) <u>'s/is staying</u> with me for
1
a few weeks. I (sleep) _____ on the sofa in the living room while she's here, and
2
she (stay) _____ in my bedroom. I always (get up) _____ at six, have
3 4
breakfast, and then (go) _____ to work. She (not/get up) _____ before
5 6
ten, and then she (eat) _____ breakfast. She only (drink) _____ fresh
7 8
juice. She usually (make) _____ oatmeal for breakfast.
9

She (not/eat) _____ meat, and she (not/drink) _____ tea or coffee.

10
11

She (use) _____ my computer, and she (drive) _____ my car while

12
13

she's here. That's OK. But she (always/make) _____ long-distance phone calls

14

on my phone. That's not OK. I'm glad she (not/stay) _____ long!

15

2 Practice

Listen to the conversation. Complete the sentences with the simple present or the present progressive. Then practice the conversation with a partner.

AUDIO
DOWNLOAD

CD1, 2

KAREN: Hi, Dan! What ___*are you doing*___ these days?

1

DAN: Hi, Karen. _____ a course in computer programming.

2
What about you?

KAREN: Oh, _____ at the library until July.

3

DAN: _____ it?

4

KAREN: Yes, _____ . Right now, they _____ me

5
6
a lot of training. Every morning, they _____ me for an hour.

7
I _____ long hours, and I _____ home until

8
9
seven. But that's OK because I _____ a lot.

10

DAN: I _____ for a job, too. It _____

11
12
harder and harder to find a job. Companies _____ for people

13
who are familiar with new software.

KAREN: _____ about all the new software in your course?

14

DAN: Yes, I _____ .

15

KAREN: How long _____ ?

16

DAN: It usually _____ for eight weeks, but I

17
_____ it in six.

18

KAREN: _____ you a certificate at the end?

19

DAN: Yes, they _____ . They also _____

20
21
students a list of companies to contact about jobs.

3 Practice

Listen to the conversations. Match the conversations that you hear with the uses of the simple present and the present progressive.

AUDIO
DOWNLOAD

CD1, 3

Simple Present	Present Progressive
a. permanent situation	d. action in progress now
b. repeated action	e. changing situation
c. general truth	f. action in progress around the present time

___a___
1

___
3

___
5

___
2

___
4

___
6

4 Practice

The following sentences are about what people generally do or how life is changing. Write *G* (what happens in general) or *C* (changing situation) next to each sentence. Then rewrite the sentences with the correct form of the verb.

___G___ **1.** People (watch) a lot of television.
People watch a lot of television.

_____ **2.** People (go) to the movies a lot these days.

_____

_____ **3.** The seasons (change) four times a year.

_____

_____ **4.** The weather (change) these days.

_____

_____ **5.** Wild animals (live) in the forests.

_____

_____ **6.** Many wild animals (become) extinct.

_____

_____ **7.** People (eat) a lot of meat.

_____

_____ **8.** These days, many people (try) to eat a balanced diet.

_____

5 Pair Up and Talk

A Practice the conversation with a partner.

A: Is anything changing in your country right now?

B: Yes. More people are moving to the cities, so the cities are getting larger.

B Continue the conversation with your partner. Ask about changes in these places:

your city/your town   your home   your school
your country   your neighborhood

1B | Nonaction (Stative) and Action Verbs

Form

Jerry **seems** very worried. I **think** he just heard some bad news.

Most verbs describe actions, but there are some English verbs that describe states and not actions. We call these *nonaction* or *nonaction stative* verbs. Sometimes we call them *nonprogressive* verbs.

Types of Stative Verbs and Examples	Verbs	
1. Verbs of the senses and perception **Do** you **smell** the coffee?	feel hear see	smell sound taste
2. Verbs of mental states	believe doubt	recognize remember

Types of Stative Verbs and Examples	Verbs	
I **remember** him.	forget know mean realize	suppose think understand
3. Verbs of possession My boss **owns** this building.	belong have	own possess
4. Verbs of feeling or emotion **I love** chocolate.	adore astonish enjoy envy fear hate like	love mind please prefer surprise wish
5. Verbs of measurement This watch is nice, but it **costs** too much.	contain cost equal	measure weigh
6. Other verbs that express states You **seem** sad today.	be exist owe	require seem

Function

Kim and Barbara **are training** for a marathon.

1. Stative verbs and action verbs have different uses.

Stative Verbs	Action Verbs

a. A stative verb describes a state. A state means that something is a certain way and stays the same.
    The school **is** big.
    We **own** our apartment.
	a. An action verb describes an action. An action means that something happens.
	    I **am reading**.
	    She **is sitting** in her favorite chair.
	    He **goes** to work every morning.

Stative Verbs	Action Verbs

b. Stative verbs cannot be in the progressive form.
   CORRECT: We have two dogs.
   INCORRECT: We ~~are having~~ two dogs.
   *EXCEPTION: My mother is having another baby.
	b. Action verbs can be in the progressive form.
	    I read a book every week.
	    This week, **I am reading** *Moby Dick*.

2. Some verbs have both a stative meaning and an active meaning.

Verb	Stative Meaning	Active Meaning
appear	She **appears** happy. (appears = seems)	She **is appearing** in a new movie. (is appearing = is starring in)
smell	The milk **smells** strange. (smells strange = has a strange smell)	He **is smelling** the milk. (is smelling = is sniffing)
taste	This food **tastes** delicious. (tastes delicious = has a delicious flavor)	She **is tasting** the food. (is tasting = checking to see if she likes it)
think	I **think** it is a good idea. (think = believe)	I **am thinking** about the problem. (am thinking = am considering)

3. *Be* + an adjective usually expresses a stative meaning.

    She **is** tall.

When we use *be* + an adjective with the progressive, it has a temporary meaning.

The adjective that follows the verb *be* must describe a behavior that the subject can control.

    He **is** polite. (character—permanent state)

    He **is being** polite because his father is in the room. (behavior—temporary state)

   CORRECT: She is beautiful. (permanent state)

   INCORRECT: She ~~is being~~ beautiful. (The subject cannot control this.)

6 Practice

Listen to the conversation. Complete the sentences with the simple present or the present progressive. Then practice the conversation with a partner.

AUDIO DOWNLOAD

CD1, 4

KEN: You _____*have*_____ a nice apartment.
           1

MARIA: Thank you. It _____ small, but it _____ a nice view.
                            2   3
           You can see the lake from here.

KEN: Yes, I _____ it. Your apartment _____ very sunny,
                      4   5
           and I _____ your furniture.
                    6

MARIA: Thank you. I _____ a very good furniture store that
                          7
           _____ great things, and they _____ much.
                8   9
           I _____ there today with a friend. You can come with us
                10
           if you want.

KEN: That _____ great! I _____ about buying a new sofa,
                     11   12
           but I _____ where to go.
                    13

7 Phrasal Verb Practice

A Complete the sentences with the correct phrasal verbs. Use the correct form of the verb. Use each verb only once. Phrasal verbs are taught in Unit 8, section H.

catch up   lie down   wake up

get up   stay up   work out

People have very busy lives. They _____*stay up*_____ late and
                                              1
_____ early. People who don't get enough sleep _____
          2   3
tired in the morning. They often have trouble sleeping. Here are some tips to help you

sleep better:

1. Don't eat or drink a lot before bedtime.

2. Get plenty of exercise. The best time to _____ is in the afternoon.
                                                        4

3. At night, _____ on a comfortable bed in a cool, quiet room.
                      5

4. Don't _____ on your sleep during the day. An afternoon nap can be

    6

good for you but can't replace a good night's sleep.

B   Match the phrasal verb with the correct definition.

1. _____ catch up   **a.** rise from bed

2. _____ work out   **b.** put the body in a flat position

3. _____ wake up   **c.** come from behind

4. _____ get up   **d.** stop being asleep

5. _____ stay up   **e.** do physical exercise

6. _____ lie down   **f.** remain awake

8 Your Turn

A Choose verbs from the following list to make the sentences below true for you. Read your sentences to a partner.

Example

I expect to have a large family.

believe	dislike	expect	know	love	think
deserve	doubt	have	like	prefer	wonder

1. I _____ a large family.

2. I _____ I will be rich.

3. I _____ how I will look in 20 years.

4. I _____ to be lucky.

5. I _____ cooking.

B   Now choose verbs from the list and words of your own to complete the following sentences.

1. My friends and I _____ .

2. I _____ and _____ .

3. I _____ to _____ .

4. _____ .

The Present Perfect and the Present Perfect Progressive

Form

> Katie **has run** six miles (9.6 kilometers).
> She **has been running** for two hours.

THE PRESENT PERFECT

1. We form affirmative statements in the present perfect with a subject + the present of *have* + a past participle. We form negative statements with a subject + the present of *have* + *not* + a past participle.

   I**'ve played** tennis for many years.

   Our team **hasn't won** any games this year.

   We form regular past participles by adding *-d* or *-ed* to a base verb. Sometimes the spelling changes when we add *-d* or *-ed*.

2. We form *yes/no* questions in the present perfect with the present of *have* + a subject + a past participle. In affirmative short answers, we use a pronoun subject + the present of *have* + *not*. We usually contract negative short answers.

   A: **Have** you ever **played** squash?

   B: Yes, I **have.**/No, I **haven't.**

3. We use the *wh-* words *what, where, when, how, which, why, who,* and *whom* to form *wh-* questions in the present perfect.

   Who has won the most games?

   How many games **have** they **won**?

Who**'s** finished?	CORRECT:	Where **have** they gone?
Where**'s** she traveled?	INCORRECT:	~~Where've~~ they gone?

4. We often use adverbs such as *ever, never, already, yet, still,* and *so far* with the present perfect. They have the following positions in a sentence:

Position	Adverb	Examples
Beginning of the Sentence	so far*	**So far,** he hasn't said anything.
Before the Auxiliary	still	He **still** hasn't said anything.
Before the Past Participle	ever	Have you **ever** been to India? I haven't **ever** been to Beijing.
	never	He has **never** been to India.
	already	Have you **already** eaten?
	just	I've **just** returned from Morocco.
End of the Sentence	already	He has left **already**.
	yet	Has he left **yet**? He hasn't left **yet**.
	so far	He hasn't said anything **so far**.

*When *so far* comes at the beginning of a sentence, we put a comma after it.

THE PRESENT PERFECT PROGRESSIVE

5. We form affirmative statements in the present perfect progressive with a subject + the present of *have + been +* a verb + *-ing*. We form negative statements with a subject + the present of *have + not + been +* a verb + *-ing*.

    They**'ve been practicing** all morning, so they're tired.

    She **hasn't been playing** basketball very long.

6. We form *yes/no* questions in the present perfect progressive with *have* or *has* + a subject + *been +* a verb + *-ing*. In affirmative short answers, we use a pronoun subject + *have* or *has*. In negative short answers, we use a pronoun subject + *'s not/hasn't* or *'ve not/haven't*.

    A: **Have** they **been winning** a lot of games?

    B: Yes, they **have.**/No, they **haven't.**

7. We use the *wh-* words *what, where, when, how, which, why, who,* and *whom* to form *wh-* questions in the present perfect progressive.

    Who has been scoring the most goals?

    Why have they **been losing** so much?

8. In speech and informal writing, we often contract *has ('s)* with the *wh-* word. In speech, we also contract *have* with the *wh-* word, but we do not usually write this form.

    Who**'s** been trying hard?

    Where**'s** she been living?

Function

1. Here are the uses of the present perfect and the present perfect progressive.

The Present Perfect	The Present Perfect Progressive
a. To talk about something that started in the past and that continues up to the present. I **have been** here for 30 minutes. (I came here 30 minutes ago, and I am still here.)	a. To emphasize the continuation of an action that started in the past and continues into the present. I **have been waiting** for your call all morning. (I have been waiting all morning, and I am still waiting.)
b. To talk about a completed action that has an importance in the present. She **has done** her homework. (Therefore, she can watch television now.)	b. To talk about an action that may or may not be completed. She **'s been doing** her homework. (Maybe she has finished it, maybe she has not.)
c. To talk about what has been achieved in a period of time. He **has written** three letters this morning.	c. To talk about how long something has been in progress. He **has been writing** all morning.
d. To describe a situation that is more permanent and that continues into the present. She **has always worked** there.	d. To describe a situation that is more temporary and that continues into the present. She's **been working** here for a couple of weeks.
	e. To talk about evidence in the present that shows that an action was happening in the recent past. A: What smells so good? B: Oh, I**'ve been making** cookies.

2. We can use the present perfect or the present perfect progressive with action verbs.

   We**'ve finished** our work.

   We**'ve been finishing** our work.

   But we do not use the present perfect progressive with stative verbs.

   CORRECT: I've had this car for five years.

   INCORRECT: I've ~~been having~~ this car for five years.

3. We often use *for* or *since* with the present perfect and the present perfect progressive.

   We use *for* to talk about a length of time. We use *since* to talk about a point in time.

   I've been waiting here **for an hour**.

   I've been waiting here **since 2:00** P.M.

4. With certain verbs used with *for* and *since*, there is little or no difference between the present perfect and the present perfect progressive. These verbs include *work, play, live, study, teach, stay, feel, compete, practice,* and *wear*.

We **have lived/have been living** in this house for 15 years.

5. We often use adverbs such as *ever, never, already, yet, still, just,* and *so far* with the present perfect.

Adverb	Meaning and Common Uses	Examples
so far	At any time up to now. Use in all types of sentences.	**So far,** I've been to three countries. I haven't been to Argentina **so far.** Have you been only to Argentina **so far**? How many cities have you visited **so far**?
still	Expected at some time before now. Use in negative statements.	He **still** hasn't visited Egypt.
ever	At any time up to the present. Use in negative statements and *yes/no* questions.	I haven't **ever** traveled to Vietnam. Have you **ever** been to Thailand?
never	At no time up to the present. Use in affirmative statements.	I have **never** sailed on a ship.
already	At some time sooner than expected. Use in affirmative statements, *yes/no* questions, and *wh-* questions.	They have **already** packed. Have you **already** bought your ticket? What have they **already** done?
just	Very recently. Use in all types of sentences.	We've **just** landed. The bus hasn't **just** arrived. It's **just** left. Has the bus **just** arrived? Where have they **just** gone?
yet	Expected at some time before now. Use in negative statements and *yes/no* questions.	They haven't called for a taxi **yet**. Have you left **yet**?

9 Practice

Complete the sentences with the present perfect or the present perfect progressive of the verbs in parentheses. Sometimes both are possible.

1. Soccer (be) _____*has been*_____ the most popular sport in the world for a long time.
2. People (play) _____ soccer in England for hundreds of years.
3. Since 1870, there (be) _____ 11 players on one side.
4. Women (compete) _____ in the Olympic Games since 1900.
5. Parachuting (be) _____ an official sport only since 1951.
6. Women (compete) _____ in singles matches at Wimbledon since 1884.
7. In the United States, baseball (become) _____ the country's favorite sport.
8. Our basketball team (practice) _____ all morning.
9. Our team (win) _____ three games so far.
10. My friends (watch) _____ that baseball game for the last two hours!

10 Practice

Listen to the TV report about Barbara Bates. Choose the correct adverb from the choices in parentheses and put it in the correct position in the sentence. Only one adverb is correct.

CD1, 5

1. She's ^*just* finished a romantic comedy. (still/just/ever)

2. She's traveled to many parts of the world. (yet/already)

3. She's done lots of comedies over the years. (already/just/yet)

4. She hasn't acted in a drama. (never/still)

5. Has she won an Oscar? (still/yet)

6. She's not won an Oscar. (so far/never)

7. She hasn't given up. (never/still)

8. She's not had the right part. (yet/never)

11 Practice

You are a newspaper reporter who is interviewing J.K. Rowling. Write *wh-* or *yes/no* questions that go with her answers. Use the simple present or the present perfect.

J.K. Rowling is an author. She has written a series of books about a boy named Harry Potter. Harry Potter is a wizard—he has magical powers. The Harry Potter books are very popular among children.

Rowling was born in the United Kingdom in 1965. In 1990, she went to Portugal to teach English. There, she married a Portuguese man and had a daughter. She wasn't happy in her marriage, so she came back to the U.K. She had no job and very little money. She started to write the first Harry Potter book. Five years later, she finished the book and sent it to publishers. The publishers did not like her book. Finally, one publisher liked it, and soon the book was in the bookstores. The book quickly became a best seller in England, and Rowling wrote more Harry Potter books.

By now, publishers have translated the Harry Potter books into 42 languages, and the books are best sellers all over the world. In fact, Rowling has sold over 100 million books. Hollywood has made movies of the books, and Rowling has made a lot of money. But the most important thing she has done is to write books that children love to read.

1. QUESTION: *What have you written?*

   ANSWER: I've written a series of books about a very special boy named Harry Potter.

2. QUESTION: _____

   ANSWER: He's special because he has magical powers.

3. QUESTION: _____

   ANSWER: I live in the U.K.

4. QUESTION: _____

   in other countries?

   ANSWER: Yes. I've lived in Portugal, too.

5. QUESTION: _____

   ANSWER: Up to now, they've been translated into 42 languages.

6. QUESTION: _____

   ANSWER: Up to now, over 100 million have been sold.

7. QUESTION: _____

   ANSWER: Hmm. I think it's to write books that children love to read.

12 Practice

Write sentences about the people using the prompts. Use the present perfect or the present perfect progressive. If both are possible, use the present perfect progressive.

A

James is a mountain climber.

1. climb/many mountains/in his career

He has climbed many
mountains in his career.

2. climb/Mount Everest

_____

_____

3. be/in the hospital many times?

_____

_____

4. climb/a lot this year?

_____

B

Maria Garcia is a singer.

1. be/on tour in the United States

_____

_____

2. sell/two million CDs a year/for
five years

_____

_____

3. win/any Grammy awards?

_____

_____

4. appear/on television yet?

_____

C

Jenny Hopkins is a TV journalist.

1. interview/many people/about the election for the last few weeks

   _____

   _____

2. travel/all over the world in her career

   _____

   _____

3. meet/the president

   _____

   _____

4. ever/have/her own TV show?

   _____

13   Pair Up and Talk

A   **Practice the conversation with a partner.**

A: What do you think this man is doing?

B: Maybe he's been waiting for a plane to arrive, and now it's flying overhead.

B   Continue the conversation with your partner. Say more about the man using the present progressive, the present perfect, and the present perfect progressive.

THE ANT AND THE GRASSHOPPER

Warm sunshine is falling on a mint leaf where a grasshopper is dozing. His forelegs are crossed casually beneath his green head. On the ground below, struggling along between the towering blades of grass, a red ant carries a huge seed.

The grasshopper awakes, stretches out his papery wings, and yawns. "Ant! You're working too hard. You're wasting this gorgeous day."

The ant, almost breathless, replies, "I'm wasting it? You're the one just sitting around on his rear segment. You'll be sorry when winter comes."

The grasshopper laughs and says, "Does this look like winter? Hey. Take a break and play some cards." The ant rolls his eyes and moves on toward his colony's food storehouse.

Months go by. Cold winds whip snowflakes past the anthill. Between the gusts of wind, the ant hears a thin flutter, like the shivering of papery wings. He puts down his supper bowl and looks out a hole which the vicious wind has opened. There stands the grasshopper, wrapped in a scrap of corn husk. "Hey, ant. Good buddy. How about a little food? Whatever you've got. I'm starving."

The ant moves a pebble toward the opening to shut out the storm. "Sorry, grasshopper. We need all the food we've got. Winter's tough. You had the chance to prepare for it, but you didn't." The pebble slips into place, and the grasshopper rustles off in search of another place to beg.

1. _____ ?   He is sleeping on a mint leaf.

2. _____   He has been gathering food for his
   _____ ?   colony's storehouse.

3. _____ ?   He seems interested only in pleasure and fun.

4. _____
   _____ ?

   He has started preparing for winter even though the weather is still warm.

5. _____
   _____ ?

   Each one thinks the other is wasting the day.

6. _____
   _____ ?

   He has come to the anthill looking for food.

7. _____
   _____ ?

   He has been starving because he failed to store up food for the winter.

8. _____
   _____ ?

   The grasshopper's carelessness has caused his own problems.

Listening Puzzle

AUDIO DOWNLOAD   CD1, 6

A Listen and check the correct answer.

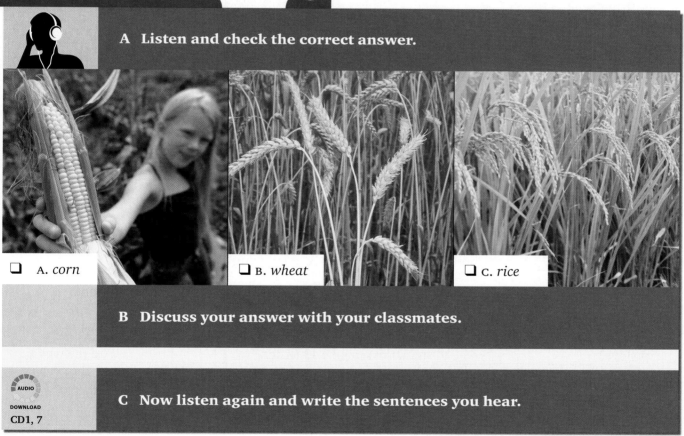

❑ A. *corn*   ❑ B. *wheat*   ❑ C. *rice*

B Discuss your answer with your classmates.

AUDIO DOWNLOAD
CD1, 7

C Now listen again and write the sentences you hear.

Review

1 Review (1a–1c)

Complete the sentences with a correct present form of the verbs in parentheses. If there are other words in parentheses, include them.

Hi Alex,

I (have) _____*'ve had*_____ a great summer! Right now, I (sail) _____ on a big
             1   **2**

sailing ship. There (be) _____ 14 other students, three teachers, and the people who
               3

work on the ship. We (sail) _____ for almost three weeks. We (wake) _____
                4   **5**

_____ up at 5:00 in the morning every day. At 6:00, we (sit) _____ at a long table and
                                                   6

(eat) _____ breakfast together. At 6:45, a bell (ring) _____ , and we
      7   **8**

(know) _____ it (be) _____ time to put our dishes away and
        9   **10**

(go) _____ up to the deck. I (be) _____ always the first.
      11   **12**

I (love) _____ to smell the sea air and (listen) _____ to the waves.
        13   **14**

I (have) _____ a job on the ship. I (take) _____ care of the safety
      15   **16**

equipment. I (know) _____ what to do in an emergency. We (not/have) _____
            17   **18**

_____ any problems so far, but you (know/never) _____ . The captain says there
                                          19

(be/always) _____ storms this time of year. I (not/think) _____ about
          20   **21**

that right now.

We (work) _____ hard on the ship, but I (love) _____ it. Since the
        22   **23**

first day that we (come) _____ on board ship, we (take) _____ sailing
                 24   **25**

lessons. Today is our day off. Right now, I (sit) _____ 26 in the front of the ship. Everything (be) _____ 27 peaceful, for now, but a light wind (blow) _____ 28 all morning, and now it (seem) _____ 29 stronger. Uh, oh! I (see) _____ 30 dark clouds. The waves (get) _____ 31 bigger. I think a storm (come) _____ 32 . I (need) _____ 33 to send a message now. Don't forget to feed my goldfish!

Pete

2 Review (1a–1c)

Complete the sentences with a correct present form of the verbs in parentheses. If there are other words in parentheses, include them.

DAVID: Hi, Martha. This (be) ____is____ 1 David. I (call) _____ 2 to
          ask you if you (enjoy) _____ 3 your vacation.

MARTHA: Oh, yes, very much. Right now, I (look) _____ 4 at the ocean outside my
          window. It (be) _____ 5 very beautiful here.

DAVID: That (sound) _____ 6 great! (you/be) _____ 7 to the
          Kilauea volcano yet?

MARTHA: Yes, we (be/already) _____ 8 there. (you/be/ever) _____ 9
          there?

DAVID: No, I haven't, but I want to go.

MARTHA: I (love) _____ 10 it here. I (already/think) _____ 11 about
          my next trip!

A Before You Read

1. What type of landscape is best for animals like cattle (cows) or bison?
2. Humans are often cited as the "greatest threat" to animals. In what sense is this true?

THE AMERICAN BISON

B Read The American bison is **back**. There are at least 350,000 of them now. One hundred years ago, there were only about 750. Bison are the largest cattle[1]-like animals in North America. Some people mistakenly call them "buffalo." The biggest males weigh more than the average car. Males and females alike have horns. A charging bison is a dangerous animal.

Bison are usually calmer than that. They spend most of their lives munching grass and producing new bison. They move throughout a wide range of territory. When they stop, they eat huge amounts of vegetation. The waste they leave behind adds nutrients to the soil. These bison droppings also burn very well. Campers and hunters often make fires with dried-out "buffalo pies." Bison appear to enjoy rolling around, or "wallowing," in muddy hollows.

They live in areas with many predators[2]. Still, bison have little to fear. Bears do not attack animals in herds[3]. Wolves try to get bison meat, but they rarely succeed. Bison are too big and they are well protected in their big herds.

Humans pose the only serious threat. People have almost wiped out wild bison. They now live only in Yellowstone National Park. About 30 percent of the bison there are wild purebreds. They have not mated with captive bison from outside. Most of them, however, carry a disease, brucellosis. It does not harm bison, but it stresses cattle herds. Cattle ranchers near Yellowstone now threaten to shoot bison. They want to keep the bison away from cattle herds.

[1.] cattle = the milk- and meat-giving animals often called "cows"

[2.] predator = an animal that kills other animals for food
[3.] herd = group of animals; usually cattle and other hoofed animals

C Notice the Grammar   Underline all simple present forms of the verbs.

Choose the best answer.

D Look for Main Ideas

1. The reading's main point about bison is that _____ .
- (A) they are endangered
- (B) their habitat is disappearing
- (C) they are numerous again
- (D) they are large and dangerous

2. What is the main topic of paragraph 4?
- (A) yellow bison
- (B) brucellosis
- (C) cattle ranchers
- (D) wild herds

E Look for Details

3. According to the passage, American bison eat _____ .
- (A) bears
- (B) humans
- (C) pies
- (D) plants

4. According to the passage, bison are protected from wolves by _____ .
- (A) other bison
- (B) predators
- (C) humans
- (D) disease

5. The passage mentions all of the following about bison EXCEPT _____ .
- (A) they are related to cattle
- (B) they are related to buffalo
- (C) some are as heavy as cars
- (D) some have been wiped out

Passages are much easier to read when we already have an idea of what they'll be about. But if we have no knowledge of the topic, a passage can be harder to understand. Before we read something, it helps to think about the topic of the reading. We may already know some facts about the topic. If we do, this personal background knowledge helps us anticipate what the reading will be about. That's why we answer prereading questions—they help us activate our background knowledge.

F Make Inferences

6. From paragraph 2, we can infer that bison wallow in order to _____ .
- (A) eat
- (B) deposit "pies"
- (C) produce new bison
- (D) have fun

7. We can infer that the author believes _____ .
- (A) wild bison will attack cattle
- (B) it is good that some wild bison still exist
- (C) wild bison will soon be wiped out by disease
- (D) no bison still in existence are truly wild

G Look for Vocabulary

8. The word *back* in the first paragraph is closest in meaning to _____ .
- (A) strong again
- (B) behind others
- (C) in the past
- (D) done traveling

Writing: Write an Informal Letter

Write an informal letter to someone you haven't seen for a long time.

1860 N. Adams St.
Santa Monica, CA 90401
March 16, 20XX

Opening → Dear Ken,

I'm still working for _____

_____

Body → _____

_____

_____

_____

Signature → Your friend,
Jill

STEP 1 **Notice the parts of a letter in this model.**

STEP 2 **Write paragraphs to tell your friend about the following.**

1. Your present situation and what you are doing in your life. For example:
   I am still working for the same company, but now I am in Los Angeles.

2. What you do every day. For example:
   The exhibit hall opens at 9:00 in the morning, and. . .

3. What is happening while you are writing this letter. For example:
   I'm writing this letter from my hotel room. The hotel is on the beach.

STEP 3 **Write a letter using the model in Step 1.**

STEP 4 **Evaluate your letter.**

   Checklist

   _____ Did you put the address and date at the top of the letter?

   _____ Did you start your letter with *Dear* and the person's name?

   _____ Did you end your letter with an ending such as *Your friend*, and your signature?

STEP 5 **Work with a partner or teacher to edit your letter. Check spelling, vocabulary, and grammar.**

STEP 6 **Write your final copy.**

Self-Test

1. For thousands of years, bread _____ a staple food for many people.

   A. is   Ⓐ Ⓑ Ⓒ Ⓓ
   B. has
   C. has been
   D. been

2. Earth's climate _____ warmer.

   A. gets   Ⓐ Ⓑ Ⓒ Ⓓ
   B. is getting
   C. have gotten
   D. have been getting

3. A person's nose and ears _____ to grow throughout his or her life.

   A. continues   Ⓐ Ⓑ Ⓒ Ⓓ
   B. are continuing
   C. continue
   D. is continuing

4. What _____ these days?

   A. are girls wearing   Ⓐ Ⓑ Ⓒ Ⓓ
   B. girls wear
   C. girls are wearing
   D. are girls wear

5. In Toronto, it _____ without stopping every day for two weeks.

   A. is raining   Ⓐ Ⓑ Ⓒ Ⓓ
   B. raining
   C. has been raining
   D. rains

6. It _____ 17 muscles to smile.

   A. takes   Ⓐ Ⓑ Ⓒ Ⓓ
   B. has been taking
   C. is taking
   D. has taken

7. Potato chips _____ popular since 1865.

   A. have been   Ⓐ Ⓑ Ⓒ Ⓓ
   B. are
   C. are being
   D. been

8. More women _____ at universities now than in the past.

   A. is studying   Ⓐ Ⓑ Ⓒ Ⓓ
   B. has studied
   C. studies
   D. are studying

9. How much _____ at birth?

   A. is a baby usually weighing   Ⓐ Ⓑ Ⓒ Ⓓ
   B. a baby usually weighs
   C. does a baby usually weigh
   D. usually a baby weigh

10. We _____ New York City many times.

   A. have been visiting   Ⓐ Ⓑ Ⓒ Ⓓ
   B. visiting
   C. visit
   D. have visited

1. Many people <u>are</u> <u>been</u> <u>exercising</u> in the United
        A   **B**   **C**
   States <u>since</u> the start of the fitness craze.
         D

   Ⓐ   Ⓑ   Ⓒ   Ⓓ

2. The cures <u>for</u> many diseases <u>has</u> <u>advanced</u>
          A   **B**   **C**
   greatly <u>since</u> the discovery of antibiotics.
        D

   Ⓐ   Ⓑ   Ⓒ   Ⓓ

3. It is warm <u>usually</u> <u>in June</u>, but this year it <u>is</u>
           A   **B**   **C**
   <u>still</u> cool.
   D

   Ⓐ   Ⓑ   Ⓒ   Ⓓ

4. What <u>people</u> <u>are</u> <u>doing</u> <u>these</u> days?
         A   **B**   **C**   **D**

   Ⓐ   Ⓑ   Ⓒ   Ⓓ

5. People in the U.S. <u>usually</u> <u>are having</u> turkey
                  A   **B**
   for Thanksgiving, but other countries <u>have</u>
                              C
   <u>something else</u>.
       D

   Ⓐ   Ⓑ   Ⓒ   Ⓓ

6. Some <u>scientists</u> <u>thinks</u> Earth <u>is</u> <u>getting</u> colder.
         A   **B**   **C** **D**

   Ⓐ   Ⓑ   Ⓒ   Ⓓ

7. Some roses <u>are</u> <u>not</u> <u>smell</u>. They <u>have</u> no scent
            A **B** **C**   **D**
   at all.

   Ⓐ   Ⓑ   Ⓒ   Ⓓ

8. People <u>have grown</u> the potato in Europe <u>since</u>
           A   **B**   **C**
   hundreds of <u>years</u>.
            D

   Ⓐ   Ⓑ   Ⓒ   Ⓓ

9. Many <u>people</u> are <u>buy</u> DVDs instead of CDs
         A   **B**
   <u>these</u> <u>days</u>.
   C   **D**

   Ⓐ   Ⓑ   Ⓒ   Ⓓ

10. Some people relax <u>never</u>. They <u>worry</u>
                   A   **B**   **C**
    <u>all the time</u>.
      D

    Ⓐ   Ⓑ   Ⓒ   Ⓓ

Unit 2
The Past

Tiger Woods played his first game of golf when he **was** one and a half years old.

The Past   **29**

Form

> Tom **was watching** television when I **came** home.

THE SIMPLE PAST

1. We form affirmative statements in the simple past with a subject + the past form of a verb.
   We form negative statements with a subject + *did not/didn't* + a base verb.
   > I **enjoyed** the movie last night.
   > I **liked** the story, but I **didn't like** the photography.
   EXCEPTION: The negative of *be* is the past form of *be* + *not*.
   > I **was not/wasn't** happy with the ending.
   > We **were not/weren't** disappointed.

2. We form the past form of regular verbs with a base verb + *-d* or *-ed*.

3. Irregular verbs form their past forms in different ways. Look at the top of the next page for some examples.

Base Form	Past Form
be*	I/He/She/It was We/You/They were
fall	fell
feel	felt
run	ran
see	saw
sit	sat

Be is the only verb that has two past forms.

4. We form *yes/no* questions with *did* + a subject + a base verb. In short answers, we use a pronoun subject + *did* or *didn't*.

A: **Did** you **hear** the concert last night?

B: Yes, I **did**./No, I **didn't**.

5. We use the *wh-* words *what, where, when, how, which, why, who,* and *whom* to form *wh-* questions in the simple past.

Who watched "The Office" on television last night?

What did you **watch** on television last night?

THE PAST PROGRESSIVE

6. We form affirmative statements in the past progressive with a subject + the past of *be* + a verb +-*ing*. We form negative statements with a subject + the past of *be* + *not* + a verb + *-ing*.

When I turned on the television, someone **was singing** the national anthem of my country.

The people in the crowd **weren't singing**. They **were cheering**.

7. We form *yes/no* questions with *was* or *were* + a subject + a verb + *-ing*. In short answers, we use a pronoun subject + *was/wasn't* or *were/weren't*.

A: **Were** you **listening** to the radio at 9:00 last night?

B: Yes, I **was**./No, I **wasn't**.

8. We use the *wh-* words *what, where, when, how, which, why, who,* and *whom* to form *wh-* questions in the past progressive.

Who was playing that loud music when I called you?

Why was the audience **laughing** at the end of the movie?

Function

1. Here are the main uses of the simple past and the past progressive.

The Simple Past	The Past Progressive
a. To describe an action that happened at a definite time in the past. We can state the time. Edmund Hillary and Tenzing Norgay **climbed** Mount Everest (in 1953).	a. To describe an action that was in progress at a specific time in the past. The action began before the specific time and might continue after that time. Mary **was working** at ten o'clock yesterday morning.
b. To talk about actions that happened in a sequence in the past. I **came** home, **picked** up my mail, and **left**.	b. To talk about two actions in the past when one action began first and was in progress when the second action happened. I **was studying** when the electricity went off.
c. With time expressions such as *yesterday, last night/week/month/year, Wednesday, four days/weeks/months/years ago*, and *in 2004*. I saw a great movie **last night**.	c. To talk about two actions in the past that were in progress at the same time. The workers **were demanding** more money while the management **was asking** for layoffs.
	d. To give background information in a story. We use the simple past for the main actions and events. It **was getting** dark. I **was walking** down a country road. I **looked** down the road and **saw** a car coming towards me.
	e. With time expressions such as *while, when,* and *all morning/day/evening*. I was working **all day**.

2. We do not use the progressive form if the verb has a stative meaning.

    CORRECT: I had an exam yesterday.

    INCORRECT: I ~~was having~~ an exam yesterday.

3. We use *when* or *while* in sentences with two actions in the past.

    When I **came** home, I **picked up** my mail.

    I **was sleeping when** the fire alarm **went** off.

    They **were watching** TV **while** I **was sleeping**.

4. Clauses with *when* or *while* can come at the beginning or at the end of a sentence. If the clause comes at the beginning, we put a comma after it.

    When the phone rang, I was watching television.

    I was watching television **when the phone rang**.

1 Practice

Listen to the conversation. Complete the sentences with the simple past or the past progressive. Then practice the conversation with a partner.

A

YUSHEN: You won't believe what happened to me this morning.

LUKE: What happened?

YUSHEN: I ___was waiting___ at the bus stop when I _____ an
                    1   **2**
accident, or almost an accident. A man _____ on his cell
                                                                  3
phone while he _____ . He _____ attention
                              4   **5**
to the road when suddenly the traffic light _____ red.
                                                                    6
A woman _____ the street at that moment.
                      7

LUKE: Wow! _____ her?
                      8

YUSHEN: Yes, he _____ the car just in time.
                          9

LUKE: _____ the woman hurt?
          10

YUSHEN: No, she _____ hurt, but she _____ lucky.
                        11   **12**

B

SONIA: Tell me about something scary that happened to you.

JIM: Well, let's see. A few months ago, I _____ at home alone.
                                                        1
I _____ a show on TV, and I _____ tired.
      2   **3**
I _____ about going to bed when I _____
    4   **5**
a noise.

SONIA: Where _____ the noise coming from?
                      6

JIM: It _____ to be coming from upstairs.
              7

SONIA: _____ you scared at that point?
          8

JIM: Yes, I _____ . Very scared. I _____ the TV,
                9   **10**
_____ the cordless phone in my hand, and
    11
_____ to walk up the stairs. Then I _____ the
    12   **13**
same noise again. I _____ the police.
                              14

2 Your Turn

Continue and complete one of the stories from Practice 1. Write at least five sentences using the simple past and the past progressive.

3 Practice

Complete the sentences with the simple past or the past progressive of the verbs in parentheses.

Ludwig van Beethoven was born in Germany in 1770. His father, who was a musician,

(give) _____*gave*_____ his son piano lessons when he was four. Ludwig (stand)
          1

_____ on the piano seat while he (play) _____ because he was so small.
     2   **3**

When his father (see) _____ how quickly his son (learn) _____ ,
                         4   **5**

he (know) _____ his son was talented. His father was a difficult man. He
               6

(hit) _____ Ludwig's hand when he (make) _____ a mistake. He often
         7   **8**

(wake) _____ Ludwig up in the middle of the night while he
           9

(sleep) _____ because he wanted Ludwig to play for him.
            10

    When he was 16, Beethoven (go) _____ to Vienna to study. While he (study)
                                        11

_____ , he (perform) _____ for important people. One day, he (play)
     12   **13**

_____ for Wolfgang Mozart. When Mozart (hear) _____ him, he was
     14   **15**

amazed at his talent.

    In his 20s, Beethoven (begin) _____ to lose his hearing. By the time he was
                                      16

50, he was almost completely deaf, so he couldn't hear the music while the orchestra

(play) _____ . In his last performance, he (continue) _____ to conduct
          17   **18**

while the audience (applaud) _____ .
                                 19

34   Unit 2

4 Practice

Use the question words to write questions for the answers that follow.
Then practice saying the questions and answers with a partner.

1. QUESTION: What _____ ?

   ANSWER: He was sleeping.

2. QUESTION: Why _____ ?

   ANSWER: Beethoven went to Vienna to study.

3. QUESTION: Who _____ ?

   ANSWER: He entertained important people.

4. QUESTION: When _____ ?

   ANSWER: He began to lose his hearing when he was in his 20s.

5. QUESTION: What _____ ?

   ANSWER: He continued to conduct while the audience was applauding.

5 Practice

Listen to the TV report on Tiger Woods. Then decide if each statement is true
or false. Pay attention to the simple past and the present perfect.

AUDIO
DOWNLOAD

CD1, 9

		T	F
1.	Tiger has played golf since 1974.	☐	☐
2.	Tiger started playing golf when he was nine months old.	☐	☐
3.	Tiger has won many tournaments since the age of eight.	☐	☐
4.	Tiger won a lot of money when he was eight.	☐	☐
5.	Tiger's father gave him some advice.	☐	☐
6.	Tiger's father said, "Always be yourself."	☐	☐

6 Pair Up and Talk

A Practice the conversation with a partner.

A: Who's your favorite musician?

B: Elton John. He was playing the piano by the age of four.

A: I didn't know that. What else did he do?

B: Early in his career, he wrote popular rock and roll songs. Then he started writing music for movies and plays. He wrote the music for *The Lion King*.

B Now think of a musician that you like. Tell your partner some interesting facts about his or her life. Use the simple past and the past progressive in your conversation.

2B | The Past Perfect and the Past Perfect Progressive

Form

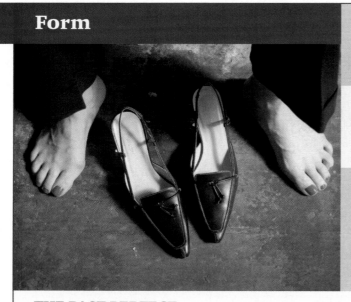

Sue took off her shoes.
She **had been wearing** her new shoes all day.

THE PAST PERFECT

1. We form affirmative statements with a subject + *had* + a past participle. We form negative statements with a subject + *had not/hadn't* + a past participle.

   I **had seen** that play before, so I didn't want to go again.

   She didn't do well on the quiz because she **hadn't studied** for it.

2. We form *yes/no* questions in the past perfect with *had* + a subject + a past participle. In short answers, we use a pronoun subject + *had* or *had not*. We usually contract negative short answers.

A: **Had** he **finished** by 2:00?

B: Yes, he **had**./No, he **hadn't**.

3. We use the *wh-* words *what, where, when, how, which, why, who,* and *whom* to form *wh-* questions in the past perfect.

   Where had Kelly **traveled** by the time she finished her trip?

THE PAST PERFECT PROGRESSIVE

4. We form affirmative statements with a subject + *had* + *been* + a verb + *-ing*.

   We form negative statements with a subject + *had not* + *been* + a verb + *-ing*.

   Susan **had been studying** the violin for only a month when she quit.

   She **hadn't been studying** it very long.

5. We form *yes/no* questions with *had* + a subject + *been* + a verb + *-ing*. In short answers, we use a pronoun subject + *had* or *had not*. We usually contract negative short answers.

6. We use the *wh-* words *what, where, when, how, which, why, who,* and *whom* to make *wh-* questions in the past perfect progressive.

Function

1. Here are the main uses of the past perfect and the past perfect progressive.

The Past Perfect	The Past Perfect Progressive
a. To talk about a past action that ended before another action or time in the past. The movie **had started** before we arrived. It is not usually necessary to use the past perfect when we use *before* or *after* in a sentence. *Before* and *after* tell us the order of the actions, so we may use the simple past. The movie **started** before we arrived.	a. To emphasize the continuation of an action that was in progress before another action or time in the past. Sara **had been working** here for two weeks when she got called away on family business.
b. To show the cause of a past action. I was tired on Monday. I **hadn't slept well** the night before.	b. To show the cause of a past action. **I had been traveling** all night, so I was tired on Monday.
c. With time expressions such as *when, after, before, as soon as, by the time, by,* and *until.* Kasey had already eaten **when** Francie stopped by to get her.	c. With time expressions such as *when, before, by the time, for, since,* and *how long.* He had been working **for** two hours when you interrupted him.

2. We do not use the progressive form with verbs that have a stative meaning.

    CORRECT: She had been tired all day.

    INCORRECT: She ~~had been being~~ tired all day.

3. We often use adverbs such as *ever, never, already, yet, so far,* and *still* with the past perfect.

    See page 15 for more information about these adverbs.

    Ellen had **never** eaten a fresh mango.

    At the end of my trip to Texas, I **still** hadn't eaten barbeque.

7 Practice

Complete the sentences with the simple past or the past perfect of the verbs in parentheses.

Janet had a bad day last Friday. She was late for class because her bus (arrive)

___*had arrived*___ late. When she (get) _____ to school, classes
      1   **2**

(already/begin) _____ .
             3

Friday (be) _____ the day of the grammar test. The test
        4

(already/start) _____ when Janet (walk) _____ into
         5   **6**

the classroom. She (take) _____ the test, but she (not/finish)
                    7

_____ because she (start) _____ late. It was a shame
      8   **9**

because she (study) _____ very hard for it the night before.
               10

That evening, Janet (decide) _____ to go to a movie, but she
                11

(not/want) _____ to go to the movies alone. It was a movie she
     12

(want) _____ to see for a long time. She (call) _____
     13   **14**

her mother, but her mother (see) _____ it before.
                       15

She (call) _____ me, but I (already/make) _____
         16   **17**

plans to go out of town. I (hear) _____ later that Janet
                     18

(do) _____ something she (never/do) _____ before—
      19   **20**

she (go) _____ to see a movie alone.
        21

8 Practice

Look at the photo of Julia. This is how she looked when you saw her yesterday. Why did she look tired? Complete the sentences using the prompts and the past perfect or the past perfect progressive.

1. She looked tired because *she had been working too much.*
   (work/too much)

2. She looked tired because _____
   (sleep/badly)

3. She looked tired because _____
   (not/eat/well lately)

4. She looked tired because _____
   (worry/about her parents)

5. She looked tired because _____
   (your idea)

6. She looked tired because _____
   (your idea)

THE SHEPHERD BOY AND THE WOLF

Once there was a shepherd boy who took care of sheep for his master. His job wasn't very exciting, and he soon got bored. One day, he thought of a plan to have fun because he'd been getting so bored.

His master had told him to call for help when he saw a wolf near the sheep. Then the people in the village would come and scare the wolf away.

So one day, the shepherd boy ran toward the village and shouted, "Wolf! Wolf!" although he hadn't seen a wolf.

As his master had told him, the villagers left their work and ran to the field. When they got there, they found the boy laughing because he'd played a trick on them.

A few days later, the boy did what he'd done before. He shouted, "Wolf! Wolf!" Again, the villagers ran to help him, and again he laughed at them.

Then one evening, a wolf really came and attacked the sheep. This time, the boy was scared and ran toward the village. He shouted, "Wolf! Wolf!" The villagers heard him, but they didn't run to help him as they'd done before.

The wolf killed many of the sheep and disappeared into the forest.

1. Why/the shepherd boy/think/of a plan to have fun
   QUESTION: Why did the shepherd boy think of a plan to have fun?
   ANSWER: He thought of a plan because he was bored.

2. What/his master/tell/him
   QUESTION: _____?
   ANSWER: _____

3. What/he/decide/to do one day
   QUESTION: _____?
   ANSWER: _____

4. he/see/a wolf
   QUESTION: _____?
   ANSWER: _____

5. What/the villagers/do
   QUESTION: _____?
   ANSWER: _____

6. Why/the boy/laugh
   QUESTION: _____?
   ANSWER: _____

7. What/the boy/do/a few days later
   QUESTION: _____?
   ANSWER: _____

8. he/laugh/at the villagers again
   QUESTION: _____?
   ANSWER: _____

9. What/the boy/do/when the wolf really came
   QUESTION: _____?
   ANSWER: _____

10. What/the villagers/do/this time
    QUESTION: _____?
    ANSWER: _____

10   Pair Up and Talk
What do you think the moral of the fable about the boy and the wolf is?
Have you ever needed help but couldn't get it? What happened?
Tell the story.

A: One time I had worked very late and I was tired and wanted someone to drive me home. But no one lived near me and I drove myself home.

B: That's too bad. How long did it take you?

11 Practice

Complete the sentences with the present perfect progressive or the past perfect progressive of the words in parentheses.

1. I am at the dentist's office now. I (wait) __'ve been waiting__ for 45 minutes.

2. I was at the dentist's office yesterday. I (wait) ___'d been waiting___ for two hours before the receptionist called my name.

3. I feel terrible because my tooth (hurt) _____ for days.

4. I felt terrible yesterday because my tooth (hurt) _____ for several days before I went to the dentist.

5. I (take) _____ aspirin for several days for the pain, but it doesn't help.

6. I (take) _____ aspirin for several days before I went to the dentist, but it didn't help.

7. I (hope) _____ that the pain would go away, but it didn't.

8. I (go) _____ to the same dentist since I was a child, so I trust him.

9. The dentist (work) _____ on my tooth for ten minutes now.

10. He (work) _____ for five minutes when I couldn't stand it anymore and ...

12 Pair Up and Talk

A Practice the conversation with a partner.

A: I was late for class today.
B: I was late, too. By the time I got to class, the teacher had arrived.

B Continue the conversation. Tell your partner what had already happened or hadn't happened in class by the time you got there. Use ideas from the list or think of your own.

all the students/sit down   the teacher/collect homework
the class/begin   the teacher/take attendance

13 Your Turn

Think about your life. Choose a particular age and list four experiences you had had by that age on a separate sheet of paper. Think about these kinds of experiences:

1. people you had met
2. places you had visited
3. things you had done
4. things you had learned to do

14 Phrasal Verb Practice

Complete the sentences with the correct phrasal verbs. Use the correct form of the verb. Use each verb only once. Phrasal verbs are taught in Unit 8, section H.

come from   figure out   send up

come up   send out   take off

The Han Chinese military flew the first kites around 180 B.C.E. A general named Hsin ordered his men to _____send up_____ a kite over enemy lines. He used the length of
₁

its string to _____ the distance between his army and the enemy. Then
₂

his soldiers dug a tunnel toward the enemy.

The Chinese military also used kites to _____ messages. Once, a
₃

general _____ with a way to cause panic among enemy troops. He
₄

attached bamboo pipes to kites and flew them over the camp of the Hans troops, their

enemy, late at night. The whistling sound that _____ the pipes sounded
₅

like "Fu Han!" That means "Beware Han!" The Hans thought it was a warning from their

guardian spirits and quickly _____ .
₆

Form

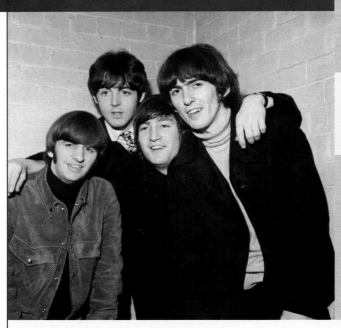

The Beatles **used to be** the most popular group in the world. We **would listen** to their songs on the radio all the time.

USED TO + BASE VERB

1. We form affirmative statements with a subject + *used to* + a base verb. We form negative statements with a subject + *did not* + *use to* + a base verb.

   CORRECT: I **used to like** rock music.

                     I **didn't use to like** rock music.

   INCORRECT: I didn't ~~used~~ to like rock music.

2. We form *yes/no* questions with *did* + a subject + *use to* + a base verb. We form short answers with a pronoun subject and *did* or *didn't*.

   CORRECT: **Did** you **use to** work there?

                     Yes, I **did**./No, I **didn't**.

   INCORRECT: Did you ~~used~~ to work there?

3. We use the *wh-* words *what, where, when, how, which, why, who,* and *whom* to form questions with *used to* + base verb when the *wh-* word is the subject. When the *wh-* word is not the subject, we form the questions with *did* + a subject + *use to* + a base verb.

   CORRECT: **Where did** you use to work?

   INCORRECT: Where did you ~~used~~ to work?

WOULD + BASE VERB

4. We form affirmative statements with a subject + *would* + a base verb. We form negative statements with a subject + *would not/wouldn't* + a base verb.

   When Tom lived in New York, he **would take** the subway. He **wouldn't take** taxis.

5. We form *yes/no* questions with *would* + a subject + a base verb. We form short answers with a pronoun subject + *would* or *wouldn't*.

> A: **Would** he **go** to the museums a lot?
>
> B: Yes, he **would**./No, he **wouldn't**.

6. We use the *wh-* words *what, where, when, how, which, why, who,* and *whom* to form questions with *would* + base verb.

> A: Where **would** he **eat** dinner?
>
> B: He**'d** usually **eat** in his apartment.

Function

1. We use *used to* to talk about a past habit which does not exist any longer. We can also use the simple past in this case with no difference in meaning.

> We **used to go** to the beach every week, but now we don't.
>
> OR We **went** to the beach every week, but now we don't.

When we give a specific time, we do not use *used to*.

> CORRECT: We went to the beach every week in 2009.
>
> INCORRECT: We ~~used to go~~ to the beach every week in 2009.

2. We can also use *would* instead of *used to* for a past habit.

> I **used to visit** my grandmother on weekends.
>
> OR I **would visit** my grandmother on weekends.

But in this meaning, we cannot use *would* with stative verbs.

> CORRECT: I used to have a red bicycle.
>
> INCORRECT: I ~~would have~~ a red bicycle.

3. We use *used to* to talk about a past situation that no longer exists.

> We **used to live** in a small apartment.

But we cannot use *would* to talk about these situations.

> CORRECT: We used to live in Poland before we moved here.
>
> INCORRECT: We ~~would~~ live in Poland before we moved here.

4. We often start a story about the past with *used to* and then use *would* to talk about the rest of the story.

> When I was a child, **I used to do** my homework first, and then **I would go out** and **play** with my friends.

5. We often use *would* to show stubbornness and that the speaker disapproves of this.

> He **would come** home whenever he wanted, and nobody could do anything about it.

6. In the negative, *would* shows refusal. We cannot replace *didn't use to* with *wouldn't* because the meaning will change.

She **didn't use to work** late. (neutral)

She **wouldn't work** late.

(She refused to work late. Maybe she didn't want to get caught in bad traffic.)

7. Do not confuse *used to* + a base verb with *be used to* + a base verb + *-ing*.

Be used to + a base verb + *-ing* means "to be accustomed to."

He **used to work** long hours.

(He did this in the past, but he does not do it anymore.)

He **is used to working** long hours.

(He is accustomed to it.)

---

15 Practice

Underline the correct form in parentheses.

1. People (<u>used to watch</u>/would watch) black and white television in the 1960s.

2. Women (used to wear/used to wearing) miniskirts in the 1960s.

3. Some young men (would not fight/didn't use to fight) in the Vietnam War.

4. Many young men (would have/used to have) long hair in the 1960s.

5. The Beatles (used to become/became) the most popular group in England in the 1960s.

6. The Beatles (used to come/came) to the United States in 1965.

7. Girls (used to scream/used to be screaming) when they saw the Beatles.

8. Other groups like the Rolling Stones, the Beach Boys, and the Bee Gees also (used to be/would be) popular in the 1960s and 1970s.

9. I (used to listen/am used to listening) to the radio when I drive to work. I hear many of my favorite songs from the 1960s.

10. People (used to be/would be) afraid of the atom bomb in the 1960s.

---

16 Practice

Look at the chart of information about Bruno Martin in the year 2000 and now. Write sentences about him that say what he used to do or would do, and what he is doing now. Use the verbs in the chart.

	Verb	2000	Now
Home	live	Brazil	Canada
Marital Status	be	single	married
Job	be	student	architect
Sports	play	soccer	hockey
Weight	weigh	160 pounds/72.5 kilos	200 pounds/90.7 kilos
Hobbies	like	movies and dancing	watching TV
Languages	speak	Portuguese	Portuguese and English
Personality	(your ideas)	(your ideas)	(your ideas)

1. *Bruno used to live in Brazil, but now he lives in Canada.*
2. _____
3. _____
4. _____
5. _____
6. _____
7. _____
8. _____

17   Your Turn

What happened when your parents or grandparents were young? What did people use to do then? What didn't they use to do? Write five sentences about this time period.

1. _____
2. _____
3. _____
4. _____
5. _____

18   Pair Up and Talk

A   Practice the conversation with a partner.

A: What TV shows did you use to like as a child?

B: I used to like cartoons. I would watch them every Saturday.

A: What do you watch now?

B: Mostly comedies.

B   Continue the conversation. Complete the chart with information about your partner. Use the chart to ask and answer questions about your lives now and when you were children.

	As a Child	Now
TV shows/like		
books/read		
food/like		
sports/play		
go on vacation		
do on the weekends		

Listening Puzzle

A Listen and check the correct answer.

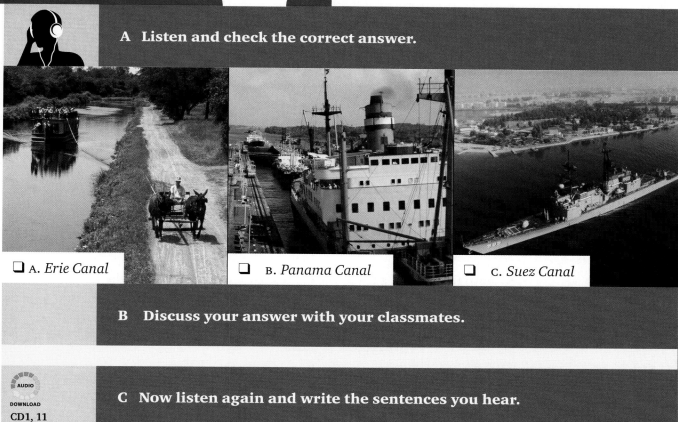

❑ A. *Erie Canal*   ❑ B. *Panama Canal*   ❑ C. *Suez Canal*

B Discuss your answer with your classmates.

AUDIO DOWNLOAD
CD1, 11

C Now listen again and write the sentences you hear.

Review (2a)

1 Review
Complete the sentences with a correct past form of the verbs in parentheses.
Sometimes more than one answer is possible. If there are other words in the parentheses,
include them.

The Maori (be) _____*were*_____ the first people in New Zealand. They first (come)
1
_____ from Polynesia in small boats as long ago as 700 c.e. While these original people
2
(live) _____ there, other Polynesians (come) _____ to their islands.
3   **4**
In the 14th century, another large group (arrive) _____ from the Society Islands. They
5
(be) _____ hungry and at war for many years before they (decide)
6
_____ to leave their islands. Later, the stories of their voyages across the Pacific Ocean
7
(pass) _____ from one generation to another. When they (land) _____
8   **9**
in New Zealand, the original people (live) _____ there for centuries. But the culture of
10
the new people (replace) _____ the old. The new people (be) _____
11   **12**
warriors¹. They (build) _____ their villages on top of hills or near a river or the sea
13
because they (need) _____ protection. It (be) _____ easy for one group
14   **15**
to insult another, so they (have) _____ wars all the time. They (fight)
16
_____ among themselves.
17
The Maoris (not/have) _____ a written language. How (they/teach)
18
_____ their children? They (tell) _____ them stories. The Maoris (be)
19   **20**
_____ also great artists and craftsmen. The Maoris (respect) _____
21   **22**
nature. They (care) _____ for the land. They (not/destroy) _____
23   **24**
anything natural. They (have) _____ many gods. They (believe) _____
25   **26**
these gods protected the sea, forest, and the crops they planted. The Maoris (have)

_____ strong families, religious beliefs, and traditions, and still do today.
27
Several years ago, New Zealanders (begin) _____ to show a great interest in the
28
Maori way of life. They (decide) _____ to teach Maori language, art, song, and dance in
29
their schools. They (realize) _____ that Maori culture is part of New Zealand's culture.
30

¹· *warriors = people who make war*

50 Unit 2

2 Review

Complete the sentences with a correct past form of the verbs in parentheses. Sometimes more than one answer is possible.

When I (be) _____ *was* _____ a child, my grandparents (live) _____ with us.

1
2

Every night, our grandmother (tell) _____ us stories about the 1950s. She

3

(not/let) _____ us go to bed until we (hear) _____ a story. We

4
5

(be) _____ very sleepy by the time she (finish) _____ her story.

6
7

Until a few years ago, I (not/think) _____ about my grandmother's stories for a long

8

time. I (start) _____ writing them down, and now I have a collection of stories for my

9

own children.

Grandma also taught us dances from the 1950s. One night, I (be) _____ late.

10

Grandma (already/start) _____ a dance by the time I came in.

11

She (show) _____ my sisters how to do the "hokey pokey" dance as I

12

(walk) _____ into the room. Grandma (put) _____ one foot in and one

13
14

foot out of the circle of dancers. Then she (shake) _____ it all around. Grandma

15

(not/let) _____ me go to bed until I (dance) _____ , too.

16
17

I (not/believe)_____ her when she said that the "hokey pokey" (be) _____

18
19

very popular in the 50s.

By 1952, people (drive) _____ a lot more. The cars then (be) _____

20
21

more comfortable than the cars of the past. In those days, more men (drive) _____ than

22

women, but more and more women (learn) _____ to drive during these years. Every

23

summer, my grandparents (pack up) _____ their car with bags and children and drive

24

hundreds of miles to a vacation spot. Over the years, they (go) _____ to the Grand

25

Canyon, to New York City, to Florida, and to the mountains of Colorado. On the trips, the children

(ask) _____ , "Are we there yet?" over and over. My children still ask this question today.

26

Some things never change.

Reading Challenge

A Before You Read

1. In what ways is it easier to travel by water than to travel by land?
2. A canal is an artificial waterway. A famous one is the Suez Canal in Egypt.
   What other canals have you heard of?

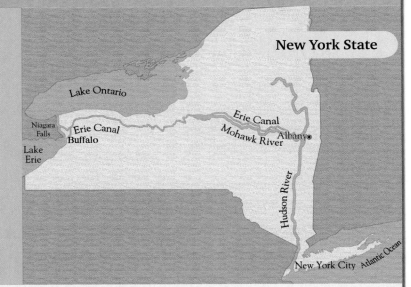

New York State

THE ERIE CANAL

DID YOU KNOW ... ?
When it opened in 1825, the Canal was only four feet deep. An average-sized man could stand in the middle of it without getting wet above his shoulders.

B Read Early European explorers in North America posed an interesting transportation question[1]. Was it possible to travel by water from the Atlantic Ocean to the western Great ⁵Lakes? A water route promised faster shipping of goods. It implied easier travel and more exploration. The great ¹⁰wealth of the interior continent could reach the world.

But nature had not provided any such route. ¹⁵You could easily get to Lake Ontario from New York City. You headed north on the Hudson River then traveled west on smaller rivers. But to get to Lake Erie, the 160-foot-high (49-meter-high) Niagara Falls ²⁰stood in the way. An artificial waterway was necessary.

By 1825, the state of New York had built one. The Erie Canal was dug from Albany westward to the Niagara River and Lake Erie. The first ²⁵140 miles (225 kilometers) or so of the canal ran alongside the Mohawk River. Then it **struck out** on its own just west of Oneida Lake in central New York State. It proceeded westward from there along a line south of the Lake Ontario ³⁰shore. The present-day Erie Canal follows this original route with only a few changes.

Through the 1800s and early 1900s, a typical canal trip depended on mule[2] power. A mule walked on a narrow trail next to the canal (a ³⁵towpath). A rope led from a harness on its shoulders to a shallow boat, called a barge. The barge usually carried goods, but passengers rode them, too.

[1] pose a question = express it for other people's consideration

[2] mule = a horse-like animal

C Notice the Grammar   Underline all past forms of the verbs.

Choose the best answer.

D Look for Main Ideas

1. This reading is mainly about _____ .
    - (A) a natural obstacle
    - (B) a water route
    - (C) a transportation question
    - (D) a typical trip

2. What is the main topic of paragraph 2?
    - (A) where the canal was built
    - (B) how the canal was built
    - (C) why the canal was built
    - (D) how fast the canal was built

E Look for Details

3. The passage mentions all of the following as benefits of a water route EXCEPT _____ .
    - (A) faster shipping
    - (B) more exploration
    - (C) the use of mules
    - (D) the export of wealth

4. Why was the Mohawk River not a good route to Lake Erie?
    - (A) It did not take a traveler below Niagara Falls.
    - (B) It did not take a traveler to one of the lakes.
    - (C) It did not take a traveler south of Lake Ontario.
    - (D) It did not take a traveler all the way to Lake Erie.

5. According to the passage, the canal _____ .
    - (A) is still the only water route to the lakes
    - (B) is still in use
    - (C) now goes to New York City
    - (D) was closed in the 1900s

F Make Inferences

6. We can most strongly infer from paragraph 3 that, for the first 140 miles, the canal _____ .
    - (A) was a river
    - (B) was in a river valley
    - (C) replaced a river
    - (D) looked like a river

7. We can most strongly infer from the reading that boats on the canal _____ .
    - (A) did not use sails or engines
    - (B) were used for recreation
    - (C) could not be used on lakes
    - (D) were very uncomfortable for passengers

G Look for Vocabulary

8. The term *struck out* in the reading is closest in meaning to _____ .
    - (A) got lost
    - (B) showed anger
    - (C) went forward
    - (D) did poorly

Writing: Write a Narrative

Write a paragraph or an essay about a person's life in the order of events. We call this type of writing a narrative. *Narrative* is another word for "story."

STEP 1   **Choose one of the following topics.**

1. A Person I Admire
2. My Life
3. The Life of (a famous person)

STEP 2   **Make notes to answer these questions.**

1. When and where was the person born?
2. Where did the person study, work, etc.? Note all the most important events in the person's life up to the present or until the person died.

STEP 3   **Make notes to answer these questions.**

Arrange the events in correct time order using time expressions such as the following:

after	**in 1989**	**one day**	**when**
finally	**next**	**then**	

STEP 4   **Write your narrative in the form of a paragraph or an essay. Make sure your paragraph or essay has a beginning, a middle, and an end. If you write an essay, each paragraph should be about a major time period in the person's life, for example, school, work, and achievements. Remember to indent your paragraph(s).**

STEP 5   **Evaluate your paragraph or essay.**

Checklist

_____ Did you write a title and put it in the right place?

_____ Did you indent the paragraph(s)?

_____ Did you use time expressions to show the correct order of events?

STEP 6   **Work with a partner or a teacher to edit your paragraph or essay.**

STEP 7   **Check spelling, vocabulary, and grammar.**

Write your final copy.

Self-Test

A Choose the best answer, A, B, C, or D, to complete the sentence. Darken the oval with the same letter.

1. By 10:00 yesterday, John _____ his test.

   A. has finished   Ⓐ Ⓑ Ⓒ Ⓓ
   B. had finished
   C. had been finishing
   D. finishing

2. When John was a boy, he _____ in the Philippines.

   A. would live   Ⓐ Ⓑ Ⓒ Ⓓ
   B. has lived
   C. used to live
   D. living

3. I didn't hear the phone. I _____ .

   A. was sleeping   Ⓐ Ⓑ Ⓒ Ⓓ
   B. slept
   C. used to sleep
   D. had been sleeping

4. TOM: Did you watch the concert on TV last night?
   SUE: _____ I was reading.

   A. No, I wasn't.   Ⓐ Ⓑ Ⓒ Ⓓ
   B. No, I didn't.
   C. Yes, I was.
   D. Yes, I did.

5. They _____ without stopping every day for two weeks.

   A. was working   Ⓐ Ⓑ Ⓒ Ⓓ
   B. were working
   C. working
   D. would work

6. BOB: I _____ a strange email message yesterday.
   JAN: Really? Who was it from?

   A. did get   Ⓐ Ⓑ Ⓒ Ⓓ
   B. was getting
   C. got
   D. have got

7. Ted _____ two hours to work, but now he lives closer to his job.

   A. used to drive   Ⓐ Ⓑ Ⓒ Ⓓ
   B. is used to driving
   C. has driven
   D. use to drive

8. How long _____ for him when he arrived?

   A. have you been waiting   Ⓐ Ⓑ Ⓒ Ⓓ
   B. had you been waiting
   C. did you wait
   D. you waited

9. Which movie _____ yesterday?

   A. you saw   Ⓐ Ⓑ Ⓒ Ⓓ
   B. did you see
   C. you did see
   D. you see

10. I _____ a test yesterday.

    A. have had   Ⓐ Ⓑ Ⓒ Ⓓ
    B. was having
    C. would have
    D. had

1. <u>Before</u> he <u>became</u> an artist, Steven <u>has</u> <u>been</u>
     A   B   C D
   a teacher.

   Ⓐ   Ⓑ   Ⓒ   Ⓓ

2. <u>As soon as</u> the alarm <u>rang</u>, he <u>got up</u> and
       A   B   C
   <u>was putting</u> on his clothes.
      D

   Ⓐ   Ⓑ   Ⓒ   Ⓓ

3. I <u>was</u> <u>driving</u> to work <u>when</u> I <u>was seeing</u>
     A   B   C   D
   the accident.

   Ⓐ   Ⓑ   Ⓒ   Ⓓ

4. What <u>do</u> people <u>use to</u> <u>do</u> when they <u>got</u> sick?
        A   B   C   D

   Ⓐ   Ⓑ   Ⓒ   Ⓓ

5. The mail carrier <u>delivered</u> this package
                 A
   <u>this morning</u> <u>while</u> you <u>were slept</u>.
     B   C   D

   Ⓐ   Ⓑ   Ⓒ   Ⓓ

6. <u>When</u> Sally <u>were</u> young, she <u>practiced</u> the
     A   B   C
   piano <u>every day</u>.
         D

   Ⓐ   Ⓑ   Ⓒ   Ⓓ

7. Rob <u>have</u> <u>been training</u> <u>for</u> three years <u>when</u> he
      A   B   C   D
   entered the tournament.

   Ⓐ   Ⓑ   Ⓒ   Ⓓ

8. <u>When</u> <u>did</u> you <u>called</u> me last <u>night</u>?
     A   B   C   D

   Ⓐ   Ⓑ   Ⓒ   Ⓓ

9. <u>When</u> I <u>was</u> a child, I <u>would like</u> to <u>do</u> things
     A   B   C   D
   with my father.

   Ⓐ   Ⓑ   Ⓒ   Ⓓ

10. They <u>have lived</u> here <u>for</u> four years <u>before</u>
         A   B   C
    they <u>moved</u>.
        D

    Ⓐ   Ⓑ   Ⓒ   Ⓓ

Unit 3
The Future

Matt says he **will be** a rock star in the future.

3A | *Be Going To* and *Will*

Form

Are you going to show me your report card, Joey?

BE GOING TO

1. We form affirmative statements with a subject + the present of *be* + *going to* + a base verb. We form negative statements with a subject + the present of *be* + *not* + *going to* + a base verb.

    I'm going to have a party for my roommate's birthday this weekend.

    I'm not going to tell him because I want it to be a surprise.

2. We form *yes/no* questions with the present of *be* + a subject + *going to* + a base verb. In short answers, we use a pronoun subject + the present of *be* (+ *not* for negatives). We usually contract negative short answers.

    A: **Are** your friends **going to make** all of the food?

    B: Yes, they **are**.

    A: **Are** they **going to make** American food?

    B: No, they**'re not**./No, they **aren't**. They're going to make Mexican food.

3. We use the *wh-* words *what, where, when, how, which, why, who,* and *whom* to form *wh-* questions.

    Who is going to make the food?

    Where are they **going to** make it?

4. In speech and in informal writing, we often contract *is* with the *wh-* word. In speech, we also contract *are* with the *wh-* word, but we do not usually write this form.

WILL

5. We form affirmative statements with a subject + *will* + a base verb. We form negative statements with a subject + *will not/won't* + a base verb.

    A: I need a big pot to make the chili in.

    B: I have one. I**'ll lend** it to you.

    A: Thanks. Could you bring it to me by 9:00 Saturday morning?

    B: Sure. Don't worry. I **won't be** late.

6. We form *yes/no* questions with *will* + a subject + a base verb. In short answers, we use a pronoun subject + *will* or *will not*. We usually contract negative short answers.

    A: **Will** your roommate **like** the surprise?

    B: Yes, he **will**. He loves parties.

7. We use the *wh-* words *what, where, when, how, which, why, who,* and *whom* to form *wh-* questions.

    I need some help. **Who will** set the table for me?

8. In speech, we often contract *will* with the *wh-* word, but we do not usually write this form.

Function

1. Here are the main uses of *be going to* + base verb and *will* + base verb.

Will + Base Verb	*Be Going To* + Base Verb

a. To talk about something we decide to do at the moment of speaking.
  A: Oh, no! I've spilled some coffee on the rug.
  B: Don't worry. I**'ll clean** it up for you.
	a. To talk about plans or something we have already decided to do.
	  I**'m going to have** lunch with my brother today.

b. To say what we think or believe will happen in the future, usually with the verbs such as *think, believe,* and *expect*; with the adverbs such as *probably, perhaps, maybe,* and *certainly*; and with expressions such as *I'm sure* and *I'm afraid.*
  They**'ll** probably **get** here late.
  I'm sure he**'ll be** there.
	b. To talk about something in the future that we can see as a result of something in the present.
	  There isn't a cloud in the sky. It**'s going to be** a beautiful day.

c. To talk about actions and events that will definitely happen in the future.
  I **will be** 20 next month.
  The sun **will rise** again tomorrow.
	c. To talk about plans, intentions, or ambitions for the future.
	  She**'s going to be** a doctor some day.

2. We often use *be going to* to talk about an intention and *will* to give details and comments.

    I **am going to have** a surprise birthday party for Ken. I**'ll invite** all his friends.

3. We can use either *will* or *be going to* to make predictions.

    They**'ll win** the game. They**'re going to win** the game.

4. We use *will* and *be going to* with time expressions such as *soon, tonight, tomorrow,* and *next Monday/week/month/year.*

5. You might occasionally notice the use of *shall* instead of *will* with the pronoun *I* or *we* to express future time. This use is more common in British English than in American English. However, in American English, we do use *shall* to make polite suggestions.

    Shall we go? It's getting late.

1 Practice

Listen to the conversation. Complete the sentences with *be going to* or *will*. Then practice the conversation with a partner.

TIM: What _____ are you going to _____ do tonight?
                          1

MIKE: I _____ see the new Steven Spielberg
                    2
movie with Melissa. How about you?

TIM: Oh, I think I _____ stay home tonight.
                        3

MIKE: Why don't you come with us? It _____
                                              4
be fun.

TIM: OK. I _____ go with you.
                5

MIKE: We _____ leave at seven, and
              6
we _____ probably get
        7
there by seven thirty.

TIM: OK. I _____ see you in front of the movie
              8
theater at 7:30 then.

2 Practice

A Read about the city of the future.

In the future, cities like Tokyo in Japan are going to be even more crowded than they are today. Japan does not have a lot of land, so where are people going to live? Japanese architects have plans for a city in the sky. At the moment, the architects do not have enough money to start their plan, but maybe they will get the money soon. They are going to find a place near Tokyo to build this city.

This city in the sky will be a glass pyramid over 2,000 meters (6,560 feet) high. The pyramid will be 500 floors. It will have residential areas with apartments, parks, and leisure centers. It will also have offices, restaurants, schools, hospitals, post offices, and everything else that a city has, but it won't have cars. The city will be climate-controlled so the weather will always be nice. Imagine. You will be able to go out for a relaxing run in the middle of winter and take the elevator to your job. People will travel in elevators, on walkways, and on special trains. The architects hope one day they will get the money to build this city.

B Write *yes/no* and *wh-* questions for the answers. The underlined words in the answer are prompts for the questions.

1. QUESTION: *Are cities like Tokyo going to be very crowded in the future?*

   ANSWER: <u>Yes</u>, cities like Tokyo are going to be very crowded.

2. QUESTION: _____

   ANSWER: They are going to build this city <u>near Tokyo</u>.

3. QUESTION: _____

   ANSWER: The shape of this city will be <u>a pyramid</u>.

4. QUESTION: _____

   ANSWER: The pyramid will be <u>2,000 meters high</u>.

5. QUESTION: _____

   ANSWER: The pyramid will be made of <u>glass</u>.

6. QUESTION: _____

   ANSWER: <u>Yes</u>, it will have apartments for people to live in.

7. QUESTION: _____

   ANSWER: <u>No</u>, it won't have cars.

8. QUESTION: _____

   ANSWER: People will travel <u>in elevators, on walkways, and on special trains</u>.

3 Pair Up and Talk

A Practice the conversation with a partner.

A: What will this city be like 25 years from now?

B: The traffic will be terrible.

A: I disagree. I think people are going to drive less. Traffic won't be so bad.

B Continue the conversation about the future of your city or town. Use ideas from the list, *be going to*, and *will* or your own ideas.

crime	neighborhoods	traffic
garbage/pollution	schools	weather

The Future   **61**

Time Clauses and Conditional Sentences in the Future

Form/Function

When we grow up, **we'll fly** in one of those planes and go all over the world.

1. All clauses have a subject and a verb. Main clauses can stand alone as complete sentences. Dependent clauses cannot. We must use them with a main clause. There are several kinds of dependent clauses. One of them is the time clause.
2. Time clauses begin with words such as *when, while, as soon as, before, after*, and *until*. Conditional clauses begin with words such as *if* and *unless*.

Main Clause	Time/Conditional Clause
I'll buy a car	**as soon as** I have enough money.
I'll get a bigger apartment	**if** I have enough money next year.

3. A time clause gives information about when something happens in the main clause.

Time Clause	Main Clause
When you get here,	we'll start the game.

4. A future conditional sentence expresses a possible situation in the conditional clause and a result in the main clause.

Conditional Clause	Main Clause
If you're late,	we'll start without you.

5. The time or conditional clause can come either at the beginning or end of the sentence. When the time or conditional clause comes at the beginning of a sentence, we put a comma after it.

Time/Conditional Clause	Main Clause
As soon as I have enough money,	I'll buy a car.
If I have enough money next year,	I'll get a bigger apartment.

6. We do not use *will* or *be going to* in a time clause even though we are talking about the future. We usually use the simple present.

Time Clause—Present	Main Clause—Future
When I see him,	I'll give him the message.
If the weather is nice,	we'll go to the beach.

7. We can also use the present perfect in a time clause to show that one action will be finished before another action.

   I'll talk with her when she **arrives**.

   OR I'll talk with her when she **has arrived**.

8. In some cases, we can use the present progressive (instead of the simple present) to talk about an action that will be in progress at a future time.

   While we **are traveling** around Mexico next summer, we will visit all the famous colonial cities.

4 Practice

A Matt is 16 years old. A TV show interviewed him about his future plans. Listen to the interview.

CD1, 13

1.   What does Matt want to be in the future?
     Matt wants to be a famous rock star in the future.

2.   When will he become a famous rock star?
     _____

3.   When will he have a lot of money?
     _____

4.   What will he do as soon as he becomes a millionaire?
     _____

5.   Where will he go as soon as he has enough time and money?
     _____

6.   When will he leave Africa?
     _____

7.   Who will he visit when he goes to China?
     _____

8.   When will he visit Japan?
     _____

9.   What will he do when he comes home?
     _____

10. What will he do if his parents want him to?
     _____

5 Your Turn

Complete the sentences with time clauses.

Example

I'll get a job as soon as I can.

1.   I'll get a job as soon as _____ .

2.   I'll live with my parents until _____ .

3.   I'll get to travel a lot _____ .

4.   I'll buy a house or an apartment _____ .

6 Pair Up and Talk

A Practice the conversation with a partner. Imagine that one of you is going hiking in the mountains for the first time.

A: What will you do if you hurt yourself?

B: I'll call for help on my cell phone.

B Continue the conversation, using the prompts below or your own ideas.

it gets dark   it rains   you get hungry   you get lost

7 Phrasal Verb Practice

A Complete the sentences with the correct form of the phrasal verbs. Use each verb only once. Phrasal verbs are taught in Unit 8, section H.

ask about   line up   look at   look forward to   stop by   walk around

Welcome to Berkeley House and Gardens. I am _looking forward to_ our tour today.

1

Please _____ behind the velvet rope while I talk to you. We're going

2

to _____ the gardens first. Our gardens have 7,000 varieties of plants,

3

shrubs, and trees. The mansion has an art gallery and a large collection. You'll have time

to _____ everything. Please feel free to _____ any part

4   5

of the gardens or collections. After the tour, we'll _____ the gift shop.

6

B Circle the correct definitions of the phrasal verbs.

1. ask about
a. demand
b. ask
c. want

2. look forward to
a. expect to enjoy
b. examine the meaning
c. watch carefully

3. line up
a. walk straight
b. draw lines on
c. move into a row

4. look at
a. see
b. remember
c. watch for

5. stop by
a. end an activity
b. make a short visit
c. decide to do something

6. walk around
a. get somewhere quickly
b. go on foot in an area
c. leave right away

Present with Future Meaning

Function

The train **leaves** at 8:15, and I**'m meeting** Mr. Sharp for an interview at 9:00.

THE PRESENT PROGRESSIVE

1. We use the present progressive for actions that we already arranged or planned for in the future.

   A: What **are** you **doing** on Sunday morning?

   B: I**'m meeting** Susan.

   We**'re flying** to New York tomorrow morning.

   When we use the present progressive in this way, we often use a time expression such as *on Monday, tonight,* or *next week.*

2. We use the present progressive more often than *be going to* with the verbs *go* and *come.*

   We**'re going** camping on Saturday, and we**'re coming** back on Sunday evening.

   I**'m going** to Toronto soon.

THE SIMPLE PRESENT

3. We use the simple present to talk about actions or events that are part of a fixed schedule.

   The train **arrives** at 8:10 in the morning.

   The movie **starts** at 9:00 in the evening, and it **ends** at 10:45.

8 Practice

Christina Lang is a famous tennis player. Complete the sentences about her trip to London next week. Use the present progressive or the simple present.

1. Christina's flight from Rio (arrive) ____arrives____ in London at 1:30 P.M.
   on Monday.

2. After she rests a little, she (have) _____ dinner with some sports reporters.

3. The next morning, she (meet) _____ with her coach at 9:00, and she
   (see) _____ her doctor at 11:00.

4. In the afternoon, she (practice) _____ for two hours.

5. On Wednesday morning, she (meet) _____ some of the other players.
   The meeting (start) _____ at 9:00 and (end) _____ at 10:30.

6. After that, she (go) _____ for a medical checkup. She
   (have) _____ an appointment with the doctor at 2:00.

7. On Thursday morning, she (rest) _____ .

8. On Thursday afternoon, she (play) _____ her match. The game
   (start) _____ at 2:00.

9. She (fly) _____ home on Friday morning. The plane
   (take off) _____ at 11:30.

9 Pair Up and Talk

A Practice the conversation with a partner.

A: What are you doing tomorrow afternoon?

B: I'm meeting my friend downtown.

A: What are you doing after that?

B: I'm shopping with my sister.

B Continue the conversation. Ask and answer questions about arrangements or plans you have made for the future. Use the time phrases below.

| next month | this Monday | tomorrow morning |
| next week | tomorrow afternoon | tonight |

10   Pair Up and Talk

A   Practice the conversation with a partner.

A: When do classes start?

B: Classes start on September 4.

B   Continue the conversation. Read this schedule of college classes. Ask and answer questions about the schedule using the simple present of the verbs in the list.

begin   end   start

> ### Schedule
>
> September 4   First day of class
> October 18–22   Fall vacation
> November 24–28   Thanksgiving vacation
> December 9   Last day of class
> December 12–17   Final exams

C   Now write a schedule of classes for your school. With a partner ask and answer questions about it as you did in part B, using the simple present.

> ### Schedule

3D The Future Progressive

Form

At this time tomorrow, **I'll be walking** on a sandy beach.

1. We form affirmative statements in the future progressive with a subject + *will* + *be* + a verb + *-ing*. We form negative statements with a subject + *will not/won't* + *be* + a verb + *-ing*.

   I can't talk to you at 10:00 this morning. **I'll be meeting** with my boss.

2. We form *yes/no* questions with *will* + a subject + *be* + a verb + *-ing*. In short answers, we use a pronoun subject + *will (not)*. We usually contract negative short answers.

   A: **Will** you **be working** when I get to your office?

   B: Yes, I **will**. Please don't interrupt me if I'm on the phone.

   OR No, I **won't**. I'll be at lunch.

3. We use the *wh-* words *what, where, when, how, which, why, who,* and *whom* to form *wh-* questions in the future progressive.

   Who will be taking the day off tomorrow?

   If I need to find you, **where will** you **be sitting**?

4. In speech, we often contract *will* with the *wh-* word, but we do not usually write this form.

   Where'll we go from here?

Function

1. We use *will be* + a verb + *-ing* to talk about something which will be in progress at a specific time in the future.

    At this time next week, I **will be walking** on a beach.

2. We also use *will be* + a verb + *-ing* to talk about something which has already been arranged or is part of a routine.

    I'll **be having** lunch with my boss tomorrow. (arrangement)

    I'll **be doing** the laundry tomorrow morning. (routine)

3. We often use *will be* + a verb + *-ing* as a polite way of asking about someone's plans in the near future, especially when those plans affect us. When we use this form, it means that we do not want the other person to change their plans for us.

    A: **Will** you **be using** the copy machine soon?

    B: No. Why?

    A: I have to make a copy of this report.

---

11   Practice

Susan Brooks is a manager. Read her schedule for Monday. Write complete sentences using the future progressive about what she will be doing at these times.

9:00	Talk to Jack Simms
9:30	Write the status report
10:30	Have a conference call with other managers
1:00	Lunch with Peter Jones
1:30	Interview Jane Pratt for the job opening
2:00	Meet with Steve
2:30	Show staff the new sales software
4:30	Answer email

1. *At 9:00 she will / she'll be talking to Jack Simms.*

2. _____

3. _____

4. _____

5. _____

6. _____

7. _____

8. _____

AUDIO
DOWNLOAD

CD1, 14

12 Practice

Listen to the conversation. Complete the sentences with *will* + base verb or the future progressive (*will* + *be* + verb + *-ing*). Then practice the conversation with a partner.

Isabel is talking to her friend Susan about going on a vacation to Barcelona, Spain. Susan's family lives there, and Isabel is going to stay with them.

SUSAN: When you arrive at the airport in Barcelona, my sister __will be waiting__
1
for you.

ISABEL: How _____ each other? We've never met.
2

SUSAN: Don't worry. She has a photo of you. Anyway, you _____ her.
3
She looks like me, and she _____ a red dress or jacket. She
4
always wears red.

ISABEL: OK. I _____ . I still can't believe it. This time tomorrow, I
5
_____ on a plane on my way to Spain.
6

SUSAN: And at one o'clock the next day, you _____ lunch with my
7
family, and then you _____ a siesta, which is what we call an
8
afternoon rest.

13 Pair Up and Talk

A Practice the conversation with a partner.

A: What will you be doing at 7:05 A.M. tomorrow?

B: At 7:05 tomorrow morning, I'll be drinking a cup of coffee.

B Continue the conversation about your plans for tomorrow, using the times below and the future progressive.

7:05 A.M.   8:00 A.M.   9:15 A.M.   4:00 P.M.

7:30 A.M.   8:55 A.M.   1:20 P.M.   6:15 P.M.

3E | Other Expressions of the Future; The Future in the Past

Form/Function

Eli **is about to throw** the ball. He **was going to throw** a slow pitch, but decided to throw a fast one.

1. We can also express the future in these ways.

Form	Function
a. *be about to* + a base verb	We use *be about to* to talk about the very near future. The movie **is about to start**.
b. *be to* + a base verb	We use *be to* + a base verb to refer to a future plan. This form is mainly used in formal English. The president **is to visit** Japan next week.
c. a present form of verbs like *plan, intend, decide,* or *mean* + an infinitive	We use these verbs + infinitive to express a future plan or intention. We **plan to buy** a house next year. He **has decided to take** the job in Baltimore.

2. We use *was/were going to* + a base verb to say that we planned something for the future at a past time. We sometimes call this "the future in the past." When we use this structure, it often means that the planned future action did not happen.

    They **were going to buy** the house, but they changed their minds at the last minute.

    We **were going to eat** at a Chinese restaurant, but it was too crowded, so we went to an Italian restaurant instead.

14 Practice

The following famous people intended to be one thing but became something else instead. Write a sentence about each one using *was going to be* in the first part of the sentence and *became* in the other.

PERSON	GOING TO BE	BECAME
1. Albert Einstein	violinist	he/physicist
2. Mahatma Gandhi	lawyer	he/great political leader
3. George Washington Carver	artist	he/chemist and botanist
4. Hans Christian Andersen	actor	he/fairy tale writer
5. Frida Kahlo	doctor	she/artist
6. Sigmund Freud	doctor	he/psychoanalyst

1. _Albert Einstein was going to be a violinist, but he became a physicist._

2. _____

3. _____

4. _____

5. _____

6. _____

15 Practice

Jane's relatives are coming for a visit. She and her husband planned to do a lot of things, but they all went wrong. Complete the sentences using *was/were about to* + the verbs in parentheses.

1. Jane (do) _was about to do_ the laundry when she realized she didn't have enough detergent.

2. She and Jim (drive) _____ to the store when the phone rang.

3. She (make) _____ a cake when she realized she didn't have butter.

4. She and Jim (do) _____ some housework when the doorbell rang.

5. Her relatives (ring) _____ the doorbell when they realized they had left their gift in the car.

6. She (tell) _____ them that they were too early, but she changed her mind.

7. She (give) _____ her aunt a cup of coffee when she dropped it on the floor.

8. She (scream) _____ , but she didn't. She just laughed.

16 Practice
Complete the sentences with *be to* or *be about to* + the verbs in parentheses.

1. The president (visit) _____ is to visit _____ the university today.

2. The ceremony (begin) _____ . The students are very excited.

3. He (enter) _____ the auditorium any minute.

4. The newspaper says that he (give) _____ a speech about more money for education.

5. This speech (help) _____ him get elected again.

6. The president of our university is standing on the stage. She (introduce) _____ the nation's president.

17 Pair Up and Talk
A Practice the conversation with a partner.

A: My sister was going to get married last month, but she didn't.

B: Why not?

A: She realized she didn't really love her boyfriend.

B Now tell your partner three things about you or other people that were going to happen but didn't. Ask follow-up questions to learn more information.

3F | The Future Perfect and the Future Perfect Progressive

Form

By this time next year, Mr. Yamasaki **will have been working** for his company for 45 years.

THE FUTURE PERFECT

1. We form affirmative statements with a subject + *will* + *have* + a past participle. We form negative statements with a subject + *will not/won't* + *have* + a past participle.

    By this time next year, the people **will have chosen** a new president.

2. We form *yes/no* questions with *will* + a subject + *have* + a past participle. In short answers, we use a pronoun subject + *will/won't (have)*.

    A: **Will** the candidates **have visited** every state before the election?
    B: Yes, they **will (have)**./No, they **won't (have)**.

3. We use the *wh-* words *what, where, when, how, which, why, who,* and *whom* to form *wh-*questions in the future perfect.

    Which candidates **will have spent** the most money?
    Why will they **have spent** so much money?

THE FUTURE PERFECT PROGRESSIVE

4. We form affirmative statements with a subject + *will* + *have* + *been* + a verb + *-ing*. We form negative statements with a subject + *will not/won't* + *have* + *been* + a verb + *-ing*.

    By the time the election is over, the candidates **will have been running** for four months.

5. We form *yes/no* questions with *will* + a subject + *have* + *been* + a verb + *-ing*. In short answers, we use a pronoun subject + *will/won't (have)*.

    A: **Will** they **have been running** for six months?
    B: Yes, they **will (have)**./No, they **won't (have)**.

6. We use the *wh-* words *what, where, when, how, which, why, who,* and *whom* to form *wh-* questions in the future perfect progressive.

    Which candidates **will have been traveling** the most?
    In **which** states **will** they **have been traveling** the most?

Function

1. Here are the main uses of the future perfect and the future perfect progressive.

The Future Perfect	The Future Perfect Progressive
a. To say that a future action will be completed before another action or stated time in the future. My computer at work is broken, but the technology department **will have repaired** it when I **get** to the office tomorrow.	a. To emphasize the continuation of an action that will be in progress up to a certain time in the future. By the end of this year, he **will have been working** for the company for 20 years.
b. With time expressions such as *by the time, by +* time, and *before*. They **will have repaired** it before 8:00 tomorrow morning.	b. With time expressions such as *by the time, by +* time, and *for*. By the time I finish my degree, **I'll have been living** here for three years.

2. When expressions such as *by the time* and *before* introduce time clauses that refer to the future, we use a present form in the clause. The main clause, with the future perfect or the future perfect progressive, can go either before or after the time clause.

Time Clause	Main Clause

By the time I **get** there, I **will have flown** for nine hours.

18   Practice

Complete the sentences about the people in this family. Then write two sentences about them with your ideas. Use the future perfect and the verbs in parentheses.

1. By next year, Carlos Sanchez (drive) _will have driven_ 10,000 miles (16,093 kilometers) on his way to and from work.

2. By next year, Rosa Sanchez (help) _____ hundreds of people in her job as a nurse.

3. By next year, their daughter (play) _____ soccer for five years.

4. By next year, their son (finish) _____ college.

5. By then, he (study) _____ at that college for four years.

6. By next year, their daughter (start) _____ college.

7. She (decide) _____ what to study for her major.

8. Carlos Sanchez (spend) _____ more of his savings on his children.

9. (your idea) _____

10. (your idea) _____

---

19   Practice
In each sentence, underline the correct future form of the verbs in parentheses.

1. Scientists (are planning/will plan) a mission to the moon.

2. They (are going to send/have been sending) some astronauts to the moon.

3. There (will be/is being) a press conference tomorrow at 9:00 to announce the mission.

4. As usual, some people (are going to be/will have been) happy about such an announcement, but others (are not/will not be).

5. The astronauts (will be preparing/will have prepared) to go to the moon for the next three years.

6. The astronauts (will have been leaving/are leaving) Earth on March 20.

7. While they are on the moon, they (will be doing/are doing) experiments.

8. They (will be looking/are looking) for signs of life.

9. They (will be collecting/are collecting) samples.

10. By the end of their stay on the moon, the astronauts (will be living/will have been living) there for four weeks.

11. By the time they get back, they (will have taken/will be taking) 5,000 photos.

20   Pair Up and Talk
Choose an age in your future. For example, if you are 25 years old, you might choose 30. What do you think you will have done by that age? Tell a partner four things using the future perfect.

Example

By the time I am 28, I will have gotten married.

21   Your Turn
Answer these questions with complete sentences. Use the future perfect progressive + *for* + length of time.

1. How long will you have been attending this school by the end of the year?

    _____

    _____

2. How long will you have been living in your house or apartment by next July?

    _____

    _____

3. How long will you have been studying English by the end of the school year?

    _____

    _____

4. How long will you have been wearing your present shoes by the end of the year?

    _____

    _____

5. How long will you have been studying with your present teacher by the end of this school year?

    _____

    _____

6. How long will you have been using this book by the end of the year?

    _____

    _____

THE GRIM VISITOR

Old Anna was not always old. Many years ago, as the young men of her village harvested hay and summer wheat, she would run on young legs from field to field, offering the men water and teasing them about being slow. She herself was the fastest person in the village—and probably the fastest in all of Hungary. She could outrace the deer of the forest.

One day, as she was about to sprint to the mill for some flour, Death appeared suddenly beside her. "Come, Anna, for it is time."

She knew Death when she saw him. His face was a waxy green and his breath smelled like a dead rat. "You must be mistaken, sir. I am not yet 20."

"For some I come early," he breathed. No matter how she pleaded, he would not leave. Just as he placed a foul hand on her sleeve to end the conversation, she made a proposition. "Grim sir, many have tried to outrun you. I believe I will succeed where they failed." Intrigued by her challenge, Death agreed. It would be a race to the riverbank. "If I reach it first," he said, "I will have my way. If not, I will leave you alone."

Of course, Anna won. That is why today she sits, frail as a stem, looking out her cottage window. Many times she has begged Death to forget that race some 150 years ago. Never once has he replied, and it is said he never will.

1. _____

She lived in a Hungarian farming village.

2. _____

She enjoyed joking with the young men harvesting their crops.

3. _____

She could run faster than anyone else she knew.

4. _____

She was about to run to the flour mill.

5. _____

He was going to end her life.

6. _____

By saying it, she meant, "I will outrun you."

7. _____

She would go willingly to her death.

8. _____

He would go away.

9. _____

She hopes Death will return and take her away.

10. _____

She will probably get older and older without dying.

A Listen and check the correct answer.

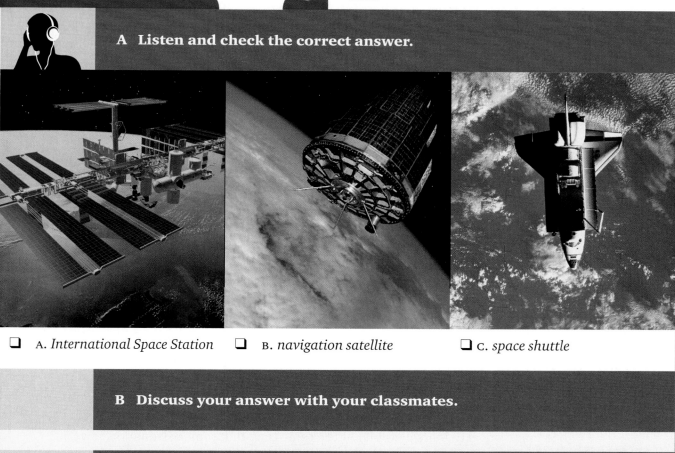

❏ A. *International Space Station*   ❏ B. *navigation satellite*   ❏ C. *space shuttle*

B Discuss your answer with your classmates.

C Now listen again and write the sentences you hear.

CD1, 16

1 Review (3a, 3f)

Complete the sentences with the correct future form of the verbs in parentheses. Sometimes more than one answer is possible. If there are other words in parentheses, include them.

(humans/ever/go) _____*Will humans ever go*_____ to Mars? I feel sure that
                                    1
humans (achieve) _____ this goal. Here's what I think
                                    2
(happen) _____ .
                        3
The International Space Station (help) _____
                                                                4
to make travel to Mars possible. At the same time that some astronauts (travel)

_____ to Mars, others (work) _____
                    5   6
_____ in the space station. By then, scientists in the space station (find)

_____ ways to keep humans healthy in space for a long
                    7
time.

By that time, they (prepare)_____ people for the long
                                                        8
and difficult trip to Mars, and many nations (join)_____
                                                                                            9
together to prepare for the first human travel to Mars.

By the time humans land on Mars, robots (be) _____
                                                                                    10
there for many years. By then, they (give) _____ us all
                                                                        11
the information we need about living on Mars. What (the first travelers/think of)

_____ life on Mars? Eventually, we (know)
                    12
_____ the answers to that question. Future missions to
                    13
Mars (give)_____ us more information about this planet.
                            14

2 Review (3a, 3c–3d)

Complete the sentences with the correct future form of the verbs in parentheses. Sometimes more than one answer is possible.

| New | Delete | Reply | Reply All | Forward | Move |

To:	alex@mg-city.edu
Cc:	
Subject:	My trip

Hi Alex,

I (fly) _____'m flying_____ to Johannesburg tomorrow.
                    1

I (be) _____ in South Africa for a month. At this time tomorrow,
                2

I (fly)_____ over the coast of Africa. I'm so excited. While I (travel)
            3

_____ around South Africa, I (see) _____ game parks,
            4   **5**

mountains, and beautiful cities. By this time next week, I (visit)_____ the
                                                                        6

Transvaal and Kruger National Park. I (take) _____ pictures of all the animals
                                                    7

with my new digital camera. On Wednesday, I (be) _____ in the park looking
                                                        8

for giraffes, elephants, and zebras!

I was going to work this summer, but I changed my mind. After all, I (work)

_____ for the rest of my life. Well, one day I (get) _____ out
            9   **10**

of school. By the end of next year, I (study) _____ to be a doctor for six years!
                                                    11

That's a long time. My plane (leave) _____ very early tomorrow morning.
                                            12

I (go) _____ to bed now.
            13

Emma

A Before You Read

1. Why do people like to go to beaches?

2. Think of a geographical feature—a beach, a wide plain, etc. What forces on Earth formed it?

WHERE WILL THE BEACHES BE?

B Read   Stop! Don't buy that beach house yet. Are you sure the beach will even be there when you're ready to swim? The Earth could be about to relocate it. The shorelines of the
5 future are going to look very different from today's shorelines.

Of course, there is the normal action of wind and weather. Water levels will rise and fall. Hills and bluffs will erode[1]
10 and sometimes collapse. Sand dunes will continue to **migrate** about two feet (0.6 meter) a year. Hurricanes will wipe out sandy islands
15 in one place and build new ones in another. Any of these changes could put your beachfront home under ten feet of water—or strand it half a mile inland.
20   Some of the world's best beaches are on the shores of the Mediterranean Sea, between Africa and Europe. Enjoy them fast, because in 100 million years, Africa will have moved north, crashed into southern Europe, and
25 raised the Mediterranean Mountains. By that time, too, California is likely to have a lot more beachfront than it has now. What is now Death Valley will be next to the beach. Western Australia may or may not still have beaches. A
30 lot depends on whether it slams into southern Asia or stops just offshore.

You might be wise to buy some land next to East Africa's Danakil Depression. Sure, it is below sea level, landlocked, and baking hot
35 now, but it won't stay that way. An ocean floor is already forming there. Somalia will continue to drift to the east. The rest of East Africa will continue moving north toward Europe. As soon as an earthquake cracks open some low
40 mountains, the Red Sea will pour in. There will be plenty of new beachfront to go around[2].

> **DID YOU KNOW ... ?**
> The world's largest desert, Africa's Sahara, was once the bottom of a huge sea.

[1.] erode = fall apart from being struck by wind or water

[2.] to go around = to be distributed

C Notice the Grammar   Underline all future forms of the verbs.

Choose the best answer.

D   Look for Main Ideas

1. This reading is mainly about factors that will _____ .
   - (A) make beaches good places to live
   - (B) threaten homes built near the water
   - (C) reshape shorelines from year to year
   - (D) eliminate some coasts and create others

2. What is the main topic of paragraph 4?
   - (A) movements of the Asian continent
   - (B) a possible new ocean forming in Africa
   - (C) a good place to buy beachfront property
   - (D) the Danakil Depression

E   Look for Details

3. Which of the following is NOT mentioned in the passage as an effect of wind and weather?
   - (A) an exciting environment for beach homes
   - (B) the destruction of hills
   - (C) changes in the location of sandy islands
   - (D) ups and downs in the depth of water

4. According to the reading, Death Valley will eventually _____ .
   - (A) move north
   - (B) become an island
   - (C) be next to the ocean
   - (D) have a sports team

5. The reading says that the Danakil region will become an ocean if _____ .
   - (A) a channel to a nearby sea is created
   - (B) the land sinks below sea level
   - (C) large enough waves occur on a nearby sea
   - (D) the region's climate changes enough

READING SKILL: Scanning

When we scan, we look for specific information we need to know, such as a name or a date. To scan, move your eyes quickly over the passage until you find the information you need. You don't have to read the whole passage carefully.

F   Make Inferences

6. What can we infer from paragraph 3 about the continents of Africa and Europe?
   - (A) They are just parts of the same continent.
   - (B) In 100 million years, they will be covered by mountains.
   - (C) They move at different speeds or in different directions.
   - (D) They will become much drier than they are now.

7. We can most strongly infer from the reading that the author thinks continental movement is _____ .
   - (A) frightening
   - (B) natural
   - (C) avoidable
   - (D) unproven

G   Look for Vocabulary

8. The term *migrate* in the reading is closest in meaning to _____ .
   - (A) fly away
   - (B) wash away
   - (C) move or shift
   - (D) flatten

Writing: Write an Essay with Supporting Examples

Write an essay about life in the year 2040. Use examples to support your ideas.

STEP **1** Work with a partner. Brainstorm the following topics. Make notes about each one.

clothes   food   shopping

computers   home   transportation

STEP **2** Choose two of the topics and write sentences about each one.

STEP **3** Write a paragraph on each topic. Write a topic sentence, a supporting sentence, and at least one example for each topic.

Topic Sentence

Supporting Sentence

Example 1

Example 2

> In the year 2040, our homes will be completely computerized. Our television, telephone, and computer will be a single machine. For example, while talking on the phone, we will see the person we are talking to. We will also exchange pictures and other information as we talk.

STEP **4** Write an introduction with a thesis statement that refers to your examples. Write a conclusion that restates the thesis statement.

STEP **5** Write a title for your essay. Center it at the top of the page.

STEP **6** Evaluate your essay.

Checklist

_____ Did you write a title and put it in the right place?

_____ Did your introduction include a thesis statement?

_____ Do your supporting paragraphs have a topic sentence, a supporting sentence, and at least one example?

_____ Does your conclusion restate the thesis statement?

STEP **7** Work with a partner or a teacher to edit your essay. Check spelling, vocabulary, and grammar.

STEP **8** Write your final copy.

Self-Test

1. By next year, I will _____ here for three years.

    A. be living   Ⓐ Ⓑ Ⓒ Ⓓ
    B. have been living
    C. live
    D. to be lived

2. She'll have graduated _____ June.

    A. for   Ⓐ Ⓑ Ⓒ Ⓓ
    B. until
    C. by
    D. already

3. I'll _____ my essay by 6:00.

    A. have finished   Ⓐ Ⓑ Ⓒ Ⓓ
    B. finishing
    C. have been finishing
    D. be finished

4. We _____ our test results tomorrow.

    A. will know   Ⓐ Ⓑ Ⓒ Ⓓ
    B. will be knowing
    C. are knowing
    D. know

5. We don't have much time. The plane _____ in 30 minutes.

    A. taking off   Ⓐ Ⓑ Ⓒ Ⓓ
    B. take off
    C. takes off
    D. will have been taking off

6. Look at those clouds! It _____ soon.

    A. is going to rain   Ⓐ Ⓑ Ⓒ Ⓓ
    B. is raining
    C. rains
    D. going to rain

7. As soon as I have enough money, I _____ a DVD player.

    A. buy   Ⓐ Ⓑ Ⓒ Ⓓ
    B. will buy
    C. buying
    D. will have bought

8. I'll give her the message when I _____ her.

    A. am seeing   Ⓐ Ⓑ Ⓒ Ⓓ
    B. will see
    C. saw
    D. see

9. ALEX: I need some help with this report.
   JULIO: Sure. _____ on it tomorrow morning? I can help you then.

    A. You will be working   Ⓐ Ⓑ Ⓒ Ⓓ
    B. Will you working
    C. Will you be working
    D. You are going to be working

10. They _____ to buy a house next year.

    A. will plan   Ⓐ Ⓑ Ⓒ Ⓓ
    B. are going to plan
    C. are planning
    D. will be planning

1. When <u>you will</u> <u>have</u> <u>completed</u> <u>all your courses</u>
       A   **B**   **C**   **D**
at the university?

       Ⓐ   Ⓑ   Ⓒ   Ⓓ

2. By the end of the year, I <u>have</u> <u>been</u> <u>studying</u> at
                   A   **B**   **C**
this college <u>for</u> three years.
          D

       Ⓐ   Ⓑ   Ⓒ   Ⓓ

3. We <u>are</u> <u>about</u> to have dinner <u>when</u> the doorbell
     A   **B**   **C**
<u>rang</u>. It was Mr. Jones.
   D

       Ⓐ   Ⓑ   Ⓒ   Ⓓ

4. Janet <u>is</u> <u>studying</u> hard right now <u>because</u> she
         A   **B**   **C**
<u>will intend</u> to go to college next year.
   D

       Ⓐ   Ⓑ   Ⓒ   Ⓓ

5. Our son <u>will</u> not <u>has graduated</u> from college <u>by</u>
        A   **B**   **C**   **D**
next summer.

       Ⓐ   Ⓑ   Ⓒ   Ⓓ

6. George <u>is going to</u> study economics, <u>but</u>
        A   **B**   **C**
he <u>changed</u> his mind and studied
    D
medicine instead.

       Ⓐ   Ⓑ   Ⓒ   Ⓓ

7. The traffic is very bad at <u>the moment</u>, <u>so</u> they
                    A   **B**
<u>are</u> probably <u>get</u> here late.
  C   **D**

       Ⓐ   Ⓑ   Ⓒ   Ⓓ

8. Where <u>she will</u> <u>be</u> <u>staying</u> when she <u>goes</u>
        A   **B**   **C**   **D**
to Canada?

       Ⓐ   Ⓑ   Ⓒ   Ⓓ

9. Next week <u>at this time</u>, <u>I'll be lying</u> on the
           A   **B**
beach <u>while</u> you <u>will studying</u>.
      C   **D**

       Ⓐ   Ⓑ   Ⓒ   Ⓓ

10. <u>Will</u> you <u>be</u> <u>go</u> to the meeting tomorrow
     A   **B**   **C**
<u>morning</u>?
  D

       Ⓐ   Ⓑ   Ⓒ   Ⓓ

Unit 4

Nouns and Expressions of Quantity

Each girl **is** wearing a traditional costume.

Form

One sheep, two **sheep**, three **sheep** … Don't fall asleep!

REGULAR PLURALS

	Singular	Plural
1. We form the plural of most nouns by adding *-s* to the singular noun.	book girl	book**s** girl**s**
2. Some regular plurals require changes in the spelling of the noun before we add *-s*.	factory knife shelf	factor**ies** kni**ves** shel**ves**

IRREGULAR PLURALS

	Singular	Plural
3. Some nouns form their plural by changing their vowels.	f**oo**t g**oo**se m**a**n m**ou**se t**oo**th w**o**man	f**ee**t g**ee**se m**e**n m**i**ce t**ee**th w**o**men
4. Some nouns form their plural by adding a syllable.	child ox	child**ren** ox**en**

	Singular	Plural
5. Some nouns have the same singular and plural form.	aircraft deer fish offspring series sheep spacecraft species	aircraft deer fish* offspring series sheep spacecraft species
6. Some nouns that come from Latin or Greek have plural endings that come from those languages.	bacterium cactus curriculum focus fungus medium memorandum thesis	bacteria cacti curricula foci fungi media memoranda theses
7. Some nouns have only a plural form. We can also use *a pair of* before these nouns.		jeans pajamas pants shorts trousers
8. Some nouns end in -s but are not plural.	economics mathematics news physics politics rabies	
9. The plural of *person* is usually *people* (not *persons*), but we can use *persons* in legal contexts. I know a **person** who works for your father. I know some **people** who work for your father. The **person** who had broken into a store was arrested. Three **persons** who had broken into a store were arrested.		

* *Fishes* is also possible, but is less common and refers to more than one *species* of fish.

Joseph Tanner is 89 years old. He is very tall and has large (foot) ____*feet*____ , a

big nose, and no (tooth) _____ at all. His (hobby) _____ are taking

(photo) _____ and fixing old (watch) _____ . He has several

(pet) _____ : three (mouse) _____ , five (fish) _____ , and

two (canary) _____ . He had two (wife) _____ during his life, but they

both died. His three (child) _____ are all grown up and now have

(life) _____ of their own.

1. The news on the Internet ___*is*___ more up-to-date than in the newspaper.

2. Physics _____ more difficult than mathematics.

3. Sheep _____ more intelligent than deer.

4. Aircraft _____ safer today than 20 years ago.

5. Bacteria _____ spread only through physical contact.

6. In some jobs, jeans _____ more common at work these days than more

   formal pants.

7. Fish _____ easier to take care of than birds.

8. Nowadays, the media _____ the biggest influence on our opinions.

9. Too many species of animals _____ now extinct.

10. The curriculum in this school _____ excellent.

A: Do you think that the news on the Internet is more up-to-date than in the newspaper?

B: Yes, I think so. The news on the Internet is more up-to-date because it can change

every minute of the day. Don't you agree?

92   Unit 4

B Continue the conversation. Discuss each of the sentences in Practice 2. Do you agree with them or not? Explain why. Use the correct singular or plural verb form in your answers.

4B Possessive Nouns; Possessive Phrases with *Of*

Form

Camels are called "the ships **of the desert**." They carry **people's** goods from place to place.

1. We use possessive nouns before singular or plural nouns.
   That **woman's** dress is very beautiful.
   The **teacher's** room is on the second floor.
2. If a noun is singular, we form its possessive by adding an apostrophe + -s ('s).
   Suzy is wearing her mother**'s** hat.
3. If a plural noun ends in -s, we form its possessive by adding only an apostrophe (').
   Today is my parents' wedding anniversary.
4. If a plural noun does not end in -s, we form its possessive by adding an apostrophe + -s ('s).
   The children**'s** toys are here.
   There is a lot of good men**'s** clothing in this store.
5. If a singular noun ends in -s, we can write the possessive form with an apostrophe + -s or just an apostrophe.
   That was Chris**'s** plan. OR That was Chris' plan.
   Sherlock Holmes**'s** hat is funny. OR Sherlock Holmes' hat is funny.
   We usually pronounce these *s'* endings as though they were written as *s's*. For example, *Chris'* is pronounced like *Chris's*, with two syllables *(chris-es)*.
6. If there are two or more nouns in a possessive phrase, we add the apostrophe to the last noun only.
   That is **Kate** and **Ben's** house.

e-Workbook 4B

Nouns and Expressions of Quantity **93**

7. We can also use a possessive noun with no noun following it. In this case, it must be clear what we are talking about.

That's not my cell phone. It's **Pete's**. (*Cell phone* is understood in the second sentence.)

8. In some cases, we use a phrase with *of* instead of an apostrophe to show possession. We usually use the possessive phrase with *of* when we refer to things.

The title **of this book** is *A Tale of Two Cities*.

Function

1. We often add the possessive *'s* to personal nouns (names like Maria and John) to show that the person owns or possesses something.

Kate's glasses look good on her.

My **brother's** school is near here.

2. We use the possessive form of nouns in some expressions of time.

Next **year's** class schedule is difficult for me.

Yesterday's news was interesting.

We can also use the possessive form of nouns to show a period of time.

He took a **week's** vacation last year.

3. With places, we can use either the possessive form of nouns or a phrase with *of*.

The **state's capital** is in Austin.

OR   The **capital of the state** is in Austin.

The **world's problems** are serious.

OR   The **problems of the world** are serious.

4. We usually use the possessive form when the first noun is a person or an animal.

First Noun	Second Noun	
My brother's	school	is very small.
The cat's	bowl	is in the kitchen.
John's	address	is 85 Valley Street.

But when the first of two nouns is a thing, we usually use *of*.

First Noun	Second Noun	
The name	of the school	is Hayes High School.
The name	of the song	is "Take My Heart."
The length	of skirts	is getting shorter this year.

4 Practice

Seven apostrophes are missing in this paragraph. Add apostrophes in the correct places.

This is a photo of my grandparents′ family. My grandmothers white dress is made of real lace. It used to be her mothers. Her aunts are sitting on either side of her. Her aunts dresses were made of silk. My grandfathers expression is very serious. He borrowed his brothers best suit for the photo. Mens suits are less formal nowadays. Womens hairstyles are more casual.

5 Your Turn

Write three sentences about the photo using the possessive forms *'s, s'* or *of*.

Example

The bride's dress is beautiful.

1. _____

2. _____

3. _____

6 Practice

Listen to the conversation. Complete the sentences. Use the words in parentheses with the possessive *'s* or *... of ...* . Sometimes you will have to add the word *the*. Then practice the conversation with a partner.

CD1, 17

HELEN: (sister/Jack) _____*Jack's sister*_____ and I went out to dinner
1
last night. The food was wonderful, but I can't remember

(name/restaurant) _*the name of the restaurant*_ . It was something like
2
(Tony/Place) _____ .
3

PETE: Where was it?

HELEN: I can't remember (name/street) _____ , but
4
it was on the opposite (side/street) _____ from
5
(Pizza/Mike) _____ . (food/freshness)
6
_____ was incredible, and you would like
7
(size/portions) _____ .
8

PETE: Was it expensive?

HELEN: (price/main courses) _____ was a little high, but
9
if you have (day/specials) _____ you won't
10
spend much.

PETE: Sounds good. Maybe I'll try it.

7 Your Turn

Complete the prompts, writing five sentences with *of*. With a partner, discuss which things are important to you when you buy clothing.

Example

The style of the pants is important, but the name of the designer isn't.

1. The price _____

2. The fit _____

3. The quality _____

4. The name of the designer _____

5. The style _____

4C | Compound Nouns

Form/Function

QUESTION: What do a **soccer ball**, a pair of **tennis shoes**, and a **paint brush** have in common?
ANSWER: They're all compound nouns!

1. A compound noun is a noun that is made of two or more simple nouns.

Simple Nouns	Compound Nouns
hair	hairbrush
brush	
can	can opener
opener	

2. We write some compound nouns as one word, for example, *bookstore*. We write others with a hyphen (-) (*T-shirt*), and others as two words (*hot dog*). There are no clear rules to tell you how to write a compound noun, and sometimes there is more than one possible way. If you are not sure how to spell a compound noun, look it up in your dictionary.

3. We can form many compound nouns by putting one noun, which acts as an adjective, in front of another noun.

   a toothbrush   a candy store

4. We usually form the plural of a compound noun by adding -*s* to the noun.

   CORRECT: two toothbrushes   two candy stores

   INCORRECT: two ~~tooths~~brushes   two ~~candies~~ stores

   Exception: Compound nouns ending in -*in-law* form plurals with the first word.

   I have one **brother-in-law**.

   My wife has three **brothers-in-law**.

5. When we use a number in a compound expression, the noun is singular and we use a hyphen between the words.

   CORRECT: We had a two-hour essay exam.

   INCORRECT: We had a two ~~hours~~ essay exam.

8 Practice

Complete the sentences with a compound noun that means the same thing as the words in parentheses.

Bob's (son who is 16 years old) _____*16-year-old son,*_____ Mark,
                                                    1
is taking a (computer course that lasts for three weeks) _____
                                                                      2
_____ . Bob is very happy about this and wants to buy him a (bicycle with ten
                                                                                3
speeds) _____ . Mark tells his father that he now
                            4
has a (license to drive*) _____ .
                                              5
Mark has found a car for sale. It's a (car with two doors) _____
                                                                            6
_____ . It's a (car that is five years old) _____
                                                                      7
_____ , but it looks great. The (person who sells cars) _____
                                                                              8
_____ tells Mark that he can take it for a (test drive for five minutes)
_____ . The man says it's a good deal. He says that it's a (car worth
2,000 dollars) _____ , but Mark can have it for
                                        9
500 dollars! And he doesn't have to pay for it now. He can get a (loan for five years)
_____ to pay for it.
                    10
*Hint: This compound noun starts with the word *driver's*.

9 Practice

Jack's class is having a sale to raise money for a trip. He is putting some things in a box to take to the sale. Write a compound noun for each thing in Jack's box. Use a word from list A and a word from list B to create each compound noun. Use *a* or *an* before each singular compound noun.

A		B	
alarm	lamp	brush	mugs
camera	neck	case	pot
coat	pencil	clock	shade
coffee	screw	driver	sharpener
computer	tea	hangers	shoes
hair	tennis	keyboard	tie

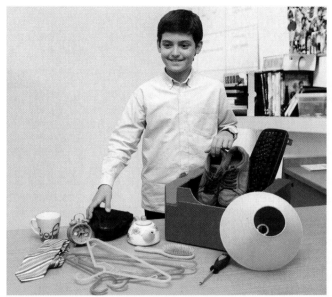

1. _____an alarm clock_____   7. _____

2. _____   8. _____

3. _____   9. _____

4. _____   10. _____

5. _____   11. _____

6. _____   12. _____

10   Your Turn

Work with a partner. Write as many compound nouns as you can with the following words and words of your own. The pair with the most compound nouns is the winner.

Example

baby blanket   *laptop computer*

baby   computer   office   shoe   telephone

bicycle   head   paper   station   time

1. _____   7. _____

2. _____   8. _____

3. _____   9. _____

4. _____   10. _____

5. _____   11. _____

6. _____   12. _____

11   Phrasal Verb Practice

A   Complete the sentences with the correct form of the phrasal verbs. Use each verb only once. Phrasal verbs are taught in Unit 8, section H.

give up   mix up   set off   take up   tear into   turn away

Wassily Kandinsky was the world's first abstract artist. Abstract art is art that does not

show real objects. Kandinsky was born in 1866 in Moscow, Russia. He studied law at

Moscow University and became a law professor. But he always wanted to

_____*take up*_____ art. In 1896, he decided to _____ law and
          1   2
become an artist. He _____ for Munich, Germany, to go to art school.
                              3
But he didn't paint like any other artist. He _____ bold colors and simple
                                                          4
designs. In 1910, he completed his first abstract painting. The public and the art critics

_____ him. They hated his work. But Kandinsky continued to paint. He
          5
refused to _____ from his art. He died in 1944 after suffering hardship
                    6
for years.

B   Match the phrasal verb with the correct definition.

_____   **1.** turn away   **a.** attack violently, especially with words

_____   **2.** set off   **b.** begin to do

_____   **3.** tear into   **c.** refuse to look at or do

_____   **4.** give up   **d.** willingly stop having or doing something

_____   **5.** mix up   **e.** put different things together

_____   **6.** take up   **f.** begin a trip

4D | Count Nouns and Noncount Nouns

Form/Function

SUE: What's that?
KUMIKO: It's **sushi**. It's made of **rice**, **fish**, **seaweed**, and other **things**. We eat it with **chopsticks**.

1. Count nouns are things that we can count: *one chair, two chairs.* Noncount nouns are things we cannot separate and count one by one. Some noncount nouns we see as a "whole" made up of individual elements, e.g. *rice, sugar.* Other noncount nouns are abstractions. We cannot see or touch them: *love, beauty.*

Count Nouns	Noncount Nouns

a. Have singular and plural forms.
   one **book**, two **books**
   a **man**, some **men**
	a. Have only the singular form. They have no plural form.
	   milk, weather, gold

b. Take singular or plural verbs.
   This book **is** good.
   Those books **are** good.
	b. Always take singular verbs.
	   Milk **is** good for you.
	   The weather **was** cold yesterday.

c. Can take *some/any/many/few/a few/a lot of* with the plural form.
   I bought **some** oranges.
   There are **few** oranges.
	c. Can take *some/any/much/little/a little/a lot of.*
	   There is **some** milk in the refrigerator.
	   There is **little** milk left.

d. Take *a/an* and numbers.
   I have **an** orange.
	d. Do not take *a/an* and numbers.
	   Milk is good for you.*

*We use *a/an, one/two/*etc. with noncount nouns such as *coffee, tea, water*, etc. when we refer to servings.
   We'd like **two coffees**, please.

Nouns and Expressions of Quantity

2. Some nouns can be count or noncount, but with a difference in meaning. Here are some examples:

Noun	Count Noun	Noncount Meaning
experience	I had a bad **experience** on a boat.	Do you have any **experience** in computer programming?
glass	Would you like a **glass** of water?	The vase is made of **glass**.
hair	He has two gray **hairs** on his head.	His **hair** is gray.
iron	I bought a new **iron**.	The pot is made of **iron**.
time	How many **times** did the phone ring?	I don't have much **time** right now.
wood	The table was made of five different **woods**.	The table is made of **wood**.

3. The following are categories of some noncount nouns.

Categories of Noncount Nouns	Examples
Abstract Words	time, love, happiness, education, information
Activities	sailing, swimming, farming
Fields of Study	history, geography, medicine
Some Kinds of Food	chocolate, meat, bread, milk
Gases	air, oxygen, pollution
Languages	Spanish, Arabic, French
Liquids	water, gasoline, blood
Materials	plastic, cotton, wood
Natural Forces	weather, wind, fire, sunshine
Particles	sand, dust, rice, hair, dirt
Recreation	football, baseball, chess, tennis

12 Practice

Complete the sentences with nouns from the list. Add articles and make the nouns plural if necessary. Then listen to the conversations to check your answers. Practice the conversations with a partner.

AUDIO DOWNLOAD

CD1, 18

experience   glass   hair   time   wood

1. A: May I have some water?

    B: Of course. Help yourself. _The glasses_ on this shelf are for water.

2. A: How was your trip to Paris?

    B: Amazing. Climbing the Eiffel Tower was _____ I will never forget.

3. A: My mother's _____ turned gray when she was only 30.

    B: I hope that doesn't happen to me. I'm 25, and I already have two gray _____ .

4. A: Do you have _____ to help me with my homework?

    B: Sure. I can help you this afternoon.

5. A: The company wanted someone with _____ in marketing or sales.

    B: That sounds perfect for you. You've worked in marketing before.

6. A: Have you met the manager before?

    B: Yes, we've met several _____ .

7. A: What an unusual office building. What's it made of?

    B: The outside is made of _____ and _____ .

8. A: I like this desk.

    B: Thanks. My brother made it. He used three different _____ .

13 Practice

Read these phrases. Write *C* next to the phrase if the article is used correctly. Write *I* if it is used incorrectly.

_____ 1. an information   _____ 6. a glass

_____ 2. pollution   _____ 7. a tennis

_____ 3. a time   _____ 8. two drinks

_____ 4. a weather   _____ 9. a dirt

_____ 5. a wood   _____ 10. a milk

14 Pair Up and Talk
A Practice the conversation with a partner.

A: Tennis is a great sport. I played yesterday with Jean. What sports do you like?

B: Baseball is fun to watch. My brother likes to watch football but I don't.

B Continue the conversation. Talk about things from the following categories that you like or dislike. Use examples from the categories on page 102 or your own ideas.

activities   fields of study   food   sports and recreation

4E | *Some* and *Any*

Form/Function

I have **some** cash. But I don't have **any** change.

1. We use *some* and *any* before plural nouns and noncount nouns to talk about an indefinite quantity.

    I have **some** paper.   I have **some** plants.

    I don't have **any** paper.   I don't have **any** plants.

2. We usually use *some* in affirmative sentences and *any* in negative sentences.

    There are **some** messages for you.   There aren't **any** messages for you.

3. We use *any* after negative-meaning words such as *never, seldom, rarely, hardly,* and *without.*

    He **never** has **any** time.   I found the store **without any** problems.

4. We usually use *any* in a question for which we don't expect any special answer.

    A: Is there **any** milk in the refrigerator?   A: Do you have **any** change on you?

    B: Yes, there is. But there isn't much.   B: Sorry, I don't.

But we usually use *some* in questions when we expect the answer *yes* or when we want to encourage people to say *yes* to an offer or request.

A: Do you have **some** money for me?   (I think you have money, and I expect the answer *yes*.)

B: Sure. Here it is.

A: Can I have **some** more cake, please?   (I want you to say *yes*.)

B: Of course. Help yourself.

5. We can use *any* to mean "it does not matter which one."

You can buy the soup at **any** supermarket.

---

15 Practice

Complete the sentences with *some* or *any*. Listen to the conversation to check your answers. Then practice the conversation with a partner.

AUDIO

DOWNLOAD

CD1, 19

MARIA: Could you go to the store for me? I want to make spaghetti tonight, and I need tomato sauce and ____*some*____ olive oil.
                                                        1

CARLA: Sure! And are there _____ other things that you need?
                              2

MARIA: Well, I don't have _____ cheese. Could you get _____
                            3   **4**
Parmesan cheese?

CARLA: Of course, about half a pound (¼ kilogram)? Oh, what kind of olive oil do you want?

MARIA: Oh, _____ kind of olive oil will do … as long as it's virgin olive oil.
            5

CARLA: Could you make _____ garlic bread to go with the spaghetti?
                        6

MARIA: Good idea! Get _____ garlic, and get _____ more bread just in
                      7   **8**
case we have _____ extra guests.
              9

CARLA: OK. I'm on my way. Oh, wait — I don't have _____ money!
                                                    10

16 Pair Up and Talk

Repeat the conversation in Practice 15 with a partner. Change the food words to those you need for one of the following dishes or one that is your own idea: stir fry, cheeseburgers, tacos, or pancakes.

A: I want to make pancakes for breakfast, but I need some eggs and some flour.

B: Do you need any milk?

Much, Many, A Lot Of, A Few, Few, A Little, and Little

Form/Function

Today, there are **few** wild rhinos left. Hunters have killed **many** for their horns.

1. Some quantity expressions such as *many* and *a few* go with plural count nouns. Others such as *much* and *a little* go with noncount nouns.

	Plural Count Nouns	Noncount Nouns
many/much/a lot of	There aren't **many apples** in this pie. There are **a lot of apples** in this pie.	There isn't **much butter** left. There's **a lot of butter** left.
a few/a little *few/little*	There are **a few eggs** in the refrigerator. There are **few bananas** left.	I have **a little milk**. These cookies require **little sugar**.

2. The choice of *many, much,* and *a lot of* often depends on whether the sentence is an affirmative statement, a negative statement, or a question.

	Affirmative Statement	Negative Statement	Question
many	There are **many** eggs in this cake. (Uncommon)	We **don't** have **many** apples.	**How many** apples are there?
much	I bought ~~much~~ rice. (Incorrect)	I **didn't** buy **much** rice.	**How much** rice is there?
a lot of	I have **a lot of** apples. I bought **a lot of** tea.	I **didn't** buy **a lot of** rice.	Did you buy **a lot of** apples?

3. We often use *much* and *many* after *too, as, so,* and *very* in affirmative sentences.

   We had just **as much** fun **as** they did.

   We enjoyed the dinner **very much**.

   He has **so many** books that he can't get them all in his backpack.

4. We use *a little* and *a few* for positive ideas.

   I still have **a little** work to do. (I have a small amount of work, but some work.)

   The new program has **a few** changes this year. (It has a small number of changes, but some changes.)

5. We use *little* and *few* for negative ideas. *Little* means "not much" or "almost no." *Few* means "not many" or "almost no." We usually use *little* and *few* in formal English.

FORMAL:	I have **little** work to do today. (I have almost no work.)
INFORMAL:	I **don't** have **much** work to do today.
FORMAL:	This year's program has **few** changes. (There are almost no changes.)
INFORMAL:	This year's program **doesn't** have **many** changes.

17 Practice

Complete the sentences with *much, many,* or *a lot of.* There is sometimes more than one possible correct answer.

JULIA: I went shopping today, and I bought _____many_____ new outfits. What do you
₁
think of this dress?

SUSAN: It's beautiful. It looks like it cost _____ money.
₂

JULIA: It didn't cost _____ money at all. I shopped at a new store on Bleecker
₃
Street. You can get _____ real bargains there. This dress had buttons
₄
missing, but it didn't need _____ new buttons. Luckily, I know
₅
how to sew, and it didn't take _____ time.
₆

SUSAN: Where are you going to wear it? You're always saying you don't get
_____ chances to get all dressed up.
₇

JULIA: I got a free ticket to the symphony, so I decided to dress up. I have so
_____ casual clothes, but not _____ formal dresses.
₈   ₉

SUSAN: What makeup are you going to wear with it?

JULIA: Oh, I don't usually wear _____ makeup.
₁₀

January 25, 2009

Dear Amy,

Can you give me ___a little___ advice? The problem is that I have _____
                      1   2
friends, and I often feel lonely. I work late every night and on weekends. I take care of my

mother, so I have _____ opportunities to go out. Can you give me
                        3

_____ tips on how to meet more people?
        4
Yours,

Busy but Lonely

January 30, 2009

Dear Busy but Lonely,

It's great that you are taking care of your mother, but you have given yourself too

_____ time for your personal life. The first thing you have to do is to set aside
        5

_____ hours every week for your social life. Then make a list of _____
        6   7
friends that you would like to spend more time with. Let them know that you would like

to spend _____ more time with them. In _____ weeks, and with just
                8   9

_____ effort on your part, your social group will start to grow.
        10
Yours,

Amy

19   Pair Up and Talk
Practice the conversation. Talk about the problem and ask your partner for advice. Use *many, much, a few, a little, few,* or *little*.

A: I always have too many bills and too little money to pay them! What should I do?

B: Well, you could make a few changes. Do you spend much money on eating out?

A: No. I don't go out to many restaurants, so I spend very little money on eating out.

4G | *Each, Each (One) Of, Every, Every One Of, Both, Both Of, All,* and *All Of*

Form/Function

> **Both of** the girls are in traditional costumes.
> **Each** costume is handmade.

1. We use *each* and *every* with singular count nouns. We usually use *each* when we talk about two people or things. We usually use *every* when we talk about three or more people or things.

CORRECT:	She is carrying a bag in **each** hand.
INCORRECT:	She is carrying a bag in ~~every~~ hand.
CORRECT:	**Every** student in the class was happy that day.
INCORRECT:	~~Each~~ student in the class was happy that day.

2. We use *every* when we are thinking of people or things together in a group as "all."

    Every student must be on time.

3. We use *each* when we are thinking of people or things separately.

    The teacher called **each** student's name.

4. We use *each (one) of* and *every one of* before plural count nouns. We use a word like *the, those, these,* or *your* before the plural count noun.

    Each one of the sisters wore the same clothes.
    I've been to **every one of these** stores.
    Every one of your answers was correct.

5. We use *both (of the)* + a plural count noun to refer to two people, groups, or things. We use *all, all the,* or *all of the* + a plural count noun or a noncount noun to refer to more than two people, groups, or things.

With *both*, we can use *both* + plural count noun OR *both of the* + plural count noun.

CORRECT: **Both movies** were good.

CORRECT: **Both of the movies** were good.

INCORRECT: ~~Both of movies~~ were good.

With *all*, we use *all* + noun if the noun is general. If the noun is specific, we can use *all of the* + noun OR *all* + noun.

A: **All Americans** like hamburgers. (*Americans* is general.)

B: That's not true. My teacher is an American, and he doesn't like hamburgers.

A: Well, **all of the Americans** that I know like hamburgers. (Here, *Americans* is specific.)

OR **All the Americans** that I know like hamburgers. (Here, *Americans* is specific.)

When we use *all* with a noncount noun, the verb is singular.

All of the information **was** useful.

All of the news **sounds** positive.

20 Practice

Match the sentence halves to create sentences that accurately describe the photos.

_____ **1.** Both girls   **a.** is smiling.

_____ **2.** Both boys   **b.** the children look happy.

_____ **3.** All   **c.** child is wearing a hat.

_____ **4.** Every child   **d.** are holding a ball.

_____ **5.** Each   **e.** are close to the camera.

21 Practice

Say or write three sentences about students in your class.

Example

Both Maria and Marta are wearing red sweaters today.

22 Practice

Listen to the news report. Then decide if the following statements are true (T) or false (F).

		T	F
1.	Both restaurants were destroyed by the fire.	☐	☐
2.	The fire reached all of the businesses on Ocean Street.	☐	☐
3.	Every one of the stores on Ocean Street is in danger from the fire.	☐	☐
4.	All of the business owners should hurry to Ocean Street.	☐	☐
5.	Both business owners and shoppers should stay away from Ocean Street.	☐	☐
6.	Fire Chief John Russell says all of the firefighters are working hard.	☐	☐
7.	Every building will have smoke and water damage.	☐	☐
8.	Each street near Ocean Street is blocked by police cars.	☐	☐

23 Read

Read the story. Then write answers to the questions.

THE DRAGON AND THE MOUSEDEER

There was a lot of rice in the village storehouse. Who would guard it while all the villagers were out planting more? In years past, every big, friendly animal they hired—the water buffalo, the tapir, the sun bear—had failed to keep out Naga, the hungry dragon who lived in the hills. What else could they do? Then a little mousedeer named Ki spoke up. "My brother Jang and I will protect your rice. A few mangoes every day for the next year is all we ask."

"Tiny, little you?" said the village headman, laughing. But the mousedeer got the job. Naga appeared on the first night the villagers were gone. As soon as she landed, she heard Ki's small voice calling out from a large cave, "A little help, please! Could you please shut us in here?"

"Why should I do that?" asked Naga.

"Because the stars are falling," said Jang. "Hurry, please. Roll some of those big rocks across the cave entrance."

Naga looked up at the night sky. Some of the stars seemed very close. "Get out of that cave," she roared. "If any creature should survive, I should." The mousedeer protested loudly, but Naga snorted fire into the cave until both of them came running out. The dragon then settled into the cave and said, "Now wake some of those water buffalo up and get them to help you. Roll the biggest rocks you can find in front of this cave entrance. Fast!" They did as they were told. When the villagers returned in a few days, their rice was safe and all was quiet—except for much angry snorting from a cave just outside town.

1. What was in the village storehouse?

    _____

    _____

2. What would the villagers be doing while they
    were gone?

    _____

3. What happened when big, friendly animals tried
    to keep out the dragon?

    _____

    _____

4. How many options did the villagers have for
    protecting their storehouse now?

    _____

5. What payment did the mousedeer request for
    protecting the rice?

    _____

6. What did Ki ask Naga to do?

    _____

    _____

7. What did Naga think she saw when she looked
    up at the sky?

    _____

8. Who came out of the cave after Naga breathed
    fire into it?

    _____

Listening Puzzle

AUDIO DOWNLOAD CD1, 21

A Listen and check the correct answer.

❏ A. *cookie*   ❏ B. *cake*   ❏ C. *pie*

B Discuss your answer with your classmates.

AUDIO DOWNLOAD CD1, 22

C Now listen again and write the sentences you hear.

Review

1 Review (4a–4b, 4d–4g)
Underline the correct answer in each sentence.

1. All of the food (was/were) good.

2. The menu had (much/a few) changes.

3. I can't meet you today. I have too (much/many) work.

4. I'd like two cups of (coffee/coffees), please.

5. There (is/are) a lot of (pollutions/pollution) in the world today.

6. Jenny met Tanya and Joseph at the airport and gave a flower to (each/all) of them.

7. I have (little/few) milk left in my glass.

8. There isn't (many/much) butter on your bread.

9. I watched several (childs/children) play with their toys.

10. You have (any/some) beautiful (cactus/cacti) in your garden.

11. Measles (makes/make) children very sick.

12. There isn't (any/some) steak in the freezer.

13. That pair of pants (looks/look) nice on you.

14. How did I know there are two (trains stations/train stations)?

15. We need a few good (idea/ideas) right now.

16. (Nancy's house/The house of Nancy) is beautiful.

17. (Little/Few) people like the new boss.

18. You can buy tickets from (any/some) student.

19. Don't play those drums! You make too (many/much) noise.

20. The (accident's cause/cause of the accident) was unknown.

21. The (wifes/wives) played tennis while their husbands played golf.

22. I think I ate too (much/many) cheese!

23. Our boss sends us about 20 (memorandum/memoranda) every day.

24. I need to do (any/some) laundry. I don't have (any/some) clean socks to wear.

25. Each one of my friends (is/are) on vacation. I need (a little/a few) time off, too!

2 Review (4a, 4c, 4d, 4f–g)

Find the errors and correct them.

TINA: Guess what? I'm going to explore the Amazon! It doesn't cost ~~many~~ *much* money.

MARIE: Really? I know there are a lot of travel bargain right now, but the Amazon?

TINA: Oh, yes. I've always wanted to go there. How much time have I told you that? All of people I know are surprised. I don't know why.

MARIE: Only a few person is that adventurous. Don't forget to pack lots of mosquitos spray.

TINA: Don't worry. The travel agent gave me a few book to read. Each book have a list of thing to bring.

MARIE: Well, I don't have a little to do today. Can I help you buy some equipments?

TINA: Sure. I need to buy so much things. I understand there will be a lot of rains. I'll need two cameras bag for my two cameras.

MARIE: You know, every one of your vacations have been an adventure. I think I've been to every one of your after-vacation party and listened to all your story. You should start your own tour company and call it "The Adventures of Tina."

TINA: That's a great idea. All of people I know would come. They'd give a lot of businesses.

MARIE: I have a few idea of my own. We can be partners. Both of us know a lot about travel.

TINA: Yes! Every one of your ideas are great. How about Brian? Maybe he can give us some offices products. You know, paper, pen, and maybe a few computers keyboard.

MARIE: I don't know. Brian never has any times. He's so busy with all his own works.

TINA: Well, there's too many work for just the two of us, don't you think?

MARIE: I don't think so. I have almost a month vacation coming to me. I can start doing a few thing while you're gone. Maybe I can get some advices about starting a business. I know a little people who can help us. With few effort, we'll have our own business!

A Before You Read

1. Do you eat breakfast cereal?
2. What kinds of breakfast cereal can you think of? Make a list.

KELLOGG'S CORN FLAKES

B Read Over 100 years ago people were just as concerned about health foods as they are today. There were health centers where people rested and ate healthy food to get better. One of these was in Battle Creek, Michigan. It was called the Battle Creek Sanitorium. Here worked two brothers, Will and John Kellogg. John, the older brother, was a doctor, and Will, who had little education, worked hard doing odd jobs.

The brothers were working on creating a new breakfast food with wheat. They boiled the wheat and then put it through rollers. One day, they had cooked some wheat but forgot about it for a day or two. When they returned, the wheat had become **moldy** but they decided to put the wheat through rollers anyway. To their surprise, they noticed the grains became flakes. They tried the process several times until they perfected it and had crispy flakes. Will persuaded his brother to serve the flakes to his patients. The patients loved the cereal and asked for more. The brothers then started a company and sold packages of flakes.

In their first year, they sold over 100,000 pounds (45,359 kilograms) of flakes. Will started to experiment with corn. He made them into flakes and added sugar. He called these tasty flakes corn flakes. Meanwhile, his brother John was getting less and less interested in the business. ■ The brothers argued and separated. ■ Will continued on his own and started the Battle Creek Toasted Corn Company. ■ In a few years, Kellogg's Corn Flakes became a huge success. ■

Will Kellogg made millions of dollars, but he wasn't comfortable being rich. He gave his wealth to many children's charities. In 1930, he started the Kellogg Foundation to help children and worked there until he died in 1951. His company had become the world's largest producer of ready-to-eat-cereal all because of an accident.

C Notice the Grammar   Underline all the nouns.

Choose the best answer.

D Look for Main Ideas

1. This passage mainly _____ .
   - Ⓐ provides interesting facts about cereal
   - Ⓑ explains how a cereal was produced by accident
   - Ⓒ analyzes the personality of the brothers
   - Ⓓ describes how the brothers made the cereal

2. Paragraph 3 mostly _____ .
   - Ⓐ describes how the corn flakes business advanced
   - Ⓑ describes Will Kellogg's charities
   - Ⓒ gives examples of his charitable work
   - Ⓓ looks at the two brothers in their old age

E Look for Details

3. According to the reading, which of the following is NOT true about Will Kellogg?
   - Ⓐ He had little education.
   - Ⓑ He was more important than his brother early in his life.
   - Ⓒ He started a successful company.
   - Ⓓ He gave away a lot of his money.

4. Will Kellogg gave away most of his time and money to _____ .
   - Ⓐ his family
   - Ⓒ charity
   - Ⓑ his house
   - Ⓓ his company

5. All of the following are true of the Kellogg brothers EXCEPT _____ .
   - Ⓐ they both worked at a sanitorium
   - Ⓑ they were both well educated
   - Ⓒ they both worked at creating a healthy cereal
   - Ⓓ they were both surprised to see the new cereal that appeared

F Make Inferences

6. We can infer from the passage that _____ .
   - Ⓐ John Kellogg didn't care about making money
   - Ⓑ John and Will argued about the popularity of the flakes
   - Ⓒ Will loved his wealth and what it could buy
   - Ⓓ Will was better at treating people at the sanitorium

G Look for Vocabulary

7. The word *moldy* in the reading is closest in meaning to _____ .
   - Ⓐ hard like wood
   - Ⓒ liquid
   - Ⓑ greenish
   - Ⓓ soft and chewy

H Sentence Addition

8. Look at the four squares ∎ that indicate where the following sentence could be added to the passage: **This was mainly due to Will's ingenious advertising.**

   Where would the sentence best fit?
   - Ⓐ at the first square
   - Ⓑ at the second square
   - Ⓒ at the third square
   - Ⓓ at the fourth square

Writing: Write a Descriptive Essay

Write an essay that describes a famous thing or place.

STEP 1   With a partner, think of some important things or places your country (or the country you are living in) is famous for. For example:

Mexico: splendid Aztec buildings, great food, beautiful beaches

STEP 2   Write as many sentences as you can to describe each of the things or places from Step 1. What do these things look like, sound like, smell like, etc? Choose two of the things or places from Steps 1 and 2 to write about.

STEP 3   1. Write your essay. Write a paragraph with a topic sentence about each of the things or places that you chose. For example:

> Many Americans think that Mexican food is nothing but tortillas, ground beef, tomato sauce, cheese, and hot peppers. In fact, there is a lot of variety in Mexican food. For example, Mexicans eat a lot of fish. It makes you feel like you are right on the beach. Everyone knows tomato salsa, but there are many other sauces in Mexico. They can be very subtle, and others can be fiery hot. Some Mexican sauces include chocolate.

2. Write an introduction and a conclusion to your paragraph or essay. Your introduction should state the two topics that you have chosen to write about. Your conclusion should summarize the points that you made.

3. Write a title for your essay.

STEP 4   Evaluate your essay.

Checklist

_____ Did you write a title and put it in the right place?

_____ Did you indent your paragraphs?

_____ Did you write an introduction, two paragraphs, and a conclusion?

STEP 5   Work with a partner or a teacher to edit your work. Check spelling, vocabulary, and grammar.

STEP 6   Write your final copy.

Self-Test

A **Choose the best answer, A, B, C, or D, to complete the sentence. Darken the oval with the same letter.**

1. That _____ clothing store has a lot of nice things.

   A. woman's   Ⓐ Ⓑ Ⓒ Ⓓ
   B. women's
   C. woman
   D. women

2. That's _____ new house.

   A. Jackie and Mike   Ⓐ Ⓑ Ⓒ Ⓓ
   B. Jackie and Mikes'
   C. Jackie's and Mike's
   D. Jackie and Mike's

3. She has a _____ .

   A. nine years old son   Ⓐ Ⓑ Ⓒ Ⓓ
   B. nine year-old son
   C. son nine year old
   D. nine-year-old son

4. He doesn't eat _____ .

   A. any meat   Ⓐ Ⓑ Ⓒ Ⓓ
   B. some meat
   C. of meat
   D. few meat

5. _____ student must take the test.

   A. All   Ⓐ Ⓑ Ⓒ Ⓓ
   B. All of
   C. Every
   D. Every one of

6. At first, she was lonely because she had _____ friends in class.

   A. a few   Ⓐ Ⓑ Ⓒ Ⓓ
   B. few
   C. little
   D. a little

7. How _____ eggs do you need?

   A. much   Ⓐ Ⓑ Ⓒ Ⓓ
   B. more
   C. little
   D. many

8. He wears _____ all the time.

   A. a jeans   Ⓐ Ⓑ Ⓒ Ⓓ
   B. a jean
   C. a pair of jean
   D. jeans

9. There are _____ in that field.

   A. some sheep   Ⓐ Ⓑ Ⓒ Ⓓ
   B. some sheeps
   C. sheeps
   D. many sheeps

10. This _____ classes are difficult.

    A. year's   Ⓐ Ⓑ Ⓒ Ⓓ
    B. years
    C. years'
    D. a year's

1. I need <u>a few</u> milk and <u>some</u> <u>flour</u> for this
        A   **B** **C**
   recipe, but I don't have <u>any</u>.
                      D

   (A)   (B)   (C)   (D)

2. The <u>women</u> and <u>children</u> of this culture cover
        A   **B**
   their <u>hairs</u> and paint designs on their hands
        C
   and <u>feet</u> on special occasions.
       D

   (A)   (B)   (C)   (D)

3. <u>Physic</u> <u>is</u> <u>Chris's</u> favorite subject, so he's going
    A   **B** **C**
   to work on a <u>two-year</u> research project.
              D

   (A)   (B)   (C)   (D)

4. We have <u>few</u> <u>time</u> to make any <u>corrections</u> in a
         A **B**   **C**
   <u>30-minute</u> essay exam.
     D

   (A)   (B)   (C)   (D)

5. <u>Babies</u> grow their first <u>teeth</u> when they are
    A   **B**
   <u>six months old</u> and keep them until they are
     C
   seven or <u>eight-years-olds</u>.
         D

   (A)   (B)   (C)   (D)

6. <u>Today's</u> <u>news</u> is interesting because two
    A   **B**
   <u>persons</u> have discovered a new <u>bacterium</u> that
    C   **D**
   helps humans.

   (A)   (B)   (C)   (D)

7. There are <u>so much</u> <u>dictionaries</u> at <u>King's</u>
          A   **B**   **C**
   that you will find one without any <u>problems</u>.
                          D

   (A)   (B)   (C)   (D)

8. In next <u>semester</u> <u>class</u> schedule, the <u>economics</u>
         A   **B**   **C**
   class I want is at the same time as the

   <u>mathematics</u> class.
    D

   (A)   (B)   (C)   (D)

9. There is <u>a lot of</u> <u>dirt</u> and <u>dusts</u> here because of
         A   **B**   **C**
   all the <u>traffic</u> and construction outside.
        D

   (A)   (B)   (C)   (D)

10. The chief cause of this <u>city's</u> <u>pollution</u> is
                     A   **B**
    <u>unleaded</u> <u>gasolines</u>.
     C   **D**

    (A)   (B)   (C)   (D)

Unit 5
Pronouns and Articles

One of the zebras looks taller than **the other**.

Form

> **My** wife and I discuss **our** finances every Sunday evening.

SUBJECT AND OBJECT PRONOUNS

1. We use personal pronouns to replace nouns when it is clear who or what we are talking about. There are three kinds of personal pronouns: subject pronouns, object pronouns, and possessive pronouns. See #3 below for information on possessive pronouns.

   Subject Pronoun: John was not in class yesterday. **He** was sick.

   Object Pronoun: The students are dressed up. Look at **them**.

2. Most of the subject and object forms are different from each other.

Subject Pronouns			Object Pronouns	
Singular	**Plural**		**Singular**	**Plural**
I	we		me	us
you	you		you	you
he/she/it	they		him/her/it	them

POSSESSIVE ADJECTIVES AND POSSESSIVE PRONOUNS

3. We use possessive adjectives in front of nouns. We use possessive pronouns without nouns.

   Possessive Adjective: I wrote a letter to **my** parents.

   Possessive Pronoun: That's not my backpack. It's **yours**.

Possessive Adjectives				Possessive Pronouns	
Singular	**Plural**			**Singular**	**Plural**
my	our			mine	ours
your	your			yours	yours
his				his	
her	their			hers	theirs
its				its	

Function

1. We use subject pronouns as the subjects of verbs.

    Dick was at home last night. **He** was studying.

    Where's Linda? **She**'s at school.

    In formal situations, such as academic writing and formal speaking presentations in business, we use a subject pronoun after the verb *be*.

    Who is it? It is **I**.

    If I were **he**, I would have complained.

    However, we normally use the object pronoun after the verb *be* in everyday speech.

    Who is it? It's **me**.

    If I were **him**, I'd have complained.

2. We use object pronouns as the objects of verbs and prepositions.

    That's Linda. I like **her**. (*her* is the object of the verb *like*)

    Those children are funny. Look at **them**. (*them* is the object of the preposition *at*)

3. We can use *you* to mean "people in general," including yourself and the person you are talking to.

    You can get a driver's license when **you** are 16 in this state.

    We can also use *one* with the same meaning. *One* is more formal and is not used much in everyday speech.

    One can get a driver's license when **one** is 16 in this state.

4. We also use *they* to mean "people in general," but not including yourself and the person you are talking to.

    They say the test is difficult, but I haven't taken it myself.

    They can also refer to the government or to the people in authority.

    They are going to build a new hospital in this neighborhood.

5. When a pronoun refers to a person whose gender (male or female) is known, we use the pronoun that matches the person's gender.

    Jane came in late for the test. **She** was not allowed to take it.

    However, some nouns such as *worker* or *student*, may refer to either gender or have a general meaning that includes people of both genders. In the past, many people used a singular masculine pronoun or possessive adjective to refer to a noun such as *worker* or *student*. This is no longer acceptable. Now we use both masculine and feminine forms to refer to such nouns.

ACCEPTABLE: A good **student** always does **his or her** homework.

NOT ACCEPTABLE: A good **student** always does **his** homework.

However, the use of *his* or *her* can be awkward. To avoid this problem, we can often make the noun plural and use a plural pronoun or possessive adjective after it.

ACCEPTABLE: Good **students** always do **their** homework.

This area of English grammar is changing. It is a good idea to ask your instructors about the pronoun uses that they will accept.

6. With group nouns such as *family, class, crowd, team, group,* and *company,* we can use a singular or plural pronoun to refer to it. We use a singular pronoun when we think of the group as one impersonal unit.

A family is important to me. **It** has the greatest value for me.

We use a plural pronoun when we think of the group as a number of people.

I have the greatest **family**. **They** always support me in whatever I do.

The **class** thinks that **they** are ready to take the test.

7. We use both possessive adjectives and pronouns to talk about ownership or relationships between people. We put a noun after a possessive adjective, but not after a possessive pronoun.

That's **her** book.

It's **hers**.

8. We usually use possessive adjectives with parts of the body and clothes.

He broke **his** leg.

She took off **her** coat.

9. The following are indefinite pronouns. Unlike other pronouns, they do not refer to a specific noun.

everyone	someone	anyone	no one
everybody	somebody	anybody	nobody
everything	something	anything	nothing

Everyone knows the answer to this question.

I saw **someone** standing outside.

Can you do **anything** about this problem?

Nobody can do the job except Sam.

In formal speech or writing, we use a singular possessive adjective (*her, his*) to refer to an indefinite pronoun. However, in everyday speech we often use a plural possessive adjective (*their*). Many, but not all, instructors will also accept this in written English.

FORMAL: **Somebody** left **his** or **her** keys on the table.

INFORMAL: **Somebody** left **their** keys on the table.

FORMAL: **Everyone** must lead **his** or **her** own life.

INFORMAL: **Everyone** must lead **their** own life.

10. We can use *it* to refer to a person when we are asking or saying who that person is.

    A: Who is **it**?

    B: **It**'s Ken.

We use *it* to talk about the weather, distance, temperature, and time.

    It's warm today.

    It's two miles (3.2 kilometers) from here.

    It's seven o'clock.

We use *it* to refer to animals, especially when we do not know the sex of the animal.

    There's a dog outside. I wonder who **it** belongs to.

    That's my dog. **She's** 10 years old.

11. Notice the difference between *its* and *it's*.

	Meaning	Example
its	Possessive adjective	I put my laptop back in **its** case.
it's	*it is* or *it has*	**It's** a nice day today. **It's** been nice all week.

1 Practice

Replace the underlined nouns with the correct subject or object pronoun. Then listen to the phone message and check your answers.

AUDIO
DOWNLOAD
CD1, 23

Ben is on a business trip. He is leaving a phone message for his wife, Rosie.

Hi Rosie, it's Ben. I left home in a big hurry this morning. Could you do a few things for me?

The electricity bill is on the bookshelf. _____ *It* _____ is due tomorrow.
                                         1

Please pay _____ for me.
                  2

    Also, I left my glasses on the table. I'm afraid _____ might get broken.
                                                                  3

Can you put _____ on the desk for me?
                         4

    Oh, and I forgot it was Jenny's birthday. _____ will be upset. Would
                                                          5

you mind getting _____ a card for me?
                    6

    What else … oh yes, remember to take Peter to his soccer game this afternoon.

_____ will be waiting for you at school. Tell _____ I
        7   8

hope his team wins. Let me see … I fed the cat this morning — the poor girl seemed

hungry! — but _____ didn't eat. Why don't you feed _____
                      9   10
a different kind of food tonight?

Rosie, I'll be back tomorrow by 7:00 in the evening. I haven't forgotten it's your

birthday. _____ both like Gino's restaurant, so I'll call and make a
                      11

reservation for _____ . Miss you, and see you soon!
                      12

2 Practice
Underline the correct word in parentheses.

I work for a small media company in New York, but (my/mine) friend works for a large
advertising company in Los Angeles. (Her/Hers) office is much bigger than (my/mine), but
                                              2   3
(my/mine) has a better view than (her/hers). (Our/Ours) working hours are 40 hours a
      4   5   6
week, but (their/theirs) are only 35 hours a week. (Their/Theirs) vacation is three weeks,
              7   8
while (our/ours) is only two weeks. (My/Mine) salary isn't bad, but (her/hers) is higher. It
        9   10   11
makes you think about looking for a new job. What would make you want to change
(your/yours)?
      12

3 Practice
A Complete the sentences with the correct pronouns (subject, object, or
   possessive) or possessive adjective. Complete the sentences with *I, me, my,*
   mine, you, your, or *yours.*

John,

I took a book from _____*your*_____ desk today. I shouldn't have done it, but I really
                          1

needed it to review for _____ exam today because I left _____ on the
                               2   3

bus yesterday. So _____ just took _____ . Please forgive _____ .
                          4   5   6

_____ promise to give it back to _____ tomorrow.
       7   8

Our neighbors went on vacation to Florida last year and had a terrible time. But my

family went this year, and we really enjoyed it. My neighbors' flight was late,

but _____ was on time. _____ hotel was far away, but _____
       1   2   3

was near the beach. _____ tour guide told _____ that _____
                           4   5   6

couldn't go to some of the theme parks, but _____ told _____ that
                                         7   8

_____ could go anywhere we wanted. Our neighbors told _____ that
   9   10

the next time _____ will use _____ travel agency!
                    11   12

George met Anna on the first day of math class. _____ fell in love with
                                                         1

_____ immediately. He gave her _____ telephone number, but she
   2   3

wouldn't give _____ to him. He asked _____ to go to the movies with
                 4   5

_____ , but _____ refused. He sent _____ flowers, but
   6   7   8

_____ sent _____ back. Finally, he wrote her a letter expressing his
   9   10

feelings for her. He hoped she would read _____ and write back
                                        11

to _____ .
   12

_____

_____

_____

_____

_____

_____

1. *All students are required to hand in their assignments on time.*

   ~~Every student is required to hand in his assignment on time~~. If any student does not understand the assignment, he must ask the instructor for further help. If any student borrows or copies another person's work and submits this as his work, the instructor may require him to withdraw from the course.

2. If my son calls this afternoon, please tell him to call me on my cell phone. I'll be unable to speak to any other caller unless his business is extremely urgent.

3. To play this game, each player will need to move his marker around the board and answer the question in the square he lands on. If a player does not know the answer to a question, he has to go back to the previous square.

1. Would the person who has parked ____*their*____ car by the main gate, please come to the front desk immediately? (informal)

2. Anyone who wishes to obtain further information should consult _____ doctor. (formal)

3. No one called for me today, did _____ ? (informal)

4. If anyone wants me to help _____ , please ask me. (informal)

5. If anyone requires assistance, would _____ please call for attention? (formal)

6. Everyone has the right to know whether any complaints have been made against _____ conduct. (formal)

7. Did you see someone here just now? I think _____ were asking for me. (informal)

8. A financial advisor should give reliable and accurate advice to every client and advise _____ of all possible risks before making an investment. (formal)

6 Phrasal Verb Practice

A Complete the sentences with the correct forms of the phrasal verbs. Use each verb only once. Phrasal verbs are taught in Unit 8, section H.

bump into   hang around   hang onto   help out   pick up   play around with

Dolphins love people. They often _hang around_ boats and swim in the waves along
                                        1
the bow. One dolphin off the coast of Ireland loves to _____ the local fishermen,
                                                            2
splashing them and pushing their crab pots. He even allowed them to _____ his
                                                                        3
fin as he pulled them through the water. Dolphins have _____ people in trouble.
                                                          4
Dolphins are intelligent creatures, too. Scientists in Australia have observed dolphins that
_____ sea sponges and put them on their nose like a glove. The sponge protects
5
the dolphins if they accidently _____ stinging creatures hidden in the sand.
                                    6

B Write *C* if the phrasal verb in the sentence is correct. Write *I* if it is incorrect.

_____ 1. Martha helped her sister pick up the color that looked best on her.

_____ 2. Play around with that song. I want to hear it again.

_____ 3. Matt helped me out by moving the computer to my new office.

_____ 4. I bumped into Julie and almost made her fall while we were playing basketball.

_____ 5. My friends and I like to hang around the shopping mall.

_____ 6. My mother is always telling me to hang onto my clothes on hangers instead of my chair.

5B | Reflexive Pronouns

Form/Function

> My doctor says people should weigh **themselves** every day. I try to remind **myself** to do that, but sometimes I forget.

Subject Pronouns	Reflexive Pronouns
I	myself
you (singular)	yourself (singular)
he	himself
she	herself
it	itself
we	ourselves
you (plural)	yourselves (plural)
they	themselves

1. We use reflexive pronouns as objects when the subject and object are the same person (for example, *I* and *myself*).

   We saw **ourselves** in the mirror.   I told **myself** to hurry.

   Reflexive pronouns are common as the objects of verbs such as *burn, hurt, cut, enjoy, teach, introduce,* and *look at*. There are also common phrases with reflexive pronouns, such as *enjoy yourself* (have a good time), *help yourself* (take something if you want), and *behave yourself*.

   He was cooking dinner when he burned **himself**.

   Are you still hungry? **Help yourself** to some more food.

2. We use reflexive pronouns to emphasize that we are speaking of a specific person and nobody else.

   I repaired the car **myself**.

   He knows about the problem. He **himself** spoke to me about it.

3. We use *by* + reflexive pronoun to mean "alone."

   My great-grandmother is 90 years old and lives **by herself**.

7 Practice

Paul and Mary have invited Tony and Linda to their house for dinner. Match the sentences on the left with the correct responses on the right. Next, complete the sentences with the correct reflexive pronouns. You may need to use *by*. Then listen to check your answers. Practice the dialogues with a partner.

CD1, 24

___e___ 1. Hello! Thanks for inviting us!

_____ 2. Mary, this cake is delicious!

_____ 3. Could I have some more cake?

_____ 4. Is this a photo of your twins when they were little?

_____ 5. Does Matthew still live at home?

_____ 6. Is that an automatic light?

_____ 7. What beautiful bookshelves!

a. Of course, Linda, please help _____ .

b. Yes, when you go into the room, it goes on _____ .

c. Yes, they taught _____ to ride bikes when they were only four years old.

d. No, he left home last year, and now he lives _____ .

e. You're welcome. Please come in and make ___yourselves___ at home!

f. Thank you, we couldn't make them _____ , so a friend made them for us.

g. Thanks, I made it _____ .

8 Pair Up and Talk

A Practice the conversation with a partner.

A: Do you cut your hair yourself?

B: No, I usually go to the hairdresser.

B Which things do you prefer to do yourself or ask someone to do for you? Talk about your preferences with a partner. Use the activities in the list below. Then share your partner's preferences with another pair of students.

cut your hair   make dinner   paint your room

fix your car   mend your clothes   solve a computer problem

5c Another, Other, Others, The Other, and The Others

Form

One woman is wearing a coat; **the others** are not.
One is talking on the phone, **another** is listening, and the **other** is going to hang up.

1. We use the different forms of *other* as adjectives or as pronouns.

		Adjective	Pronoun
Indefinite	Singular	*another* + singular noun	another
	Plural	*other* + plural noun	others*
Definite	Singular	*the other* + singular noun	the other
	Plural	*the other* + plural noun	the others*
	*Only plural pronouns take -s.		

2. Do not use *others* before a plural noun.
    CORRECT: There are other bicycles in the garage.
    INCORRECT: There are ~~others~~ bicycles in the garage.

Function

1. *Another* means one more. We use *another* with singular count nouns.
    Can I have **another** cup of coffee?
2. We use *another* + *two, three, few,* etc. + noun with expressions of time, money, and distance.
    We are going to stay here for **another few days**.
    The place is **another five miles** (8 kilometers) from here.
    I need **another ten dollars**.
3. *Other* and *others* (without *the*) refer to a part of a group beyond those already mentioned.
    Our guest was from Brazil. **Another** guest came from China. **Other** guests were from Europe.
    Others were from Africa.

4. We can also use *others* to mean other people.

   Some people enjoy playing football; **others** like watching it.

5. *The other* and *the others* means the rest of a group we are talking about.

   The movie star has two homes. One is in Malibu, California, and **the other** is in New York City.

   The movie star also has three expensive cars. One is a Porsche, and **the others** are Ferraris.

6. Here are some common expressions with *other*. *Each other* and *one another* indicate that people do the same thing, feel the same way, or have the same relationship.

   We understand **each other**.

   OR We understand **one another**. (I understand you, and you understand me.)

   Every other means every second one.

   We have a test **every other** week.

   The other day means a few days ago.

   I saw Jim **the other day**.

---

9 Practice

Complete the sentences with a word or phrase from the list.

another	every other	others	~~the other~~
each other	one another	the other	

I saw Sammy in the park ___the other___ day. We had seen _____ before, but
                              1   **2**

we had never spoken to _____ . Some people go to the park to walk by the lake,
                              3

while _____ like to sit on a bench or feed the ducks. I like to go there at least
            4

_____ day. One day, I noticed Sammy on a bench near the lake. He was looking
      5

down, and he seemed to be talking to himself. Several little boys were near Sammy. One

boy was sitting on the bench beside him. _____ boy was looking at Sammy
                                                  6

curiously. I went over to talk with Sammy. Then I saw that he was holding a small baby

duck in one hand and feeding it some bread with _____ .
                                                        7

---

10 Your Turn

Write four sentences about the topic. Use different forms of *other* as an adjective or pronoun.

Example

The park is a good place to meet other people.

5D The Indefinite Articles *A* and *An*; *One* and *Ones*

Form

A zebra has stripes. Each **one** has different **ones**.

1. We use the article *a* before words beginning with a consonant sound.*
   a book   **a** girl

2. We use the article *an* before words beginning with a vowel sound.*
   an apple   **an** umbrella

   If a *u* or *eu* sounds like "yoo," we use *a*: **a** university, **a** European.

3. We can sometimes use *one* before a noun instead of *a* or *an*.
   I need **one ticket**, not two.

4. We can use *one* and *ones* as pronouns.
   If there aren't any large cakes, get a small **one**.
   If there aren't any large cakes, get two small **ones**.

   Some letters of the alphabet start with a vowel sound, so we use *an*: **an** X-ray
   (*x* sounds like "ecks"), **an** MA (*M* sounds like "em"), but for letters that start with a consonant
   sound, we use *a:* **a** BA, **a** YMCA.

   *It is the sound, not the letter, that determines whether you use *a* or *an*. If an *h* is silent, we use
   an: **an** hour; **an** honest man. But if it is not silent, we use *a*: **a** hotel; **a** horse.

Function

A AND AN

1. We use *a* and *an* with singular count nouns when we talk about them in general.

   I saw **a** man outside. (The listener does not know which man.)

2. We do not use a singular count noun alone. We always use *a* or *an, the, my,* etc. before it.

CORRECT:	It's a computer.
INCORRECT:	~~It's computer.~~

3. We do not use *a* or *an* with noncount nouns or plural count nouns.

CORRECT:	I like music.
INCORRECT:	I like ~~a~~ music.
CORRECT:	Students from all over the world are here.
INCORRECT:	~~A~~ students from all over the world are here.

4. We use *a* or *an* + a noun when we say what someone or something is.

   She's **an** architect.

   It looks like **an** address book, but it's really **a** computer.

   But we don't use *a* or *an* if the noun is noncount.

   A: What's in that bowl?

   B: It's flour and sugar.

5. We use *a* and *an* to show certain measures.

Measure	Example
Price in relation to weight	It costs $2.00 **a** pound.
Frequency	He goes to the doctor once **a** year.
Distance in relation to speed	He was driving 70 miles (112.6 kilometers) **an** hour.

A, AN, AND ONE

6. We use *a* or *an* when we talk about something or one thing that is not specific. We use *one* when we want to emphasize the number and to be more specific.

   I have **an** umbrella. (not a specific umbrella)

   I have **one** umbrella.

   I was disappointed to get just **one** card for my birthday.

7. We can use *one day* to refer to the future.

   One day, all cars will run on electricity.

8. We use *a, an,* or *one* with no difference in meaning when we count or measure. We use *one* when we need to emphasize that there is only one (or when we need to show we are precise).

   I have **a/one** bottle of water.

   It costs **a/one** hundred dollars.

ONE AND ONES

9. We usually use *one* or *ones* to avoid repeating a noun. We use *one* for the singular and *ones* for the plural.

 This apartment is bigger than my old **one**. (my old apartment)

 These pants are nicer than the other **ones**. (the other pants)

10. We use *a* or *an* with *one* if there is an adjective before *one*.

 I want to buy a shirt. I'm looking for **one** right now.

 I'm looking for **a blue one**.

11. We can use *one* or *ones* after *the* if we are referring to a specific noun or nouns.

 This movie is better than **the one** we saw last week.

 I don't like these oranges. I prefer **the ones** we bought yesterday.

12. We can use *one* after *this* or *that*.

 Which computer do you prefer, **this one** or **that one**?

13. We use *which one(s)* in questions.

 I like these shoes best. **Which ones** do you like?

11	**Practice**
	Complete the questions with *a* or *an*.

Which do you prefer:

1. ___*a*___ telephone call or ___*an*___ email message?

2. _____ one-story house or _____ two-story house?

3. _____ oral exam or _____ written exam?

4. _____ honest man who is unfriendly or _____ friendly man who is dishonest?

5. _____ one-dollar coin or _____ one-dollar bill?

6. _____ island in the Caribbean or _____ mountain in the Andes?

7. _____ European car or _____ American car?

8. _____ MRI or _____ X-ray?

12 Pair Up and Talk

A   Practice the conversation with a partner.

A: Which do you prefer: a telephone call or an email message?

B: It depends. I prefer a telephone call with family members. It's more personal. I prefer an email message when I'm making plans with friends. It's faster.

B   Now share your answers to the questions in Practice 11 with a partner. Explain the reasons for your choices.

13 Practice

A   Complete the sentences with *a, one,* or *ones*.

George Crum invented the potato chip in 1853. Crum was _____*a*_____ chef in
1

Saratoga Springs, New York. French fries were very popular in his restaurant.

_____ day, _____ customer complained that the French fries were too
2   3

thick. Crum made some thinner _____ , but the customer still didn't like them.
4

So Crum made French fries which were too thin to eat with _____ fork and hoped
5

to annoy the picky customer. But the customer was happy—and that's the story of potato

chips! Now potato chips are _____ big industry in the United States. The average
6

person there eats seven pounds (3 kilograms) of potato chips _____ year. It takes
7

about four pounds of potatoes to make _____ pound of potato chips.
8

B   Answer these questions with complete sentences.

1.   What was George Crum's job? *He was a chef.* _____

2.   What kind of French fries did he make?

     _____

3.   Why did he make them?

     _____

4.   How many pounds of potato chips does the average American eat each year?

     _____

14　Practice

Listen to the conversation at a bakery. Complete the sentences with *one* or *ones* + *the, this, that, which,* or other words that you hear. Then practice the conversation with a partner.

AUDIO DOWNLOAD

CD1, 25

CUSTOMER:　A loaf of bread, please.

SALESPERSON:　Which kind?

CUSTOMER:　I'm not sure. What's ___this one___ in front called?
                                            1

SALESPERSON:　It's called country farmhouse white.

CUSTOMER:　And what's _____ over there called?
                                2

SALESPERSON:　_____ on the top shelf? It's called German rye.
             3

CUSTOMER:　I'll take two of _____ , please.
                              4

SALESPERSON:　Would you like them sliced?

CUSTOMER:　I'd like _____ sliced, and _____ unsliced, please.
                      5   **6**

SALESPERSON:　Anything else?

CUSTOMER:　Yes, I'd like four cupcakes.

SALESPERSON:　I have cupcakes with orange or chocolate frosting. _____ do
                                                                   7
you want?

CUSTOMER:　_____ with the orange frosting.
             8

SALESPERSON:　Small or large?

CUSTOMER:　_____ , please. I don't like large _____ .
             9   **10**

138　Unit 5

Function

The Leaning Tower of Pisa is in Italy. Many people visit **the** tower every year.

We Use *The*	We Do Not Use *The*
1. With count and noncount nouns when it is clear from the situation which people or things we mean or when the noun is mentioned for the second time or is already known. 　　Can you pass me **the** milk, please? 　　(the milk that is on **the** table) 　　I met a man and a woman in **the** hallway. 　　I didn't like **the** man, but **the** woman was nice.	1. With plural count nouns and noncount nouns when we talk about something in general. 　　Roses smell sweet. 　　Milk is good for you. (milk in general)
2. When there is only one of something, for example, *the sun, the moon, the Earth, the sky*. 　　Would you like to travel around **the** world?	2. With names of days, months, celebrations, drinks, meals, languages (without the word *language*), sports, and games. 　　I'm working on Monday, and I'm playing tennis after lunch on Friday.
3. With countries when they include a count noun, for example, *union, republic, states*, and *kingdom*. 　　**the** United Kingdom 　　**the** Federal Republic of Germany With names of plural countries. 　　**the** Netherlands 　　**the** United Arab Emirates	3. With most countries. 　　India 　　China 　　Brazil 　　Canada

We Use *The*	We Do Not Use *The*

4. With other place names.
Oceans and seas:
    the Pacific, **the** Mediterranean
 	
Rivers, canals:
    the Mississippi
 	
Deserts:
    the Sahara
 	
Island groups:
    the Azores
 	
Mountain ranges:
    the Andes
 	
Hotels, theaters, museums, galleries:
    The Ritz, **the** Wang Theater, **the** Guggenheim
	4. With other place names.
	Continents:
	    Africa, Antarctica
	
	Most countries:
	    India, China, Brazil, Canada
	
	Cities, towns, states:
	    Tokyo, Pleasantville, California
	
	Individual islands:
	    Long Island, Puerto Rico
	
	Lakes:
	    Lake Ontario, Lake Chad
	
	Individual mountains:
	    Mount Everest, Mount Fuji
	
	Streets, parks, squares:
	    Main Street, Central Park, Trafalgar Square

5. Before names that end with a prepositional phrase with *of*.
    the Statue of Liberty
    the Leaning Tower of Pisa
    the University of London
	5. With names of hotels or restaurants named after the people who started them.
	    McDonald's
	    Macy's
	    Harrods

6. With the names of musical instruments and scientific inventions.
    He can play **the** guitar.
    Marconi invented **the** radio.
	6. With some nouns such as *school, college, prison, church,* and *bed,* when we are thinking about the main purpose of the place.
	    He is at school right now.
	    BUT I didn't like **the** school that I went to last year.

7. Before nationality words ending *in -sh,-ch,-ans,* or *-ese* such as *English, Italians,* and *Japanese,* to mean people of that country.
With other nationality endings, we can use or not use *the.*
    The Americans love hamburgers.
    OR **Americans** love hamburgers.
	7. With means of transportation such as *by car/bus/ plane/train,* etc., to talk about how we travel.
	    I go to school by bus.
	    BUT I left on **the** 7:15 bus this morning.

8. With adjectives and adverbs in the superlative form.
    He bought **the most expensive** car.
Also, before some adjectives such as *young, old, rich,* and *poor* with a general meaning.
    The rich should help **the poor**.
	8. With names of illnesses.
	    He has pneumonia.
	But we can say **the** flu, **the** mumps, **the** measles.

We Use *The*	We Do Not Use *The*
9. With a singular count noun to mean something in general. **The horse** is a beautiful animal. We can also use *a* or *an* to express a general meaning. **A horse** is a beautiful animal. Or we can use a plural count noun alone. **Horses** are beautiful animals.	9. With seasons, we may or may not use *the*. I love (**the**) spring in this part of the country.
10. Some expressions with *the* have a general meaning, for example, *the countryside, the mountains, the rain, the wind,* and *the snow*. I love to hear the sound of **the rain**. We usually go to **the mountains** in the summer.	

15 Practice

Complete the sentences with *a, an, the,* or *X* (no article).

Madagascar is _____ island in _____ Indian Ocean,
          1   2
off _____ east coast of Africa. It is _____ fourth largest island in
      3
_____ world. It is sometimes known as _____ Great Red Island. The
     5   6
people of Madagascar speak _____ many different languages, but
                          7
_____ official language is French. _____ capital is Antananarivo. It
     8   9
is _____ picturesque city with _____ narrow streets. Archaeologists
    10   11
believe that _____ first humans arrived here from _____ Indonesia
           12   13
and _____ Malaysia around 2,000 years ago. Madagascar has mountains in
    14
_____ central region. It also has _____ tropical rainforests, grasslands,
    15   16
and deserts in _____ west. After _____ island split from _____
         17   18   19
mainland of _____ Africa 88 million years ago, many unique species of
        20
_____ plants and _____ wildlife developed there.
    21   22

16 Practice

Write a short description of the country you are from on a separate piece of paper.

THE SLEEPING BEAR

A forest fire, the worst one ever in the North Woods, raced toward Mother Bear and her two baby cubs. They were trapped between it and the cold water of the endless lake. Mother Bear knew they had no choice. They would have to swim.

"But, Mother," said one of the cubs. "The old ones say this lake has no other shore. We will have to swim forever."

"No, my precious children. There is a shore. I have seen it." She was not being honest. She did not know what was on the other side. But her lie calmed them. They followed her into the water and began swimming east. For days they paddled, seeing nothing but bright water all around them. When they grew hungry, they caught fish. They certainly did not lack water to drink. But they could not sleep or even stop moving their legs to rest. Mother Bear was angry with herself for leading her cubs on such a hopeless journey.

Then on their fifth day in the water, Mother Bear saw a dark line on the horizon. It was land.

Mother and cubs swam harder, struggling to keep their tired bodies moving. Finally, Mother Bear stepped ashore. She turned around to welcome her cubs to this new land, but she saw neither of them. "They are small," she thought to herself. "They cannot swim as fast as I can. I will wait for them here on the beach." So she waited and, in her exhaustion, fell asleep.

She sleeps there still, covered by the great sand dune[1] we call "Sleeping Bear." Her cubs will never swim ashore, for they were too tired to complete their journey. But the Great Spirit took pity on the cubs and their mother. He raised the drowned cubs up and turned them into two sandy islands. They are just offshore from where she sleeps. When she wakes up, she will see two shining islands and feel in them the spirits of her two beautiful cubs.

[1.] *sand dune = a hill of sand near the sea or in a sand desert.*

1. How did the bears escape the forest fire? _____
   _____.

2. Why were the cubs afraid to swim out into the lake? _____
   _____.

3. How did Mother Bear calm her cubs' fears? _____
   _____.

4. What did the bears eat while they were out in the lake? _____
   _____.

5. Why were the bears unable to rest? _____
   _____.

6. How did Mother Bear feel about their journey? _____
   _____.

7. Where is Mother Bear right now? _____
   _____.

8. Why is the Great Spirit important in this story? _____
   _____.

Listening Puzzle

AUDIO DOWNLOAD CD1, 26

A Listen and check the correct answer.

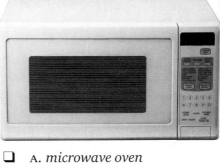  

❑ A. *microwave oven*   ❑ B. *gas grill*   ❑ C. *refrigerator*

B Discuss your answer with your classmates.

AUDIO DOWNLOAD CD1, 27

C Now listen again and write the sentences you hear.

1 Review (5a–5b, 5d)

Complete the sentences with pronouns, possessive adjectives, articles, or *one*. Write X for no article. There may be more than one correct answer.

Dear Lisa,

How are _____you_____ ? Thanks for your email message. I enjoyed reading
1

_____ .
2

I have some news, too. I'm going on vacation next week to _____ New York
3

City. Unfortunately, _____ is only for three days. Imagine! I haven't seen
4

_____ Statue of Liberty or been to _____ show on Broadway! I don't
5   6

want to go by _____ , so I'm going with Melissa. We can share a room so it will
7

be cheaper for _____ . Melissa is a shopaholic[1], and I'm not, so I'll let her go
8

shopping by _____ and I'll go to _____ museum. There are so many of
9   10

_____ . I want to go to a different _____ every day. I want to take
11   12

_____ photos so I can remember everything. The only problem is that my
13

camera doesn't work, but Melissa said I can use _____ . She has _____
14   15

digital _____ .
16

I'll write to you when I come back, and tell you what _____ was like.
17

Take care,

Annie

[1] shopaholic = informal and sometimes humorous term for someone who shops a lot

2 Review (5a, 5c)

Complete the sentences with pronouns, possessive adjectives, forms of *other*, or articles. Write X for no article. There may be more than one correct answer.

LOUISA: Hi Ken, how are you? We always seem to run into each _____other_____ .
1

KEN: Hi Louisa. You're right, we see each _____ almost every _____ day.
2   3

LOUISA: I saw your brother, Tony the _____ day. He was driving
4

_____ red car, but I don't think he saw _____ .

5   **6**

KEN: He didn't tell _____ he saw _____ . By the way, that's his new car. His old

                         7   **8**

_____ broke down and he sold _____ . _____ old car was red, too.

9   **10**   **11**

LOUISA: _____ red car! What's the matter with _____ ?

             12   **13**

KEN: He just likes _____ color red.

                         14

3 Review (5d–5e)

Find and correct the errors in pronouns and articles. Add pronouns and articles where necessary.

1. The word *Olympic* comes from the name of the town Olympia in ~~the~~ Greece where ^the first games started.
2. The athletes in the first modern Olympic Games in 1896 were only the men, as in ancient Greece. In 1900, the women became eligible to participate in Games.
3. In 1932, the women could not participate in more than the three events.
4. The five rings on Olympic flag represent five geographic areas of the world: the Europe, Asia, Africa, the Australia, and the Americas.
5. Muhammad Ali won an Olympic gold medal in boxing in 1960. At the time, he called him Cassius Clay. In 1996, he returned to Olympics and lit Olympic flame at the opening ceremony.
6. Before Olympic Games start, runners carry torch all the way from Greece to a site of the games. On first day, the last runner lights a huge torch. This flame burns until last day.
7. Olympic Games have taken place every four years since 1896, except for 1916, 1940, and 1944, during two World Wars.
8. Summer Games were seen on the television for the first time in 1936.
9. In ancient Greece, the prize for the winner was not gold medal. It was branch from a olive tree; however, the winners became very famous and were like celebrities in hometowns.

A Before You Read

1. Name an inventor you have heard of. What did this person invent?
2. Is electricity an invention? Explain your answer.

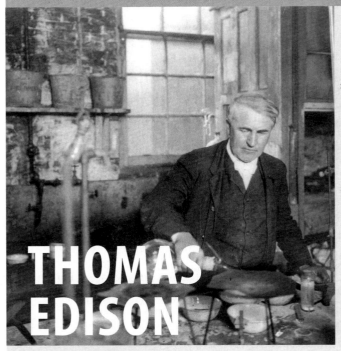

THOMAS EDISON

DID YOU KNOW ... ?
Thomas Edison, a pioneer of sound-recording technology, was almost entirely deaf since childhood.

B Read Thomas Alva Edison invented many devices which we use in our everyday lives. Think of him when you turn on an electric light. Or go to a movie. Or listen to recorded music. He was born in Milan, Ohio, in 1847. He grew up there and in Michigan. At the age of 12, Edison rescued a three-year-old boy from an oncoming train. It was a turning point[1] in Edison's life. As a reward, the little boy's father gave Edison free lessons in operating a telegraph[2]. **They** eventually led to a series of jobs in the telegraph field.

Edison pushed himself and worked hard. He came up with now-forgotten inventions like an electric pen. Others were soon to come. In 1876, he set up a new lab in Menlo Park, New Jersey, and hired many assistants. Edison expected them to work as hard as he did. Not many of them could. He allowed himself very little sleep, which he considered an inconvenient habit instead of a need. He respected hard work more than brilliance. Others praised his "genius." He himself called it, "one percent inspiration and 99 percent perspiration[3]."

The Menlo Park team soon produced the phonograph. It could record voices and music on a thin sheet of metal. In hopes of making an electric light, they also kept trying to make threads of various elements **glow**.

Carbon turned out to be the right one. By enclosing carbon "filaments" in an airless bulb, they created a dependable source of light. It could burn for hours without getting too hot. This made their light bulb a far better bulb than anyone else's. Edison showed it off in 1879 by lighting up the entire Menlo Park lab. By 1882, a square mile in New York City was lit by a system Edison had invented.

Later he would invent many other things, including a movie projector. The name "Edison," however, is most strongly linked to electricity. No one could invent it, but he made it widely usable.

[1.] turning point = event that causes a great change
[2.] telegraph = a device for sending messages in a special code
[3.] perspiration = sweat; Edison used the word to mean "hard work"

C Notice the Grammar Underline all the pronouns.

Choose the best answer.

D Look for Main Ideas

1. This reading is mainly about
   Edison's _____ .
   Ⓐ childhood
   Ⓑ work
   Ⓒ philosophy
   Ⓓ laboratory

2. What is the main topic of paragraph 3?
   Ⓐ the phonograph
   Ⓑ Menlo Park's inventions
   Ⓒ a new electric light
   Ⓓ the lighting of New York City

E Look for Details

3. According to the reading, when Edison
   was 12 years old, _____ .
   Ⓐ he saved a boy's life
   Ⓑ he got a job operating telegraphs
   Ⓒ he produced his first invention
   Ⓓ he set up a laboratory

4. The reading mentions that Edison's light
   bulb was better than earlier bulbs
   because _____ .
   Ⓐ it was hotter
   Ⓑ it was brighter
   Ⓒ it cost less
   Ⓓ it lasted longer

5. When Edison's light bulb was burning, which
   of the following could NOT be found
   inside it?
   Ⓐ a filament
   Ⓑ carbon
   Ⓒ air
   Ⓓ heat

F Look for Inference

6. We can most strongly infer from
   the reading that Edison _____ .
   Ⓐ did not really invent many things
      credited to him
   Ⓑ produced fewer inventions because
      he lacked sleep
   Ⓒ thought of many inventions while he
      was asleep
   Ⓓ had help producing many of his
      inventions

G Look for Vocabulary

7. The term *glow* in the reading is closest in
   meaning to _____ .
   Ⓐ produce light
   Ⓑ catch fire
   Ⓒ get bigger
   Ⓓ stay together

H Look for References

8. The word *they* in the reading refers
   to _____ .
   Ⓐ the father and the boy
   Ⓑ lessons
   Ⓒ the father and Edison
   Ⓓ telegraphs

Writing: Write a Review of a Movie

Think of a movie that you enjoyed or one that you thought was terrible. Write a five-paragraph review about it.

STEP 1 — Use the following guidelines to organize and write your review. The sentence starters may help you as you write.

Paragraph 1: Write an introduction that gives basic facts about the movie (title, director, screenplay writer, actors).

The movie was directed by … and written by … . Its star is (name of actor) in the title role and (name of actor) in the supporting role …

Paragraph 2: Introduce the setting (the place and time of the action) and the characters.

The story is set in (Tokyo, Los Angeles, outer space) … .
The story takes place (in the early 1800s, during the war in … , in the present) …

Paragraph 3: Describe the story. Use two paragraphs if necessary.

It tells the story of (a character) OR It is based on the real-life story of (a person) … . As the story develops, we learn that … Finally … OR In the end …

Paragraph 4: State your reactions and the reasons why you did or didn't like it.

The story was convincing/not convincing because …
(Actor's) performance in the movie was exciting/disappointing because …

Paragraph 5: Write a conclusion.

This movie is/isn't successful because …
The movie's story was very engaging, but unfortunately …

STEP 2 — **Evaluate your review.**

Checklist

_____ Did you write an introduction that presented basic facts about the movie?

_____ Did you describe the time and place of the movie in the second paragraph?

_____ Did you summarize the story in the third paragraph?

_____ Did you state your reactions to the movie in the fourth paragraph?

_____ Did you summarize your reactions in the fifth paragraph?

STEP 3 — **Work with a partner or a teacher to edit your review. Check spelling, vocabulary, and grammar.**

STEP 4 — **Write your final copy.**

Self-Test

A   Choose the best answer, A, B, C, or D, to complete the sentence. Darken the oval with the same letter. A dash (–) in an answer means that no word is needed.

1. He is 92 and lives _____ .

    A. himself   Ⓐ Ⓑ Ⓒ Ⓓ
    B. by himself
    C. by himselves
    D. by hisself

2. It costs $2.50 _____ .

    A. the pound   Ⓐ Ⓑ Ⓒ Ⓓ
    B. pound
    C. one pound
    D. a pound

3. I see better with these glasses than with _____ .

    A. the other ones   Ⓐ Ⓑ Ⓒ Ⓓ
    B. the other one
    C. other one
    D. one other

4. Richard went to _____ United Kingdom on business.

    A. an   Ⓐ Ⓑ Ⓒ Ⓓ
    B. a
    C. the
    D. –

5. The satellite will be above _____ Earth.

    A. an   Ⓐ Ⓑ Ⓒ Ⓓ
    B. a
    C. other
    D. the

6. Brenda is _____ architect now. She has just finished her degree.

    A. an   Ⓐ Ⓑ Ⓒ Ⓓ
    B. a
    C. the
    D. –

7. That's not my book. It's _____ .

    A. your   Ⓐ Ⓑ Ⓒ Ⓓ
    B. yours
    C. yourself
    D. yours book

8. The town is _____ ten miles from here.

    A. more   Ⓐ Ⓑ Ⓒ Ⓓ
    B. other
    C. another
    D. a

9. BILL: I flew to Chicago _____ day, and your sister had the seat next to me.
   LINDA: No kidding! That's amazing!

    A. the other   Ⓐ Ⓑ Ⓒ Ⓓ
    B. another
    C. other
    D. each other

10. We tried not to look at _____ during the meeting.

    A. every other Ⓐ Ⓑ Ⓒ Ⓓ
    B. the other
    C. each other
    D. each one

1. There are <u>the salads</u>, sandwiches, and <u>desserts</u>
        A   **B**
   on <u>the tables</u>, so please help <u>yourselves</u>.
       C   **D**

   Ⓐ   Ⓑ   Ⓒ   Ⓓ

2. We had spoken to <u>each</u> <u>another</u> before Ken
                    A   **B**
   introduced <u>us</u> <u>a</u> week ago.
             C D

   Ⓐ   Ⓑ   Ⓒ   Ⓓ

3. My friend gave <u>me</u> the name of a <u>dentist</u>, so I
                  A   **B**
   made <u>an appointment</u> to see <u>a dentist</u>
        C   **D**
   next week.

   Ⓐ   Ⓑ   Ⓒ   Ⓓ

4. <u>They</u> say it's very cold in <u>winter</u> on <u>an east</u>
    A   **C**   **B**
   <u>coast</u> of <u>the United States</u>.
    C   **D**

   Ⓐ   Ⓑ   Ⓒ   Ⓓ

5. He was born in <u>Canada</u>, went to school in
              A
   <u>Australia</u> and <u>the United States</u>, and
     B   **C**
   worked in <u>United Arab Emirates</u>.
            D

   Ⓐ   Ⓑ   Ⓒ   Ⓓ

6. <u>The Chinese</u> eat a lot of <u>the rice</u>, but they don't
     A   **B**
   drink a lot of <u>milk</u> like <u>the Americans</u>.
            C   **D**

   Ⓐ   Ⓑ   Ⓒ   Ⓓ

7. In <u>the United States</u>, <u>people</u> say that <u>the time</u>
       A   **B**   **C**
   is <u>money</u>, but I don't agree with this.
     D

   Ⓐ   Ⓑ   Ⓒ   Ⓓ

8. There are two solutions. <u>One</u> would be
                     A
   <u>a miracle</u>, and <u>other</u> is <u>a possibility</u>.
    B   **C**   **D**

   Ⓐ   Ⓑ   Ⓒ   Ⓓ

9. Zebras all seem to be <u>the same</u>, but in fact
                   A
   <u>each ones</u> <u>has</u> its <u>own</u> particular stripes.
    B   **C**   **D**

   Ⓐ   Ⓑ   Ⓒ   Ⓓ

10. The chief cause of this <u>city's</u> <u>pollution</u> is
                      A   **B**
    <u>unleaded</u> <u>gasolines</u>.
      C   **D**

    Ⓐ   Ⓑ   Ⓒ   Ⓓ

Unit 6
Modals I

You **should** try to watch Oprah Winfrey's talk show. She always has great guests on it.

6A | Introduction to Modal Verbs

Form/Function

They **might** be late for their flight.

1. We use modal verbs with a main verb. Modal verbs add meaning to a main verb.

   | | **Modal** | **Main Verb** | |
   Betsy is only four, but she **can** **ride** a bicycle.

   The modal *can* expresses the idea that Betsy has the ability to ride a bicycle. Modals often have several meanings, and two or three modals can share the same meaning.

You **may** take another piece of candy.	*May* expresses permission.
I **may** be late for your party.	*May* expresses possibility.

I **might** be late.	*Might*, *may*, and *could* all express possibility.
I **may** be late.	
I **could** be late.	

2. Here is a list of modals.

   | can | may | shall | will | must |
   | could | might | should | would | ought to |

3. We form statements and questions the same way with all modals. Here are summaries and examples of how modals work.

   Affirmative Statements: Subject + Modal + Verb

   You **should see** a doctor about that cough.

   Negative Statements: Subject + Modal + *Not* + Verb

   They **can't speak** Chinese very well.

   Yes/No **Questions: Modal + Subject + Verb**

   Short Answers: *Yes/No* + **Pronoun + Modal (+ *Not*)**

   A: **Could** you **swim** when you were five?   B: Yes, I **could.**/No, I **couldn't.**

   Wh- **Questions:** *Wh-* **Word + Modal + Subject + Verb**

   When should the children **eat** their dinner?

4. Modal phrases such as *be able to* also add meaning to a main verb. In their function, they are like modals, but they are in a different form. We will address both modals and modal phrases in Units 6 and 7.

Modals	Examples of Modal Phrases
can/could	be able to
must	have to
will	be going to *
should	be supposed to
would	used to *
may/might	be allowed to

* See page 44 for *used to* and page 58 for *be going to*.

6B | *Can, Could,* and *Be Able To* to Express Ability

Function

Could you speak more loudly, please? I **can't** hear you.

1. We use *can* to talk about ability in the present and future.
   Can you drive?
   I **can** play the piano.
   When Tom comes home, he **can** help you with your homework.
2. We use *could* to talk about ability in the past.
   I **could** swim when I was three years old.
3. We can also use the modal phrase *be able to* with the same meaning as *can* and *could*. *Be able to* is not used as often as *can* and *could*.
   Are you able to drive? (present)
   I was able to swim when I was three years old. (past)

4. When we want to say that someone had the ability or opportunity to do something in a particular situation which resulted in an action, we use *was/were able to* and not *could*.

   Although the president of the company was at a meeting, we **were able to** speak to him for a few minutes.

   The office was closed today, so I **was able to** do things that needed to be done at home.

5. When we talk about a future ability that we do not have in the present, we use *will be able to*, not *can*.

   CORRECT: He**'ll be able to** walk after his leg heals.

   INCORRECT: He ~~can~~ walk after his leg heals.

6. We must use *be able to*, not *can*, with some grammatical structures, such as with another modal and in the perfect form.

   CORRECT: We **might be able to** finish before the library closes.

   INCORRECT: We might ~~can~~ finish before the library closes.

7. In particular situations, we usually use *can* or *could* and not *be able to* with stative verbs such as *see, hear, smell, taste, feel, understand,* and *remember.*

   COMMON: When I opened the door, I **could** smell gas.

   UNCOMMON: When I opened the door, I ~~was able to~~ smell gas.

---

1 Practice
Listen to the conversations. Complete the sentences with the correct form of *be able to, can,* or *could* and the verb that you hear. Then practice the conversations with a partner.

CD1, 28

1. A: Stan is such a great swimmer!

    B: I know. But he ___*wasn't able to swim*___ until he was 15 years old!

2. A: So are we going to the concert this weekend?

    B: I have to think about it. I _____ a decision right now.

3. A: I regret that I _____ the meeting next Tuesday.

    B: That's all right. Thank you for notifying me in advance.

4. A: Anne broke her right arm last year.

    B: You're kidding! She _____ it very well now when she

        plays tennis.

x

x

154   Unit 6

5. A: They _____ a decision at the meeting yesterday.

   B: I can't believe it. The meeting lasted six hours!

6. A: It's necessary to have a car in Los Angeles. Everything is so far apart.

   B: Then I guess I'm at a big disadvantage there because I _____ .

7. A: _____ me home now?

   B: Sure, I'd be happy to.

8. A: The tech people are going to work on the server this afternoon.

   B: Oh, no. We _____ our email.

2 Pair Up and Talk
A Practice the conversation with a partner.

A: Can you do this activity outside?

B: Yes, you can./No, you can't.

B Think of one unusual skill that you have or activity you like to do. Your partner will ask you questions to try and guess what the skill or activity is. You will answer *yes* or *no* to each question. You can give hints. When your partner has guessed the skill or activity, tell your partner as many details as you can about it.

Function

You **have to** stop at a stop sign.
You**'ve got to** stop at a flashing yellow light and red light, too.

1. We use *must* or *have to* to express obligation or necessity.

    You **have to** take an English exam when you enroll at the university.

    You **must** take an English exam when you enroll at the university.

2. In everyday English, *have to* is more common than *must*. In spoken English, *have to* may sound like *hafta*.

3. We use *must* when we write forms, signs, and notices.

    The last person to leave the office **must** lock the door.

4. We usually use *must* when the necessity to do something comes from the speaker. We usually use *have to* when the necessity comes from outside the speaker.

    | TEACHER: | You **must** give me all your essays by tomorrow. |
    | STUDENT TO A FRIEND: | I **have to** write my essay by tomorrow. (The teacher says so.) |

5. *Must* usually shows urgent necessity.

    We **must** get her to a doctor right away.

6. *Have got to* has the same meaning as *have to*, but we use it mostly in informal spoken English. We use it in affirmative statements. We do not often use it in negative statements or questions. We do not use *have got to* in the past tense.

    | CORRECT: | I have got to go now. |
    | CORRECT: | I haven't got to go now. |
    | CORRECT: | Where have you got to go now? |
    | INCORRECT: | I ~~had got to~~ go early last night. |
    | CORRECT: | I had to go early last night. |

    In rapid speech, *got to* sounds like *gotta*.

We can contract *have got to* with the subject, but we can't contract *have to*.

CORRECT:	I have to buy a new computer.
INCORRECT:	I've to buy a new computer.
CORRECT:	I have got to buy a new computer.
CORRECT:	I've got to buy a new computer.

7. We can use *have to* for all forms. There is no past form of *must* or *have got to*. We rarely use *must* for questions.

	Statement	Question
Present or Future	I **must study** for the test now/tomorrow. I **have to study** for the test now/tomorrow.	**Do** I **have to study** for the test now/tomorrow?
Past	They **had to study** for the test yesterday.	**Did** they **have to study** for the test yesterday?

3 Practice

Write rules for each of the following situations. Use the prompts and *must* or *have to*.

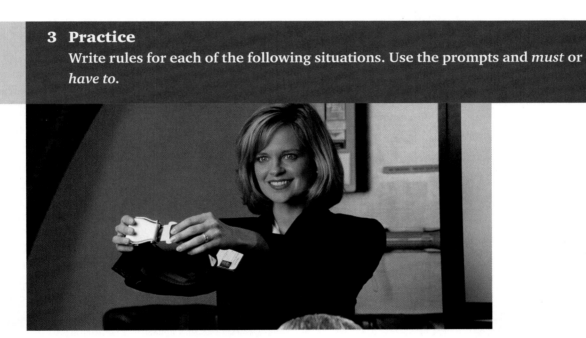

1. sit in your assigned seat
   You must sit in your assigned seat./You have to sit in your assigned seat.

2. fasten your seat belt when the seat belt sign is on

3. stay seated when the seat belt sign is on

4. turn off your cell phone

5. talk quietly—if at all

6. buy your food or drinks at the theater

_____

7. buy a ticket

_____

8. respect the animals

_____

4 Your Turn

Do you think the following rules should be set by the school or by the classroom teacher? If you think it should be a school rule, complete the sentence with *must*. If you think the teacher should set the rule, complete the sentence with *have to*.

Rules

1. You _____*must*_____ pay your fees before you start the class.

2. You _____ attend all the classes.

3. You _____ come to class on time.

4. You _____ turn off your MP3 player in class.

5. You _____ bring a dictionary to class every day.

6. You _____ be quiet when the teacher is talking.

7. You _____ complete all the assignments on time.

8. You _____ take all exams.

5 Pair Up and Talk

A Practice the conversation with a partner.

A: Do I have to pay the fees before I start class?

B: Yes, you have to pay them when you register.

B You and your partner will take the roles of teacher and student. Ask and answer questions about the rules in your school. Think of some rules to add to the ones in Practice 4.

Function

Miguel is calling his friend.
He **doesn't have to do** any homework today.

1. *Have to* and *must* have similar meanings in the affirmative, but in the negative, they have very different meanings.

   We use *not have to* to show that something is not necessary. There is another possibility or choice.

   > You **don't have to help** me today. (It's not necessary. I don't need your help today; you can help me another day.)

   We use *must not* express prohibition. It means that something is not allowed or is against the law. There is no choice.

   > You **must not drive** over 60 miles (96.5 kilometers) an hour. (It's against the law. You are not allowed to drive over 60 miles an hour.)

2. We usually use *must not* to show prohibition in official written forms, notices, and signs. We usually do not use *must not* when we talk to an adult, but we sometimes use *must not* when we tell a child something is not allowed.

   > Billy, you **must not go** near the fire.

3. We can use *not have to* in all forms. We can use *must not* only to talk about the present and the future.

   > You **must not park** in front of the doorway now/later. (present or future)

   > I **didn't have to take** a driver's test when I moved to this state. (past)

   > I **won't have to renew** my driver's license for another five years. (future)

6 Practice

Complete the sentences with *must* or *don't have to*. Then decide which place each sentence describes. Sometimes more than one place is possible.

airplane   airport   art gallery   hotel   museum   restaurant   theater   zoo

                                                            Place

1. Visitors _____*must*_____ buy a ticket before entering.   _*museum*_

2. Children under six _____ pay.   _____

3. Guests _____ tip the waiter—service is included.   _____

4. You _____ be quiet during the performance.   _____

5. Guests _____ sign in at the reception desk.   _____

6. Passengers _____ have their hand luggage screened.   _____

7. You _____ switch off your cell phones.   _____

8. Visitors _____ hand in their audio players after the tour.   _____

7 Practice

Complete the sentences with *must, have to, must not, mustn't,* or *don't have to* and the verbs in parentheses. Change the forms as necessary.

When I started my new job, I saw that most of the employees were wearing sweaters and casual shirts. I'm happy that men (wear) _*don't have to wear*_ a jacket and tie.
                                                                            1
In my previous job, we (keep) _____ our jackets on all day. Here, only
                                              2
the manager (wear) _____ a tie, but he (keep) _____
                              3   4
his jacket on.

On the other hand, some rules are quite strict. For example, you

(clear) _____ your work space at the end of every day, and you
                    5
(put) _____ any personal pictures up. You (be) _____
                6   7
late because there is a staff meeting every day at 8:00 A.M. You

(be) _____ absent unless it is absolutely necessary. My friend was sick
              8
for three days, and she (get) _____ a doctor's note.
                                              9

8 Pair Up and Talk

A Practice the conversation with a partner.

A: What are some differences between your old job and your new job?

B: Well, at my old job, we didn't have to come in at any specific time. We chose our own hours. But in my new job, we mustn't ever be late or we'll get in trouble.

B Compare your previous job and your present job, your previous school and your present school, or your previous residence and your present residence. Talk with your partner about the work, school, or house rules using *must*, *have to*, *must not*, *mustn't*, or *don't have to*.

9 Phrasal Verb Practice

A Complete the sentences with the correct forms of the phrasal verbs. Use each one only once. Phrasal verbs are taught in Unit 8, section H.

apply for   pick out   reach for   set aside   strike out   take part in

My parents want to buy me a car when I graduate from college. We're supposed to go to a dealer today to _____*pick out*_____ the one I want. I know I should be happy,
    1
but I don't want a car now. My parents want me to _____ a job, but I
                                                              2
want to _____ on my own and see the world. I'm not even engaged, but
            3
my parents have already _____ money for my wedding! I want to have
                              4
a family some day, but right now I want to _____ the stars—to achieve
                                                  5
my highest goals. One of these goals is to _____ the global effort to end
                                                6
hunger and poverty.

B Match the phrasal verbs with the correct definition.

_____   **1.** take part in   **a.** save for a special purpose

_____   **2.** reach for   **b.** request something in writing

_____   **3.** strike out   **c.** go on one's own

_____   **4.** set aside   **d.** choose

_____   **5.** pick out   **e.** seek

_____   **6.** apply for   **f.** participate in some activity

6E | *Should, Ought To,* and *Had Better* to Give Advice

Function

We **shouldn't** pollute the air. Factories **ought to** use better air filters in the smokestacks.

1. We use *should* and *ought to* to ask for and give advice, to say what is right or good in general, or to talk about an obligation or duty.

   You **should** learn to drive.
   You **ought to** learn to drive.
   You **shouldn't** tell lies.
   You **ought not** to tell lies. (uncommon)

   In general, we use *should* more than *ought to*.

2. We use *had better* to express a strong recommendation in a specific situation. *Had better* suggests a warning or a threat of bad consequences. It is stronger than *should* or *ought to*. In statements, we usually contract *had* to *'d*.

   You**'d** better leave now, or you'll miss the flight.

3. Even though *had better* contains the word *had*, it refers to the present or the future, not to the past.

4. We use *should* for questions. We do not usually use *had better* for questions. Questions with *ought to* are very rare.

10 Practice

Listen to Laura's description of her problems at work. What should Laura do? Write four sentences using *should, shouldn't,* or *ought to.*

CD1, 29

1. *She should talk to her supervisor about her workload.*
2. _____
3. _____
4. _____
5. _____

11 Your Turn

Work with a partner. Write a conversation between Laura, from Practice 10, and a friend. The friend gives advice. Laura responds using expressions like the ones listed below:

That's a good idea!   I hadn't thought of that!   No, that wouldn't work because …

~~I've tried that.~~   That's not a bad idea, but …

FRIEND: *I think you should talk to your supervisor about your workload.*

LAURA: *I've tried that. She said that she couldn't change it.*

FRIEND: _____

LAURA: _____

FRIEND: _____

LAURA: _____

FRIEND: _____

LAURA: _____

12 Pair Up and Talk

A   Practice the conversation with a partner.

A: I don't have anyone to speak English with. What should I do?

B: You should find an English-speaking key pal on the Internet.

B   Think of three problems that you have. Ask your partner for advice about each one.

6F | *Should Have* and *Ought To Have* to Express Regret or a Mistake

Form

This man is in handcuffs because he was arrested for stealing a car. He **shouldn't have** committed that crime.

1. We call this form of modal —modal + *have* + past participle—a perfect modal. Perfect modals refer to the past.

Affirmative and Negative Statements

Subject	Modal (*Not*)	*Have*	Past Participle
I/You He/She/It We/They	should should not shouldn't ought to ought not to	have	**gone** there.

We rarely use *ought to* in the negative.

Yes/No Questions and Short Answers

Modal	Subject	*Have*	Past Participle	Yes,		No,	
Should	I/we he/she you they	have	**gone** there?	you he/she I/we they	**should have.**	you he/she I/we they	**shouldn't have.**

Yes/no questions with *ought to* are extremely rare.

Wh- Questions					
	Subject (*Wh- Word*)	*Should Have*			**Past Participle**
Wh- Word is the Subject	**Who** **Which** (boy)	**should have**			**left** early? **won** the race?
	Wh- Word	*Should*	*Subject*	*Have*	**Past Participle**
Wh- Word is not the Subject	**What**	**should**	I	**have**	**done** to help you?
	Where		she		**gone**?
	When		they		**taken** the test?
	How		he		**completed** the form?
	Which (car)		you		**repaired**?
	Why		he		**left** early?
	Who*		they		**talked to**?

* In formal written English, the *wh-* word could be *whom*.

Wh- questions with *ought to* are rare.

2. In speech, we contract *should have* to *should've* when *should have* comes before a past participle, or when it is used in a short answer. It is very common to say this, but we do not often write it. Do not make the mistake of writing the contracted form of *should have* as *should of*.

CORRECT: I **should have** brought more money. (*Should have* sounds like "should've" or "should'a".)

INCORRECT: I **should** ~~of~~ brought more money.

Function

We use the perfect modal form of *should* or *ought to* to say that something was the best thing to do, but we didn't do it.

I **should have taken** a map with me. (I didn't, and I got lost.)

You **ought to have taken** the job. (You didn't take it. That was a mistake.)

He **shouldn't have missed** the test. (He did miss it. Now he regrets it.)

13 Practice

Listen to the conversation about Gary and Julia's vacation. Write five sentences about the conversation using *should have* and *shouldn't have*.

DOWNLOAD

CD1, 30

1. They should have booked the trip with a travel company that they knew about.

2. _____

_____

3. _____

_____

4. _____

_____

5. _____

_____

6. _____

_____

14 Pair Up and Talk

A Practice the conversation with a partner.

A: Anna failed her math exam. What should she have done differently?

B: She should have studied harder. And she shouldn't have spent so much time watching TV!

B Think of three situations that went wrong for someone you know. Discuss with a partner what the person should or shouldn't have done in each situation.

6G | *Be Supposed To* to Express Expectation

Function

You**'re supposed to study** in the library.
Are you supposed to sleep in the library?

1. We use *be supposed to* to talk about what we expect to happen because it is the normal way of doing things or because of an arrangement, duty, or custom.

    You **are supposed to take** something to the host when you go for dinner.

2. There is often a difference between what is supposed to happen and what really happens.

    I **am supposed to go** to the conference tomorrow, but instead I'm going to stay in the office and catch up on my work.

    She **was supposed to call** me yesterday, but she didn't.

3. We can use *be supposed to* in the past by using *was* or *were* instead of *am*, *is,* or *are*.

    The plane **was supposed to arrive** at 9:30, but it arrived an hour late.

    The soccer players **were supposed to practice** on Sunday, but it rained.

15 Practice

Complete the sentences with the correct form of *be supposed to*.
Then match the sentences with the phrase that describes what the
sentence is about. Some phrases will be used more than once.

The sentence is about …

___d___ **1.** I (go) __*was supposed to go*__ to the dentist
Tuesday, but I had too much work.

a. a generally agreed last
upon custom.

_____ **2.** (you/not be) _____
in a meeting right now?

b. a rule or regulation.

_____ **3.** My cousins (visit) _____
us last April, but they canceled their trip.

c. a scheduled event.

_____ **4.** I (not/tell) _____
you this, but I think they are going to give you a
surprise party.

d. a scheduled event that
did not take place.

_____ **5.** In Japan, you (take off) _____
your shoes before you enter someone's house.

_____ **6.** You (not/drive) _____
without a license. It's against the law.

e. an action carried out
against the rule.

_____ **7.** If you fail the test, the examiner (tell)
_____ you why.

_____ **8.** (I/put) _____
my luggage on the bus myself?

16 Pair Up and Talk

A Practice the conversation with a partner.

A: What are you supposed to do for a burn? I heard you're supposed to put butter on it.

B: Putting cold water on a burn is supposed to help it. You're not supposed to put butter
on it.

B Talk about things that you are supposed to or not supposed to do to help the
following problems:

a burn   a fever   a toothache

a cold   a headache   sunburn

THE LOYAL QUILL[1]

Ben and Simon went to school together in a city near the sea. One day, just before a test, Simon turned to Ben. "I forgot my pen!" he said. "Ben, you've got to help me."

Once again, Simon had forgotten to do something he was supposed to do. "You should have checked before you left home this morning!" Ben said angrily. Still, Ben was a kind person. "I shouldn't do this, Simon," he said, "but I'll lend you my extra pen." Simon used Ben's sturdy quill during the test. After class, he absentmindedly slipped Ben's pen into his own bag. For months, Simon promised to give it back and then forgot. After about a year, Ben grew tired of asking Simon to return it. Because of that, Simon thought, "Ben must not care about getting it back. I guess I don't have to worry about it." The pen continued to serve

Simon well as he grew into a young man and built a successful business. Eventually, Simon became the richest person in the city.

Ben went into the shipping business. He did well, but his business could not grow unless he bought another ship. He did not have enough money, but he knew Simon did. He sent Simon a letter. "Ha!" Simon said as he saw Ben's papers asking for a loan. "Ben thought he was so much smarter than me. Who's smart now? He ought to manage his money better." Simon grabbed the quill to write "No" on Ben's loan papers. But when the tip of the quill reached the paper, all it would write on the loan papers was "Yes!" Simon dropped the disobedient pen. It stood up on its own and added Simon's signature.

[1] quill = a kind of pen made from a feather and used for writing long ago

1. _____

He should have brought his own pen.

2. _____

They had to take a test.

3. _____

He should have given Ben his pen back.

4. _____

He did not remember to do so.

5. _____

He thought he did not have to give it back.

6. _____

Simon kept it for many years.

7. _____

He must not have been as lucky as Simon.

8. _____

He was not able to expand his business without one.

9. _____

He must have felt Ben had a bad opinion of him.

10. _____

It remained loyal to its original owner.

A   Listen and check the correct answer.

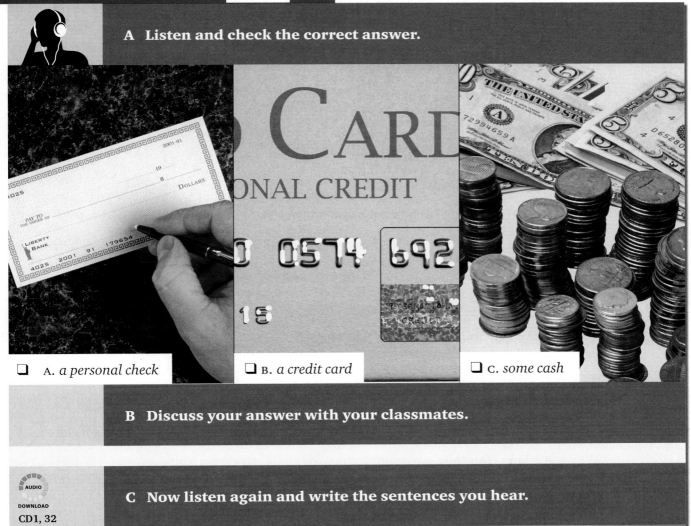

❏ A. *a personal check*   ❏ B. *a credit card*   ❏ C. *some cash*

B   Discuss your answer with your classmates.

AUDIO

DOWNLOAD

CD1, 32

C   Now listen again and write the sentences you hear.

Review

1 Review (6a–6c, 6e, 6g)
Underline the correct answers.

What (<u>Can</u>/ought to) happen if you don't prepare for an interview? Will you
¹
(be able to/better not) get the job you really want? If you don't prepare, you'll leave
²
thinking about what you (should/mustn't) have done and said. You say you want a better
³
job? Then you (are supposed to/had better) learn how to interview for one. You (aren't
⁴
supposed to/don't have to) attend a class to do it. Just read the following information.
⁵

First, you (ought/should) remember PPPQ. That's Preparation, Practice, Personal
⁶
Presentation, and Questions. To prepare for your interview, you (should/couldn't)
⁷
read as much as you can find about the company. You (don't have to/must not) know
⁸
everything. You (ought to/aren't supposed) to be an expert, but (you aren't able/you've
⁹   ¹⁰
got) to show the interviewer that you're interested in the company.

Practice is very important. You (must/are supposed to) practice answering questions
¹¹
with someone. You (might not/cannot) think this is important, but you really
¹²
(could/ought to) understand how it feels to answer questions and communicate well.
¹³
What clothes (ought/should) you wear? Personal presentation is very important. You
¹⁴
(might/should) get away with wearing a bathing suit if you want to be a lifeguard, but
¹⁵
in most cases, you (could/had better) wear more formal clothes to an office interview.
¹⁶
You're (supposed to/able to) look like a professional. You (aren't able to/shouldn't) walk
¹⁷   ¹⁸
into an interview wearing a wrinkled shirt or a pair of jeans. You (should have/must)
¹⁹
wear something that you feel good in. You (can/ought to) look and feel confident.
²⁰

SUSAN: (you/find) ___*Can you find*___ someone else to help you study your lines for
1

your play today? I (go) _____ to my aunt's house. She's
2

not well.

JOHN: Of course. You (not/help) _____ me today. I can get
3

someone at the theater to read my lines with me. I (know) _____
4

my part by tomorrow night. Don't worry about me.

You (leave) _____ now before you miss your bus.
5

SUSAN: Oh, I have plenty of time. You know, I (stay) _____ with my
6

aunt for two days, but instead I'm coming home tomorrow afternoon. That

way I (go) _____ to your dress rehearsal.
7

JOHN: Oh, don't remind me! I'm not ready. I (take) _____ some time
8

off from work yesterday to study my script, but I was too busy. Now I don't know

half my lines. What (I/do) _____ ? Stay up all night? Oh, I
9

(not/take) _____ this part.
10

SUSAN: We (not/go) _____ to the theater that night. Then you
11

never would have seen the notice.

JOHN: You know how much I love to be on stage, but I (never/try out)

_____ for this role. I (know) _____ that I
12   13

wouldn't have the time. I (do) _____ this sort of
14

thing when I was in school. But I'm working full-time now.

SUSAN: I know it's hard, but I really think that you (do) _____ it.
15

I (come) _____ home by noon tomorrow. Then, I'll come over
16

to help you. Oh, I (never/agree) _____ to go there tonight.
17

A Before You Read

1. What happens on a typical TV talk show?
2. Why are some people on TV especially popular?

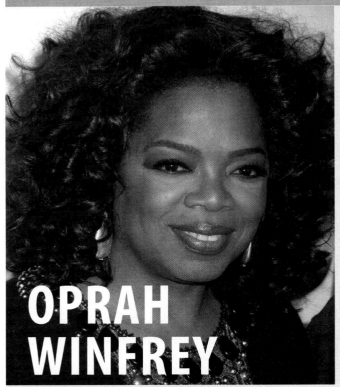

OPRAH WINFREY

DID YOU KNOW ... ?
Oprah is the first African-American female to make *Fortune* magazine's list of billionaires.

B Read When Oprah Winfrey talks, people listen. Every time she hosts her television talk show, "The Oprah Winfrey Show," more than 100 million people tune in. Books that she recommends on her show can become famous overnight. She often tops[1] lists of the most influential women in the world.

Such success must seem unreal to anyone who knew Oprah as a child in Milwaukee. From the age of six she lived there with her mother in an unstable, dangerous home. She suffered poverty and abuse. Then at 13, she saw that she had better run for her life. She ran away to Chicago and was eventually sent to live with her father in Tennessee. Life in her mid-teens became more **settled** under Vernon Winfrey's rules. She had to be home at a specific time every evening. She had to read a book every week. She was even supposed to write a report for her father on every book she read. She began to see that her life did not have to be so aimless and tough.

She studied performance techniques at Tennessee State University and moved around through jobs as a radio and TV show host. Then she got a job with a TV talk show in Chicago. She joined the show in 1984 and, in one year, turned it into a success. The station managers realized they should just name the show after her. "The Oprah Winfrey Show" went national[2] in 1986 and soon became a worldwide favorite. Oprah became famous in the movies. She played an abused girl in the 1985 movie *The Color Purple*. Oprah could easily understand the character. Her performance was nominated for an Academy Award. Many people think she should have won. Because of her great influence, she has often appeared before the U.S. Congress to say that the government must do more to help abused children.

[1] top = appear at the top of

[2] went national = became available nationwide

C Notice the Grammar Underline all the modals discussed in this chapter.

Choose the best answer.

D Look for Main Ideas

1. This reading is mainly about Oprah Winfrey's _____ .
   - (A) TV show
   - (B) troubled childhood
   - (C) rise to success
   - (D) charitable activities

2. What is the main topic of paragraph 3?
   - (A) Oprah's movie career
   - (B) Oprah's training as a performer
   - (C) Oprah's rise to success
   - (D) Oprah's move to Chicago

E Look for Details

3. How old was Oprah when she moved to Milwaukee?
   - (A) under 3
   - (B) 6
   - (C) 13
   - (D) in her mid-teens

4. Which of the following happened first?
   - (A) Oprah got a job in Chicago.
   - (B) The movie *The Color Purple* was released.
   - (C) Oprah's show went national.
   - (D) Oprah addressed the United States Congress.

5. The passage mentions that Oprah has done all of the following EXCEPT _____ .
   - (A) help other actors become famous
   - (B) take part in a movie
   - (C) host a radio show
   - (D) run away from home

Vocabulary questions ask the meaning of a word in the reading. Some vocabulary questions ask which answer choice can be best substituted in the sentence without changing its meaning. To answer this kind of vocabulary question, look for context clues in the reading that tell the true meaning of the word.

F Make Inferences

6. From paragraph 2, we can most strongly infer that Vernon Winfrey _____ .
   - (A) thought Oprah's bad behavior was hopeless
   - (B) did not want Oprah to live with him
   - (C) believed Oprah could benefit from discipline
   - (D) knew Oprah could succeed if she learned how to read

7. We can infer most strongly from the reading passage that, in 1985, Oprah _____ .
   - (A) won an award
   - (B) almost won an award
   - (C) gave someone an award
   - (D) refused to take an award

G Look for Vocabulary

8. The word *settled* in the reading is closest in meaning to _____ .
   - (A) decided
   - (B) stable
   - (C) exciting
   - (D) relaxed

Writing: Write an Expository Essay

An expository essay explains something. In this essay, you will explain how a visitor should and should not act when going for a meal in a home in your country.

STEP 1

Work with a partner and make notes about what a visitor from another country should remember when going to a home for a meal in your country. Make notes for each part of the visit. Use the following ideas or your own. Then write your essay.

1. **Arrival**

   Being punctual: When to go?

   Greeting: How to?

   Bringing a gift: Necessary or not? What to bring? Whom to give the gift to?

   Ask for a tour of the house?

2. **At the table**

   What to talk about?

   How to eat: Utensils (use of chopsticks, spoons, fingers, etc.)? Where to put your hands?

   OK to make noise while eating?

   How to refuse food or ask for more?

   What to say about the food?

3. **After the meal**

   How long to stay?

   How to thank your host?

   Offer to help after the meal?

   What to say before you leave?

STEP 2

Evaluate your essay.

Checklist

_____ Did you write an introduction that stated the purpose of the essay?

_____ Did you write three paragraphs in the body?

_____ Did the paragraphs explain what a visitor should do in the three parts of the visit?

_____ Did you write a conclusion that summarized your points in the body?

STEP 3

Work with a partner or a teacher to edit your essay. Check spelling, vocabulary, and grammar.

STEP 4

Write your final copy.

Self-Test

1. You _____ be late for your interview tomorrow. It will not look good.

    A. had better not   Ⓐ Ⓑ Ⓒ Ⓓ
    B. better not
    C. had no better
    D. 'd better

2. He _____ to call yesterday, but didn't.

    A. is supposed   Ⓐ Ⓑ Ⓒ Ⓓ
    B. was supposed
    C. supposed
    D. supposing

3. You _____ drive without a seat belt. It's the law.

    A. have to   Ⓐ Ⓑ Ⓒ Ⓓ
    B. are supposed to
    C. must not
    D. don't have to

4. When _____ to help us?

    A. will you be able   Ⓐ Ⓑ Ⓒ Ⓓ
    B. you will be able
    C. you be able
    D. are you be able

5. I have a bad sunburn. I _____ sat in the sun so long.

    A. should have   Ⓐ Ⓑ Ⓒ Ⓓ
    B. shouldn't have
    C. musn't have
    D. musn't

6. A few months ago, I _____ to use a computer, but now I even use it to chat with my family.

    A. am not able   Ⓐ Ⓑ Ⓒ Ⓓ
    B. couldn't
    C. wasn't able
    D. couldn't able

7. Tim _____ to wash the dishes. There are no more clean ones.

    A. must   Ⓐ Ⓑ Ⓒ Ⓓ
    B. have got
    C. got
    D. has

8. You _____ to clean your room today. You can do it tomorrow.

    A. have   Ⓐ Ⓑ Ⓒ Ⓓ
    B. don't have
    C. mustn't
    D. can't

9. RICK: _____ go now?
    ANNIE: Yes, that's a good idea.

    A. Shouldn't I   Ⓐ Ⓑ Ⓒ Ⓓ
    B. Had better I
    C. Had I
    D. Better had I

10. You _____ tell lies.

    A. shouldn't   Ⓐ Ⓑ Ⓒ Ⓓ
    B. ought to
    C. ought better not
    D. had not better

1. We <u>are supposed</u> <u>to go</u> camping last Saturday,
        A   **B**

   but we <u>had to</u> <u>cancel</u> it because of the weather.
        C   **D**

   Ⓐ Ⓑ Ⓒ Ⓓ

2. You <u>should ask</u> <u>your counselor</u> <u>for advice</u>, or
         A   **B**   **C**

   you <u>call</u> the department at the university.
      D

   Ⓐ Ⓑ Ⓒ Ⓓ

3. I work from home, so I <u>haven't</u> <u>have to</u> drive
                 A   **B**

   much, but my husband <u>has to</u> <u>do</u> a lot
               C   **D**

   of driving.

   Ⓐ Ⓑ Ⓒ Ⓓ

4. When he <u>was</u> <u>a child</u>, he <u>couldn't read</u>, but he
         A   **B**   **C**

   <u>was able use</u> a computer.
    D

   Ⓐ Ⓑ Ⓒ Ⓓ

5. We <u>have</u> a test tomorrow, so we <u>had better</u> <u>not</u>
      A   **B**   **C**

   <u>to go</u> out tonight.
    D

   Ⓐ Ⓑ Ⓒ Ⓓ

6. She <u>have</u> <u>got to</u> take the test this year or else
       A   **B**

   she <u>won't</u> <u>be able to</u> apply for college.
        C   **D**

   Ⓐ Ⓑ Ⓒ Ⓓ

7. In most high schools, students <u>must not</u> <u>to call</u>
                           A   **B**

   their teachers by their first names, but

   in college, students <u>are able</u> <u>to call</u> their
                   C   **D**

   professors by their first names if the professor

   allows them to do so.

   Ⓐ Ⓑ Ⓒ Ⓓ

8. You <u>not</u> <u>have to</u> finish high school <u>in order</u>
       A   **B**   **C**

   <u>to get</u> a driver's license.
    D

   Ⓐ Ⓑ Ⓒ Ⓓ

9. We <u>should</u> <u>not have wash</u> the car yesterday
       A   **B**

   because <u>it's going</u> <u>to rain</u>.
          C   **D**

   Ⓐ Ⓑ Ⓒ Ⓓ

10. You <u>don't have</u> <u>got to</u> show your passport when
         A   **B**

    you <u>fly</u> within the United States, but you
        C

    <u>must show</u> your driver's license or another
       D

    form of photo identification.

    Ⓐ Ⓑ Ⓒ Ⓓ

Unit 7
Modals II

Could I check this book out of the library?

Shall, Let's, How About, What About, Why Don't, Could, and *Can* to Make Suggestions

Form/Function

ANNE:	**Let's get** a cup of coffee after class.
ERIK:	Good idea. **How about going** to the new café next to the library?

1. We can make suggestions with *shall, let's, why don't, how about,* and *what about*. Notice that all of these, except *let's*, are questions and must end with a question mark.

Shall		
Shall	**Subject**	**Base Verb**
Shall	we	**leave** now?

How About and What About	
How/What About	**Gerund*/Noun**
How about	**going** to dinner?
What about	**dinner?**

* A gerund is a base verb + *-ing* that we use as a noun.

Let's	
Let's	**Base Verb**
Let's	**leave** now.
Let's not	

2. A question starting with *why don't* can be a suggestion or a normal question. We expect an agreement or a disagreement in response to a suggestion. We expect an explanation in response to a normal question.

A: **Why don't you eat** now?

B: That's a good idea. (The response to the suggestion is an agreement.)

OR

B: Because I'm not hungry. (The response to the normal question is an explanation.)

3. Statements with *could* and *can* are sometimes suggestions. Words and phrases such as *maybe* and *if you like* can show that a statement is a suggestion. *Could* is usually more polite than *can* in these suggestions.

Could **and** Can			
Maybe	**Subject**	**Modal + Base Verb**	**(If You Like)**
Maybe	we	**could** leave now	**if** you **like.**
	I	**can** leave now	

Let's and *let us* can also mean that the speaker expects the listener to agree to what the speaker says. The uncontracted form, *let us* is usually formal.

Doctor to a child:	Let's listen to your heart.
In a speech:	Let us never forget this senator's contribution to our country.
In a religious service:	Let us pray.

1 Practice

Complete the sentences with *how about, why don't, shall, could,* or *can*. Listen to the conversation to check your answers. Then practice the conversation with a partner.

CD2, 2

Rick and Olivia are having a cup of coffee between classes.

RICK: _____*Shall*_____ we go to the movies tonight?
              1

OLIVIA: Great Idea! _____ going to that new film at the Avon Cinema?
                                2

RICK: OK. _____ I pick you up at 5:30?
                     3

OLIVIA: Sure. Maybe we _____ go out to eat afterwards?
                            4

RICK: Great! Or we _____ eat at my place, if you like.
                        5

OLIVIA: _____ we pick up some take-out Chinese food on the way to
             6

your house? Then you don't have to cook.

RICK: Perfect!

2 Pair Up and Talk

A Practice the conversation with a partner.

A: Let's go bowling on Saturday.

B: Hmm. I don't really like to bowl. How about going dancing?

A: We went dancing last weekend. Shall we try to get tickets for the ballet instead?

B: Ugh. I hate the ballet. What about a concert?

B You and your partner can't agree on what to do this weekend. Use *shall, let's, how about, what about, could,* and *can* to make suggestions until you agree on the same activity. Use activities from the list or your own ideas.

a baseball game	a movie	dancing	skating
a concert	a party	shopping	swimming

7B | *Prefer, Would Prefer,* and *Would Rather* to Express Preferences

Form

They**'d prefer eating** pizza **to** salad.

PREFER AND WOULD PREFER

Statements			
Subject	**(Would) Prefer(s)**	**Object**	**(To + Object)**
I/You He/She/It We/They	prefer(s) would prefer	coffee	to tea.
		drinking coffee	to tea. to drinking tea.
		to **drink coffee.**	*

*We do not use *to* + object if the first object is an infinitive.

Yes/No Questions					Short Answers	
Auxiliary	Subject	Base Verb	Object	(*To* + Object)	Yes,	No,
Do	I/we				you **do**.	you **don't**.
	you		coffee?		I/we **do**.	I/we **don't**.
Does	they	**prefer**			they **do**.	they **don't**.
	he/she				he/she **does**.	he/she **doesn't**.
Would	I/we				you **would**.	you **wouldn't**.
	you		coffee	to tea?	I/we **would**.	I/we **wouldn't**.
	he/she				he/she **would**.	he/she **wouldn't**.
	they				they **would**.	they **wouldn't**.

1. The objects that follow *prefer* and *would prefer* can be nouns, gerunds, or infinitives.

    I prefer **television** to **movies**. (noun object)

    He prefers **watching** television to **watching** movies. (gerund objects)

    We prefer **to watch** television. (infinitive object)

2. *To* + object is optional if both speakers understand what the second object is.

    I prefer **coffee**. (The listener knows that they are talking about coffee and tea.)

3. After *(would) prefer,* we do not use *to* + object if the first object is an infinitive.

    CORRECT: We prefer to watch movies.

    INCORRECT: We prefer to watch movies ~~to watch television~~.

4. When the object after *prefer* is an infinitive, we can add *than* + another infinitive. We can omit the *to* in the second infinitive.

    I prefer to see movies **than (to) rent** videos.

WOULD RATHER

Affirmative and Negative Statements				
Subject	Would Rather (*Not*)	Base Verb	Object	(*Than* + Object) (*Than* + Base Verb + Object)
I/You/He/She/ We/They	**would rather** **'d rather**	**have**	**tea**	than coffee.
				than have coffee.
I/You/He/She/ We/They	**would rather not**	**have**	**tea.**	

5. Some verbs (intransitive verbs) do not have objects. In these cases, objects are not necessary with *would rather*.

> I'**d rather** leave now than leave later.
> I'**d rather** not arrive too early.

6. These phrases with *than* are optional if both speakers understand what the object is.

Yes/No Questions					
Would	**Subject**	*Rather*	**Verb**	**Object**	(*Or* + Object) (*Or* + Base Verb + Object)
Would	I/you he/she/it we/they	**rather**	**have**	tea?	
				tea	**or coffee?** **or have coffee?**

Answers	
Question	Possible Answers
Would he **rather** have tea?	Yes, he **would**./No, he **wouldn't**.
Would they **rather** have coffee or tea?	They'd **rather** have tea.

Function

1. We use *prefer*, *would prefer*, and *would rather* to say that we like one thing more than other things. We usually use *prefer* to state our general preferences, but we use *would prefer* or *would rather* when we are talking about a specific choice, as in a restaurant.

> Which do you **prefer**, beef or chicken? **Would** you **prefer** a steak or a hamburger? I **prefer** Chinese food to Indian.
> I'**d prefer** to have Chinese food to Indian.

2. When we want to refuse an offer, we usually answer by saying *I'd rather not*.

> A: Would you like some coffee?
> B: I'**d rather not**. It makes me nervous.
> CORRECT: I'd rather not.
> INCORRECT: ~~I wouldn't rather.~~

3. When we want to compare two things, we can use *to* after *prefer* + object.

> Helen **prefers** books **to movies**. (noun objects)
> Helen **prefers** reading books **to watching movies**. (gerund objects)

Bob completed this questionnaire about his preferences. Use the questionnaire to write nine sentences about Bob using *prefer, would prefer,* and *would rather*.

Preferences Quiz

Write your preferences on a scale of 1-5.

1 = love, 2 = like a lot, 3 = like, 4 = OK, 5 = dislike

	1	2	3	4	5
Fish	1	(2)	3	4	5
Meat	(1)	2	3	4	5
Tofu	1	2	3	4	(5)
Jogging	1	(2)	3	4	5
Tennis	(1)	2	3	4	5
Classical music	1	2	(3)	4	5
Rock music	(1)	2	3	4	5
Chess	(1)	2	3	4	5
Eating out	(1)	2	3	4	5
Eating at home	1	2	3	(4)	5
Sending email messages	(1)	2	3	4	5
Writing letters	1	2	3	4	(5)

1. _Bob prefers fish to tofu._

2. _____

3. _____

4. _____

5. _____

6. _____

7. _____

8. _____

9. _____

10. _____

4 Pair Up and Talk

A Practice the conversation with a partner.

A: Do you prefer jogging to tennis?

B: No, I don't. I like tennis because it's more competitive.

A: Do you like eating out?

B: Yes. I would rather eat out than eat at home. It's less work.

B Use the questionnaire in Practice 3 to ask questions about your partner's preferences. Your partner will answer the questions and give reasons for his or her choices.

7C *May, Could,* and *Can* to Ask Permission

Form

Could I **check** this book out of the library?

Yes/No Questions			Short Answers			
Modal	**Subject**	**Base Verb**	**Yes,**		**No,**	
May **Could** **Can**	I/we	**use** your phone?	you	**may.** **could.** **can.**	you	**may not.** **couldn't.** **can't.**
	he/she		he/she		he/she	
	they		they		they	

Function

1. We use *may, could,* and *can* to ask permission. We use *may* or *could* with people we do not know or who are in authority. We can use *could* in any situation. We use *can* with friends and family members.

    Ms. Brown isn't at the office. **May** I take a message?

    Could Sally have another piece of cake, please?

    Pete, **can** I borrow your dictionary?

    Remember that *can* and *could* sometimes express ability.

    I **can** make cakes, but I **can't** make pies.

    She **couldn't** swim until last year.

2. It is polite to use *please* when we ask permission. *Please* usually goes after the subject or at the end of the sentence. We put a comma before it if it is at the end of the sentence.

    Could I **please** borrow the car?

    Could I borrow the car, **please**?

3. When we use *could* to ask permission, it refers to the present or future. Remember that *could* also has the meaning of past ability.

    Could she **take** some more potatoes, please? (permission)

    Could she **swim** when she was five? (*could* = past ability)

4. When we ask permission with *could*, the short answer uses *may* or *can*.

    A: **Could** I borrow your dictionary?

    CORRECT: B: **Yes, of course** you can/may.

    INCORRECT: B: Yes, of course you ~~could~~.

5. We can use expressions other than short answers to answer requests for permission.

    A: **Could** I use your phone?

    B: **Yes, of course.**

      OR Sure.

      OR No problem.

      OR Go ahead.

6. When we refuse to give permission, we usually also offer an apology and/or an explanation.

    A: **May** I sit here?

    B: I'm sorry, but I'm saving this seat for my friend.

5 Practice

Complete the sentences about a zoo with *can* or *can't*. Then identify the meaning of *can* or *can't* by writing *permission* or *ability* on the line.

1. You _____ can _____ buy popcorn there.   _____ ability _____

2. You _____ feed the giraffes. It isn't good for them.   _____

3. You _____ take photos. It doesn't hurt the animals.   _____

4. You _____ see the snakes when they hide in the rocks.   _____

5. You _____ see the elephants. They are next to the giraffes.   _____

6. You _____ stay after dark. The zoo is closed then.   _____

7. You _____ see everything today. The zoo is too large.   _____

8. Children under five _____ get in free.   _____

6 Practice

A Listen to each conversation. Write the word you hear—*may*, *could*, or *can*—to complete each request. Then practice the conversations with a partner.

AUDIO
DOWNLOAD

CD2, 3

1. EMPLOYEE: _____ Could _____ I leave work a little early today?

    BOSS: Certainly. That's fine.

2. PASSENGER A: _____ I borrow your newspaper for a moment?

    PASSENGER B: Of course.

3. CUSTOMER: _____ I have another cup of coffee?

    SERVER: Sure! Right away!

4. TEACHER: _____ Susan come to school early tomorrow? I want to help her with her math.

   PARENT: Of course. What time should she be there?

5. STUDENT: _____ I hand in my paper a day late?

   TEACHER: I'm sorry, but the date can't be changed.

6. CHILD: _____ you give me five dollars, please?

   PARENT: Certainly not! I've already given you your allowance this week.

7. HUSBAND: _____ I close the window?

   WIFE: Good idea. It's getting cold in here.

B Write *formal* or *informal* for each of the situations in Practice A.

1. _____formal_____   5. _____
2. _____   6. _____
3. _____   7. _____
4. _____

7 Pair Up and Talk
A Practice the conversation with a partner.

A: May I close the window? It's cold in here.

B: Sure. That's fine. (OR I'd rather you didn't.)

B Work with a partner. Choose two of the situations from the list below, or use two of your own ideas. For each situation, take turns making a request and responding to your partner's request.

An employee wants to miss a meeting this afternoon.

A boss wants to talk to an employee about the schedule.

A patient wants to cancel an appointment at a doctor's office.

A friend wants to reschedule a lunch date with another friend.

A passenger on a bus wants to change seats with another passenger.

Form

ROBBY: **Could** you **make** a copy of this for me?

Tom: Sure. **Would you mind** waiting until I finish copying this report?

ROBBY: Of course.

WILL, CAN, COULD, AND *WOULD*

Request			Possible Answers	
Modal	**Subject**	**Base Verb**	**Accept**	**Decline**
Will	you	**pick up** my mother at the airport?	Yes, of course.	Sorry, I can't.
			I'd be happy to.	
Can			Certainly.	I'm not sure. When?
Would			Sure.*	No way!*
Could			No problem. *	

Sure, No problem, and *No way!* are informal. *No way!* is sometimes also humorous.

WOULD YOU MIND

Request		Possible Answers	
Would You Mind	**Gerund**	**Accept**	**Decline**
Would you mind	**mailing** this for me?	Of course.	Sorry, I can't.
		(No,) I'd be happy to.	I won't have time. Sorry.
		(No,) I'd be glad to.	No way!
		Sure.	

Function

1. We use *would* and *could* to make polite requests.

   BOSS TO EMPLOYEE: **Could** you **make** a copy of this, please?

   Would you **answer** these letters for me, please?

2. We use *will* and *can* for more direct and informal requests.

   MOTHER TO DAUGHTER: **Will** you **turn** down the TV, please?

   Can you pass me the salt?

3. We use *please* to make a request more polite. We can put *please* at the end of the sentence or between the subject and the verb. If we put *please* at the end of the sentence, we put a comma before it.

   Could you make a copy of this, **please**?

   Could you **please** make a copy of this?

4. We may agree to do a polite request. However, when we cannot do it, we usually apologize and give a reason.

   BOSS: Could you finish that report for me this morning?

   EMPLOYEE: I'm sorry, I can't. I'll be in a meeting.

5. We can also use *would you mind* + a gerund to make a polite request.

   A: **Would you mind waiting** a few minutes longer?

   B: No, that's OK. OR Yes, I would. I've already been waiting for an hour.

6. Compare these answers to polite requests.

   Requests with *would/could* + base verb. (Do not answer with *would* or *could*.)

   BOSS: **Would/Could** you **come** to my office?

   EMPLOYEE: Yes, of course. INCORRECT: Yes, I would/could.

   Requests with *would you mind* + gerund (You can answer with *would*.)

   RECEPTIONIST: **Would you mind waiting** a few minutes longer?

   VISITOR: No, that's OK. OR Yes, I would. I've already been waiting for an hour.

   A negative answer to *would you mind* means that you will do what the person wants. A positive answer — *Yes, I would* — means that you are not willing to do it.

8 Practice

For each of the following situations, write three different requests and responses that would be appropriate to the situation.

1. It's very hot and stuffy in your office. The windows are all closed. The heat is on high. The door is closed. There are two co-workers in the office with you. What requests could you make?

    Request A: *Would you mind opening the window?*
    Reply: *I'd be happy to.*
    Request B: _____
    Reply: _____
    Request C: _____
    Reply: _____

2. You are on the train that you take every day to work. You realize that you left your train pass at home. It costs a lot to buy a ticket on the train, and you don't want to do that. What requests could you make to the train conductor?

    Request A: _____
    Reply: _____
    Request B: _____
    Reply: _____
    Request C: _____
    Reply: _____

9 Phrasal Verb Practice

A Complete the sentences with the correct forms of the phrasal verbs. Use each verb only once. Phrasal verbs are taught in Unit 8, section H.

call off	leave behind	pack up
fix up	lie around	run off

RON: Let's _____ the yearbook meeting today and go on a hike instead.
                        1

PETER: I'd rather _____ the house and watch TV.
                          2

RON: How about taking a drive to the beach? I just _____ my car and I want
                                                                    3
        to test it.

PETER: OK. The beach is a good idea. Let's _____ our work and have some fun.
                                                    4

RON: Oh, no! I almost forgot. I can't _____ anywhere today. I have to help
                                                5
        Fiona. She's moving and needs someone to help her _____
                                                                    6

her books. She must have over 200! Do you want to help us?

PETER: No thanks. I think I'll have the yearbook meeting after all.

B   Match the phrasal verb with the correct definition.

_____ **1.** lie around   **a.** make better and more attractive

_____ **2.** call off   **b.** put one's belongings in cases or boxes

_____ **3.** run off   **c.** go away

_____ **4.** fix up   **d.** not take or bring

_____ **5.** leave behind   **e.** cause not to take place

_____ **6.** pack up   **f.** be lazy; do nothing

10   Pair Up and Talk

A   **Practice the conversation with a partner.**

A: In dance class today I forgot the steps to our new dance.

B: So what did you do?

A: I finally asked the teacher, "Could you please show me the steps to the new dance?"
     She said, "Sure."

B   Think of three requests that you have made recently. In what kind of situations did you make them? What kind of replies did you receive? Tell a partner about the requests and replies.

7E | *May, Might,* and *Could* to Express Possibility

I **could be** in this traffic jam for a long time. I **might miss** my meeting.

PRESENT

Subject	Modal (*Not*)	Base Verb
I/We He/She/It You We/They	may may not might might not could*	be there.

*No negative for *could* in this meaning.

Yes/No Questions			Short Answers			
Modal	Subject	Base Verb	Yes,		No,	
Could	I/we	get there early?	you	could.	you	couldn't.
	you		I/we		I/we	
	he/she/it		he/she/it		he/she/it	
	they		they		they	

1. We do not contract *may not* or *might not* when they express possibility.
   CORRECT: He may not be there yet./He might not be there yet.
   INCORRECT: He ~~mayn't~~ be there yet./He ~~mightn't~~ be there yet.
2. When *could* refers to the present, we do not use it in the negative.
   CORRECT: They may/might not be on time.
   INCORRECT: They ~~could~~ not be on time.

3. We can form *yes/no* questions about possibility with *could*, but not with *may* or *might*. However, we often respond to *yes/no* and *wh-* questions in the present progressive or the future with *may* or *might*.

    A: Are you leaving soon?   A: Is John still in his office?

    B: I don't know. **I might/may**.   B: He **might/may be**.

4. *Maybe* and *may be* both express possibility, but they have different forms. *Maybe* is an adverb. It is one word and always comes at the beginning of a sentence.

    Maybe that's Ted at the door. That **may be** Ted at the door.

    May be is a modal + a verb (*be*). It is always two words.

    Pronunciation Note: *Maybe* is pronounced with stress on the first syllable. *May be* is pronounced with stress on both syllables.

        MAYbe that's Ted at the door. OR MAYbe it's Grace.

        Ted MAY BE in the library.

PAST

5. We use the perfect modal form (modal + *have* + a past participle) to express possibilities with these modals in the past.

Affirmative and Negative Statements			
Subject	**Modal (Not)**	**Have**	**Past Participle**
I/You He/She/It We/They	**may/may not*** **might/might not*** **could** (no negative**)	**have**	**been** there yesterday.

*The contraction of *may not* and *might not* is very rare.

**Could not* expresses past impossibility.

Yes/No Questions				Short Answers			
Modal	**Subject**	**Have**	**Past Participle**	**Yes,**		**No,**	
Could	I/we	**have**	**taken** the wrong road?	you	**could have.**	you	**couldn't have.**
	you			I/we		I/we	
	he/she			he/she		he/she	
	they			they		they	

6. In statements and short answers, we can contract a modal + *have* to "may've," "might've," and "could've." We do not usually write this contraction. Although they sound like "may of," "might of," and "could of," be sure that you do not spell these speech contractions with *of*.

Function

PRESENT AND FUTURE

1. We use *may, might,* and *could* to talk about present and future possibility.

    I **may be** there tomorrow.

    I **might b**e there tomorrow.

    I **could b**e there tomorrow.

    A: Who is at the door?

    B: I don't know. It **may** be Ken.

    I'm not sure what I'm going to do tomorrow. I **might** go to the library.

    Where is Ted? I'm not sure, but he **could** be in his room.

2. We use *may not* and *might not* (but not *could not*), to express that something will possibly not happen.

    She **might not** come tomorrow. (Possibly she will not come.)

    The rain has stopped. I **may not** need an umbrella. (Possibly I won't need an umbrella.)

PAST

3. We use the perfect modal form (modal + *have* + past participle) of *may, might,* or *could* to express that something was possible in the past.

    He **may have** already **gone**.

    Maria is late. She **might have missed** her train.

    I can't find my glasses. I **could have left** them at work.

4. We use the negative with *may have* and *might have* (but not *could have*) to say that something possibly did not happen in the past.

    I **may not have put** my glasses in my bag as usual.

    They **might not have heard** about it yet.

5. We use *could have* and *might have* (but not *may have*) when something was possible in the past, but it did not happen.

    We were lucky. There **could have been** a bad accident.

    It was dangerous to climb that wall. You **might have fallen**.

6. We use *couldn't have* to say that something was impossible in the past.

    You **couldn't have seen** Mary on the street. I know she's in Beijing!

11 Practice

A   Listen to the TV documentary on Agatha Christie.

CD2, 4

B   Write sentences in response to the following questions that express possibilities of what may, might, or could have happened to Agatha Christie. Try to think of two or three possible answers for each question.

1.   Why did Agatha Christie suddenly disappear? _____
     She might have been so sad that she needed to be alone for awhile.

2.   Why did she go to a small hotel? _____
     _____

3.   Why did she use a different name? _____
     _____

4.   Why didn't she tell anyone where she was going? _____
     _____

5.   How do you think the police were able to find her? _____
     _____

6.   Why do you think she never talked about the incident again? _____
     _____

12 Your Turn

Your friend was absent from class yesterday. What happened? Write five possibilities with *may have, might have,* or *could have* + a past participle.

Example

He could have had a dental appointment.

Modals II   **197**

7F | *Should* and *Ought To* to Express Probability

Carlos is concerned because his friends aren't here yet. They **should be** here by now.

1. We use different modals for different degrees of certainty.

    I **will be** there tomorrow.   100% sure

    I **should be** there tomorrow.   90% sure

    I **ought to be** there tomorrow.   90% sure

2. We use *should* or *ought to* to say that something is probable at the time of speaking or in the future.

    Maria **should be** at work now. She's usually there at this time.

    I **ought to pass** the English test easily. I have studied hard and know everything.

3. We use the perfect modal form of *should* or *ought to* when we think something has probably happened, but we don't know for sure.

    Their plane **should have landed** by now.

    Their plane **ought to have landed** by now.

    We also use this form when we expect something to happen that has not happened.

    I was surprised to hear that he didn't pass the test. He **should/ought to have passed** it.

13 Practice

Read about Jim. Write sentences using *should* or *ought to* and one of the phrases from the list. Some sentences require a modal + a base verb; others require a perfect modal. Some sentences may be negative.

Jim is a reliable, punctual, hardworking person. He is a sales manager in a computer software company and has worked there for four years. He thinks his job is a little boring. He goes to a night school, and he recently applied for the position of senior sales manager in his company.

be at the office by now	**get an interview soon**
be in good physical shape	**get the new job**
earn a higher salary	**have to borrow money**
feel tired by noon	**need repairs yet**
finish it before going home	**reply to it by now**
get a high grade	

1. It is after 9:00 A.M.
   Jim *should be at the office by now.*

2. You left him a phone message this morning.
   He _____

3. He started writing a report yesterday morning.
   He _____

4. He's just had a week's vacation.
   He _____

5. He earns a good salary.
   He _____

6. He's studied hard for his Spanish exam next week.
   He _____

7. He's just bought a new car.
   It _____

8. He swims at the gym every day.
   He _____

9. He applied for a better job in the company two weeks ago.
   He _____

10. His job performance reviews are excellent.
    He _____

11. When he is senior sales manager, _____
    _____

14   Pair Up and Talk

A   Practice the conversation with a partner.

A: Do you think you'll get into a good college or university next year?

B: Yes, I should get into a good university because my grades have been excellent. I ought to make the soccer team, too, as I'm a pretty good player. What about you?

B   Tell your partner two things that will probably happen in your future. Use *should* and *ought to*. Ask each other questions about each event.

7G   *Must, Must Not,* and *Can't* to Make Deductions

Form

Maura is wearing slippers, so she **must be** at home.

PRESENT

Subject	Modal	Base Verb	
I/You He/She/It We/They	**must (not) can't**	**be**	hungry.

PAST

Subject	Modal	*Have*	Past Participle	
I/You He/She/It We/They	**must (not) can't**	**have**	**been**	hungry.

1. In this meaning, we use *must* in the affirmative and the negative *(must* or *must not),* but we use *can* only in the negative *(can't).*
2. In this meaning, we do not contract *must not.*
3. Questions in these forms are very rare.

Function

PRESENT

1. We use *must (not)* to express deductions (or a good guess) based on information we have about a present situation, and when we are almost 100 percent sure that something is true.

    Dana **must know** New York City very well. She has lived in the city all her life.

    Eddie comes to class every day, but today he isn't in class. He **must not feel** well.
2. We use *can't* to make a deduction that is, in our opinion, 100 percent true.

    I saw Rob a minute ago, so he **can't be** at home.

    We had lunch half an hour ago. You **can't be** hungry.

PAST

3. We use the perfect modal form of *must* or *can't* for deductions about the past.

    You did a lot of walking yesterday. You **must have been** tired.

    She **can't have seen** us on campus yesterday. We weren't there.

    We can also use *couldn't have* instead of *can't have* in this meaning.

    She **couldn't have seen** us on campus yesterday.

    What **can** she **have seen**? What **could** she **have done**?

15 Practice

You are talking about your neighbors. Complete the sentences using *must* or *can't.*

1. There are no lights on. They _____ *must* _____ be out.

2. They bought a new car. They _____ make a lot of money.

3. The husband comes home late and looks tired. He _____ work a lot.

4. People do not come to their house. They _____ have many friends.

5. The woman leaves in the morning and comes home in the evening.

    She _____ work.

6. She wears expensive suits. She _____ work in a factory.

1. People (die) ___*must have died*___ when they had infectious diseases because there were no antibiotics.

2. Travel to faraway places (be) _____ long and dangerous without trains or planes.

3. Europeans (go) _____ to Australia because they didn't know it existed.

4. Many children (have) _____ a good education because there were no schools for them.

5. Many people (work) _____ at home or a farm because the economy was not industrialized as it is today.

6. Many children (work) _____ to help their parents because it was difficult to make a living then.

7. Big castles (be) _____ cold places in winter.

8. Life (be) _____ easy for many people then.

17   **Practice**
A   **Read about Rapa Nui.**

Rapa Nui, also called Easter Island, is a small island in the middle of the South Pacific Ocean. It is over 2,000 miles (3,218 kilometers) from Tahiti and Chile, and it is one of the most isolated places on Earth. It is best known for the mystery of the moai—giant statues that stand on high cliffs around the island. Each statue has a human form, and a few of them have a separate stone of red volcanic rock on their heads.

We do not know where the original people of Rapa Nui came from, or what these giant statues represent. We also do not know how they transported the statues from the quarries[1] to the ceremonial sites around the island. Each statue weighs about 14 tons! The people had no metal tools or machinery of any kind. They transported 288 statues to their final locations, but there were 397 statues, all fully carved, still in the quarry. There were also 92 statues abandoned on the road from the quarry to their final location. Some statues were later knocked down and damaged. The stone for these statues did not come from the ceremonial sites but from the quarries. Archaeologists have discovered that the island was once covered with thick palm forests, but today there are no trees and not enough vegetation to support a population. At one time, the population of Rapa Nui reached 10,000, but today there are no descendents of this culture. There are no written records to explain the mystery of the island.

[1] quarries = holes in the ground from which people get building stones

B Write your conclusions about what must have happened, must not have happened, or can't have happened on the island.

1. How did the ancient people transport these giant statues?
    They can't have used machines.

2. Why were some statues abandoned on the road?

3. What did the statues represent?

4. Did the ancient people of the island carve the statues before or after they transported them to their final locations?

5. Why did the ancient people of the island go to so much trouble to carve and transport these statues?

6. How and why did the ancient population disappear?

7. Why did they leave no written records?

8. How did archaeologists discover facts about Rapa Nui's population?

18   Pair Up and Talk

A   Practice the conversation with a partner.

A: I wonder where our instructor is. Do you think something has happened to him?

B: I don't know. He might have had an accident. Whatever happened, he must not be able to call.

B   Imagine that your instructor hasn't come to class for two days. Discuss what must, might, could, or can't have happened. Think of at least five ideas.

7H   The Progressive and Perfect Progressive Forms of Modals

Form

Danielle **must have been sleeping** all through the class.

THE PROGRESSIVE FORM

Affirmative and Negative Statements			
Subject	**Modal (*Not*)**	***Be***	**Verb + *-ing***
I/You He/She/It We/They	**may** **may not** **might** **might not** **could** **could not** **couldn't** **should** **should not** **shouldn't** **must** **must not**	**be**	**working.**

Yes/No Questions				Short Answers			
Modal	Subject	*Be*	Verb + -*ing*	Yes,		No,	
Could	I/we you he/she they	be	working?	you I/we he/she/it they	could (be).	you I/we he/she/it they	couldn't (be).
Should				you I/we he/she/it they	should (be).	you I/we he/she/it they	shouldn't (be).

THE PERFECT PROGRESSIVE FORM

Subject	Modal (*Not*)	*Have Been*	Verb + -*ing*
I/You He/She/It We/They	may may not might might not could could not couldn't should should not shouldn't must must not	have been	working.

Yes/No Questions				Short Answers	
Modal	Subject	*Have Been*	Base Verb + -*ing*	Yes,	No,
Could	I/we you he/she/it they	have been	working?	you I/we he/she/it they **could have been.**	you I/we he/she/it they **couldn't have been.**
Should				you I/we he/she/it they **should have been.**	you I/we he/she/it they **shouldn't have been.**

1. In speech, we often contract the modal + *have: may've, might've, could've, should've,* and *must've.* They sound like *might of, could of,* etc., but be sure not to spell the *'ve* part of the contraction as *of.*

    CORRECT: She should have been here by now.

    INCORRECT: She should ~~of~~ been here by now.

2. We can form *yes/no* and *wh-* questions with *could* and *should* in the progressive and progressive perfect forms.

    It's midnight, and John's light is still on. **Could** he **be studying**?

    The test is tomorrow. What **should** I **be studying**?

    I saw John's light on at midnight last night. **Could** he **have been studying?**

    Why **should** he **have been studying** at that time?

Function

1. We use the progressive form of modals to say that something is in progress at the time of speaking.

    He **may be staying** at his uncle's house. (He's not home right now.)

2. We use the perfect progressive form of modals to say that something was in progress at a time in the past.

    They **must have been eating** dinner when we called.

---

19   Practice

Complete the sentences with the progressive or perfect progressive form of a modal and the verbs in parentheses.

1. A man is sitting on a bench in a train station early one morning. He has no luggage. He (wait) _could be waiting_ for someone.

2. His raincoat and hair are wet. The floor is wet. It (rain) _____ .

3. He looks very tired. He (work) _____ late last night.

4. There is a used and folded newspaper next to him. He (read) _____ it.

5. There is an empty paper coffee cup next to the newspaper.

    He (drink) _____ coffee.

6. There is also a bouquet of red roses next to him. The person he is meeting

must be his wife or girlfriend. The man is looking at his watch. The person (come)

_____ on the next train.

7. The train comes from Medham, but there are other towns where the train

    stops on the way. She (come) _____ from Medham.

8. There is a big university in Medham. She (study) _____ there.

9. The train is coming and has now stopped. The woman (get off) _____

    _____ the train any minute.

10. The two meet. They are looking at each other and smiling. They (feel) _____

    _____ very happy.

20 Practice

Read the situations and write sentences about each one with *may, might, could,* or *must* in the progressive or perfect progressive form. Use one of the following prompts for each situation. Then listen to the conversations to check your answers. Practice the conversations with a partner.

CD2, 5

they/celebrate a birthday	they/have an argument
they/cook on the grill	new neighbor/move in
they/expect a lot of guests	they/plan this party for some time
the neighbors/have a party	they/play music too loud to hear anything

1. A: What's happening next door? I heard people shouting this morning.

    B: *They must have been having an argument.* _____

2. A: I live in a five-story building. I heard a lot of noise on the stairs yesterday.

    B: _____

3. A: The front door of the neighbor's house is open, and all the hall lights are on.

    B: _____

4. A: I can hear a lot of loud music next door and people laughing and talking.

    B: _____

5. A: There is smoke and the smell of delicious food coming from the back yard.

    B: _____

6. A: They sent out invitations several weeks ago.

    B: _____

7. A: A delivery man from Christine's Bakery took a huge cake box into their house.

    B: _____

8. A: I called them to complain about the noise, but no one answered the phone.

    B: _____

21   Pair Up and Talk
A   Practice the conversation with a partner.

A: I hear a lot of music and laughter. What do you think they're doing over there?

B: They must be having a party.

B Imagine that you hear some different noises coming from the classroom next door. Use ideas from the list below or use your own ideas. Discuss things that must, might, may, or can't be happening. Think of at least three ideas for each situation.

You hear music and laughter   You hear animal noises

You hear a lot of coughing and sneezing   You hear complete silence

You hear singing and clapping

HOW THE NORTH COUNTRY GOT ITS LAKES

This winter was the coldest one Babe could remember, and Babe, a giant blue ox, knew cold. In fact, she was blue because she was born in midwinter and just never warmed up. Her giant human friend, Paul Bunyan, was using the cold as an excuse to be lazy. He and his (much shorter) lumberjack friends sat around their camp talking. Each man's words froze into his beard as soon as they came out of his mouth. The lumberjacks might have to wait until April to find out what each had said.

Babe pulled Paul inside the cookhouse for a talk. Babe then started to complain, "You can't just stop working and let all these logs go undelivered."

"Well, Babe," Paul said in unfrozen words, "we can't pull them out of the woods. The road is in bad shape, and in this cold air the tiniest bump would snap our log sleds."

The blue ox knew what she could do.

In about an hour, Paul and his men heard clanking and sloshing. Babe approached with a huge water tank on her back. Each of her heavy footsteps punched through the snow and into the ground. As she walked, water from the tank spilled into the holes and over the whole road. It was soon a smooth highway of ice, perfect for the log sleds. And each of her footprints ought to be a great place to swim in the summer.

1. _____

   Because she was born at a very cold time of year.

2. _____

   He and Babe were both very, very large.

3. _____

   Because their words might stay frozen until then.

4. _____

   Because he wasn't doing the work he was supposed to do.

5. _____

   They were supposed to be delivering logs that had already been cut.

6. _____

   It would be a problem because the bumps might break the log sleds.

7. _____

   The extreme cold made them brittle and therefore easier to break.

8. _____

   It could freeze and make a smooth road of ice.

9. _____

   Because the weight of the water tank made her heavier than usual.

10. _____

   Because the water in each footprint should melt in the summer to become a lake.

A   Listen and check the correct answer.

❑ A. *New Zealand*

❑ B. *Japan*

❑ C. *England, Scotland, and Wales*

B   Discuss your answer with your classmates.

 AUDIO DOWNLOAD CD2, 7

C   Now listen again and write the sentences you hear.

1 Review (7a–7e)

Complete the sentences using the words and phrases from the list. Sometimes there is more than one correct answer.

can't	let's not	must	why don't
could	may	prefer	will
could have	may not	rather not	would you mind
couldn't have	maybe	should have	

1. Margaret isn't here right now. ___*Could/May*___ I ask who's calling?

2. The sun seems to be coming out. I _____ need an umbrella after all.

3. You _____ gone to the soccer game today. It was cancelled!

4. It's four o'clock. They _____ been here by now.

5. He _____ know a lot about plants. He's been working at the garden center for years.

6. She _____ be in the office today. She's on vacation.

7. _____ you call Mr. Winters, please? I need to confirm our schedule.

8. _____ we go out for dinner? There's a great new restaurant in the mall.

9. _____ stay home today. It's a great day for the beach!

10. I _____ going to the movies tonight to going shopping.

11. It was a terrible day, but it _____ been worse.

12. I'm very busy right now. I'd _____ go to that meeting.

13. It's a good thing that you didn't drive into the city. You _____ been caught in that traffic jam.

14. I know you're in a hurry. _____ we could finish this another time.

15. _____ changing my appointment? I won't be in town tomorrow.

16. _____ you please turn down that radio? It's too loud!

BRENDA: Good morning, Neil. How ~~is~~ about getting a cup of coffee?

NEIL: Sorry, I can. I'm late for a meeting with Foster.

BRENDA: Then you'll be happy to hear that Foster isn't in the office today.
He can't be out sick.

NEIL: But that can't not be true! I thought I saw him coming into the
building an hour ago. I musn't be mistaken. What a relief!

BRENDA: Well, that's lucky for you. Now, I'm going to get some coffee.
Would you like some?

NEIL: Actually, I would rather tea.

BRENDA: Fine. By the way, has David left for Jakarta yet?

NEIL: Yes, he's on the way. He would be there in three hours. No, wait.
I forgot about the time difference. Actually, his plane ought to land an hour ago.

BRENDA: He can know Jakarta very well by now. He's been there at least a dozen times.

NEIL: Yes, he has. Oh, that reminds me. I should be going to Mexico City next week. It isn't
certain yet, but may you check on flight times for me this morning?

BRENDA: No.

NEIL: Oh, no problem. I can have some time to do it myself this afternoon. By the way,
does everyone know that we're having a group meeting at 3:00 today?

BRENDA: I think most people know, although a few could not have heard about it yet.

NEIL: Then how don't we make an announcement? I'll write it down and give it to Betty.

Reading Challenge

A Before You Read

1. What kinds of underground structures might a city contain?

2. *Trespassing* means "entering restricted property without permission." Why might someone trespass?

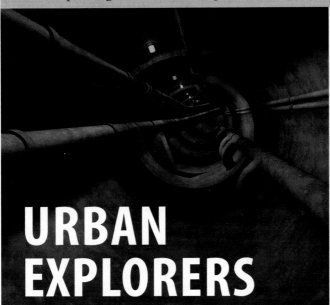

URBAN EXPLORERS

DID YOU KNOW ... ?
Students at the Massachusetts Institute of Technology used to explore the college's steam tunnels, just for fun. Their adventures evolved into the hobby known as "urban exploration."

B Read In 2002, criminals took more than 850 people hostage[1] in a Moscow theater. The
5 Russian government turned for help to the city's underworld. Literally. The Diggers of the Underground Planet crawl
10 through sewer[2] pipes and old tunnels under Moscow. They do it just for fun. Could the Diggers help the police sneak into the occupied theater? They
15 could and did, through the sewers they knew so well.

---

[1] take [someone] hostage = to hold someone as a kind of prisoner, to be released only if the police or other authorities give you what you want

[2] sewer = a channel, usually underground, for carrying away excess water, human waste, and other unwanted substances

Groups like theirs are dedicated to going where they shouldn't. Hidden passages, such as empty subway tunnels, are some of their
20 favorites. They are called Urban Explorers, or UE. Explorers launch expeditions into intriguing places that might have secrets to uncover. They do not go into places that are currently inhabited, no matter how interesting
25 they may be.

Serious UE enthusiasts follow a code of conduct. Their main **tenet** is, "Take nothing but pictures; leave nothing but footprints." They do not steal from or damage the places they
30 explore. A true urban explorer would rather be photographed next to a hidden treasure than carry it away. In the UE world, a good reputation is priceless. You want other explorers to think you must have been to some really
35 cool places without wrecking things. To count as "cool," a space might have several features. It could be hard to get to, or perhaps mysterious. Finding a space that might be undiscovered is very cool. Getting past fences, guard dogs, or
40 other security enhances the coolness.

UE is usually illegal. Only a few explorers would pretend that they are breaking no laws. This might present a dilemma if an urban explorer stumbles across something the police
45 really should know about—a chemical spill, stolen property, or even a dead body. By reporting it, the explorer might be admitting that he or she was somewhere illegally. On the other hand, silence about such a thing could be really bad for your reputation.

C Notice the Grammar Underline all forms of modals.

Choose the best answer.

D Look for Main Ideas

1. This reading is mainly about _____ .
   Ⓐ the Diggers of the Underground Planet
   Ⓑ how urban explorers help fight crime
   Ⓒ the activities of urban explorers
   Ⓓ the hidden structures below an average city

2. What is the main topic of paragraph 3?
   Ⓐ the rules of behavior accepted by most urban explorers
   Ⓑ disagreement among urban explorers about proper behavior
   Ⓒ efforts made by urban explorers to clean up the places they visit
   Ⓓ building a good reputation as an urban explorer

E Look for Details

3. The Russian government approached the Diggers for _____ .
   Ⓐ weapons
   Ⓑ tunneling equipment
   Ⓒ extra security officers
   Ⓓ information

4. What is the purpose of UE?
   Ⓐ recreation
   Ⓑ archaeology
   Ⓒ fighting crime
   Ⓓ agriculture

5. The passage mentions that urban explorers target all of the following EXCEPT _____ .
   Ⓐ old tunnels
   Ⓑ waste-disposal channels
   Ⓒ unused subways
   Ⓓ family homes

READING SKILL: Restatement

To answer reading comprehension questions you must do one of two things: identify restated information or retell information using your own words. For example, read this sentence: *Half of the people in the world never set foot in school.* A restatement of this sentence might be: *About 50% of the world's population don't or will never go to school.* Try it yourself. Choose a sentence from the reading and write three different restatements of it.

F Make Inferences

6. What can we infer from paragraph 4 about the way most urban explorers view trespassing laws?
   Ⓐ The laws do not actually ban UE.
   Ⓑ The laws are harmful.
   Ⓒ Breaking the law is all right in some cases.
   Ⓓ UE is likely to be wiped out by the laws.

7. We can infer from the reading that most urban explorers pursue their hobby in order to _____ .
   Ⓐ get rich
   Ⓑ have adventures
   Ⓒ protest social problems
   Ⓓ prepare for a conflict

G Look for Vocabulary

8. The word *tenet* in the reading is closest in meaning to _____ .
   Ⓐ rule
   Ⓑ obstacle
   Ⓒ grip
   Ⓓ muscle

Writing: Write a Business Letter

Write a business letter in which you complain about a product or a service.

STEP 1 With a partner, brainstorm ideas for your letter. Think of (or imagine) something you have bought and were unhappy with. Write down your ideas, and make notes about what you would like to tell the company.

STEP 2 Pay attention to the format and organization of this letter. Notice that a business letter is short and direct, but also polite.

126 Longwood Avenue
Boston, MA 02116
March 30, 2009

Mr. James Smithson
President, Real Mobility, Inc.
2003 N. Mountain Avenue
Los Angeles, CA 90027

Dear Mr. Smithson:

Introduction:
State the problem simply and briefly. →

I am writing to express my disappointment with my cellular phone service with your company.

Body:
Give specific information about the problem. →

I signed a contract with Real Mobility on February 15, 2009. The service was supposed to start on February 16, but it didn't start until February 20. When I called your customer service department, the representative …

Conclusion:
Summarize your position and tell what you want. →

I think you will agree that it is unfair for me to have to pay for phone service that I can't use all the time. Would you please arrange for me to receive a full refund of the money that I have paid? My account number is 100-265-983.

Signature:
Sign your name and type it below your signature. →

Sincerely,
Sarah MacKay
Sarah MacKay

STEP 3 Write a letter of complaint in the format above, on a computer if possible.

STEP 4 Evaluate your letter.
Checklist

_____ Did you use the format of the example letter?
_____ Is your letter short, direct, and polite?
_____ Did you sign your name in writing and also type it?

STEP 5 Work with a partner or a teacher to edit your letter. Check spelling, vocabulary, and grammar. Then write your final copy.

Self-Test

A   Choose the best answer, A, B, C, or D, to complete the sentence. Darken the oval with the same letter.

1. Would you mind _____ me tomorrow?

    A. meet   Ⓐ Ⓑ Ⓒ Ⓓ
    B. to meet
    C. meeting
    D. if you meet

2. I'd rather _____ home. I'm too tired to go out.

    A. stay   Ⓐ Ⓑ Ⓒ Ⓓ
    B. staying
    C. not stay
    D. to stay

3. _____ go home. It's getting late.

    A. Why don't   Ⓐ Ⓑ Ⓒ Ⓓ
    B. Let's
    C. Can
    D. How about

4. May I _____ my dictionary during the test?

    A. use   Ⓐ Ⓑ Ⓒ Ⓓ
    B. using
    C. to use
    D. rather use

5. There's someone at the door. Who _____ it be?

    A. must   Ⓐ Ⓑ Ⓒ Ⓓ
    B. may
    C. will
    D. could

6. He _____ arrived home by now. It only takes 20 minutes to get here from the airport.

    A. might   Ⓐ Ⓑ Ⓒ Ⓓ
    B. should have
    C. should
    D. ought to

7. People wait six months for an appointment with him. He _____ a very good doctor.

    A. must be   Ⓐ Ⓑ Ⓒ Ⓓ
    B. may be
    C. should have been
    D. would rather be

8. John's light is still on. _____ studying?

    A. Could he   Ⓐ Ⓑ Ⓒ Ⓓ
    B. Should be
    C. Could he be
    D. Must he be

9. JENNY: Was that Franco in that car?
   VALERIE: It _____ him. He is on vacation.

    A. could have been   Ⓐ Ⓑ Ⓒ Ⓓ
    B. couldn't
    C. couldn't have been
    D. shouldn't have

10. ED: Will the flight be delayed this evening?
    ROSA: It _____ . It is still snowing.

    A. can't be   Ⓐ Ⓑ Ⓒ Ⓓ
    B. won't
    C. may be
    D. maybe

1. The extreme weather conditions could <u>causing</u>
                                 A

   droughts, <u>and</u> <u>food</u> may <u>get</u> expensive.
              B   **C**   **D**

             Ⓐ Ⓑ Ⓒ Ⓓ

2. <u>Would</u> you prefer <u>eat</u> here or <u>in</u> a <u>restaurant</u>?
   A   **B**   **C**   **D**

             Ⓐ Ⓑ Ⓒ Ⓓ

3. <u>It's</u> summer south of the Equator, so <u>it</u> <u>should</u>
   A   **B** **C**

   <u>been</u> warm in Argentina.
   D

             Ⓐ Ⓑ Ⓒ Ⓓ

4. <u>Would</u> you <u>mind</u> <u>work</u> <u>an extra hour</u> on Friday?
   A   **B**   **C**   **D**

             Ⓐ Ⓑ Ⓒ Ⓓ

5. Jack <u>prefer</u> <u>a video game</u> <u>to</u> <u>a walk</u> in the park.
       A   **B**   **C** **D**

             Ⓐ Ⓑ Ⓒ Ⓓ

6. <u>I'm</u> hungry, so <u>let's</u> <u>us</u> <u>start</u> dinner soon.
   A   **B** **C** **D**

             Ⓐ Ⓑ Ⓒ Ⓓ

7. <u>May</u> Matt <u>uses</u> your computer tonight, <u>or</u> <u>do</u>
   A   **B**   **C** **D**

   you need it?

             Ⓐ Ⓑ Ⓒ Ⓓ

8. Why <u>we don't</u> <u>leave</u> early so we can <u>get</u> <u>there</u>
        A   **B**   **C** **D**

   on time?

             Ⓐ Ⓑ Ⓒ Ⓓ

9. He <u>must</u> <u>have sleeping</u> <u>when</u> I <u>called him</u>
      A   **B**   **C**   **D**

   last night.

             Ⓐ Ⓑ Ⓒ Ⓓ

10. I <u>can't</u> help you, <u>but</u> <u>may be</u> Tony <u>can</u>.
    A   **B**   **C**   **D**

             Ⓐ Ⓑ Ⓒ Ⓓ

Unit 8

The Passive Voice, Causatives, and Phrasal Verbs

It is said that chocolate is actually good for you.

Form

The Colosseum in Rome **was built** by the Romans. Competitions **were held** there. Today, some sports arenas **are named** after this building.

1. To form the passive voice, we change the object of an active voice sentence into the subject of a passive one. The subject of the active sentence can become the agent in a passive sentence. The agent tells who or what did the action in a passive sentence. It is introduced with the preposition *by*.

	Subject	Verb	Object
Active Voice	The pilot	**flew**	the airplane.
Passive Voice	The airplane	**was flown**	by the pilot.

2. We form the passive voice with a form of the verb *be* + a past participle. Questions use an auxiliary verb before the subject.

Subject	Be	(Other Auxiliary Verb)	Past Participle	
The Great Wall	**was**		**built**	by the Chinese.
The tourists	**are**	**being**	**shown**	around by the guides.

Yes/No Questions				
Auxiliary Verb	Subject	(Other Auxiliary Verb)	Past Participle	
Was	the Great Wall		**built**	by the Chinese?
Has	it	**been**	**visited**	by many people?

Wh- Questions				
Wh- Word	Auxiliary Verb	Subject	(Other Auxiliary Verb)	Past Participle
When	was	the Great Wall		built?
How many people	has	it	been	visited by?

3. We form passive voice sentences with transitive verbs, which take objects. We cannot form passive voice sentences with intransitive verbs.

TRANSITIVE VERB:	**fly**
ACTIVE SENTENCE:	The pilot **flew** the plane.
PASSIVE SENTENCE:	The plane **was flown** by the pilot.
INTRANSITIVE VERB:	**arrive**
CORRECT:	The plane **arrived** on time.
INCORRECT:	The plane ~~was arrived~~ on time.

Some common intransitive verbs are *appear, arrive, become, come, go, happen, occur, rain,* and *stay*. Motion verbs such as *go, come, walk, run,* and *arrive* are often intransitive.

Some transitive verbs do not have passive forms. These include stative verbs such as *cost, fit, have, resemble, suit,* and *weigh*.

CORRECT:	You resemble your father.
INCORRECT:	Your ~~are resembled by your father~~.

Some verbs can be either transitive or intransitive. A good dictionary will tell you which verbs are transitive, intransitive, or both. Here are some examples.

Verb	Transitive Use	Intransitive Use
leave	She **left** her keys at home.	She **left** early.
move	I can't **move** that box.	Don't **move**. There's a snake next to your foot.
drive	I can **drive** a truck.	I'm tired. Would you **drive**?
play	We **play** soccer on weekends.	The children **play** nicely together.
work	Can you **work** this machine?	This computer won't **work**.

4. We use the passive voice in the following forms. Note that the form of *be* is in the same form as the active verb.

	Active Voice	Passive Voice
Simple Present	He **washes** the car.	The car **is washed** by him.
Present Progressive	He **is washing** the car.	The car **is being washed** by him.
Present Perfect	He **has washed** the car.	The car **has been washed** by him.
Simple Past	He **washed** the car.	The car **was washed** by him.
Past Progressive	He **was washing** the car.	The car **was being washed** by him.

	Active Voice	Passive Voice
Past Perfect	He **had washed** the car.	The car **had been washed** by him.
Future with *Will*	He **will wash** the car.	The car **will be washed** by him.
Future with *Be Going To*	He **is going to wash** the car.	The car **is going to be washed** by him.
Future Perfect	He **will have washed** the car.	The car **will have been washed** by him.

We do not use the passive voice with some forms because they sound awkward. These are the present perfect progressive, the future progressive, the past perfect progressive, and the future perfect progressive.

5. Object pronouns (*me, him, her,* etc.) in the active voice become subject pronouns (*I, he, she,* etc.) in the passive voice.

Active Sentence			Passive Sentence		
Subject	**Verb**	**Object**	**Subject**	**Verb**	
Thousands of people	elected	**her.**	**She**	was elected	(by thousands of people).
The Chinese	built	**it.**	**It**	was built	(by the Chinese).

Function

1. We use the passive voice when the agent (who or what does something) is not known or unimportant.
   The Great Wall **was built** hundreds of years ago. (The people who built the wall are not important to the meaning of the sentence.)

2. When we use *by* + an agent, it is usually because the subject of the sentence is more important than the agent, but we want to express them both.
   The economy was hurt **by last year's bad weather**.
   We do not use *by* + an agent when the agent is a pronoun such as *you* or *they* used with a general meaning.
   ACTIVE SENTENCE: In this school, you obey the rules. (*you* = people in general)
   PASSIVE SENTENCE: In this school, the rules are obeyed ~~by you~~.
   Sometimes we do not use *by* + an agent because we do not want to mention the agent.
   TEACHER: Some very basic grammar errors **were made** in last week's test.
   (The teacher doesn't want to say who made the errors.)

3. We often use the passive voice to make a sentence more impersonal in situations involving rules, instructions, announcements, advertisements, or processes.
   Passengers **are requested** to show their passports along with their boarding passes.
   The time of the press conference **will be announced** later today.

4. We often use the passive when the agent is obvious from the meaning of the sentence.
   Olive oil **is used** a lot ~~by Italians~~ in Italy. (It is obvious that Italian people use it.)

| Alexander Graham Bell | calcium | earthquakes | Greece |
| Brazil | | discs | Edmund Hillary and Tenzing Norgay |

1. Coffee is grown in Italy.
   Coffee is not grown in Italy. It is grown in Brazil.

2. The telephone was invented by Picasso.
   _____

3. Bill Gates started Microsoft.
   _____

4. The Taj Mahal in India was built by an emperor in memory of his wife.
   _____

5. The summit of Mount Everest was reached by Marco Polo.
   _____
   _____

6. The world's first Olympic Games were held in France.
   _____
   _____

7. Blood pressure is measured on the Richter scale.
   _____
   _____

8. *Hamlet* was written by Shakespeare.
   _____

9. Sugar is needed for strong bones.
   _____

10. Data on a computer is stored on plates.
    _____

2 Practice

Rewrite the headlines as complete sentences. Use the present perfect passive or simple past passive. Make any other changes that are necessary. (Remember that headlines often omit articles and words like *people*.)

1. Movie Star Questioned in Murder Case

   A movie star has been questioned in a murder case.

   OR *A movie star was questioned in a murder case.*

2. Higher Wages Demanded by Teachers

   _____

   _____

3. Twelve Injured in Friday's Earthquake

   _____

   _____

4. Plane Captured by Hijackers

   _____

   _____

5. Airport Closed; All Flights Canceled (Write two sentences.)

   _____

   _____

6. Ten Hospitalized after Gas Explosion

   _____

   _____

3 Practice

Rewrite the following news stories in the passive voice where appropriate. State the agent if it is important to the story. Listen and check your answers.

AUDIO

DOWNLOAD

CD2, 8

1. Snowstorms have cut off many towns in the north. Snow has blocked the main highway to the north. People are unable to clear the road because the snow is still coming down heavily.

   Many towns in the north have been cut off by snowstorms.

   The main highway ...

   _____

2. Somebody has stolen a total of two million dollars from the National Bank in New York City. Medical Emergency workers took two guards to the hospital. The police have arrested three men in connection with the robbery. They are questioning another man.

_____

_____

3. The Coast Guard found two teenage boys in a small boat far off shore yesterday. The boys and the boat have been missing since last Friday. The two boys were alive but weak. They took the boys to the hospital. Doctors expect them to recover soon.

_____

_____

_____

4. The police are seeking* two men in connection with a robbery at a gas station. They held up the cashier, but they did not injure him. While they were stealing the money, one of the men tied up the cashier. The men escaped in a black truck which the police think they used in other robberies in the same area.

_____

_____

_____

* _Seek_ means "look for." The past participle of _seek_ is _sought._

4 Your Turn

Find or make up three newspaper headlines. Ask a partner or the class to make a passive sentence from each. Discuss: Can we write all headlines in the passive voice?

Example

HEADLINE: Local Student Chosen for Big Scholarship

PASSIVE VOICE SENTENCE: _A local student has been chosen for a big scholarship._

1. _____

2. _____

3. _____

Form

Certain animals **should be protected.** These tigers **are going to be moved** to a wild animal park in a few weeks.

1. To form the passive voice of a modal expressing the present or the future, we use a modal + *be* + a past participle.

Subject	Modal	*Be*	Past Participle	
The sign	can		seen	by everyone.
The report	may		finished	on Tuesday.
The car	could*		repaired	in two days.
The work	might		given	to us.
The garbage	should		thrown out.	
His decision	ought to	be	respected.	
The rules	must		obeyed.	
Claudia	has to		told	the truth.
The workers	had better		paid	this week.
We	are supposed to		informed	about the delay.
We	will		invited	to the reception.
The date	is going to		changed.	

* *Could* can refer to the past, present, or future, depending on the context.

2. To form the passive voice of a perfect modal (modal + *have* + past participle), we use a modal + *have been* + a past participle.

Subject	Modal	*Have Been*	Past Participle	
The project	should		finished	this week.
The Great Wall	must	have been	built	a long time ago.
We	ought to		informed	of the change.
The house	had better		cleaned.	

3. To form the past passive of expressions with *be* or *have*, we use the past forms of those verbs.

Subject	*Be/Have* Expression	Past Participle	
The students	had to be	told	that the trip had been canceled.
The house	was supposed to be	painted	the next day.
The computers	were going to be	repaired,	but weren't.

Function

1. We use the passive of *will* or *going to* to talk about the future.
    A new drug **will be produced** soon.
    More tests **are going to be performed** soon.
2. We use *can* to talk about ability in the present and future. We use *could* to talk about ability in the past.
    Our lives **can be extended** by this drug.
    The computer **could be repaired**, but the monitor **couldn't**.
3. We use *may, might,* and *could* to talk about present or future possibility.
    The new drug **may be tested** on patients this year.
    The drug **could be sold** in pharmacies in a year or two.
4. We use *should, ought to, had better,* and *must* to express advice or necessity.
    It **should be sold** to anyone who wants it.
    It **must be regulated** by law.
5. We use perfect modals with *can, could, should, ought to, may, might, must,* and *had better* to refer to the past.
    They **should have been told** about the change in the schedule.
    The report **must have been written** by one of the students.
    They **can't have been held up** in traffic. The roads are clear at this hour.

Elephants are very important in Sri Lanka. They are important culturally, as they often lead religious processions. They are also important economically, as they (can/use) _____can be used_____ to haul timber. There used to be tens of thousands
                                1
of wild elephants in Sri Lanka, but now there are only around 3,000. Why did so many elephants disappear? Some of the working elephants (may/mistreat)

_____ when they got old or sick. Some of the wild elephants
          2
(may/shoot) _____ by villagers who were trying to protect their crops.
          3
Other elephants (may/force) _____ to leave the forests as the human
                                          4
population increased over the years.

   What (can/do) _____ to help save them? How (can/more elephants/
                          5
save) _____ ? Sri Lankan authorities have
                          6
decided that in the future many elephants (will/move) _____ to
                                                                  7
protected areas so people and crops won't be hurt and the elephants (can/preserve)

_____ in safety. Better conservation programs
                          8
(will/establish) _____.
                                          9

Example

There are too many cars in the city where I live. Cars should be banned from downtown. Downtown should be reserved as a pedestrian area. Parking lots could be built near downtown, and people could be taken to the stores and businesses by train or bus.

8C The Passive Voice with *Get*; *Get* + Adjective

Form

The girls **got dirty** during their game. They have to **get washed** soon.

1. We sometimes use *get* in place of *be* in passive voice sentences.

Subject	Get	Past Participle	
I	got	hurt	by the falling tree branch.
You	get	frightened	by thunderstorms.
She	gets	bored	by long movies.
We	will get	paid	early this month.
They	might get	delayed	by the snowstorm.

2. We can also use *get* + an adjective. We can use *get* in any form.

Subject	Get	Adjective
I	**will get**	**angry** if I'm late.
You	**got**	**cold.**
He/She/It	**gets**	**full** after a big meal.
We	**are getting**	**hungry.**
They	**get**	**thirsty** after a run.

3. The past participles of many verbs can be adjectives. We can use them after *get*.

Subject	Get	Past Participle as Adjective	
I	**will get**	**tired**	before the day ends.
He	**gets**	**bored**	quickly.
You	**got**	**scared,**	didn't you?

Function

1. We often use *get* + a past participle or *get* + an adjective in conversation instead of *be* + a past participle or *be* + an adjective. We rarely use the passive voice or *get* + an adjective in formal writing.

2. We use *get* to emphasize action or change. We often use *get* in this way to suggest that something happens accidentally, unexpectedly, or unfairly.

   The vase **got broken** when I bumped into the table. (accidentally)

   She **got awarded** a big prize. (unexpectedly)

   I **got blamed** for losing the money. (unfairly)

3. When we use *get* + a past participle or an adjective, *get* usually means *become*.

   I **got hungry** by 11:00 in the morning. (I became hungry by 11:00 in the morning.)

4. In some expressions, *get* does not mean *become*.

   get washed (wash oneself)

   get dressed (dress oneself)

   get started (begin doing something; or begin a trip)

5. We usually use *get*, not *become*, before the words *engaged, married*, and *divorced*, in speech and in writing.

   They **got engaged** last month. (It is possible to say *become engaged*, but this is rather formal.)

   They **got married** at the end of the year. (We do not use *become* with *married*.)

   We **got divorced** in January. (We do not use *become* with *divorced*.)

7 Practice

A Read about Princess Diana's life. Use *get* + one of the words from the list to complete the missing information. Use the correct form. (Use *involved* twice.)

blamed	depressed	engaged	jealous	married
criticized	divorced	involved	killed	

Princess Diana was born on July 1, 1961. It was in 1980, on a trip to visit the royal family at Balmoral Castle, that she _got involved_ romantically with Prince Charles.
_____1_____

Diana and Charles _____, and from that moment on, Diana was
                            2

followed everywhere by photographers and journalists. Diana and Charles

_____ on July 29 1981 in St. Paul's Cathedral in London. But after
        3

her marriage, Diana _____ about her life with Charles and the royal
                              4

family. People said that Charles _____ because of Diana's popularity.
                                          5

She was beautiful and glamorous, but she understood the lives of ordinary people.

They had two sons, but their marriage was not happy. They _____ on
                                                                          6

August 28th, 1996. Afterwards, Diana _____ in humanitarian cases,
                                              7

helping people with AIDS, and campaigning against land mines. On September 6th,

1997, Diana and her friend Dodi Al Fayed _____ in a car crash in Paris.
                                                    8

The Queen wanted a private funeral. But the British public wanted a public funeral to

express their grief. The Queen _____ for not showing enough emotion
                                        9

about Diana's death. In the investigation, the driver of the car, Henri Paul,

_____ for causing the crash by driving when drunk.
        10

B Work with a partner. Ask your partner questions about the facts in the story.

Example

YOU: What happened in 1980?

YOUR PARTNER: Diana got romantically involved with Prince Charles.

8 Practice

A Listen to statements about Janice. What kind of person is she? Write *B* for the sentences in which *get* means *become*. Write *O* for sentences with other meanings of *get*.

DOWNLOAD

CD2, 9

1. ___*O*___   7. _____

2. _____   8. _____

3. _____   9. _____

4. _____   10. _____

5. _____   11. _____

6. _____

B Discuss Janice with a partner. Give a reason why each of these characteristics applies (or doesn't apply) to her.

1. Janice is (a) punctual (b) lazy (c) confident.

2. Janice is (a) efficient (b) hardworking (c) impatient.

3. Janice is (a) energetic (b) ambitious (c) nervous.

9 Pair Up and Talk

A Practice the conversation with a partner.

A: When do you get irritated?

B: When I get held up in traffic. What about you?

A: That doesn't bother me, but I do get irritated when I have to wait in line for a long time.

get angry	get depressed	get scared
get bored	get irritated	get worried

8D *It* + a Passive Voice Verb + a *That* Clause

Form/Function

> **It is said that** chocolate is actually good for you.

1. We can use *it* + a passive voice verb + a *that* clause to avoid mentioning an agent. We use this structure with past participles such as *believed, confirmed, considered, estimated, feared, hoped, known, mentioned, reported, said,* and *thought.*

Active Sentence	Passive Sentence		
	It	**Passive Verb**	**That Clause**
People said that he is a billionaire.	**It**	**is said**	**that** he is a billionaire.

2. We can also use the subject of the active *that* clause as the subject of the passive sentence.

Active Sentence	Passive Sentence		
	Subject	**Passive Verb**	**To Be**
People said that he is a billionaire.	He	**is said**	**to be** a billionaire.

10　**Practice**

Rewrite the sentences using *It is … that …*

1.　We believe that calcium builds strong bones and teeth.
　　It is believed that calcium builds strong bones and teeth.

2.　We know that fruits and vegetables are important for our health.

　　_____

3.　Many doctors think that some fruits and grains can help to prevent cancer.

　　_____

4.　People say that fruit improves your immune system.

　　_____

5.　We believe that nuts help to lower cholesterol.

　　_____

6.　Dentists know eating a lot of sugar can be bad for our teeth.

　　_____

11　**Your Turn**

Complete the following statements with a noun + a passive voice verb.
Use the past participles of verbs like *think, say, expect, report,*
or *consider* + the infinitive in parentheses.

1.　(to be) _____ *Norah Jones is thought to be* _____ the best singer of the decade.

2.　(to taste) _____ delicious,

　　but I have never eaten it/one/them.

3.　(to win) _____ the World Cup this year.

4.　(to have) _____ a financial recovery soon.

5.　(to be) _____ good for your health.

12　**Pair Up and Talk**

A　Practice the conversation with a partner.

A:　What are the Japanese known for?

B:　They're known to have a healthy diet.

8E | Present and Past Participles Used as Adjectives

Form

> Sheila felt **frustrated**.
> She is playing a game that is **frustrating**.

1. We can use present participles* and past participles as adjectives.

Base Verb	Present Participle	Past Participle as Adjective
tire	My job is **tiring**.	I'm **tired**.
relax	We had a **relaxing** vacation.	We felt **relaxed**.
excite	The game was **exciting**.	Everyone was **excited**.
shock	The **shocking** news spread quickly.	**Shocked** citizens demonstrated in the streets.

*Present participle is another term for verb + -ing

Function

Present and past participles used as adjectives generally describe feelings. The two forms have different meanings.

1. Present participle adjectives describe someone or something that causes a feeling.

The game was **exciting** (to me).

Ted is **boring** (to Sandra).

2. Past participle adjectives describe someone who experiences a feeling.

     I am **bored** (by the movie).

     He is really **confused** (by the question).

3. Here are some common participles used as adjectives.

Present Participle	Past Participle
amazing	amazed
amusing	amused
boring	bored
confusing	confused
depressing	depressed
embarrassing	embarrassed
exhausting	exhausted
frightening	frightened
interesting	interested
relaxing	relaxed
shocking	shocked
surprising	surprised

4. Use an -ed adjective if the noun experiences a feeling. Use an -ing adjective if the noun causes a feeling.

     The **excited** children watched the **exciting** game.

13 Practice
Read the story. Underline the correct adjectives.

I had a (terrified/<u>terrifying</u>) experience when I went to Michigan a few years ago. I
          1

had been driving all day, and I was completely (exhausted/exhausting). I stopped at the
                                                                2

first hotel I could find. The hotel looked a little run down, and its dark windows were

quite (depressed/depressing), but I was so (tired/tiring) that I couldn't drive any farther.
          3   **4**

The desk clerk looked very (surprised/surprising) that I had stopped there. The hotel
                                  5

wasn't cheap, and when I saw the room, it was a little (disappointed/disappointing).
                                                        6

I tried to watch TV, but all the programs were (bored/boring). So I read until I felt
                                            7

(relaxed/relaxing) enough to fall asleep. Suddenly, I heard a strange creaking noise
      8

outside my door. I was really (frightened/frightening). Then I heard the sound again,
                                        9

so I leapt out of bed and opened the door. There was nothing there, but I noticed the door was covered in scratch marks. I packed my things and ran for my car. I have never been so (terrified/terrifying) in my life.
10

14   Pair Up and Talk
Practice the conversation with a partner. Then think of your own story and tell your partner.

A: I had an embarrassing experience the other day.

B: Really? What happened?

A: I was really tired yesterday so I overslept. I rushed to class and opened the door. I said "Sorry" to the teacher. Everyone just stared at me. They looked amused. The teacher looked shocked, and I was confused. Then I realized I was in the wrong classroom!

8F Causative Sentences with *Have, Get,* and *Make*: Active Voice

Form

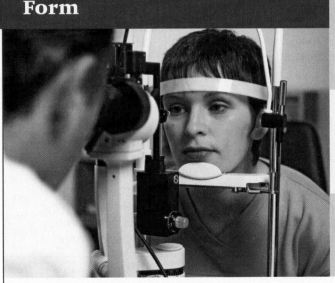

> I **have** the optometrist **check** my eyes every year. Sometimes he puts drops in my eyes, so I **get** my sister **to drive** me home.

1. We can form causative sentences with *have, get,* and *make* as the main verb.

THE CAUSATIVE WITH *HAVE* AND *MAKE*

Subject	Have/Make	Object	Base Verb
We	**have**	our son	**do** the dishes.
She	**had**	her assistant	**copy** the report.

Subject	Have/Make	Object	Base Verb
The boss	**is going to make**	everyone	**work** late.
Tom's mother	**will make**	him	**stay** home tonight.

THE CAUSATIVE WITH *GET*

Subject	Get	Object	To + Base Verb
Tom	**gets**	his sister	**to do** the dishes for him.
I	**got**	my friend	**to drive** me here.
We	**are going to get**	the store	**to give** us a refund.
The boss	**should get**	the staff	**to work** late tonight.

2. We use a base verb after *have* and *make,* but we use *to* + a base verb after *get*.
3. We can use any form or modal that makes sense in causative sentences.
4. We use the normal rules to form negative statements, questions, and short answers with the causative.

Negative Statements	We **don't make** our son do the dishes. She **didn't have** her assistant copy the report. The boss **isn't going to make** everyone work late. Tom's mother **might not make** him stay home tonight. Tom **didn't get** his sister to do the dishes for him.	
Yes/No Questions and Answers	**Do** you **have** your son do the dishes? **Did** she **have** her assistant copy the report? **Is** the boss **going to make** everyone work late? **Can** Tom's mother **make** him stay home tonight? **Did** you **get** your friend to drive you here?	No, I **don't**. Yes, she **did**. No, he's **not**. Yes, she **can**. Yes, I **did**.
Wh- Questions and Answers	Who **gets** his sister to do the dishes for him? Who **does** Tom **get** to do the dishes for him? What **does** Tom **get** his sister to do? Who **made** Tom do the dishes? What **did** she **have** her assistant copy? Where **did** they **have** the taxi take them? When **will** you **have** the students take the test? Why **did** you **make** the children go to bed?	Tom **does**. His sister. The dishes. His mother **did**. The report. To the train station. Tomorrow. Because they were tired.

Function

1. We use the causative to talk about something that we require or arrange for someone else to do.
   I **had** the stylist **cut** my hair really short. (It's the stylist's job to cut my hair. I told him to cut it really short.)

2. We use *have* in a causative sentence when we normally expect someone, like a salesperson in a store, to do something for us.

He **had** the salesperson **show** him 12 pairs of shoes.

My boss **had** us **prepare** a progress report every week.

3. We use *get* when there is some difficulty involved or when we have to persuade someone to do what we want.

It took a long time, but I finally **got** my boss to **let** me take a week off.

The teenager **got** his parents to **let** him take the car, but they told him to be very careful.

4. We use *make* when one person has power and/or authority over another. The person who does the action does not want to do it.

The children's mother **made** them go to bed. (The mother has authority and power.)

The robber **made** the clerk give him the money. (The robber does not have authority but does have power.)

---

15   Practice

A famous film director, Robert Ebbits, is traveling to New York City. His personal assistant is giving the hotel instructions. Rewrite the sentences as causatives. Then listen and check your answers.

AUDIO DOWNLOAD

CD2, 10

ASSISTANT: Mr. Ebbits will be arriving at your hotel tomorrow, and I want to make sure that everything is arranged for him.

HOTEL RECEPTIONIST: Yes, of course. What can I do for you?

1. He likes to wake up at 6:00 A.M. (have/the front desk/call him)
   Please have the front desk call him at 6:00 A.M.

2. He likes to read three daily newspapers first thing in the morning.
   (have/bellman/deliver)

3. He likes to have fresh fruit and coffee for breakfast at 7:00 A.M.
   (have/room service/bring)

4. He doesn't like fresh flowers in his room. (have/the florist/put)
   Don't

5. He needs three shirts to be washed every day. (have/the laundry/wash)

6. He needs a fax machine and a flat-screen TV installed in his room before he checks in.
(get/the technical staff/install)

_____

7. He wants his shoes polished and left outside his door every morning.
(have/the bellman/polish)

_____

8. He needs a limousine waiting for him in front of the hotel each day at 9:00 A.M.
(get/a chauffeur/bring)

_____

16   Pair Up and Talk

A   Practice the conversation with a partner.

A: Mr. Ebbits likes to wake up at 6:00 A.M. Please have the front desk call him.

B: Certainly. I'd be happy to have the front desk call him.

B Role-play the conversation between the personal assistant and the hotel receptionist. Use the sentences you wrote in Practice 15. The receptionist should respond using positive or negative phrases listed below. If the receptionist cannot fulfill a request, explain why.

Certainly.	I wish I could, but …	That's no problem.
I'd be happy to …	My pleasure.	Unfortunately, …
I'm sorry.	Of course.	

8G | Causative Sentences with *Have* and *Get*: Passive Voice

Form

The restaurant is **getting** its carpets **cleaned** for the wedding season.

1. We can form passive causative sentences with *have* and *get*, but not with *make*.

Subject	*Have/Get*	Object	Past Participle	
I	**have**	my hair	**styled**	by Lorenzo.
We	**have had**	our car	**serviced**	twice this year.
She	**had**	her winter coat	**cleaned**	last week.
He	**is getting**	his car	**washed**	this afternoon.
You	**should get**	your eyes	**tested**	soon.

2. When we use *have* or *get* in a passive causative sentence, we do not use *to* with the past participle.

   CORRECT: He **got** his hair cut.

   INCORRECT: He **got** his hair ~~to cut~~.

3. We can use the causative with modals and in all forms.
4. We use the normal rules to form negative statements, questions, and short answers.

Negative Statements	I **don't have** my hair styled by Lorenzo. He **isn't getting** his car washed this afternoon.	
Yes/No Questions	**Did** she **have** her winter coat cleaned last week? **Should** I **get** my eyes tested?	Yes, she **did**. No, you **shouldn't**.
Wh- Questions	Who **had** the car serviced? What **did** John **have** serviced?	John **did**. The car.

Function

1. We use the passive form of the causative when we want to stress what was done and not who did it. We do not use *by* + an agent when we don't know who did it, or when it is not important who did it.

   She **has** her hair **styled** every week.   I **got** the refrigerator **fixed**.

2. We use *by* + an agent when it is important to mention the person doing the service.

   She **has** her hair **styled** by Lorenzo. (The speaker wants to mention the agent, Lorenzo.)

   I must **get** my suit **cleaned** this week. (The speaker is not interested in mentioning the agent.)

3. We use the causative with *have* when something unpleasant or unexpected happens to someone.

   We **had** our passports **stolen** when we went on vacation.

---

17 Practice
Write a sentence about what you can have done (or get done) at these places.

1. copy shop   3. dry cleaner's   5. hair salon

2. dentist's office 4. garage   6. laundromat™

1. *You can get copies made at a copy shop. You can also get them bound.*

2. _____

3. _____

4. _____

5. _____

6. _____

18 Pair Up and Talk
A   Practice the conversation with a partner.

A: If you were in the hospital, what would you like to have done for you?

B: I'd have my husband bring me something to read, and I would have flowers delivered every day.

B Discuss the situations below or think of one of your own. Use the Part A conversation as a model. What would you like or need to have done?

if you had car trouble   if you were in the hospital   if it was your birthday

Form/Function

Dakota and Jane **are putting on** makeup. Then they're going to **dress up** and **go out** to eat with their parents.

1. Phrasal verbs are very common in English. A phrasal verb consists of a verb + a particle. A particle is an adverb such as *up, down, away, out*. A verb followed by a particle has a different meaning from the verb alone. Sometimes we can guess the meaning of a phrasal verb.

    We **stood up**. (We got on our feet from a seated position.)

2. Sometimes we cannot guess the meaning of a phrasal verb. In these cases, we have to learn the special meaning of the phrasal verb.

    I'll **look up** the word. (I'll find information about the word in a dictionary, thesaurus, etc.)

INTRANSITIVE PHRASAL VERBS

3. Some phrasal verbs are intransitive. They do not take objects.

Subject	Verb + Particle
My car	**broke down** last night.
They	**eat out** every Saturday night.

Below and on page 244 are some common intransitive phrasal verbs.

Phrasal Verb	Meaning	Phrasal Verb	Meaning
break down	stop working (as a machine)	go out	leave the house; not stay home
break out	happen suddenly and unexpectedly	grow up	become an adult
break up	separate	hang up	end a phone conversation

Phrasal Verb	Meaning	Phrasal Verb	Meaning
dress up	put on nice clothes	show up	appear; be present
eat out	eat in a restaurant	speak up	speak loud/louder
fall down	fall to the ground	stand up	arise from a sitting position
get up	arise from a bed or a chair	start over	begin again
give up	stop trying to do something	stay up	remain awake
go down/up	increase/decrease	take off	go up (as an airplane) suddenly succeed (as a business) leave (informal)
go on	continue	work out	exercise

Some of these phrasal verbs can take objects, but the meaning is different. Phrasal verbs, like other verbs, can have different meanings.

The plane **took off** on time. (intransitive)

We **took off our coats** because it was too warm. (transitive; *take off = remove a piece of clothing*)

4. Some intransitive phrasal verbs can be followed by a prepositional phrase, but the meaning of the phrasal verb does not change.

Bob and June **broke up**.

June **broke up** with Bob.

I **get up** at 7:00 every day.

She **got up** from her chair when the visitor arrived.

TRANSITIVE PHRASAL VERBS

5. Most phrasal verbs are transitive. Transitive verbs take objects.

Phrasal Verb   **Object**
Take off   your shoes.

There are two kinds of transitive phrasal verbs: separable and inseparable. Separable phrasal verbs are very common. Inseparable phrasal verbs are less common.

6. With separable phrasal verbs, the particle can go before or after a noun object. But when the object is a pronoun, the particle always follows the object.

Separable Phrasal Verbs					
	Subjects	Verb	Particle	Object	Particle	
Noun Object	I	take	out	the garbage		every morning.
	I	take		the garbage	out	every morning.
Pronoun Object	I	take		it	out	every morning.

INCORRECT: I take ~~out it~~.

7. With inseparable phrasal verbs, the particle always goes before the object.

Inseparable Phrasal Verbs				
	Subject	**Verb**	**Particle**	**Object**	
Noun Object	She	**got**	**over**	**her cold**	quickly.
Pronoun Object	She	**got**	**over**	**it**	quickly.

INCORRECT: We ~~came an interesting~~ museum across.
INCORRECT: She ~~got her cold over quickly~~.

Here are some common separable and inseparable phrasal verbs and their meanings. Some of these phrasal verbs have additional meanings. Check a dictionary for other meanings.

Separable Phrasal Verbs	Meaning	Separable Phrasal Verbs	Meaning
bring up	raise a child; state something/someone as a topic	set up	arrange for something
call off	cancel something	start over	start something again
call up	telephone someone	tear down	destroy something completely
do over	do something again	think over	reflect on someone/something
drop off	leave someone/something somewhere	think up	invent something
give up	quit something	turn down	lower the volume on something
leave out	omit someone/something	turn up	increase the volume on something
pick up	meet someone and take him/her somewhere	use up	use something until there is no more
put back	place something in its original location	wake up	cause someone to stop sleeping
put off	postpone someone/something		
put on	place a piece of clothing on your body		

Inseparable Phrasal Verbs	Meaning
call for	come get someone
check into	register at a hotel; inquire into something
come across	find or discover someone/something by chance
get over	recover from something
go over	review something

Inseparable Phrasal Verbs	Meaning
look after	take care of someone/something
look into	investigate something
put up with	tolerate someone/something
run into	meet someone by chance

19   Practice

Read Mr. Jackson's schedule. Then answer the questions. Use pronouns in your answers. Remember that the position of pronouns is different for separable and inseparable phrasal verbs.

From: Company Management Tour Services

To: Interglobal Corporation, Inc.

Re: Mr. Jackson's Schedule, April 16 - 18, 2009

16 April

- Pick up Mr. Jackson from the airport at 6:45 P.M.

- Drop off Mr. Jackson at his hotel at 7:30 P.M.

- Mr. Jackson will check into the hotel at 7:35 P.M.

- Meet the tour guide who will look after Mr. Jackson during his stay.

17 April

- Tour guide will call for Mr. Jackson at 7:00 A.M.

- Set up a meeting to discuss the contract with the president at 9:00 A.M.

- If the president decides to call off the meeting, we will call up Mr. Jackson immediately.

- Afternoon and evening free; guided tour of city.

18 April

- Pick up Mr. Jackson from the hotel at 10:30 A.M.

- Meeting with the president to go over the contract from 11:00 A.M. to 12:30 P.M.

- Drop off Mr. Jackson at the airport at 1:15 P.M.

1. What time will they pick up Mr. Jackson from the airport?
   They will pick him up at 6:45 P.M.
   _____

2. What time will they drop off Mr. Jackson at his hotel?
   _____

3. What time will Mr. Jackson check into his hotel?
   _____

4. Who will look after Mr. Jackson during his stay?
   _____

5. What time will the tour guide call for Mr. Jackson the next morning?
   _____

6. For what time will they set up a meeting with the president?
   _____

7. What will they do if the president decides to call off the meeting?
   _____

8. What time will they pick up Mr. Jackson from the hotel on the final day?
   _____

9. When will Mr. Jackson go over the contract with the president?
   _____

10. What time will they drop off Mr. Jackson at the airport?
    _____

20 Practice

A   Complete the sentences with particles from the list. Use *down* two times.
     Use *up* four times. Then listen and check your answers.

CD2, 11

across	down	over
after	out	up

I was born and brought _____up_____ in Madrid. I was left alone a lot as a child and
                          1

learned to look _____ myself. I did a lot of reading. One winter, while I was
                     2

getting _____ the flu, I came _____ a book about Sherlock Holmes, the
             3   4

famous fictional detective. I loved it! And that's when I started thinking _____
                                                                                5

mystery stories of my own and writing them _____ . I designed elaborate covers
                                                6

for the books and used _____ all the paper in the house. I gave them as presents
                            7

to my family and challenged them to work _____ solutions to the crimes in my
    8
stories. My mother tried to get me to give _____ mystery stories and try some
    9
other form of fiction, but it was no good. Even now that I am older, I still read mysteries
in my spare time. There's nothing like a good mystery to calm you
_____ after a hectic day.
    10

B Here is a list of synonyms for the phrasal verbs in Part A. Write each phrasal verb next to the correct synonym.

1. find by accident   *come across*
2. invent   _____
3. make a note of   _____
4. quit   _____
5. raise   _____

6. recover from   _____
7. relax   _____
8. solve   _____
9. take care of   _____
10. use all of   _____

8I Prepositions Following Verbs, Adjectives, and Nouns; Other Combinations with Prepositions

Form/Function

Alberto is **responsible for** the computer sales for his company. He is **thinking about** today's sales meeting.

We use prepositions not only to show time, place, manner, and agent, but also in combination with verbs, adjectives, and nouns, and in many common expressions.

1. We use many verbs with specific prepositions.

   You must **concentrate on** your work!

   I love to **listen to** the birds in the early morning.

   Here are some common examples of verb and preposition combinations.*

Preposition	Examples			
about	dream about	think about	worry about	
at	laugh at	shout at	smile at	
for	account for	fight for	search for	wait for
from	come from	derive from	recover from	
in	believe in	delight in	result in	
of	dream of	think of		
on	concentrate on	depend on	plan on	rely on
to	belong to	contribute to	listen to	speak to

* Some verbs can take more than one preposition. For example, if you think **about** something, you consider it. If you think **of** something, it comes to your mind.

   I **thought about** the problem all night.

   I **thought of** a great place to go on Saturday night.

2. We use many adjectives with specific prepositions.

   Are you **worried about** the test?

   We are very **proud of** her.

Preposition	Examples			
about	angry about	excited about	worried about	
at	bad at	expert at	good at	surprised at (also *by*)
for	responsible for			
from	free from			
in	interested in	successful in (also *at*)		
of	afraid of	aware of	envious of	fond of
	proud of	tired of	typical of	
to	compared to	essential to	married to	opposed to
	related to	similar to		
with	bored with (*also* by)	disappointed with	pleased with	

3. We use many nouns with specific prepositions.

The **cost of** food has risen.

The senator didn't like the **results of** the government's policies.

I didn't know the **answer to** her question.

Preposition	Examples				
for	demand for	need for	reason for		
in	change in	decrease in	increase in	rise in	
of	cause of	cost of	danger of	evidence of	example of
	possibility of	result of	supply of	trace of	use of
on	effect on	impact on	influence on		
to	answer to	invitation to	reaction to	reply to	solution to
	threat to				

4. Here are some other common expressions that end in prepositions.

Preposition	Examples			
of	as a result of	because of	in spite of	in view of
	on account of	on behalf of	with the exception of	
to	according to	prior to		

5. There are also many common expressions that begin with prepositions.

Preposition	Examples			
at	at first	at last	at present	at the moment
	at times			
by	by accident	by chance	by land	by sea
	by air	by day	by night	
in	in common	in existence	in general	in the future
	in the past			
on	on fire	on land	on purpose	on the other hand
	on the whole			

A

Nouns + Prepositions

a threat to   an increase in   one example of

an impact on   changes in

What is global warming? Global warming is ___*an increase in*___ Earth's
                                           1

temperature, which in turn causes many _____ climate. These changes
                                              2

may have _____ plants, wildlife, and humans. _____ a
              3   **4**

change caused by global warming is the rise in sea level, which may be

_____ coastal communities and the people and animals that live there.
       5

B

Adjectives + Prepositions

essential to   opposed to

free of   responsible for

What causes global warming? Most of the energy that is _____
                                                             1

the creation of the light and heat in our homes is produced by burning coal and gas,

which produces carbon dioxide. The carbon dioxide traps heat in Earth's atmosphere.

Carbon dioxide is _____ about half of our global warming. Many
                        2

environmentalists are _____ fossil fuels like coal and gas. They say we
                            3

should try to develop energy that is _____ pollution, such as wave or
                                           4

wind energy. Then it will be possible to protect the climate as well as the animals and

people who live on Earth.

C

Verbs + Prepositions

account for	contribute to	result in
come from	recover from	

Another cause of global warming is a reduction in ozone in the outer layer of Earth's atmosphere. Ozone is a gas that absorbs ultraviolet (UV) rays that

_____ the sun. Chlorofluorocarbons (CFCs) are chemicals that are used
          1
in aerosols, air conditioners, refrigerators, and throwaway food containers. Scientists

believe that CFCs _____ the destruction of the ozone layer and
                          2
_____ a thinner layer of ozone in the outer atmosphere. This
          3
_____ an increase in cases of skin cancer. What can we do? Using
          4
CFC-free products is one way to help our planet to _____ the damaging
                                                              5
effects of ozone depletion.

22   Pair Up and Talk

A   Practice the conversation with a partner.

A: What do you worry about when you think about the world?

B: I worry about global warming. People should be more responsible for the environment.

A: Can you think of ways for people to do that?

B: Well, I'm no expert at conservation, but people could do small things that would have a big impact on the environment. For example, they could rely on cars less and travel by bike more.

B   Discuss one or more problems from the list below, or your own ideas. Discuss possible solutions. Use some of the noun, verb, and adjective + preposition combinations from Practice 21 or the charts in 8i.

crime in your city/town	global warming	overcrowded schools
destruction of rainforests	health care costs	traffic in your city/town

CHICKEN LITTLE

Chicken Little was afraid of almost everything. To him, his shadow was a big black bird. The moo[1] of a cow in the farmyard meant ghosts were searching for him. One day, a rain shower moved over the farm. The rain cloud, the breeze—all of it made him very nervous. As usual, he knew something was wrong. Then a raindrop hit him on the head. And another. And another.

"The sky is falling!" he shouted in his squeaky voice. He ran wildly through the farmyard. The others had to be warned. By this time, the rain shower had passed. The sun was shining. His shadow appeared behind him, which made him run faster. The hens[2] heard him, thought of their eggs, and panicked. Their frightened clucking[3] made the goats try to leap over the fences. All the confusion got the pigs squealing loudly, even though they were not sure why.

Finally, Big Red, the oldest and wisest rooster[4] in the yard, came to see what was going on[5]. He saw Chicken Little running madly around, leading dozens of wild-eyed farm animals. Stepping suddenly in front of Chicken Little, Big Red made the whole crowd slide to a stop. "What's the problem here?" he shouted to a goose. "I don't know," said the goose, "but it must be really bad!" Finally, Chicken Little spoke up, "The sky is falling!"

Big Red looked up at the sky. He looked at Chicken Little. Then he reached out a wing feather toward a wet drop on the little bird's head. "This doesn't look like sky to me," he clucked calmly. Soon, Chicken Little had lost his following. He stood in the farmyard, alone except for his shadow.

[1] moo = the sound a cow makes   [2] hen = a female chicken

[3] clucking = the sound a chicken makes

[4] rooster = a male chicken

[5] going on = happening

1. _____

   He was frightened of almost everything.

2. _____

   It made him think ghosts were trying to get him.

3. _____

   Some drops of rain hit him on the head.

4. _____

   They made him believe the sky was falling.

5. _____

   The hens got worried about their eggs and panicked.

6. _____

   It made them try to leap over the fences.

7. _____

   They did not really know why there was so much confusion.

8. _____

   They were stopped by a rooster named Big Red.

9. _____

   He made them realize that all the excitement was over nothing.

10. _____

   He was left alone in the farmyard when the crowd went away.

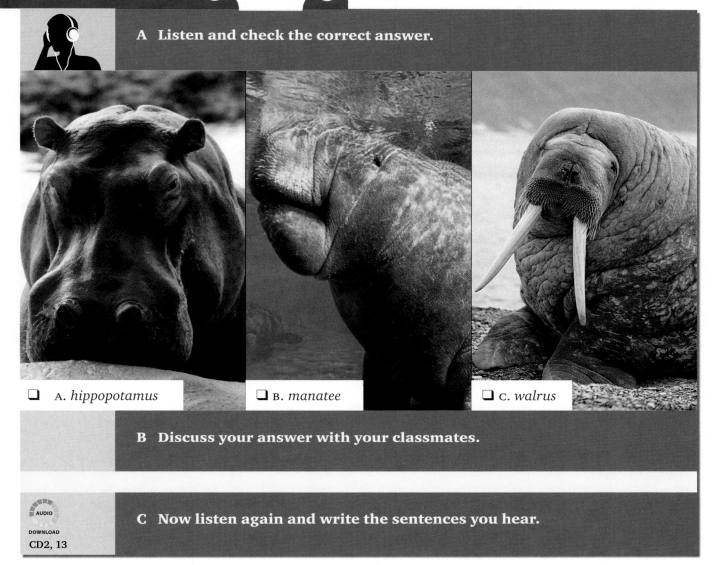

A Listen and check the correct answer.

❑ A. *hippopotamus*   ❑ B. *manatee*   ❑ C. *walrus*

B Discuss your answer with your classmates.

AUDIO
DOWNLOAD
CD2, 13

C Now listen again and write the sentences you hear.

Review

1 Review (8a, 8e, 8i)
Underline the correct words.

Wouldn't you like to be able to (have/<u>get</u>) the weather to do what you want? Do you ever
₁

(get angry/have anger) because the weather is (depressing/depressed) and you want to have a
₂   ₃

(relaxing/relaxed) day at the beach? Well, you're not alone. Everyone would like their wishes to
₄

(be obeyed/obey). However, the weather (is obeying/obeys) no one. Everyone should delight (in/about)
₅   ₆   ₇

that fact because the weather has a big impact (on/for) our planet and is essential (on/to) our survival.
₈   ₉

The sun (got worshipped/was worshipped) by ancient people. They believed (in/on) its importance
₁₀   ₁₁

to life on Earth even though they didn't understand how it makes plants grow and how it affects the

weather. The sun is (amazed/amazing). Our air, oceans, and land (are heated/heat) by the sun's energy.
₁₂   ₁₃

As the seasons change, Earth (is/has) bathed in different amounts of energy from the sun. The result
₁₄

(for/of) this is a planet that has areas of hot and cold. The weather (gets/is getting) powered by these
₁₅   ₁₆

differences. Huge areas of hot and cold air (have/are) created by the heat and cold coming off water and
₁₇

land. These air masses must (have moved/move) or the cold areas (would get/are getting) colder, and
₁₈   ₁₉

the hot areas (would get/are getting) hotter. Fortunately, Earth keeps everything (on/in) balance by
₂₀   ₂₁

moving cold water and air from the poles towards the tropics, while warm water and air flow from the

tropics toward the poles. As these areas of heat and cold move (around/over) and meet, wind, rain, and
₂₂

storms (are/have) produced. Crops grow, rivers run, and life on our planet goes (about/on).
₂₃   ₂₄

Complete the sentences using *have*, *get,* or *make* and the verbs in parentheses in the active or passive voice. Use the correct form.

1. Even though we're busy, I _____*got*_____ my boss (give) _____ me the day off tomorrow.

2. When I was a child, I didn't like to do housework, but my mother _____ me (clean) _____ my room before I could go out to play.

3. I _____ my computer (upgrade) _____ twice since I've owned it.

4. I _____ the painter (paint) _____ the room again after he painted it with the wrong color.

5. How does that teacher _____ her students (stay) _____ so quiet?

6. My knee has been hurting for a week. I really have to _____ it (examine) _____ by a doctor.

7. My son's grades are too low. From now on, I _____ him (finish) _____ his homework before he goes out to play with his friends.

8. When will you _____ the students (take) _____ their examinations?

9. Who will John _____ (help) _____ him paint his apartment?

10. How can I _____ her (wear) _____ this dress if she doesn't want to?

3 Review (8c, 8h)
Find the errors and correct them.

MELINDA: Did you hear that Joe and Marian are ~~being~~ *getting* married?

PATRICK: No way! They broke last month.

MELINDA: They did, but I guess they decided to start out. Anyway, I don't know how she puts with him.

PATRICK: Him! You're not trying to have me believe that he's the problem, are you?

MELINDA: No, you're right. Their problems must cause by both of them. I still can't believe they're engaged. Do you think we can get them change their minds?

PATRICK: I doubt it. Remember what write by Shakespeare: "Love is blind." Anyway, don't be so worry. They'll work up their problems. They'll probably end over being very happy.

Reading Challenge

A   Before You Read
1. What can you see when you look up at the sky at night?
2. An asteroid is a piece of rock moving through space. What happens when one hits a planet?

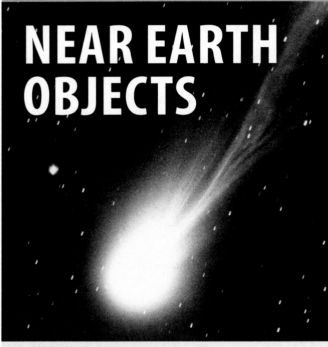

NEAR EARTH OBJECTS

DID YOU KNOW ... ?
In April 2019, an asteroid (a piece of rock in space) will come close enough to Earth to be seen without a telescope.

B   Read   On March 8, 2002, Earth was nearly punched by an asteroid. Now called 2002 EM7, it got almost as close as the moon is. It was the size of a soccer field. This is not especially big for an asteroid, but it is big enough. When a much
10 smaller object exploded in Earth's atmosphere in 1908, a huge expanse of a Siberian forest was wiped out. If the larger EM7 had collided with[1] Earth, millions of people would probably have been killed.
15   EM7 was not even noticed until two days
20 after it had passed Earth. The problem was that it came from the direction of the sun. The bright background made it invisible to the human eye and to astronomers' **instruments**. Not until it was on the other side of Earth's
25 orbit could it be seen against a dark sky. The EM7 incident and other close calls have made scientists nervous. New efforts to track objects like these asteroids have been launched.

Asteroids, comets[2], and other space
30 bodies that pass close to Earth are called Near Earth Objects (NEOs). Keeping track of[3] the thousands and thousands of known NEOs would make any system dizzy. That is why astronomers focus on those that measure
35 at least one kilometer (0.6 mile) across. It is generally believed that only such a large NEO could cause a global catastrophe. By these standards, 2002 EM7 is too small to be important. It might kill millions, but the planet
40 as a whole would survive.

About 1,000 of these big NEOs are now being tracked. More get added to the list nearly every month. The system for detecting them is being made more reliable as instruments
45 get more sensitive. Also, scientists from more nations have gotten involved. This gives Earth more observation points, which widens our perspective. The hope is that careful watching will reveal any problems far in advance. Then there might be time to knock an NEO harmlessly off its collision course.

[1.] collide with = run into; hit

[2.] comet = an object similar to an asteroid but containing large amounts of ice   [3.] keeping track of = making an effort to know something's location

C   Notice the Grammar   Underline all the passive verbs.

Choose the best answer.

D Look for Main Ideas

1. This reading is mainly about _____ .
   - Ⓐ NEOs
   - Ⓑ 2002 EM7
   - Ⓒ collisions
   - Ⓓ tracking

E Look for Details

2. Why was EM7 not seen as it approached Earth?
   - Ⓐ It was behind the sun.
   - Ⓑ It was too small.
   - Ⓒ The sun was too bright.
   - Ⓓ The sky was cloudy.

3. The reading mentions all of the following about NEOs EXCEPT_____ .
   - Ⓐ one entered Earth's atmosphere in 1908
   - Ⓑ each month, many of them hit Earth
   - Ⓒ some are known to be at least one kilometer across
   - Ⓓ they include comets and asteroids

4. According to the reading, why is it good to have scientists from many nations tracking NEOs?
   - Ⓐ The NEOs can be observed from more points of view.
   - Ⓑ The costs of tracking NEOs can be spread among many nations.
   - Ⓒ Scientists get a chance to meet and talk if they work together.
   - Ⓓ Knocking an NEO off course must be an international effort.

F Make Inferences

5. What can we infer from paragraph 3 about NEOs?
   - Ⓐ Astronomers focus on those that measure less than one kilometer.
   - Ⓑ Tracking even the very small ones is needed.
   - Ⓒ There are more of them than astronomers are able to keep track of.
   - Ⓓ Astronomers track only those large enough to be seen with the human eye.

6. We can infer from the reading that _____ .
   - Ⓐ any NEO that threatened Earth would be destroyed before it could collide with the planet
   - Ⓑ if a big NEO is on a collision course with Earth, nothing can be done to prevent it
   - Ⓒ some NEOs have already been pushed off course so they would not collide with Earth
   - Ⓓ no one knows if an NEO can be pushed off course because it has not yet been done

G Look for Vocabulary

7. The word *instruments* in the reading is closest in meaning to _____ .
   - Ⓐ senses
   - Ⓑ partners
   - Ⓒ skills
   - Ⓓ tools

Writing: Write a Cover Letter

When you send an application form or a résumé to a company or a school, you send a cover letter with it. The purpose of a cover letter is to make the reader interested in reading your résumé or application. A cover letter has the format of a business letter (see page 216).

STEP 1   **Pay attention to the format and organization of this letter.**

224 Brinker Avenue
Fort Lee, NJ 07024
May 1, 2009

Anderson and Sons
3099 East Street
Union, NJ 07083

Dear Sir or Madam:

Introduction:
Tell where you heard about the job. Summarize your experience. →

I am sending you my résumé in response to your advertisement for a bookkeeper in the Daily News of June 6, 2009. I have two years of experience as a bookkeeper, and I am fully qualified for the job.

Body:
State your most important qualifications. →

As you can see from my résumé, I am responsible for both accounts receivable and accounts payable in my current job for Hunter Electronics. I am a conscientious person and enjoy problem solving.

Conclusion:
Offer to be contacted. Thank the person. →

Please feel free to call me at (203) 555-9999 to set up an interview. Thank you for your consideration.

Signature:
Sign your name and type it below the signature. →

Sincerely,
Alexandra Balmas
Alexandra Balmas

STEP 2   **Write a cover letter for a job that you would like to have. Type it on plain white paper (use a computer if possible). When you send a cover letter, send an original, not a photocopy.**

STEP 3   **Evaluate your letter.**
Checklist
_____ Did you use the format of the example letter?
_____ Did you follow the organizational model of the example letter?
_____ Do you think your letter would interest the reader? Would you get an interview?

STEP 4   **Edit your letter with a partner or teacher.**

STEP 5   **Write your final copy.**

Self-Test

A Choose the best answer, A, B, C, or D, to complete the sentence. Darken the oval with the same letter.

1. You have to get a photo _____ for your passport.

   A. taking   Ⓐ Ⓑ Ⓒ Ⓓ
   B. took
   C. taken
   D. to take

2. This is an example _____ a multiple-choice question.

   A. of   Ⓐ Ⓑ Ⓒ Ⓓ
   B. in
   C. at
   D. to

3. I am going to the dentist next week to have _____ .

   A. my teeth clean   Ⓐ Ⓑ Ⓒ Ⓓ
   B. clean my teeth
   C. my teeth cleaned
   D. cleaning my teeth

4. The tests results _____ next Monday.

   A. will have posted   Ⓐ Ⓑ Ⓒ Ⓓ
   B. will posted
   C. will post
   D. will be posted

5. Hurry up and _____ !

   A. get dress   Ⓐ Ⓑ Ⓒ Ⓓ
   B. get dressed
   C. to get dressed
   D. getting dressed

6. _____ there was once water on the planet Mars.

   A. It is said that   Ⓐ Ⓑ Ⓒ Ⓓ
   B. It is said to
   C. They say it was
   D. Says it

7. Ted is _____ about what to do.

   A. confuse   Ⓐ Ⓑ Ⓒ Ⓓ
   B. confusing
   C. confused
   D. get confused

8. _____ the facts, we need more time.

   A. In view to   Ⓐ Ⓑ Ⓒ Ⓓ
   B. In view of
   C. On view of
   D. By view of

9. He was late, so I _____ .

   A. woke up him   Ⓐ Ⓑ Ⓒ Ⓓ
   B. woke him up
   C. wake him
   D. him wake up

10. She's very _____ her job.

    A. a success in   Ⓐ Ⓑ Ⓒ Ⓓ
    B. successful in
    C. successful for
    D. successful with

1. Today's meeting <u>was put off</u> <u>because of</u> a
   A B
   schedule conflict and a new time for the

   meeting <u>will been</u> <u>announced</u> later today.
   C D

   (A) (B) (C) (D)

2. There has been an <u>increase in</u> demand for the
   A
   buildings that <u>were built</u> in this area at the
   B
   turn of the century; that is why they <u>are be</u>
   C
   <u>renovated by</u> investors.
   D

   (A) (B) (C) (D)

3. Diamonds <u>are found</u> <u>in</u> different colors and,
   A B
   <u>on general</u>, only shine when they
   C
   <u>are cut and polished</u>.
   D

   (A) (B) (C) (D)

4. A strange <u>coincidence</u> <u>was happened</u> when the
   A B
   news <u>was</u> <u>announced</u> this morning.
   C D

   (A) (B) (C) (D)

5. Some kinds of <u>fish cannot</u> <u>be ate</u> <u>because of</u>
   A B C
   contamination <u>from</u> industrial waste.
   D

   (A) (B) (C) (D)

6. In the past, <u>it was said</u> <u>that computers</u> were
   A B
   too <u>complicating</u> for people to use and
   C
   <u>would be used</u> only for scientific purposes.
   D

   (A) (B) (C) (D)

7. <u>It is best</u> not <u>to leave out</u> multiple-choice
   A B
   questions on a test and <u>go them over</u>
   C
   <u>at the end</u>.
   D

   (A) (B) (C) (D)

8. Everyone <u>was amazing</u> that the painting
   A
   <u>was stolen</u> with <u>all the security precautions</u>
   B C
   that <u>were taken</u>.
   D

   (A) (B) (C) (D)

9. After the ancient artifacts <u>discovered</u>,
   A
   construction on the site <u>was stopped</u>
   B
   <u>by the</u> <u>city</u>.
   C D

   (A) (B) (C) (D)

10. We <u>will have</u> <u>our computers service</u> next week
    A B
    <u>by a company</u> that <u>was recommended</u> by
    C D
    the bank.

    (A) (B) (C) (D)

Unit 9
Gerunds and Infinitives

In order to score a goal in soccer, the ball must go into the net.

Form

Daydreaming is useful.
Wanda **enjoys daydreaming**.

1. A gerund is a base verb + -*ing* that works like a noun. A gerund can be a subject or an object in a sentence.

GERUND AS SUBJECT

Gerund Subject	Verb	
Painting	is	my favorite hobby.
Cycling	is	good exercise.
Scuba diving	takes	a lot of money.

GERUND AS OBJECT

Subject	Verb	Gerund Object
I	enjoy	**painting**.
He	stopped	**cycling**.

2. A gerund is always singular. When one gerund is the subject of a sentence, it takes a singular verb.

   Painting makes me happy.

   But if two gerunds form a subject, the verb is plural.

   Cycling and **diving are** my favorite sports.

3. Do not confuse a gerund with the present progressive.

   Cycling is a good sport. My favorite sport is **cycling**. (*Cycling* is a gerund.)

   He is **cycling** in the park right now. (*Cycling* is part of the present progressive verb.)

Function

1. We use a gerund as a noun.
   Painting is relaxing for me.

2. We can use a gerund after the following verbs and verb phrases.

admit	finish	quit
appreciate	give up	recall
avoid	imagine	resent
can't help	involve	resist
consider	keep/keep on	risk
continue	(not) mind	stand
delay	postpone	suggest
deny	practice	tolerate
discuss	prevent	understand
enjoy	put off	

   Have you **finished doing** your homework?
   I **enjoy walking** in the rain.

3. We usually use *go* + a gerund to describe recreational activities.
   We **went sightseeing** yesterday.
   Let's **go surfing**.

   Here are some expressions with *go* + a gerund.

go biking	go hiking	go shopping
go bowling	go hunting	go sightseeing
go camping	go jogging	go skating
go canoeing	go running	go skiing
go dancing	go sailing	go surfing
go fishing	go scuba diving	go swimming

1 Practice

Complete the sentences with the gerund form of the verbs from the list.

camp	cycle	exercise	sail	sleep
climb	dive	jog	ski	swim

We are a very active family. In the winter, when there is snow, we pack up our skis and go

____*skiing*____ every weekend. In the summer, we take our tents and go _____
      1   2

in the mountains. Our son Mark prefers mountain _____ . We often go to the coast
                                                        3

and do a lot of _____ , _____ , and _____ . During the week, I
                      4   5   6

take my running shoes to work so I can go _____ on my lunch break if the weather
                                                 7

is good. And when my husband gets home from work, he takes his bike and goes

_____ for an hour or so. _____ regularly is very good for our health, and
      8   9

we're usually so tired at the end of the day that we don't have any problems _____
                                                                                    10

at night.

2 Practice

Tim and Erica feel the same way about their health. Use gerunds to complete Erica's sentences to express the same information as in Tim's sentences. Listen to check your answers. Then practice the conversation with a partner.

CD2, 14

1. TIM: The doctor said I could get heart disease.

    ERICA: Really? My doctor said I risk ____*getting heart disease*____ , too!

2. TIM: "It might be a good idea to go on a diet," she said.

    ERICA: My doctor also suggested _____ .

3. TIM: I'm making other changes to improve my health. I decided not to drink coffee.

    ERICA: I decided to give up _____ myself.

4. TIM: It's difficult not to drink coffee when I'm tired.

    ERICA: For me, it's difficult to avoid _____ in the mornings.

5. TIM: I think that I shouldn't eat ice cream.

    ERICA: Me, too. In fact, I want to stop _____ and all

    other desserts.

6. **TIM:**   I sometimes buy a small bag of potato chips. They are so good!

   ERICA: I know. Sometimes I can't resist _____ .

7. **TIM:**   I thought dieting would be hard. But it's OK to count calories at meals.

   ERICA: I don't mind _____ either.

8. **TIM:**   I used to cook a lot of rich food.

   ERICA: I used to enjoy _____ , too.

9. **TIM:**   I have to learn to make new dishes with fewer calories.

   ERICA: I know what you mean. I have to practice _____

   healthier meals.

10. **TIM:**   It's hard to make changes, but I want to take care of my health while I'm

    still young.

    ERICA: I feel the same way. I don't want to put off _____ .

3   Pair Up and Talk

A   Rank the following list of activities in order from the most dangerous (1) to the least dangerous (9) in your opinion. Discuss your opinions and reasons with a partner.

_____ cycling   _____ scuba diving

_____ flying in an airplane   _____ skateboarding

_____ hiking   _____ skydiving

_____ jogging   _____ snowboarding

_____ mountain climbing

B   Practice the conversation with a partner. Then discuss your opinions using your ranked list in Part A.

A: I think that scuba diving is the most dangerous because there may be sharks in the water.

B: I disagree. I don't think that sharks attack people very often. I put scuba diving as number five on my list.

Gerunds as Objects of Prepositions; Gerunds after Certain Expressions

Form

> Am I really interested **in studying** plant life in Antarctica? **It's no use wasting** time thinking this way. I need to finish this research.

1. Prepositions are words like *about, against, at, by, for, in, of, on, to, with*, and *without*. The noun or pronoun that comes after a preposition is the object of the preposition. A gerund works like a noun and therefore can also be the object of a preposition.

   She is interested **in him**.   (pronoun)

   She is interested **in seeing him**.   (gerund)

   Here are more examples of prepositions + gerunds.

	Preposition	Gerund	
What do you like	**about**	**living**	in a big city?
I am good	**at**	**learning**	languages.
He has plans	**for**	**decorating**	the house.
She stops him	**from**	**coming**	here.
He is interested	**in**	**working**	for us.
She is tired	**of**	**doing**	this job.
He insists	**on**	**checking**	my work.
They look forward	**to**	**seeing**	us tomorrow.
There's no point	**in**	**having**	a car in the city.

2. We use a gerund after many common expressions.

Expression	Example
Be busy	I'll **be busy doing** housework tomorrow.
Can't stand	He **can't stand waiting** in long lines.
Have difficulty/trouble	She **has difficulty learning** languages.
It's a waste of time/money	**It's a waste of time washing** the car because it's going to rain later.
*It's no use	**It's no use worrying** about it. There's nothing you can do.
It's not worth	**It's not worth waiting** in line for hours to see the game. We can see it on television.

*We can also say *there's no use (in) worrying about it.*

4 Practice
Jane has recently gone to an interview for a new job. Match the two halves of the interviewer's statements and questions.

_____h____ 1. Thank you
_____ 2. We are excited
_____ 3. We are thinking
_____ 4. Are you interested
_____ 5. Tell us about a time when you succeeded
_____ 6. Are you capable
_____ 7. Are you good
_____ 8. What are your plans
_____ 9. What would stop you
_____ 10. We look forward

a. of taking on responsibility?

b. in solving a problem.

c. in working on databases?

d. about talking to you regarding this opportunity.

e. to seeing you again.

f. of hiring someone to manage our computer databases.

g. at dealing with stressful work situations?

h. for coming to this interview.

i. for developing your career?

j. from coming to work for us?

5 Practice

Listen to the statements. For each one, circle the letter, a, b, or c, of the sentence with the same meaning.

CD2, 15

1. a. I can type my report but not yours.
    b. I can't type your report and mine, too.
    c. I'll type your report after I type mine.

2. a. The films are not good enough to watch in the theater.
    b. You might as well wait for the DVD to come out.
    c. Going to the cinema is too expensive.

3. a. If you don't go out, you don't benefit from living in the city.
    b. You don't have to go out if you live in the city.
    c. If you like to go out, you shouldn't live in the city.

4. a. If you don't complain, the service will be bad.
    b. If you complain, they will waste your time.
    c. The service will be bad whether you complain or not.

5. a. Worrying about the exam will not help you now.
    b. You can't worry about the exam because it is over.
    c. You don't have to worry about the exam now that it's over.

6. a. I don't ever spend all of my money before the end of the month.
    b. Spending all of my money before the end of the month is OK with me.
    c. I really don't like spending all of my money before the end of the month.

6 Pair Up and Talk

A Practice the conversation with a partner.

A: I'm really good at drawing. I'm interested in video games. But I'm tired of the ones my roommates like to play.

B: I'm good at playing basketball, but I'm tired of getting injured. I'm interested in video games, too!

B Tell a partner two things that you are good at, interested in, and tired of.

9c | Verbs Followed by Infinitives

Form

They **want to see** if they have passed the test.

1. We form an infinitive with *to* + a base verb. With some verbs, we use the verb + an infinitive.

Subject	Verb	Infinitive
We	agreed	**to look** after the children.
My parents	promised	**to visit** me this summer.
Everybody	wants	**to succeed**.

Here are some verbs that take infinitives.

afford	expect	need	refuse
agree	hope	plan	seem
appear	learn	pretend	threaten
decide	manage	promise	want

He can't **afford to buy** a computer.

She **threatened to resign** from the committee.

2. After some verbs, we can use the verb + an object + an infinitive.

Subject	Verb	Object	Infinitive
They	encouraged asked persuaded	her	to stay.

Here are some verbs that follow the pattern of verb + object + infinitive.

advise	invite	prefer	tell
allow	order	remind	warn
ask	permit	require	
encourage	persuade	teach	

3. With some verbs, we can use either of the structures in points 1 and 2 on page 271.

ask	help	want
expect	need	would like

The teacher **wants to leave** early. (The teacher will leave early if he can.)
The teacher **wants us to leave** early. (We will leave early because the teacher wants this.)

7 Practice

Our neighbor, Rose, phoned us last night and this is what she said. Rewrite the sentences using the verbs in parentheses. Remember that some verbs need an object.

1. She said, "Please come to my house for a barbecue* with us on Saturday." (invite)
   She invited us to come to her house for a barbecue on Saturday.

2. She said, "Don't forget to bring the children." (remind)
   _____

3. She said, "Don't knock on the door loudly, or you'll wake up the baby." (warn)
   _____

4. She said, "Could you please bring a salad?" (would like)
   _____

5. She said, "I'm going to make a big chocolate cake. You'll love it." (promise)
   _____

6. She said, "Please come at 6:00 P.M." (want)
   _____

7. She said, "Try to be on time." (encourage)
   _____

8. She said, "You will be able to cook your own meat if you want." (allow)
   _____

barbecue = An informal meal which is cooked and usually eaten outdoors

8 Pair Up and Talk

A Practice the conversation with a partner.

A: Does your teacher expect you to do much for class?

B: Yes, he expects us to do homework every single night.

A: What else does he want you to do?

B: He told us to watch English movies every week for practice.

A: Does he require you to watch certain movies?

B: No, we're allowed to pick our own movies.

B With a partner, ask and answer questions about what people expect, want, and allow you to do. Choose two people from the list or use your own ideas.

your boss   **your husband/wife/friend**   **your parents**   **your teacher**

9D Verbs Followed by a Gerund or an Infinitive

Form/Function

Celia **loves to draw**.
She **loves drawing**.

Some verbs can take either an infinitive or a gerund. With some verbs, there is no difference in meaning, but with other verbs there is a difference in meaning.

1. These verbs can take either an infinitive or a gerund with no difference in meaning.		
begin	hate	love
continue	like	start

It **started to snow.** OR It **started snowing.**

2. With these verbs, there is a difference in meaning between the infinitive and gerund forms.

Verb	We Use Verb + Gerund	We Use Verb + Infinitive
forget	To say that we forget something after we have done it. **I forgot going** to their house. (I went there but I forgot about it.)	To say that we forget something and don't do it. **I forgot to go** to the post office. (I was supposed to go there, but I didn't because I forgot.)
regret	To say that we regret something we have already done in the past. **I regret telling** him that I bought a car. (I told him that I bought a car.)	To say that we regret something we have to do now. **I regret to tell** you that you have failed the test.*
remember	To say that we remember something after we have done it. **I remember going** to their house. (I went there, and I remember it.)	To say that we remember something before we do it. **I remembered to go** to the post office. (First I remembered, then I went there.)
stop	To say what we are doing before we stop. The class **stopped talking** when the teacher entered the room.	To say why we stop. The teacher **stopped to talk** to the principal when he entered the classroom.
try	To say that we intend to do an experiment to see what happens. I'll **try switching** the computer on and off to see if it will work.	To say that we intend to make an effort to see if we can do something. I **tried to fix** the computer, but I couldn't.

* Regret + infinitive is usually formal English.

9 Practice

Sherry is on the phone with her sister Susan. Read their conversation and underline the correct form. Circle both forms if both are correct.

SUSAN: I've been thinking about our trip to Vermont last fall.

SHERRY: Yeah. It was really great. Do you remember (to climb/<u>climbing</u>) up that
¹
steep mountain?

SUSAN: Yes. I'll never forget (to walk/walking) under all those red and gold leaves.
²
I love (to hike/hiking) in the mountains.
³

SHERRY: You know, I don't have copies of your photos. Please don't forget (to send/sending)
⁴
them to me. Mine are terrible. I always try (to take/taking) them at special angles,
⁵
but they never come out well.

SUSAN: Sure. I'm sorry that I forgot (to mail/mailing) them. Sherry, how about another trip
⁶
next year? I was thinking that we could try (to go/going) on one of those organized
⁷
tours. I know you hate (to travel/traveling) by bus, but it's really inexpensive.
⁸

SHERRY: I know, but you don't have any freedom.

SUSAN: It's not that bad. They let you stop (to take/taking) photos along the way, and you
⁹
get time on your own. I started (to look/looking) for some information on the
¹⁰
Internet, but I got too busy and couldn't finish.

10 Your Turn

Write a short paragraph that could be part of an email message to a family member or a friend. Write three or four sentences and use at least three verbs from the list.

begin	enjoy	hate	remember	stop
continue	forget	love	start	try

Example

You know how much I love skiing. Did you know that I began to ski when I was only four years old? ...

9E | Infinitives after Certain Adjectives, Nouns, and Indefinite Pronouns

Form

Ella has a lot of **homework to do**. She is **determined to finish** it by 5:00.

1. We use infinitives after certain adjectives.

	Adjective	Infinitive	
It is	**important**	**to know**	a foreign language.
He was	**pleased**	**to see**	me.
We were	**disappointed**	**to hear**	the news.

Here are some adjectives that take infinitives.

afraid	determined	hesitant	proud
ashamed	eager	likely	ready
careful	happy	pleased	willing

2. We can use infinitives after nouns or after indefinite pronouns like *something* or *anything*.

	Noun/Pronoun	Infinitive
Do you have	**anything**	**to read?**
I have	**something**	**to eat.**
It's	**time**	**to leave.**
I have some	**letters**	**to write.**

Function

1. The adjective in many adjective + infinitive combinations describes a feeling or attitude.

   She was **happy to hear** the news.

   We were **eager to try** the new restaurant.

2. When an infinitive follows a noun, it often means that there is an obligation or a necessity.

   I have some **letters to write**. (I must write some letters.)

   It's **time to leave**. (It's necessary for us to leave now.)

3. We use *for* + a noun or an indefinite pronoun when we need to say who does an action in the infinitive.

   It's convenient **for everyone** to have a computer in the classroom.

   I have some work **for James** to do.

11   Practice
Complete the sentences with the infinitive form of the verbs from the list.

aim for	**do**	**finish**	**hear**	**think**
be	**find out**	**have**	**plan**	**travel**

Dear Henry,

I was very happy ___to hear___ that you have decided to apply for graduate school next
                     1

year. As you know, your mother and I were very concerned _____ that you were
                                                            2

thinking of taking a year off. Of course, we'll support you, whatever you decide. But I'm

sure you realize that it's very important for you _____ your education. After you
                                                   3

graduate from college, you'll have time _____ and do other things. But now it's
                                          4

good to have something _____ . It's good for everyone _____ a goal in life.
                        5   **6**

That has always been my philosophy. When you are young, it's easy _____ that the
                                                                    7

future is not important. But believe me, and I know from experience, the time

_____ for the future is when you are young, not when it's too late _____
8   **9**

anything about it. Take my advice. Finish your education. It'll make your mother and me so

proud _____ there on your graduation day.
       10

Love,

Dad

12 Pair Up and Talk

A Practice the conversation with a partner.

A: It's never too late to learn new things.

B: What do you mean?

A: Well, my grandmother learned to use a computer this year.

B Complete one of the sentences below with your own opinion. Explain your reasons to your partner.

It's never too late to …

It's very important to …

It's nice to have someone to …

There is never enough time to …

9F   *Too* and *Enough* Followed by Infinitives

Form

Madison is **too** young **to use** a computer. She isn't old **enough to use** a computer.

1. *Too* comes before an adjective or adverb. We use *for* + an object when we need to say who does the action in the infinitive.

Subject	Verb	*Too* + Adjective/ Adverb	(*For* + Object)	Infinitive
It	is	**too cold**	(for the girls)	**to go** to the beach.
He	spoke	**too quickly**	(for me)	**to understand.**
It	isn't	**too late**	(for us)	**to go.**

2. *Enough* comes after an adjective or an adverb.

Subject	Verb	Adjective/Adverb + Enough	(For + Object)	Infinitive
It	isn't	warm enough	(for the girls)	to go to the beach.
He	spoke	loudly enough	(for us)	to understand.
She	is	old enough		to go.

3. *Enough* comes before a noun.

Subject	Verb	Enough + Noun	(For + Object)	Infinitive
There	isn't	enough time	(for them)	to finish.
We	have	enough money		to buy the CDs.

Function

1. When we use *too*, it has a negative meaning. It means that something is more than necessary or more than is wanted.

    She is **too** young to drive. (It is impossible for her to drive.)

    I'm **too** tired to go. (I cannot go.)

   Do not confuse *too* with *very*. *Very* means to a great degree; to a great extent. It does not suggest more than necessary.

    POSITIVE MEANING: I am **very** busy, but I can help you. (I am busy, but it is possible for me to help you.)

    NEGATIVE MEANING: I am **too** busy to help you. (I can't help you because I am busy.)

2. When we use *enough* in an affirmative sentence, it has a positive meaning. It implies that there is as much of something as is needed.

    She is **old enough** to drive.

   But when we use *enough* in a negative sentence, it means that something is less than necessary or less than is wanted.

    This coffee is **not warm enough** to drink.

3. *Enough* usually comes before a noun. However, in formal English it occasionally follows a noun.

    INFORMAL: I have **enough** time.

    FORMAL: There is time **enough**.

13   **Practice**
Rewrite the sentences about a restaurant using *too* and *not ... enough* and
the words in parentheses.

1.   The tea was so hot that we couldn't drink it.

(hot/for us) _The tea was too hot for us to drink._

(cool/for us) _The tea wasn't cool enough for us to drink._

2.   The server spoke so fast that I couldn't understand her.

(fast/for us) _____

(slowly/for us) _____

3.   The words on the menu were so difficult that I couldn't pronounce them.

(difficult/for me) _____

(easy/for me) _____

4.   The room was so dark that I couldn't see the food.

(dark/for me) _____

(bright/for me) _____

5.   The music was so loud that we couldn't have a conversation.

(loud/for us) _____

(quiet/for us) _____

6.   I was so shy that I couldn't complain.

(shy) _____

(brave) _____

7.   We were so disappointed that we didn't leave a tip.

(disappointed) _____

(satisfied) _____

8.   We were so tired that we couldn't walk home.

(tired) _____

(energetic) _____

_____

14 Pair Up and Talk
A Practice the conversation with a partner.

A: In the morning, I'm often so sleepy that I don't want to get out of bed. Sometimes I feel so lazy that I don't even make breakfast for myself. That's fine, because I'm usually not that hungry anyway.

B: My partner is usually too sleepy to get out of bed in the morning. Sometimes he's too lazy to make breakfast, but that's OK because he's usually not hungry enough to eat anyway.

B Tell a partner about yourself using *so* + adjective/adverb + *that*. Then ask your partner to tell the class about you using *too* or *not … enough*. Use the words in the list or your own ideas.

ambitious	friendly	optimistic	shy
athletic	hungry	outgoing	sleepy
busy	lazy	pessimistic	thirsty
energetic	lucky	scared	

9G Showing Purpose

Form

We went to the jewelry store **to look at** rings.

1. We can use an infinitive to talk about the purpose of an action. It explains why we do something.

I am saving **to buy** a new car.   (My purpose in saving is to buy a new car.)

I went to Miami **to see** Susan.   (My purpose in going to Miami was to see Susan.)

2. We can also use *in order to* + a base verb instead of an infinitive to explain a purpose. This is usually more formal.

> I drank a lot of coffee **in order to stay** awake.
>
> We left early **in order to get** there in time.

3. In formal English, we use *in order not to* to express a negative purpose. In informal English, we usually use a clause with *so*.

> FORMAL: All employees should attend the meeting **in order not to** miss important news.
>
> INFORMAL: All employees should attend the meeting **so** they won't miss important news.

4. We can also use *for* + an object to show purpose.

> I went to the pharmacy **for** some medication.
>
> I went to the pharmacy **to buy** some medication.

15   Practice

Jan is planning a trip to Colorado. Write sentences using the infinitive of purpose to tell what she will need these items for. Use the phrases from the list.

| boil water | find her way | keep mosquitoes away | sleep in |
| carry things | keep food cold | see in the dark | start a fire |

1. matches   *She needs matches to start a fire.* _____

2. a tent _____

3. insect repellent _____

4. a cooler _____

5. a kettle _____

6. a flashlight _____

7. a backpack _____

8. a compass _____

16   Pair Up and Talk

A   Practice the conversation with a partner.

A: What do you do before going on vacation?

B: I usually go to the drugstore to get some air sickness pills and some sunscreen. What about you?

A: I sometimes go to the bookstore to look for guidebooks about the places I'm going.

9H Perfect Infinitives and Perfect Gerunds; Passive Voice of Infinitives and Gerunds

Form

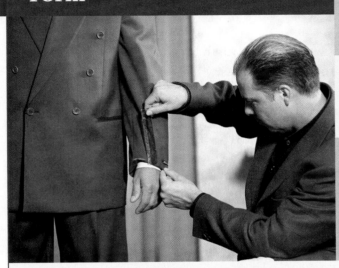

The sleeves needed **to be shortened**. The tailor hoped **to have finished** the work by 4:00, but he couldn't.

Active Forms of Infinitives and Gerunds	
Form	**Example**
Simple Infinitive	Bob wanted **to do** the work by 5:00.
Simple Gerund	I enjoy **going** to parties.
Perfect Infinitive	Bob hoped **to have completed** the project by 5:00, but he wasn't able to.
Perfect Gerund	I enjoyed **having gone** to Amy's party.

Passive Forms of Infinitives and Gerunds*	
Form	**Example**
Simple Infinitive	She was lucky **to be awarded** the prize (by the judges).
Simple Gerund	I enjoy **being invited** to parties (by my friends).
Perfect Infinitive	She was lucky **to have been awarded** the prize (by the judges).
Perfect Gerund	I enjoyed **having been invited** (by Amy) to Amy's party.

* The agent may or may not be stated.

Function

1. We use the perfect infinitive or perfect gerund to talk about something that happened at a time earlier than the main verb.

     My English seems **to have gotten** better. (My English got better before the time of speaking.)

     I remember **having met** her a year ago. (I met her before the time of speaking.)

2. We can also use the simple and perfect forms of infinitives and gerunds in the passive voice. The agent may or may not be mentioned. As in the active voice, we use the perfect form to talk about something that happened at a time earlier than the main verb.

     Thomas didn't expect **to be called** into the meeting (by his boss). (simple infinitive)

     He was glad **to have been called** into the meeting (by his boss). (perfect infinitive)

     Chloe dislikes **being given** extra work (by her boss). (simple gerund)

     She disliked **having been given** extra work last week (by her boss). (perfect gerund)

3. We can use the simple and perfect gerunds as introductory phrases.

     Before **deciding** on my destination, I talked to friends.

     Having decided to go on vacation, I called my travel agent.

4. We usually use an infinitive after the verb *need*.

     I **need to go** to the bank.

   But sometimes we use a gerund after *need*. In these cases, the gerund has a passive meaning. It usually shows that it is necessary to improve or fix something.

     My suit **needs cleaning**.

     His car **needs servicing**.

   The passive infinitive can also be used with the same meaning.

     My suit **needs to be cleaned**.

     His car **needs to be serviced**.

---

17   Practice

Complete the sentences with the simple or perfect form of infinitives or gerunds of the verbs in parentheses. Some answers must be in the active voice; others must be in the passive. Write one word on each line.

1. Kate was relieved (hear) _____*to*_____ _____*have*_____ _____*heard*_____ the news.

2. She was not really surprised (choose) _____ _____

   _____ _____ as the best student by the class.

3. (receive) _____ _____ the highest score in every test, she was

   very happy.

4. She was pleased (be) _____ _____ so successful.

5. It had been hard for her (spend) _____ _____ _____ so much of her time studying.

6. She missed (not/see) _____ _____ _____ the latest movies.

7. (tell) _____ _____ _____ by her parents she would not get any more money, she had no choice.

8. She also wanted (recognize) _____ _____ _____ as the intelligent child in her family instead of her brother!

18   Practice
Listen to Joe telling a friend about his first job. Complete the sentences using the perfect gerund form of the verbs that you hear. Some sentences require the active voice. The others require the passive.

My first job was as a journalist for a local newspaper. _Having spent_ four years
                                                              1
in college earning a degree in English, I thought I would be able to do the job easily.

I was pleased at _____ the perfect job. After _____ many
                       2   **3**
corrections on my first article, my boss advised me to work harder. I tried hard, but I

couldn't do better. After _____ that I could lose my job,
                                              4
I started to worry. I think most people would get worried after _____
                                                                          5
_____ that they would lose their job. I felt like a complete failure. I felt angry at

_____ unfairly. I told my uncle that after _____
                  6   **7**
_____ this job, I thought I would never find a job again.

_____ that, my uncle offered me a job as his personal assistant working for
          8
his magazine!

19   Practice

Rewrite the sentences using *need* + a gerund and *need* + a passive infinitive. Use verbs from the list.

buy	cut	paint	sweep
clean	do	repair	wash

We've just rented a house, but there are a lot of problems.

1.   The windows are dirty.
      They need cleaning./They need to be cleaned.

2.   The front gate is broken.
      _____

3.   The grass is too long.
      _____

4.   The floors are dusty.
      _____

5.   The paint is coming off the walls.
      _____

6.   The curtains are dirty.
      _____

7.   The gas stove in the kitchen is old. We need a new one.
      _____

8.   We have a lot of things to do!
      _____

20   Pair Up and Talk

A   Practice the conversation with a partner.

A: What things need to be done in your house or apartment?

B: My windows need to be cleaned.

A: What else?

B   What things need to be done in your house or apartment? Tell your partner at least four things.

Form

> I **saw** a man **playing** music to a snake.

After some verbs of perception such as *see, hear, feel, smell, listen to, look at, notice, watch,* and *observe*, we can use an object + a base verb + *-ing* (form) or a base verb.

Subject	Verb	Object	Base Verb + *-ing* / Base Verb
I	heard	Susan	**playing** the piano.
I	heard	Susan	**play** the piano.
We	saw	them	**leaving**.
We	saw	them	**leave**.

Function

There is usually little difference in meaning between the base verb + *-ing* and the base verb. However, in general, we use the base verb + *-ing* when we perceive (*hear, see, notice*) part of the action in progress.

I saw him **sleeping** in front of the television.

We use the base form when we perceive the whole action from beginning to end.

I saw him **sleep** through the whole movie from beginning to end.

21 **Practice**

Listen to the following questions. Is the question about a single complete action or an action in progress? Underline the form that you hear.

AUDIO

DOWNLOAD

CD2, 17

What would you do if … ?

1. What would you do if you saw someone (<u>steal</u>/stealing) your car?

2. What would you do if you saw someone (leave/leaving) their car lights on?

3. What would you do if you heard someone (break/breaking) into your house at night?

4. What would you do if you heard someone (scream/screaming) and (fall/falling) down the stairs?

5. What would you do if you noticed a mouse (crawl/crawling) towards your chair?

6. What would you do if you saw a spider (sit/sitting) on your computer?

22 **Pair Up and Talk**

Practice the conversation with a partner. Then with a partner, ask and answer the questions in Practice 21.

A: What would you do if you saw someone steal your car?

B: If I saw someone steal my car, I'd call the police right away.

9J Person + Gerund

Form/Function

The referee insisted on **my leaving** the game.

1. In informal English, when we use a gerund to talk about what a person is doing, we usually use an object pronoun (*me, you, her,* etc.) + a gerund, or, if it is a person's name, the name (*David*) + a gerund.

e-Workbook 9J

They insisted on **us going** with them.

We were surprised at **David forgetting** to attend.

In formal English, we usually use a possessive pronoun or noun.

They insisted on **our going** with them.

We were surprised at **David's forgetting** to attend.

2. In both informal and formal English, we use the object form after perception verbs such as *see, hear,* and *feel.*

CORRECT: I saw him arriving.

INCORRECT: I saw ~~his arriving~~.

---

23 Practice

Rewrite the sentences with a person + a gerund on a separate sheet of paper. Give answers in both informal and formal English.

1. David forgot to call me on my birthday. I was surprised.

   I was surprised at David forgetting to call me on my birthday.

   I was surprised at David's forgetting to call me on my birthday.

2. He often phones me at work when I am busy. I don't like it.

3. He phones in the evening before 9:00. I don't mind.

4. He takes me dancing every Saturday night. My parents don't approve of it.

5. His friends talk on their cell phones all the time. I can't stand it.

6. I sometimes go out with other friends. He doesn't like me for it.

7. My parents tell me that David is not good enough for me. I don't listen to them.

8. My parents are always telling me what to do. I am tired of it.

---

24 Your Turn

Complete the sentences with true facts about yourself.

Example

I can't stand people telling me what to do.

1. I can't stand people _____

2. I don't mind people _____

3. My friend criticized me for _____

THE TORTOISE AND THE DUCKS

A tortoise was very sad because he saw birds flying above him and other animals running by him all the time. He, too, wanted to see the world, but the house on his back was too heavy and his legs were too short.

One day he met two ducks. He told them he was tired of staying in the same place all the time and he longed to see the world. The ducks agreed to help him. "This is our plan to carry you up in the sky: First, you have to take hold of this stick with your teeth. We'll then carry you far up in the air and you'll see the whole countryside. But you must not talk or you will be sorry."

The tortoise was happy for now he could enjoy seeing the world like the other animals. He held the stick with his teeth. Each duck took one end of the stick and they flew up high in the sky. Just then a crow flew by. He was surprised at what he saw and said, "This must be the king of tortoises!"

"Why certainly …" the tortoise began to say as he couldn't help speaking.

But he stopped holding on to the stick to say these foolish words and fell down to the ground.

1. _____

   The tortoise wanted to see the world.

2. _____

   He couldn't see the world because his back was too heavy and his legs were too short.

3. _____

   The tortoise was tired of staying in the same place all the time.

4. _____

   He longed to see the world.

5. _____

   He met two ducks.

6. _____

   The ducks decided to help him.

7. _____

   They planned to carry him up into the sky.

8. _____

   He could now go and see the world.

9. _____

   "This must be the king of tortoises!"

10. _____

    The tortoise couldn't help speaking.

11. _____

    He stopped holding on to the stick.

26 Phrasal Verb Practice

A Complete the sentences with the correct form of the phrasal verbs. Use each verb only once. Phrasal verbs are taught in Unit 8, section H.

jump on   live with   lose out   mark up   save up   sit around

One day, Grace decided that she was too old to _____ a lot of roommates. It
was time to find an apartment of her own, She had been _____ for this day for
three years. Now she had enough money for the first and last month's rent and some
furniture. Every day, she _____ the newspaper with red circles around the
rental listings. One morning, she was sure she had found the perfect place. She read
the description. "I have to _____ this right away. I can't _____ here or
I'll _____ on getting my dream place." She hurried out the door and ran to the
address in the advertisement. But wait! The apartment was right next door!

B Circle the correct definition of the phrasal verb.

1. mark up

a. draw lines around

b. spend time on

c. take note of

2. live with

a. follow certain rules

b. produce an income

c. share a home with others

3. save up

a. avoid wasting

b. keep for later use

c. make safe from danger

4. sit around

a. take another's place

b. rise to a sitting position

c. do nothing while others act

5. lose out

a. not understand

b. not get or obtain

c. not have value

6. jump on

a. start something late

b. be eager to accept an opportunity

c. disagree with someone

A Listen and check the correct answer.

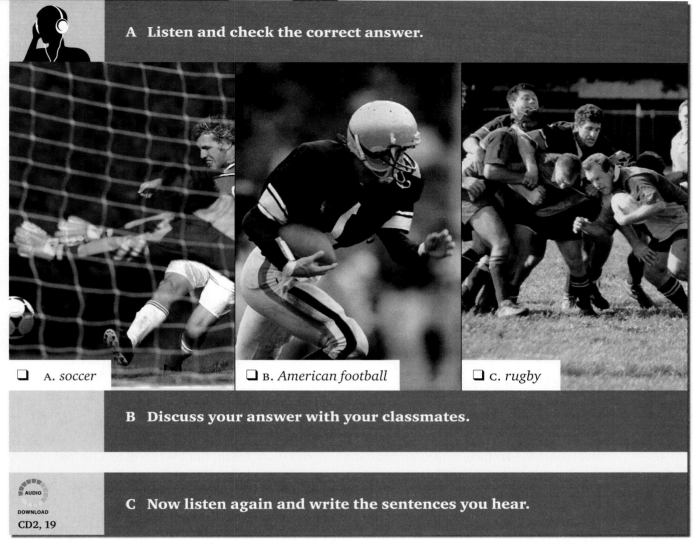

❏ A. *soccer*   ❏ B. *American football*   ❏ C. *rugby*

B Discuss your answer with your classmates.

AUDIO DOWNLOAD CD2, 19

C Now listen again and write the sentences you hear.

Review

1 Review (9a–9d, 9f–9g, 9i)
Complete the sentences with a gerund or an infinitive.

JACK: I heard you went (camp) ___camping___ over the weekend. I thought you hated
   1

(do) _____ any outdoor activity.
   2

BETTY: I like (shop) _____ in flea markets, don't I? Flea markets are outdoors!
   3

JACK: Yes, (shop) _____ is your favorite pastime. But who persuaded you
   4

(sleep) _____ under the stars?
   5

BETTY: You know I have trouble (say) _____ no. Anyway, I couldn't avoid
   6

(go) _____ . It was Stephanie's birthday. Besides, none of us had enough money
   7

(stay) _____ in a hotel.
   8

JACK: I see. Well, tell me about it. I can't wait (hear) _____ what happened.
   9

BETTY: Do you really want to hear me (talk) _____ about it? It's a very sad story.
   10

It all started at 5:00 Saturday morning. I was trying (get) _____ some sleep
   11

when the phone rang. "It's time (get) _____ up!" Stephanie said. Three
   12

hours later, we arrived at the campground. We put up our tent, but I was still too sleepy

(do) _____ anything! I was also very upset because I'd forgotten (bring)
   13

_____ my feather pillow. After the tent was up, we went (hike) _____ .
   14   15

At first, I refused (go) _____ . But I was too afraid (stay) _____
   16   17

alone. We hiked and hiked. It was awful. Terry warned me (stay) _____ on
   18

the path. But I saw some wild flowers (grow) _____ in a field. I can't resist
   19

(pick) _____ flowers. How did I know there was poison ivy[1] there! Now I'm going
   20

crazy with all the (itch) _____ . Not to mention the insect bites. I had forgotten
   21

(bring) _____ my insect spray. Finally, we got back to camp. All I thought about
   22

was (eat) _____ dinner. But they said it was too early (eat) _____ .
   23   24

[1]*poison ivy = a plant that irritates the skin and makes it itch*

They had (swim) _____ on their minds. By that time I was too tired (argue)
_____ ₂₆ . After they left, I thought I'd try (do) _____ some (cook)

_____ , but there wasn't a stove. I tried (start) _____ a fire in the

fire pit. After an hour, I got a small stick of wood (light) _____ . Then it started

(rain) _____ . There was no use even (think) _____ about dinner. I

decided I needed (go) _____ to bed. I had big plans for (sleep)

_____ . Then I discovered the leak in my tent.

---

2 Review (9b–9c, 9e, 9g–9h)
Complete the sentences with the correct gerund or infinitive form of the verbs from the list.

be	cycle	meet	rest	see	swim	work
compete	do	prepare	run	sleep	win	worry

I have dreamed about ____*competing*____ in a triathlon. Tomorrow, I'll see that dream come true.

I'm nervous, but there's no use _____ about it. It's more important for me

_____ part of this competition than _____ it. I'm sure I'll have difficulty

_____ tonight. But I'll have plenty of time _____ my sore muscles tomorrow

night. I'm looking forward to _____ all the other athletes at 5:00 in the morning. At 7:00,

we'll start the triathlon by _____ in the lake for 2.4 miles (3.8 kilometers). The next event

requires us _____ over mountains and through deserts for 112 miles (180 kilometers).

Those who are left can look forward to _____ 26.2 miles (42 kilometers) through the city

streets. I insist on _____ this event though it's very difficult. _____ very hard

_____ for this event, I want _____ my dream come true.

A Before You Read

1. Have you ever searched for information on the Internet? Describe the process you used.
2. Is information from the Internet as good as information from a library? Explain.

THE GOOGLE GUYS

DID YOU KNOW ... ?
Users can choose to display Google in more than 100 languages. Some of these (such as Klingon) are fictional languages that no one has ever spoken as a native language.

B Read In the late 1990s, it took a long time to find a piece of information on the Internet. The search
5 engines[1] then were good at finding websites with key words in them. However, they were not very good at ranking these sites from
10 most to least helpful. People wasted a lot of time looking at websites they did not need. Then Sergey Brin and Larry Page came up with a new approach. They are the Google
15 Guys.

The two men were born in the early 1970s—Brin in Russia and Page in Michigan. They met as graduate students at Stanford University in California. Page asked Brin to work with him
20 on a research project. The aim was to **invent** a new search engine. In a list of hits[2] for a given

[1.] search engine = computer software that finds information on the World Wide Web [2.] hit = a website found through a search; a visit by one reader to one website

set of key words, it would be able to show the most popular sites first. Brin and Page realized that a site's popularity could indicate its quality.
25 Identifying the most popular sites was easy. Each site on the Web automatically counts how many "hits" (visits from Internet users) it gets.

They decided to name their engine "Google," an alternate spelling of googol. This is the name
30 for the number 10^{100} (10 followed by 100 zeroes). After releasing it on the Stanford University computer network, they saw it become very popular. ∎ They knew they had a winner. ∎ They formed a company in 1998 to market Google far
35 beyond Stanford. ∎ It is now one of the richest companies on the planet. ∎

Google is a part of daily life for many computer users. The search engine is so widely used that its name has become a verb in
40 English. To "google" something is to search for it on the Web. At the company's headquarters in California, employees enjoy a relaxed atmosphere that encourages creativity. This reflects the casual style of Brin and Page. It is rare
45 to find a photograph of them wearing neckties.

C Notice the Grammar Underline all the gerunds and the infinitives.

Choose the best answer.

D Look for Main Ideas

1. What is the main topic of paragraph 2?
   - (A) how Brin and Page met
   - (B) how Google got started
   - (C) what a search engine does
   - (D) what makes a site popular

E Look for Details

2. According to the reading, what could Internet search engines in the 1990s NOT do well?
   - (A) find sites containing certain key words
   - (B) keep users coming back to use them more than once
   - (C) indicate how helpful a site might be
   - (D) waste time looking at unneeded sites

3. According to the reading, which of the following is true about Brin and Page?
   - (A) neither one is American
   - (B) they were born in different countries
   - (C) they both studied in Russia
   - (D) english isn't their first language

4. How does Google determine how popular a site is?
   - (A) by how often it is visited
   - (B) by how many key words it contains
   - (C) by how many comments its users make
   - (D) by how useful it is

F Look for Vocabulary

5. The word *invent* in the reading is closest in meaning to _____ .
   - (A) create   (C) test
   - (B) improve   (D) discover

G Make Inferences

6. What can we infer from the reading about Google's headquarters?
   - (A) some employees live there
   - (B) it is part of Stanford University
   - (C) it contains some sports facilities
   - (D) employees do not have to wear suits

7. We can infer from the reading that _____ .
   - (A) there is no evidence to show that popularity does not indicate quality
   - (B) the Google Guys were right to use popularity as an indicator of quality
   - (C) high-quality sites are not popular
   - (D) the quality of a site usually drops after it becomes popular

H Sentence Addition

8. Look at the four squares ▪ that indicate where the following sentence could be added in the reading.
   The Google Guys themselves are among the world's youngest billionaires.
   Where would the sentence fit best?

   - (A) at the first square
   - (B) at the second square
   - (C) at the third square
   - (D) at the fourth square

Writing: Write an Essay of Analysis

An essay of analysis gives reasons or causes of something.

STEP 1 — **Work with a partner or a group and analyze the topics. Make notes of the causes or reasons for each topic.**

1. the causes of heart disease
2. the major causes of pollution in the world
3. how weather affects our lives
4. why marriage is good

STEP 2 — **Choose one of the topics in Step 1, or think of your own.**

STEP 3 — **Write your essay.**

1. Write an introduction to the topic. In your introduction, write a thesis statement: state your method of analysis (for example, causes or reasons) and state your organizational method (for example, number of causes or reasons). Also summarize your key points. Here is an example of an introductory paragraph. The thesis statement is in bold.

2. Write a paragraph on each of the causes or reasons you have listed in your thesis statement. Make sure you have supporting examples and details for each.

> Preventing heart disease is a major public health effort in the United States. Some researchers say that heart disease appears to be on the decline, but we must persuade more people to pay attention to the risk that they face. One way to do this is by educating them about the causes of heart disease. **There are many causes of this deadly disease; however the three major causes are high blood pressure, genetic predisposition, and an unhealthy lifestyle.**

3. Write a conclusion. Restate your thesis statement and also state that there may be causes other than the ones you have listed.

4. Write a title for your essay.

STEP 4 — **Evaluate your essay.**
Checklist

_____ Did you write an introduction with a thesis statement?
_____ Did you write a paragraph about each of the points in the thesis statement?
_____ Are your reasons or causes clear? Do they support the thesis statement?

STEP 5 — **Edit your essay with a partner or a teacher. Check spelling, vocabulary, and grammar.**

STEP 6 — **Write your final copy.**

Self-Test

A   Choose the best answer, A, B, C, or D, to complete the sentence. Darken the oval with the same letter.

1. _____ a foreign language can sometimes be difficult.

   A. To learning   Ⓐ Ⓑ Ⓒ Ⓓ
   B. Learning
   C. Learn
   D. Be learning

2. I enjoyed _____ him write his essay.

   A. helping   Ⓐ Ⓑ Ⓒ Ⓓ
   B. to help
   C. help
   D. for to help

3. He_____ correcting my pronunciation.

   A. insist on   Ⓐ Ⓑ Ⓒ Ⓓ
   B. insist
   C. insists on
   D. insist to

4. We advised _____ .

   A. to him not to go   Ⓐ Ⓑ Ⓒ Ⓓ
   B. him not go
   C. him not to go
   D. not him to go

5. On the way home, we stopped _____ some gas.

   A. getting   Ⓐ Ⓑ Ⓒ Ⓓ
   B. get
   C. to get
   D. for getting

6. We were eager _____ the new game.

   A. to try   Ⓐ Ⓑ Ⓒ Ⓓ
   B. trying
   C. try
   D. for to trying

7. We _____ to finish the test.

   A. didn't enough have time   Ⓐ Ⓑ Ⓒ Ⓓ
   B. didn't have enough time
   C. had not time enough
   D. did not enough time have

8. The teacher saw_____ during the test.

   A. the student to cheat   Ⓐ Ⓑ Ⓒ Ⓓ
   B. cheat the student
   C. the student cheating
   D. cheating the student

9. He left a note for himself in order _____ forget.

   A. not   Ⓐ Ⓑ Ⓒ Ⓓ
   B. not for
   C. not to
   D. for not

10. We have an important issue _____ .

    A. for discuss   Ⓐ Ⓑ Ⓒ Ⓓ
    B. for discussing
    C. to discussing
    D. to discuss

1. Drinking enough water is important
      A   **B**   **C**
   in order not get dehydrated.
        D

   (A) (B) (C) (D)

2. After I finished doing my homework, I
         A   **B**
   decided go for a walk.
      C   **D**

   (A) (B) (C) (D)

3. The teacher was pleased see her students
               A
   do well on their final exam before graduating.
   B   **C**   **D**

   (A) (B) (C) (D)

4. We had been told by our teacher not using the
      A   **B**   **C**
   Internet for our research.
         D

   (A) (B) (C) (D)

5. After having a wonderful time hiking and
        A   **B**
   seeing friends at the camp, I look forward to go
   C   **D**
   there again next year.

   (A) (B) (C) (D)

6. MEG: Could you help me with these

             math problems?

   MATT: Sorry. I don't have time enough now,
                      A   **B**
          but I can help you later.
            C   **D**

   (A) (B) (C) (D)

7. We decided to go on a trip to the mountains
      A
   but forgot taking the map, so we stopped
         B   **C**
   to buy one at a gas station.
   D

   (A) (B) (C) (D)

8. Watching bears in the wild are exciting
      A   **B** **C**
   and fun, but we must remember to keep
                     D
   our distance.

   (A) (B) (C) (D)

9. In order to be not late for the flight and have
   A   **B**
   enough time for breakfast, I suggest getting up
   C   **D**
   at five in the morning.

   (A) (B) (C) (D)

10. I always enjoy to go to the airport because it's
            A
    nice to sit and watch the planes taking off
        B   **C**
    and landing.
       D

    (A) (B) (C) (D)

Unit 10

Agreement and Parallel Structure

All the students **are** happy that graduation day is finally here.

Form/Function

All the students in the photo **have** graduated. **Everyone is** happy.

In an English sentence, the subject and the verb must agree in number. This means that a singular subject must have a singular verb, and a plural subject must have a plural verb.

SINGULAR: John **is** a lawyer.

(*John* is a singular subject, and *is* is a singular form of the verb *be*.)

PLURAL: John and Alice **are** lawyers.

(*John and Alice* is a plural subject, and *are* is a plural form of the verb *be*.)

We form singular and plural forms of *be* differently from other verbs.

	Singular		Plural	
The verb *be* (present and past)	I	am/was	we	are/were
	you	are/were	you	
	he/she/it	is/was	they	
Other verbs in the present *	I	run	we	run
	you		you	
	he/she/it	runs	they	

*Note: *I* is a singular pronoun and *you* can also be a singular subject, but they both take the base form of the verb. Only third person singular subjects (*he, she, it, Tom,* etc.) take the *-s* form.

Most of the time, subject-verb agreement is clear, but in some cases, even native speakers have to be careful. Here are some rules for special situations.

1. A sentence with two subjects joined by *and* takes a plural verb.

    The physics laboratory **and** the library **are** located on the first floor.

2. Some words like *mathematics* and *news* end in *-s*, but they are singular and take a singular verb.

    Mathematics **is** not my favorite subject.

    The news **is** good.

    Other examples are *politics, physics, economics, aeronautics, electronics,* and *measles.*

3. When we use a gerund as the subject, it is always singular.

    Swimming **is** my favorite sport.

    But if a subject has two gerunds, it is plural.

    Swimming and biking **are** my favorite sports.

4. When we use *each, every,* or *any* as an adjective in front of a subject, it takes a singular verb. This also includes indefinite pronouns like *everyone* and *anything.*

    Each of the subjects in a sentence **has** to agree with its verb.

    Everyone **wants** something from us.

5. When we use *all, almost all, most,* or *some* in front of a subject or as a subject, the subject takes a plural verb.

    All the students **eat** lunch at 12:00.   (*all* + a subject)

    Most eat in the cafeteria.   (*most* is the subject)

    Some of the students **eat** at home.   (*some* is the subject)

6. Two singular subjects joined by *or* take a singular verb. See page 317 for information on *either . . . or* and *neither . . . nor.*

    Thursday or Friday **is** the best day to go.

    Two plural subjects joined by *or* take a plural verb.

    Are the boys or the girls going to leave first?

    If one subject is singular and the other is plural, the verb agrees with the subject that is closest to it.

    I think that the potatoes or the chicken **is** burning.

    I think that the chicken or the potatoes **are** burning.

1 Practice

Complete the sentences using the singular or plural form of the verbs in parentheses.

Every student whose first language is not English and who wants to go to college in the United States (have) _____has_____ to take an exam called TOEFL® (Test of English as a

1

Foreign Language). This exam tests your knowledge and skills in grammar, vocabulary, reading, writing, and listening. Mathematics (be) _____ not included in the

2

test. Reading (be) _____ the subject most students have difficulty with. But

3

listening and writing (be) _____ also difficult for many students. Each student

4

(apply) _____ to take the test individually. The test can be taken on a computer

5

or with a pen and paper. Neither the handwritten test nor the computerized test (be)

_____ marked by a person. Everything, except the essays, (be) _____

6   **7**

scored by computer. Each student (receive) _____ a score by mail a few weeks

8

later. Most colleges in the country (require) _____ a certain score on this exam.

9

Taking tests (be) _____ a skill that requires a lot of practice.

10

2 Your Turn

What is the process of applying for college in your country? Write four sentences explaining what every student has to do, what most students have to do, etc. Share your information with the class.

Example

Every student has to write an essay.
Most students have to go to an interview.

1. _____

2. _____

3. _____

4. _____

Form/Function

> **Here is** your paper. **There are**
> only two mistakes. You got an A.

1. Prepositional phrases do not affect the verb. The verb always agrees with the subject.

   The value of his investments **is** dropping every day.

Subject	Prepositional Phrase	Verb	Complement
The value	of his investments	**is** dropping	every day.
One	of the students	**is**	here.
The directions	for operating this machine	**are**	confusing.

   Phrases like *along with, together with, accompanied by, as well as,* and *in addition to* also do not affect the verb.

   The surgeon, together with his team of doctors, **is** visiting the patient.

   My parents, along with my brother, **are** going to visit me tomorrow.

2. When we begin a sentence with *here* or *there*, the verb may be singular or plural depending on the noun that follows.

   There **are** many students in class today.

   Here **is** the result of all your efforts.

3 Practice

Complete the sentences with a singular or plural form of the verb *be*. Then listen and check your answers.

There _____are_____ 20 students in my daughter's class. Elena, along with all the
        1

other students, _____ taking a test right now. The subject of the test
                        2

_____ mathematics. All of the children _____ allowed to use a
      3   4

calculator, which makes it easier. The instructions for the exam _____ on the
                                                                          5

board. There _____ a separate answer sheet for each section of the exam. The
                    6

answers _____ written in pencil. My daughter, along with all the other students
              7

in the class, _____ trying hard to pass the exam. All of the children, except
                    8

Elena, _____ having trouble with the questions. Elena is one of the few students
              9

who _____ able to finish all the questions on time.
          10

4 Your Turn

Write at least four sentences describing this photo. What are all the people
doing? What are some of the people doing? What is one person doing?

One person is using the ATM. _____

_____

_____

_____

_____

_____

_____

10c Subject-Verb Agreement with Quantity Words

Form/Function

> **Sixteen dollars is** the cost of that CD. **A number of** them **have been sold** today.

1. We usually use a singular verb with expressions of time, money, distance, weight, and measurement. We do this because we think of the subject as a single unit.

    Ten dollars is all the money I have.

    Three miles (4.8 kilometers) is not far to run.

    Three days is a long time to wait for the results of the test.

    Twenty minutes is not enough time for an essay.

    Two cups of milk **is** what we need for this recipe.

    Two-thirds of this box of cereal **has** been eaten.

2. We use the subject *the number of* + a plural noun with a singular verb.

    The number of students in our class **is** 20.

    We use the subject *a number of* + plural noun with a plural verb.

    A number of important people **are** here today.

3. When we use expressions of quantity such as *some of, a lot of,* and *three-quarters of* as the subject, the verb agrees with the pronoun or noun that follows *of*.

    Some of the **orange is** still good. (*some of the orange* = a part of the orange)

    Some of **it is** still good.

    Some of the **oranges are** still good.

    Some of **them are** still good.

However, we use a singular verb with these subjects: *one of the* + plural noun, *each of the* + plural noun, *every one of the* + plural noun, and *none of the* + plural noun.

> **One of the** students **is** sick.
> **Each of the** students **is** ready for the test.
> **Every one of** the students **is** on time for the test.
> **None of the** students **is** late.

In informal speech, we often use a plural verb with *none of the*.

> **None** of the students **are** late.

5 Practice

A Look at the photo of the women having a friendly game of cards. Complete the sentences with the following quantity words.

a number of	none of the	the number of (use twice)
each of the	one of the	

1. _The number of_ women playing cards is four.
2. _____ women is playing cards.
3. _____ women is not playing cards.
4. _____ women are playing cards.
5. _____ women is looking at her cards carefully.
6. _____ cards in their hands is unclear.

B Write two sentences about the photo.

1. _____

2. _____

6 Practice

Read the sentences about a survey of student activities. Fill in the correct form of the verbs in parentheses.

STUDENT SURVEY				
	Eat Dinner	**Do Homework**	**Watch TV**	**Talk on the Phone**
Student 1	20 mins.	60 mins.	90 mins.	45 mins.
Student 2	20 mins.	120 mins.	30 mins.	90 mins.
Student 3	20 mins.	60 mins.	90 mins.	15 mins.
Student 4	20 mins.	30 mins.	45 mins.	0 mins.
Student 5	60 mins.	90 mins.	120 mins.	30 mins.
Student 6	20 mins.	120 mins.	0 mins.	45 mins.
Student 7	60 mins.	60 mins.	30 mins.	20 mins.
Student 8	20 mins.	90 mins.	45 mins.	50 mins.
Student 9	20 mins.	60 mins.	60 mins.	120 mins.
Student 10	60 mins.	90 mins.	15 mins.	30 mins.
Student 11	60 mins.	30 mins.	45 mins.	45 mins.
Student 12	20 mins.	60 mins.	90 mins.	75 mins.
Student 13	20 mins.	120 mins.	120 mins.	15 mins.
Student 14	20 mins.	90 mins.	30 mins.	20 mins.
Student 15	20 mins.	30 mins.	90 mins.	0 mins.
Student 16	60 mins.	30 mins.	60 mins.	20 mins.
Student 17	20 mins.	90 mins.	120 mins.	0 mins.
Student 18	60 mins.	60 mins.	30 mins.	20 mins.

1. There (be) _____are_____ 18 students in this survey.

2. Two-thirds of the students (spend) _____ 20 minutes eating dinner.

3. One-third of the students (spend) _____ one hour on eating dinner.

4. None of the students (do) _____ homework for more than two hours.

5. All of the students (spend) _____ some time on homework.

6. One of the students never (watch) _____ TV.

7. Half of the class (watch) _____ TV for an hour or more.

8. Two-thirds of the class (talk) _____ on the phone for less than an hour.

9. One-sixth of the class (talk) _____ on the phone for more than an hour.

10. A number of students (not talk) _____ on the phone.

7 Your Turn
Answer the following questions.

1. How long is a long time to talk on the phone?
2. How long is enough time to finish your homework?
3. How long is enough time to spend on eating dinner?
4. Is two hours enough time to spend watching TV?

8 Pair Up and Talk
A Practice the conversation with a partner.

A: How much time is right for you when you exercise?

B: Thirty minutes every day is enough for me.

B Interview six students in your class. Ask them how much of their time they spend on each of these activities every day. Take notes. Then tell the class about the results of your survey.

| exercising | sleeping | talking on the phone |
| instant messaging | surfing the Internet | watching TV |

9 Your Turn
Write a paragraph about the results of your survey on student activities.

_____

_____

_____

_____

_____

_____

_____

Form/Function

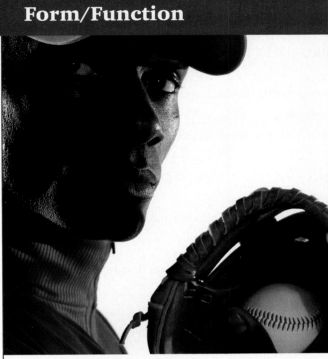

A good baseball player needs **stamina**, **concentration**, and **skill**.

1. We can use the conjunctions *and, but, or,* and *nor* to connect words or phrases. The words before and after these conjunctions must have the same grammatical form. When this is the case, there is parallel structure.

Grammatical Form	Example
Nouns	The essay had mistakes in **grammar** and **organization**.
Adjectives	His speech was neither **short** nor **good**.
Verbs	She **arrives** at seven and **leaves** at nine.
Adverbs	Does she work **slowly** or **quickly**?
Gerunds	**Dancing** and **watching** movies are my favorite weekend activities.
Infinitives	I like **to swim** but not **to fish**.

2. When a parallel structure has more than two parts, we use a comma to separate each part.
   The book contained **stories, poems**, and **plays**.
   His chores are **washing the dishes, cleaning the bathroom**, and **watering the flowers**.
   The instructor expects students **to attend** every class, **to do** all the assignments, and **to hand in** homework on time.
3. If a parallel structure has only two parts, we do not use a comma between them.
   I can speak **Chinese** and **English**.

10 Practice

Underline the parallel structure in the following sentences. Then write the grammatical form (nouns, adjectives, verbs, adverbs, gerunds, or infinitives) the parallel structure contains.

1. The colors you choose for your <u>clothes</u> and for your <u>home</u>, <u>office</u>, and <u>car</u> can have an effect on you. _____nouns_____

2. Colors have been known to ease stress, to fill you with energy, and even to reduce pain and other physical problems. _____

3. When you decide to paint your apartment, you shouldn't choose colors quickly or carelessly. _____

4. For example, the colors blue and green have a calming, relaxing, and peaceful effect. _____

5. On the other hand, the color red excites, stimulates, and warms the body. _____

6. The color yellow also energizes and stimulates the body, but not as much as the color red. _____

7. The color yellow is good for remembering things and relieving depression. _____

8. If you are sleeping and eating poorly, then orange is the color for you. _____

11 Practice

Underline and correct the errors in parallel structure. Some sentences have no errors. Then listen to the statements and check your answers.

CD2, 21

1. In order to maintain youth and good <u>healthy</u>, we need to have a combination of exercise
   health
   and proper <u>nutritional</u>.
   nutrition

2. Exercise is good for our physical health and psychologically.

3. Regular exercise improves digestion, increases energy, burns fat, and lowering blood cholesterol.

4. It also reduces stress and anxious, which are the main reasons for many illness and conditions.

5. Also, regular exercise elevating mood, increases feelings of well-being, and reduces anxious and depression.

6. When you start an exercise program, remember to start out slowly, listen to your body, and gradually increase the difficulty and long of the exercise.

7. There are many different forms of moderate exercise including daily walking, bicycling, or even gardening.

12 **Your Turn**

Complete each sentence with your own words using parallel structure.

1. The night before a test, it is important to _____ , _____ ,
   and _____ .

2. On the day of the test, you must be _____ , _____ ,
   and _____ .

3. During the test, you must _____ , _____ , and _____ .

4. After the test, you can, _____ , _____ , and _____ .

13 **Read**

Read the story. Then underline and correct the errors in parallel
structure in the sentences that follow.

MING AND HIS STEPMOTHER

Ming's mother died when he was a baby. His father married again and had two more sons. Ming's new mother wasn't always nice to him. She always dressed her own sons in thick, warm coats, but she gave Ming only an old, thin coat. She bought new shoes for her own sons but didn't buy any for Ming. However, Ming never complained about anything to his father who was always away at work and never saw anything.

One winter day, it happened that Ming's father saw that his oldest son was wearing an old, tattered coat. This disturbed him very much and he immediately told his second wife to leave the house. Ming begged his father to forgive his stepmother. He said, "If she stays, one son will be freezing. But if she leaves, all three sons will be freezing." After these words, his father changed his mind, and his stepmother was kinder to Ming.

1. Ming's father remarried and <u>having</u> two more sons. _____*had*_____
2. She took care of her sons but neglecting Ming. _____
3. Ming had neither a new nor warmth coat. _____
4. Ming had a patient, unselfish and honesty character. _____
5. He was a well-behaving, hardworking and uncomplaining son. _____
6. Ming always wanted to help and pleased his elders. _____
7. Ming insisted on forgiving and forget the mistakes of his stepmother. _____

10E Coordinating Conjunctions

Form/Function

The ostrich is a bird, **yet** it doesn't fly.

1. We use a conjunction like *and, but, or, so, yet,* and *for* to connect two main clauses. We usually put a comma before the conjunction in the main clause.

   Susan has many problems, **but** she always looks happy.

   We can begin a sentence with *and* or *but*. Some instructors do not accept this usage. Check with your instructor.

   Susan has many problems. **But** she always looks happy.

2. We also use *so, for,* and *yet* to join two independent clauses. We usually use a comma before these conjunctions.

   I was very hungry, **so** I ate the whole cake.

   The actor doesn't appear in public, **for** he doesn't like publicity.

   He told me he would give back my money, **yet** he didn't.

   So, for, and *yet* also have other meanings.

   She is **so** smart. (adverb: *so* = *very*)   I haven't finished **yet**. (adverb)

   I bought it **for** you. (preposition)

He

Terry Fox was born in 1958 in Canada. ~~he~~ played soccer and basketball in high school for he loved sports when he was 18 he had problems with his knee so he went to the doctor the doctor told him he had bone cancer needed an operation and would lose his leg this was a terrible shock yet Terry had an idea he decided he could help people even with one leg his idea was to run across Canada to collect money to fight cancer after the operation he got an artificial leg and started to prepare for the run his progress was very slow but he did not give up in 1980 he started his run and called it the "Marathon of Hope" he ran 26 miles (41.8 kilometers) a day, seven days a week this was amazing but it was more amazing because he only had one leg later that year Terry got sick again and had to stop running he received letters from all over the world and Canadian television showed a program about him the program collected $10 million for the Canadian Cancer Society Terry Fox collected almost $24 million for cancer he died in 1981 but his story did not end there. Terry Fox events started all over the world raising millions of dollars to fight cancer.

Practice

Punctuate the sentences with commas and periods. Use capital letters where necessary. Do not add other words.

They

Dolphins live in the sea, yet they are mammals. ~~they~~ breathe air and give live birth to their young dolphins are intelligent and sensitive animals their brains are almost as large as ours and they have a language of more than 30 sounds for communicating with each other they live in groups of several hundred and always help any dolphins that may be in danger.

Dolphins are friendly to humans and there are many reports of dolphins helping people in danger in one case in 1983, a helicopter crashed into the Java Sea and it was a dolphin that saved the pilot's life the dolphin pushed the rubber raft for nine days until it reached the coast.

16 **Your Turn**

Write a paragraph describing your classroom. Use coordinating conjunctions and the correct punctuation.

Example

Our classroom has a board, desks, and chairs, but it doesn't have computers.

Form/Function

> Malaika Mills is appearing **not only** in a movie **but also** in a play this year.

1. Correlative conjunctions come in two parts, for example, *both … and*. We use these conjunctions to compare two ideas. We use the same grammatical form after each part of a correlative conjunction. Here are some examples of parallel structure with correlative conjunctions.

Parallel Structure	Example
both + verb + *and* + verb	Ben **both** studies **and** works.
not only + adjective + *but also* + adjective	Mary is **not only** generous **but also** intelligent.
either + noun + *or* + noun	I have to do **either** my homework **or** my chores.
neither + gerund + *nor* + gerund	He enjoys **neither** skiing **nor** hiking.

2. When we connect two subjects with *both … and*, we use a plural verb.

    Both his brother **and** sister **are** in town.

3. When we connect two subjects with *not only … but also, either … or,* or *neither … nor,* we use a singular or plural verb depending on the subject that is closest to the verb.

    Neither the doctor **nor** the nurse **is** with the patient.

    Neither the doctor **nor** the nurses **are** with the patient.

17 Practice

Underline the correct form of the verbs in parentheses. Then listen to the statements and check your answers.

AUDIO

DOWNLOAD

CD2, 22

1. Both vitamin C and calcium (is/<u>are</u>) important for good health.
2. Both your teeth and bones (need/needs) calcium.
3. Either milk or products from milk (contain/contains) a lot of calcium.
4. Both children and the elderly (require/requires) calcium.
5. Neither chicken nor pork (have/has) much calcium.
6. Not only milk products but also green vegetables (contain/contains) calcium.
7. Neither the liver nor the blood (make/makes) calcium.
8. Either food or drink (give/gives) the body the calcium it needs.

18 Practice

Combine the sentences into one with *both … and*, *not only … but also*, *either … or*, or *neither … nor*. Write them on a separate sheet of paper.

1. Fruits have vitamin C. Vegetables have vitamin C.
   Both fruits and vegetables have vitamin C.
2. Heat destroys vitamin C. Exposure to air destroys vitamin C.
3. You can take vitamin C naturally in food. You can take vitamin C in tablet supplements.
4. Rice does not have vitamin C. Pasta does not have vitamin C.
5. Oranges have a lot of vitamin C. Lemons have a lot of vitamin C.
6. They say vitamin C prevents heart disease. They say vitamin C prevents colds.
7. Vitamin C does not prevent cancer. Vitamin C does not prevent infection.
8. Natural vitamins are good for the body. Synthetic vitamins are good for the body.

19 Phrasal Verb Practice

A   Complete the sentences with the correct phrasal verbs using the correct form.

clean up   miss out   range from   search for   take over   work on

Robotics is the science of making machines that _____ the jobs done by

1

humans. In the near future, robots will do tasks that _____ the most common,

2

like _____ our homes, to saving lives. Researchers are experimenting with

3

rescue robots that can _____ survivors buried under rubble. Other scientists are

4

_____ ways for robotic machines to help people with missing limbs not
 5

_____ on a normal life. They can wear mechanical legs, arms, knees, and hands.
 6

B Match the phrasal verb with the correct definition.

_____ **1.** search for   **a.** make neat and tidy

_____ **2.** take over   **b.** use effort to do something

_____ **3.** range from   **c.** lose a chance to gain advantage or enjoyment

_____ **4.** miss out   **d.** reach from one limit to another

_____ **5.** clean up   **e.** look through or examine thoroughly to find something

_____ **6.** work on   **f.** take control of or responsibility for something

Listening Puzzle

AUDIO DOWNLOAD CD2, 23

A Listen and check the correct answer.

☐ A. *cotton*   ☐ B. *leather*   ☐ C. *polyester*

B Discuss your answer with your classmates.

AUDIO DOWNLOAD CD2, 24

C Now listen again and write the sentences you hear.

Review

Animals with a backbone (is/<u>are</u>) vertebrates. Scientists have recently discovered Earth's smallest
            1
vertebrate. It is the "stout infantfish." When scientists first looked under the microscope, they instantly

recognized it as something special. It is not only the world's smallest fish, but also (light/the lightest).
                                                                                                    2
This new species (are/is) no longer than the (wide/width) of a pencil. Both the male and the female
                    3   **4**
(is/are) quite small. The female stout infantfish (measure/measures) a third of an inch (0.7 centimeter).
5   **6**
The male (is/are) just over one quarter of an inch (0.6 centimeter). Each of these fish (weigh/weighs)
            7   **8**
very, very little. A load of 500,000 stout infantfish (weigh/weighs) barely one pound (0.45 kilogram).
                                                          9
Of course, no one (have/has) that many. As a matter of fact, there (is/are) only six specimens of this fish
                    10   **11**
in laboratories today. The stout infantfish (are/is) very rare.
                                            12
    Neither the males (or/nor) the females (have/has) color, except for the eyes. Every one of these fish
                      13   **14**
(lacks/lack) teeth, scales, and certain characteristics typical of other fish. Two months (is/are) not very
15   **16**
long, but that (is/are) how long the stout infantfish live.
                17
    Everyone (want/wants) to know more about this tiny fish, but they are very hard to find. Fishing
                  18
(is/are) not the way to catch them, of course. The only ways (is/are) diving and (to explore/exploring)
19   **20**   **21**
the deep ocean.

Neil Armstrong and Buzz Aldrin walked on the moon on July 21, 1969. Neither of them ~~are~~ *is* still there,

of course, and one of their experiments are. Armstrong and Aldrin wasn't only walking and jumped

around on the moon. They was busy placing instruments on the surface and conducted experiments.

About an hour before the end of their final moonwalk, they set up a science experiment, a two-foot

(0.6 meter) wide panel with 100 mirrors. This panel, along with many other objects, is still on the moon

today, for no one have gone back to get them. Neither the U.S. or any other country have gone back to

the moon. The exact number of objects on the moon is unknown. However, astronauts landing on the

moon today would find only one piece of equipment that are still working—the panel. None of the other

experiments are still running. The panel, called a "lunar laser ranging retroreflector array," is small and

simplicity, or it give scientists lots of important information.

The operation of the panel is simple. The mirrors on the panel points at Earth. A laser pulse shoots out

of a telescope on Earth, crossing the Earth-moon space, so hits the mirrors. The mirrors sends the pulse

straight back. On Earth, scientists measure the travel time and determining the moon's distance, not

only quickly, but very accurate. For decades, scientists, along with an occasional researcher, has traced

the moon's orbit and learned many remarkable things.

Everyone seem to have something to gain. The lunar laser ranging retroreflector array have provided

information to many fields of science. Physics are a good example. Physicists has used the laser results

to check Einstein's theories of gravity and relativity. So far, Einstein are still considered correct, so who

know whether the lunar laser ranging retroreflector array will someday tell us something different!

A Before You Read

1. Many celebrities hire bodyguards to follow them when they go out. Why?
2. Even in war, soldiers must obey some rules. Name some of these.

THE SAMURAI

B Read Japan's samurai do not exist anymore. However, many people still admire them. Their fighting
5 skill and their strict code of conduct are legendary.

The samurai started around the year 1000 as private armies for the emperor and for powerful families. The word
10 *samurai* comes from a Japanese term meaning "one who serves." Many early samurai were farmers who had become too poor to farm.

They fought partly to have a job and partly to chase away tax collectors. Early on, they fought
15 on horseback, mostly with bows and arrows. Later, they fought with swords and became famous for their sword fighting skill. As time went on, the samurai had to not only fight but also be familiar with poetry and culture.

20 They followed a code called *bushido*, the "way of the warrior." Bravery and loyalty are **valued** among soldiers in many cultures. Courtesy, compassion, honesty, and honor were also common values. ▪ The remaining principle
25 in bushido is not often associated with warriors. The samurai code, however, ranked it number one. ▪ A good samurai had to use both his brain and his heart in making decisions. ▪ An action he chose should not only make sense but also
30 feel correct. ▪

From about 1600 to the 1860s, the samurai held a high place in Japanese society. They still worked in the private armies of local lords. **These** often waged war against each other, so a
35 lord depended on the samurai for his life. He was happy to grant the samurai many privileges but they could not own land. But among the Japanese who were not landowners, the samurai had the highest status. They were in
40 a class of their own. They ranked higher than the other three classes—farmers, craftspeople, and merchants. It was illegal for anyone but a samurai to own a sword. Still, the samurai did not live in comfort. To stay tough, they typically
45 slept in rough barracks. They also avoided fancy food and fine clothing.

C Notice the Grammar Underline all the parallel constructions.

Choose the best answer.

D Look for Main Ideas

1. What is the main topic of paragraph 2?
   - Ⓐ how the samurai's role developed
   - Ⓑ expectations placed on the samurai
   - Ⓒ cultural contributions of the samurai
   - Ⓓ Japan in A.D. 1000

E Look for Details

2. The samurai are best known for fighting with
   _____ .

   - Ⓐ bows and arrows   Ⓒ horses
   - Ⓑ cultural pursuits   Ⓓ swords

3. The reading says that your social class in
   Japan determined _____ .
   - Ⓐ what you could own
   - Ⓑ what you could say
   - Ⓒ where you could live
   - Ⓓ whom you could marry

4. The reading mentions all of the following
   as part of *bushido* EXCEPT _____ .
   - Ⓐ using your brain and heart
   - Ⓑ treating others politely
   - Ⓒ following your conscience
   - Ⓓ taking care of your family

F Make Inferences

5. From the reading, which of the following
   can we most strongly infer about Japanese
   society between 1600 and the 1860s?
   - Ⓐ We know about it mostly from the
     writings of the samurai.
   - Ⓑ Some records of it must exist.
   - Ⓒ Most of what is known is inaccurate.
   - Ⓓ No one really knows much about it.

G Look for Vocabulary

6. The word *valued* in the reading is closest in
   meaning to _____ .
   - Ⓐ put into practice
   - Ⓑ tested
   - Ⓒ ignored
   - Ⓓ considered important

H Look for References

7. The word *these* in the reading refers
   to _____ .
   - Ⓐ principles   Ⓒ swords
   - Ⓑ samurai   Ⓓ lords

I Sentence Addition

8. Look at the four squares ▪ that indicate where
   the following sentence could be added to
   the passage:
   **The samurai emphasized them more than
   most soldiers would.**
   Where would the sentence best fit?
   - Ⓐ at the first square
   - Ⓑ at the second square
   - Ⓒ at the third square
   - Ⓓ at the fourth square

Writing: Write an Essay of Definition

An essay of definition gives the writer's opinion of the meaning of a concept.

STEP 1   Look at the terms below. With a partner or a group, brainstorm ideas about what these terms mean. Think of specific examples or situations that explain them.
1. friendship   3. a stranger
2. happiness   4. good parents

STEP 2   Choose one of the terms above, or think of your own.

STEP 3   Write your essay.
1. Write an introduction that defines the term you have chosen. You may define the term using a dictionary (name the dictionary and quote from it). In your thesis statement, tell how you are going to define it and give two or three aspects of the definition that you will write.

> Friends play a major role in a person's life. When you find a friend, your life changes. All of us have a different definition of what a friend is. According to the *American Heritage College Dictionary*, a friend is "a person whom one knows, likes, and trusts." For me, too, a friend is someone I know, like, and trust, but a friend is also someone with whom you share the same moral values, whom you support in times of need …

2. Write your body paragraphs. Each paragraph of your essay must illustrate a part of the definition stated in your thesis. Support each part with examples.
3. Write a conclusion that summarizes your definition. Give a final comment on the term.
4. Write a title.

STEP 4   Evaluate your essay.
Checklist
_____ Did you write a thesis statement in your introduction?
_____ Did you give details, examples, or situations that support your thesis statement?
_____ Did you summarize and comment on your term in the conclusion?

STEP 5   Work with a partner or a teacher to edit your essay. Check spelling, vocabulary, and grammar.

STEP 6   Write your final copy.

Self-Test

1. Kate runs and _____ .

   A. lifts weights   Ⓐ Ⓑ Ⓒ Ⓓ
   B. is lifting weights
   C. weight lifting
   D. is doing weight lifting

2. The doctor recommended eating healthier meals and _____ .

   A. to do exercise   Ⓐ Ⓑ Ⓒ Ⓓ
   B. exercising
   C. exercise
   D. to exercise

3. The store sells not only vitamins _____ .

   A. but also food   Ⓐ Ⓑ Ⓒ Ⓓ
   B. also sells food
   C. but sells food
   D. but also is selling food

4. Neither his grammar _____ good.

   A. or his reading
      skills are   Ⓐ Ⓑ Ⓒ Ⓓ
   B. nor his reading skills is
   C. nor his reading skills are
   D. or his reading skills are not

5. He told me he would help me, _____ he didn't.

   A. so   Ⓐ Ⓑ Ⓒ Ⓓ
   B. for
   C. and
   D. yet

6. Both the students _____ at the meeting.

   A. and also the teachers   Ⓐ Ⓑ Ⓒ Ⓓ
   B. and the teachers was
   C. and the teachers were
   D. but also the teachers were

7. He exercises regularly, _____ he is in good health.

   A. so   Ⓐ Ⓑ Ⓒ Ⓓ
   B. but
   C. yet
   D. for

8. I hope to go to college _____ .

   A. and study economic   Ⓐ Ⓑ Ⓒ Ⓓ
   B. or study economics
   C. and also to study economics
   D. and to study economics

9. She wants to take either _____ next semester.

   A. physics nor chemistry   Ⓐ Ⓑ Ⓒ Ⓓ
   B. physics and chemistry
   C. physics or chemistry
   D. physic or chemistry

10. Air _____ .

    A. both contains oxygen
       and water   Ⓐ Ⓑ Ⓒ Ⓓ
    B. contains both oxygen and water
    C. both oxygen and water contains
    D. both contain oxygen and water

1. <u>Each</u> <u>of the students</u> in the class <u>have</u>
      A   B   C

   <u>a grammar book</u> and a reading book.
        D

   (A)   (B)   (C)   (D)

2. <u>Having</u> <u>a cold</u> can make you feel tired,
     A   B

   <u>miserable</u>, and <u>weakness</u>.
       C   D

   (A)   (B)   (C)   (D)

3. The number of <u>students</u> <u>who</u> passed the test
                A   B

   <u>were</u> <u>fewer</u> than expected.
     C   D

   (A)   (B)   (C)   (D)

4. Mathematics <u>are</u> my favorite class, <u>but</u> I also
             A   B

   <u>like</u> <u>physics</u> and chemistry.
    C   D

   (A)   (B)   (C)   (D)

5. <u>The principal of the school</u>, <u>along with</u> the
           A   B

   teachers <u>and</u> custodians, <u>were</u>
         C   D

   present at the meeting.

   (A)   (B)   (C)   (D)

6. <u>The news</u> about the economy <u>are</u> <u>both</u> a
      A   B C

   surprise <u>and</u> a relief.
        D

   (A)   (B)   (C)   (D)

7. <u>Each of the students</u> agrees <u>that</u> twenty
         A   B

   minutes <u>are</u> <u>not enough</u> for an essay exam.
       C   D

   (A)   (B)   (C)   (D)

8. Many people in the world <u>has</u> <u>neither</u> food to
                   A   B

   eat <u>nor</u> clean <u>water</u> to drink.
      C   D

   (A)   (B)   (C)   (D)

9. Our teacher <u>expects us</u> to be <u>on time</u>, <u>to do</u> all
           A   B   C

   our homework, and <u>sitting</u> quietly in class.
              D

   (A)   (B)   (C)   (D)

10. <u>Everybody</u> in our class <u>enjoy</u> <u>doing</u> <u>quizzes</u>.
       A   B   C   D

    (A)   (B)   (C)   (D)

Unit 11

Noun Clauses and Reported Speech

I wonder **if people realize how famous James Dean was in his day**.

11A Noun Clauses Beginning with *That*

Form

I hope **that it doesn't rain today**.
We want to go sightseeing.

Main Clause	Noun Clause (with *That*)
I think	**(that) she's a movie star.**
She hopes	**(that) people won't notice.**

1. Noun clauses act as nouns in a sentence. In this unit, most of the noun clauses act as objects. In the first example above, the noun clause *that she is a movie star* is the object of the verb *think*.
2. We use an object noun clause with a main clause. The main clause always comes first. We do not use a comma between the two clauses.

Function

1. We use *that* clauses after certain verbs that express feelings, thoughts, and opinions. Here are some of them:

agree	expect	hope	presume	remember
assume	fear	imagine	pretend	suppose
believe	feel	know	prove	suspect
decide	figure out	learn	read	show
discover	find	notice	realize	teach

doubt	forget	observe	recognize	think
dream	guess	predict	regret	understand

2. We often omit *that* from a noun clause, especially when we speak. The meaning of the sentence does not change.

    LINDA: I think **it's raining**.
            OR I think **that it's raining**.
    JOHN: I hope **we don't get wet**.
            OR I hope **that we don't get wet**.

3. When the introductory verb is in the present, the verb in the noun clause can be in the present, past, or future, depending on the meaning of the sentence.

    I believe he**'s** here now.
    I believe he**'ll** be here (in a few minutes).
    I believe he **was** here (a few minutes ago).

4. In conversation, to avoid repeating the *that* clause after verbs such as *think, believe,* and *hope,* we can use *so* or *not* in response to a *yes/no* question.

    KEN: Is Nancy here today?
    PAT: I **think so**. (I think that Nancy is here today.)
    KEN: Are we having dinner soon?
    PAT: I**'m afraid not**. (I want us to have dinner soon, but we are not going to.)

	With These Verbs	Question	Answer
Positive Verb + *So*	think		I **think so**.
	believe		I **believe so**.
	be afraid		I**'m afraid so**.
	guess		I **guess so**.
	hope		I **hope so**.
Negative Verb + *So*	think	Has the rain stopped?	I don't **think so**.
	believe		I don't **believe so**.
Positive Verb + *Not*	be afraid		I**'m afraid not**.
	guess		I **guess not**.
	hope		I **hope not**.

5. In formal English, a noun clause can also be the subject of a sentence. In this case, we cannot omit the word *that*.

    That prices are going up is clear.

It is more common to say the same thing with the word *it* as the subject and with the noun clause at the end.

    It is clear **(that) prices are going up**.

1 Practice

Match the two halves of the sentences to make predictions about the future.

What will happen by the year 2050?

__d__ **1.** Population experts predict

_____ **2.** Food scientists expect

_____ **3.** Energy scientists think

_____ **4.** Astronauts will prove

_____ **5.** Robots will figure out

_____ **6.** People will realize

a. that renewable energy will replace fossil fuels.

b. that they are smarter than humans.

c. that it is possible to survive on Mars.

d. that the world population will be over nine billion.

e. that everyone needs to speak one language.

f. that most of our food will be genetically modified.

2 Pair Up and Talk

A Practice the conversation with a partner.

A: In your opinion, will people stop using cars in the future?

B: I think so. Gas will become too expensive. Do you think people will stop using cars?

A: I hope not. I love to drive.

B With a partner, ask and answer questions about the future predictions listed below. Answer with *think, believe, be afraid, guess,* or *hope + so* or *not.*

People will stop using cars.

Hunger in the world will disappear by the year 2050.

Scientists will figure out a way for humans to live on Mars.

Everyone will speak the same language.

Online classrooms will replace traditional classrooms.

3 Your Turn

Write five predictions about the future. Use verbs from the list.

discover   expect   predict   prove   think

Example

I predict that everyone will learn English on the Internet by the year 2050.

Form

I don't know **why he takes his computer on camping trips**.

Main Clause	Noun Clause (Indirect Question)*
She wanted to know	who I was.
	where they came from.
	why he called.
I don't know	when he arrives.
	what she said.
	how they did it so fast.

Indirect question is the name of this type of noun clause.

1. Noun clauses may also begin with *wh-* words. Sentences with noun clauses beginning with *wh-* words are also called indirect questions.

    DIRECT QUESTION: Why did he call?

    INDIRECT QUESTION: I don't know why he called.

2. Although *wh-* clauses begin with a question word, they do not follow question word order. Instead, they use statement word order.

    CORRECT: I know where **she is**.

    INCORRECT: I know where ~~is she~~.

3. We use a question mark at the end of a sentence if the main clause is a direct question and a period at the end of a sentence if the main clause is a statement.

	Main Clause	Noun Clause (Indirect Question)
Main clause is a question	Can you tell me	where the televisions are?
Main clause is a statement	I wonder	where the elevators are.

Function

1. We usually use an indirect question to express something we do not know or to express uncertainty.

    I don't know **how much it is**.

2. We often use indirect questions to ask politely for information.

    DIRECT QUESTION: What time does the train leave?

    INDIRECT QUESTION: Can you tell me what time the train leaves?

4 Practice

Listen to the questions someone asks a potential employer at a job interview. Rewrite each question as a main clause + a *wh-* noun clause. Be sure to use correct punctuation at the end of the sentences.

CD2, 25

1. Can you tell me *how many people your company employs?* _____

2. I'd like to know _____

3. Can you tell me _____

4. Can you tell me _____

5. I wonder _____

6. Can you tell me _____

7. I'd like to know _____

8. Can you tell me _____

5 Pair Up and Talk

A Practice the conversation with a partner.

A: Can you tell me how many people your company employs?

B: We currently employ 300 people.

B   Work with a partner. Imagine you are at a job interview. Ask and answer the questions in Practice 4.

6 Practice

Rewrite each direct question as an indirect question (a main clause + a *wh-* noun clause). Be sure to use correct punctuation at the end of the sentences.

You have a job interview tomorrow, and you are asking a friend to help you prepare. Your friend is telling you about the questions that they will probably ask you.

1. They will probably ask ___what your current job title is.___

   (What is your current job title?)

2. They will want to know _____

   (What are your job duties?)

3. They will ask _____

   (What qualifications do you have?)

4. They will want to know _____

   (Who was your previous employer?)

5. They will ask _____

   (How long did you work in your last job?)

6. They will want to know _____

   (Why did you leave your last job?)

7. They will ask _____

   (What was your salary?)

8. They will want to know _____

   (Why do you want the job?)

7 Your Turn

Work with a partner. Think of an unusual job. Imagine that you went to a job interview for this job and write five *wh-* questions the interviewer asked you. Tell the class about the questions using a main clause + a *wh-* noun clause. Your classmates should guess the job.

Example

(The unusual job was a lion tamer.)

They asked (me) why I was interested in lions.

Form

I wonder **if my cat Peanut understands me**. Can you tell **whether or not he understands me?**

Yes/No Question	Main Clause	Noun Clause (Indirect *Yes/No* Question)
Did he see you?	Do you know	**if/whether he saw you (or not)?**
Are they angry?	I don't know	**if/whether they're angry (or not).**
Is she at home?	I wonder	**if/whether she's at home (or not).**

1. Noun clauses with *if* or *whether* are indirect *yes/no* questions.

   DIRECT QUESTION: Are they angry?

   INDIRECT QUESTION: I don't know if they are angry or not.

2. *If* and *whether* noun clauses must begin with *if* or *whether*. They do not follow question word order. Instead, they use statement word order.

   CORRECT: Do you know if this is the director's office?

   INCORRECT: Do you know ~~is this~~ the director's office?

3. We can add the phrase *or not* to the end of an *if/whether* clause if the clause is short.

   I don't know if she's here **or not**.

   I don't know whether she is here **or not**.

   We can also put *or not* immediately after *whether*, but not after *if*.

   CORRECT: I don't know whether or not she is here.

   INCORRECT: I don't know if ~~or not~~ she's here.

Function

1. *If* and *whether* at the beginning of a noun clause have the same meaning. We usually use *whether* in more formal situations.
2. We usually use *if/whether* clauses following verbs of mental activity.
   I can't remember **if I turned off my computer**.
   I wonder **whether he has sent me a message**.
3. We use *if/whether* clauses in polite questions.
   Do you know **if Mr. Gallo is in the office today**?
   Can you tell me **whether Flight 213 has arrived or not**?

8 Practice

Listen to the conversation. Rewrite each question with the *if/whether* clause + main clause that you hear. Then practice the conversation with a partner.

DOWNLOAD

CD2, 26

Alice is thinking of having a birthday party at the Paradise Restaurant. She is asking her friend Todd about the restaurant.

ALICE: Did we eat lunch there together last year, or didn't we?

TODD: I can't remember *if we ate lunch there together last year.*

1

ALICE: Did we like the food?

TODD: I can't remember _____

2

ALICE: Are they open for lunch on Saturday?

TODD: I don't know _____

3

ALICE: Is there a fixed price lunch menu?

TODD: I don't know _____

4

ALICE: Are there enough tables for 50 guests?

TODD: I don't know _____

5

ALICE: Do they have live music?

TODD: I can't say _____

6

ALICE: Can they order a special birthday cake?

TODD: Good question. I wonder _____

7

9 Pair Up and Talk

A Practice the conversation with a partner.

A: I wonder if the hotel has a fitness center.

B: Of course. They have a huge fitness center with an Olympic-sized pool.

B Imagine that you are planning to stay at an expensive hotel. Your partner knows the hotel well. Find out five things about the hotel from your partner.

10 Phrasal Verb Practice

A Complete the sentences with the correct form of the phrasal verbs. Use each verb only once.

pass up   sign up   sink in   sit tight   wind down   wrap up

I hadn't had a moment to think about my summer vacation until today. This morning, I called my travel agent, Molly. She told me to ___*sit tight*___ while she did some research.
1

A few hours later, the phone rang. "I've found something you just cannot _____,"
2

said Molly. "It's a seven-day cruise for a real bargain. They only have one place left. If you

want it, you must _____." It took a few moments for her words to _____.
3   4

"Yes, of course I want to go!" I replied. "Great. The cruise leaves in two weeks," she said.

"That's just enough time for me to _____ my project at work. Then I can use my
5

trip to _____ from my busy life and relax." I was feeling relaxed already.
6

B Write C if the phrasal verb in the sentence is correct. Write I if it is incorrect.

1. _____ Professor O'Neill asked me why I didn't sign up for her philosophy class.

2. _____ Masha couldn't pass up the new clothing store without going in and browsing.

3. _____ "Let's wrap up this meeting and go home," said Mr. Fox.

4. _____ She studied the math formulas for two hours before they finally sank in.

5. _____ My acting coach told me to wind down my performance and give it more energy.

6. _____ Our flight attendant told us to sit tight and enjoy the film.

Form/Function

James Dean said, "**Dream as if you'll live forever. Live as if you'll die today.**" He died at the age of 24 when his car crashed.

We use quoted speech to show the exact words someone uses. We use quoted speech in novels, stories, and newspaper articles. In these examples, notice where the *said* phrase is. Notice that it can go before or after its subject.

Story about James Dean: "Dream as if you'll live forever.
Live as if you'll die today," **James Dean said**.
OR **James Dean said**, "Dream as if you'll live forever.
Live as if you'll die today."

Newspaper article: "I will not vote for this law," **said Senator Smith**.

THE TRAVELERS AND THE PURSE

Two men were traveling together along a road when one of them picked up a purse.

"How lucky I am," he said, "I've found a purse. Judging by its weight it must be full of gold."

Don't say *I* have found a purse said his companion. Instead, say *we* have found a purse and how lucky *we* are. Travelers should share the fortunes and misfortunes of the road.

No, no replied the other angrily. *I* found it and *I* am going to keep it

Just then they heard a shout of "Stop! Thief!" and when they looked around, they saw a mob of people with clubs coming down the road.

The man who had found the purse began to panic.

We'll be in trouble if they find the purse on us he said

No, no replied the other you wouldn't say *we* before, so now stick to your *I*. Say *I* am in trouble

Example

My teacher said, "Please do the exercises on quoted speech by tomorrow."

11E   Reported Speech: Statements

Form

Benjamin Franklin said **that nothing was certain except death and taxes**.

1. *Say* and *tell* are examples of reporting verbs. If a reporting verb is in the present, there is no change in form in reported speech. We can omit *that* with no change in meaning.

   QUOTED SPEECH: Mary **says**, "I **am** happy."

   REPORTED SPEECH: Mary **says** (that) she **is** happy.

   Say and *tell* are sometimes confused. Remember we use *say* with or without a prepositional phrase with *to*.

   CORRECT: Mary said that she is happy. OR Mary said to me that she is happy.

   INCORRECT: Mary ~~said me~~ that she is happy.

   We always use *tell* with an object. We do not use a prepositional phrase with *to* after *tell*.

   CORRECT: Mary told me she is happy.

   INCORRECT: Mary told ~~that~~ she is happy. OR Mary told ~~to~~ me that she is happy.

2. If the reporting verb is in the past (*said, told*), the verb form changes when we report it. Here are some common verb form changes.

Quoted Speech	Reported Speech
Mary said, "I **do** all the work."	Mary said that she **did** all the work.
Mary said, "I**'m doing** all the work."	Mary said that she **was doing** all the work.
Mary said, "I **did** all the work."	Mary said that she **had done** all the work.
Mary said, "I**'ve done** all the work."	Mary said that she **had done** all the work.
Mary said, "I**'ve been doing** all the work."	Mary said that she **had been doing** all the work.
Mary said, "I**'ll do** all the work."	Mary said that she **would do** all the work.
Mary said, "I **can do** all the work."	Mary said that she **could do** all the work.

3. Pronouns can change in reported speech. The change depends on the meaning. Here are some common examples.

	Quoted	Reported	Quoted Example	Reported Example
Subject Pronouns	I	he, she	Sam said, "**I**'m leaving."	Sam said that **he** was leaving. (Sam was leaving.)
	you (singular)	I	Sam said, "**You**'re leaving."	Sam said that **I** was leaving. (The speaker is leaving.)
		he, she	Sam said, "**You**'re leaving."	Sam said that **he** was leaving. (Sam was talking to a boy or a man.)
	we	they	Sam said, "**We**'re tired."	Sam said that **they** were tired. (*They* include Sam and other people.)
	you (plural)	we	Sam said, "**You**'re tired."	Sam said that **we** were tired. (*We* include the speaker and other people but not Sam.)
		they	Sam said, "**You**'re tired."	Sam said that **they** were tired. (*They* include a group of other people but not Sam or the speaker.)
Object Pronouns	me	him, her	Sam said, "It's for **me**."	Sam said that it was for **him**. (It was for Sam.)
	you (singular)	me	Sam said, "It's for **you**."	Sam said it was for **me**. (It was for the speaker.)
		him, her	Sam said, "It's for **you**."	Sam said it was for him/her. (Sam was talking to a man/woman.)

		Quoted	Reported	Quoted Example	Reported Example
Object Pronouns	us	us		Sam said, "It's for **us**."	Sam said that it was for **us**. (*Us* includes the speaker.)
			them	Sam said, "It's for **us**."	Sam said it was for **them**. (*Us* includes Sam but not the speaker.)
	you (plural)	us		Sam said, "It's for **you**."	Sam said that it was for **us**. (*Us* includes the speaker and other people but not Sam.)
			them	Sam said, "It's for **you**."	Sam said it was for **them**. (*Them* includes other people but not Sam or the speaker.)
Possessive Forms	my	his, her		Sam said, "**My** son is sleepy."	Sam said that **his** son was sleepy. (The son is Sam's.)
	your (singular)	my		Sam said, "**Your** son is sleepy."	Sam said that **my** son was sleepy. (The son is the speaker's.)
		his, her		Sam said, "**Your** son is sleepy."	Sam said that **her** son was sleepy. (The son belongs to a woman, not Sam or the speaker.)
	our	their		Sam said, "**We** have a gift for **our** neighbors."	Sam said that **they** had a gift for **their** neighbors. (The neighbors are not the speaker's.)
	your (plural)	our		Sam said, "**Your** garden is beautiful."	Sam said that **our** garden was beautiful. (The garden belongs to the speaker and other people.)
		their		Sam said, "**Your** garden is beautiful."	Sam said that **their** garden was beautiful. (The garden belongs to other people but not to Sam or the speaker.)

4. Time expressions can also change in reported speech. Again, it depends on the meaning. Here are some common changes.

Quoted	Reported
now	then
today	that day
tonight	that night
yesterday	the day before
tomorrow	the next day
this week/month/year	that week/month/year
last week/month/year	the week/month/year before
next week/month/year	the week/month/year after
two weeks/months/years ago	two weeks/months/years before

QUOTED SPEECH: She said, "I'm going on vacation **today**."
REPORTED SPEECH: She said that she was going on vacation **that day**.

QUOTED SPEECH: Tom explained, "I finished all of the work **yesterday**."
REPORTED SPEECH: Tom explained that he had finished all of the work **the day before**.

5. Here are two additional common changes:

Quoted	Reported
here	there
come	go

QUOTED SPEECH: They said, "We'll be **here** when you arrive."
REPORTED SPEECH: They said that they would be **there** when we arrived.

QUOTED SPEECH: My mother said, "I hope you can **come** over for dinner."
REPORTED SPEECH: My mother said that she hoped I could **go** over for dinner.

---

13 Practice

It's a very busy time at the office, so the manager asked the staff to work on Saturday morning. Report the answers the staff gave him.

1. Susan said, "I can't work on Saturday because I am having my car fixed and won't be able to get here."
Susan said she couldn't work on Saturday because she was having her car fixed and she wouldn't be able to get there.

2. Mary Ann said, "I have made other arrangements, and I can't change them now."

_____

3. Ted explained, "I'll be out of town. I'm taking my children to see their grandparents."

_____

4. Stanley complained, "I'm too tired. I need Saturday and Sunday to relax."

_____

5. Steve insisted, "I'll work on Saturday morning, but only if I get paid double."

_____

6. Kate wondered, "Why do I have to come in if the others aren't?"

_____

_____

14 Practice

Your friend asked you to listen to her phone messages. Write the messages using reported speech. Listen more than once if necessary.

Message 1

Cindy called from the dentist's office. She was calling to remind you that you have a dental appointment tomorrow at 10:00.

Message 2

_____

_____

Message 3

_____

_____

Message 4

_____

_____

Message 5

_____

_____

Message 6

_____

_____

11F Reported Speech: Questions

Form/Function

Dr. Marshall asked me **how I felt**. I told her **I felt very tired**. She wanted to know **if I was under a lot** of stress.

1. Like indirect questions, questions in reported speech use statement word order.

DIRECT QUESTION:	Will it rain this afternoon?
INDIRECT QUESTION:	I want to know if it will rain this afternoon.
REPORTED QUESTION:	She asked me if it would rain this afternoon.
DIRECT QUESTION:	Where is my CD player?
INDIRECT QUESTION:	She wonders where her CD player is.
REPORTED QUESTION:	She asked me where her CD player was.

2. Reported questions use a reporting verb such as *ask*. They report someone else's words.

3. Reported questions use the same form, pronoun, and time expression changes as reported statements (see pages 339-342).

4. After *ask*, we can use an object (*me, Nancy*) to say who asked the question.

I **asked Nancy** if she was busy. (In formal English, *was* would be *were*.)

He **asked me** where I had gone.

He **asked me** to leave early.

5. After the verb *tell* we must use an object.

CORRECT:	He told me what he wanted.
INCORRECT:	He ~~told what~~ he wanted.

15   Practice

Sue lived in Los Angeles for a few years, and now she is back in her home town. She meets an old friend, Jeff. Rewrite Sue's questions as reported.

1. JEFF: How are you?

    He asked her how she was.

2. JEFF: When did you get back?

    _____

3. JEFF: Did you like Los Angeles?

    _____

4. JEFF: Why didn't you stay there longer?

    _____

5. JEFF: Are you living in your old neighborhood?

    _____

6. JEFF: Are you still living alone?

    _____

7. JEFF: What are you doing for a living now?

    _____

8. JEFF: Would you like to play tennis with me again, like old times?

    _____

16   Pair Up and Talk

A   Practice the conversation with a partner.

A: What subject do you want to study in college?

B: I want to study chemistry.

B   Think of four questions to ask your partner about his or her future. Your partner will answer. Then tell the class what you asked and how your partner answered.

Example

I asked my partner what subject she wanted to study in college. She told me that she wanted to study chemistry.

Form/Function

I was driving too fast in my neighborhood. The police officer **warned me not to do it** again.

VERB + OBJECT + (*NOT*) + INFINITIVE

	Quoted Speech	Reported Speech			
		Subject	**Verb**	**(Object)**	**(*Not* +) Infinitive**
Commands	"Wait."	They	**told**	**me**	**to wait**.
	"Don't get lost."	She	**told**	**us**	**not to get** lost.
Requests	"Talk quietly, please."	We	**asked**	**them**	**to (please) talk** quietly.
	"Could you not drive so fast?"	I	**asked**	**him**	**not to drive** so fast.
Advice	"You should call her."	He	**advised**	**me**	**to call** her.
	"We shouldn't eat so much."	She	**advised**	**us**	**not to eat** so much.
Invitations	"Would you like to have lunch with us?"	They	**asked**	**me**	**to have** lunch with them.
Warnings	"You'd better not be late."	She	**warned**	**them**	**not to be** late.
	"We'd better be careful."	He	**warned**	**us**	**to be** careful.

VERB + (NOT) + INFINITIVE

	Quoted Speech	Reported Speech		
		Subject	**Verb**	**(Not +) Infinitive**
Threats	"I won't give you the money."	She	**threatened**	**not to give** me the money.
Promises	"I'll take you to the movies tomorrow."	I	**promised**	**to take** her to the movies the next day.
Offers	"Can I help you?"	He	**offered**	**to help** me.

Notice that the verbs *tell, ask, advise,* and *warn* are followed by an object + (*not*) + an infinitive. *Tell, advise,* and *warn* must be followed by an object.

CORRECT: They told us to come early.

INCORRECT: They told to come early.

We can use *ask* with or without an object.

WITH OBJECT: George asked Alex to play the guitar. (George wants Alex to play the guitar.)

WITHOUT OBJECT: George asked to play the guitar. (George asked permission to play the guitar.)

17   Practice

Listen to a teacher giving some instructions before a test. Rewrite each statement using the reporting verbs in parentheses.

AUDIO

DOWNLOAD

CD2, 28

1. (tell) *He told us to listen carefully.* _____

2. (tell) _____

3. (ask) _____

4. (ask) _____

5. (warn) _____

6. (threaten) _____

7. (advise) _____

8. (promise) _____

9. (invite) _____

10. (offer) _____

18 Pair Up and Talk

A Practice the conversation with a partner.

A: My sister promised to send me a present for my birthday.

B: That's nice. My sister offered to send me one, but I told her not to. I know she doesn't have much money this year.

B Make sentences using the cues below. Your partner will respond to the sentence with his or her own ideas.

father/advise   friend/invite   student/ask   teacher/offer

11H The Subjunctive in Noun Clauses

Form/Function

The judge **demanded** that the courtroom **be** quiet. Then he **insisted** that it **stay** quiet for the rest of the day.

1. The subjunctive form is the base form of the verb. It has no present, past, or future form. It has no singular or plural. We put *not* before the base verb to form the negative.
2. We use the subjunctive form in *that* clauses following certain verbs of command, urgency, or request. Here are some verbs that are followed by the subjunctive in noun clauses.

advise	desire	request
ask	insist	require
command	propose	suggest
demand	recommend	urge

Our teacher **insists** that we **be** on time.

The officer **asked** that he **show** his passport.

They **recommended** that he **not try** to fix the computer himself.

3. We can also use *should* after the verbs *suggest* and *recommend*.

I **suggested** that she **should take** the test soon.

4. We also use the subjunctive form in *that* clauses following adjectives of urgency. These statements are similar to commands, but they are impersonal and therefore softer.

It's **vital** that you **make** a decision right now.   (impersonal and softer)

Make a decision right now! I insist that you make a decision right now.   (strong)

Here are some adjectives of urgency.

advisable	critical	essential	important	urgent
best	desirable	imperative	necessary	vital

19   Practice

Rewrite the sentences using the subjunctive. Listen and check your answers.

CD2, 29

A 17-year-old boy was arrested for stealing CDs from a music store. He was sent to a youth correctional facility for a month. What were the opinions of the people involved in the case?

1.   The judge: Go to jail for two months.

The judge recommended *that he go to jail for two months*.

2.   The parents: He must get another trial.

The parents demanded _____

3.   The lawyer: Why doesn't he do community service?

The lawyer suggested _____

4.   The police officer: He must repay the money to the store owner.

The police officer insisted _____

5.   The store owner: Could he please return the CDs?

The store owner requested _____

create	improve	reduce	stop
develop	protect	restrict	try

1. Many wildlife species are endangered.

    It is urgent _____

2. We are running out of fossil fuel.

    It is imperative _____

3. Our cities are overcrowded.

    It is desirable _____

4. There are too many cars.

    It is essential _____

5. Our climate is heating up too rapidly.

    It is critical _____

6. We produce too much plastic waste.

    It is advisable _____

7. Too many people are dying from hunger.

    It is vital _____

8. There are too many wars.

    It is critical _____

21 Your Turn
In groups, choose one of the following cases. Imagine the opinions or reactions of different people involved in the case. Write four sentences on a separate sheet of paper about the case using *recommend, insist, suggest,* and *demand.*

Cases

1. A 15-year-old boy was traveling on a train alone. He didn't have a ticket. (People involved: boy, train conductor, other passengers)

2. A friend of yours spent over 3,000 dollars on a credit card to buy luxury clothes and jewelry. (People involved: friends, you, spouse/partner of the friend)

3. A man pretended that his car had been stolen so that he could claim insurance. Actually, the car had broken down, and he couldn't afford to repair it. (People involved: man, insurance company representative, man's wife)

Example

(Situation 1): *The train conductor insisted that the boy get off at the next station.*

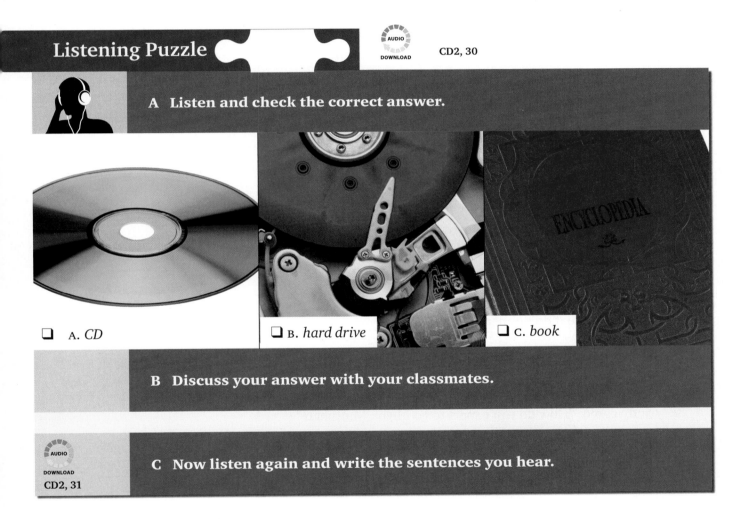

Listening Puzzle

AUDIO DOWNLOAD   CD2, 30

A Listen and check the correct answer.

❑ A. *CD*   ❑ B. *hard drive*   ❑ C. *book*

B Discuss your answer with your classmates.

AUDIO DOWNLOAD
CD2, 31

C Now listen again and write the sentences you hear.

1 Review (11a–11c, 11e–11g)
Rewrite the quotes as reported speech.

1. Cindy said, "Matthew, get out of bed, or you'll be late for your interview."

   Cindy told *Matthew to get out of bed or he'd be late for his interview.*

2. Matthew said, "Why didn't you get me up earlier?"

   Matthew wanted to know _____

3. Cindy said, "I went to the gym."

   Cindy said that _____

4. Matthew said, "Did I set my alarm clock or not?"

   Matthew couldn't remember _____

5. Cindy suggested, "Matthew, you'd better hurry if you want to get that job."

   Cindy suggested that _____

6. The interviewer had said, "Be here on time."

   The interviewer had insisted _____

7. Cindy said, "Why did you sleep so late?"

   Cindy said she didn't understand _____

8. Matthew explained, "I was preparing for the interview until 2:00 A.M."

   Matthew explained that _____

9. Cindy asked, "How do you expect to get there, Matthew?"

   Cindy asked _____

10. Matthew asked, "Can you drive me there?"

    Matthew wondered if _____

11. Cindy asked, "How far is it to the office?"

    Cindy wanted to know _____

12. Matthew said, "It's about 20 miles (32 kilometers)."

    Matthew explained that _____

"I want more excitement," said one traveler.

I want different things to do said another.

When asked, many travelers have insisted that we don't want to do just one thing while we're on vacation. In response, many tour operators now offer combination packages, or "combos." David Rose of High Roads Traveled says We now offer combo packages that mix several activities in one outing. Mr. Rose recommends that a traveler takes a combo if he or she likes fun and adventure. People love these trips is very clear, he adds.

Combo packages mix hiking, biking, climbing, rafting, horseback riding, or other activities. Ron Clair of Ways Traveled says, "Combos are his most popular trips.

"Sunbathing at the beach all week is a thing of the past, says Margaret Erikson, author of *Your Adventure*. Can I tell you why are combos so popular? she asks. She continues today travelers demand tour operators that will give them a variety of adventures. Will this trend continue? I believe so. Sometimes I wonder the old car trip will eventually fade away.

Some people wonder if or not they must be a superior athlete to take a combo adventure. Top athletes do things on their own says Mary Miller of High Mountain Bike Tours. She adds that my company is oriented toward vacations for the average person. She does say that I talk to a client first and advises he or she prepare. She says, "It's important that you are doing some cycling or hiking before you go on any adventure vacation. But I urge that every client remembers that our tours are designed to be enjoyed at your own pace and in your own style.

Do you know where are you going on your next vacation? If you're into major thrills, a combo adventure just may be what are you looking for.

A Before You Read
1. Look up the words *millennium, century,* and *decade*. Did any of them start in the year 2000?
2. What would happen if most computers stopped working all at once?

THE Y2K PROBLEM

B Read As January 1, 2000 was approaching, computer users were nervous. Would the clocks inside computers switch to the New Year? Would the computers think it

5 was the year 0 instead of the year 2000? Many feared that banks would lose track of their money. Others wondered if the huge mass of data[1] in computers would be lost. Governments worried that entire electricity systems or water

10 systems might crash. Together, these date-change problems were called "Y2K."

The basic problem with Y2K is commonly misunderstood. Many

15 people believe that it involved the "2" at the beginning of "2000." Actually, it centered on the last two digits in the

20 name of the year. Each New Year's Day, computer software changed the year upward. The software knew that '97 became '98 and '98 became '99. What would happen when '99 turned into '00? Some earlier programs

25 used two digits to save space. They expressed 1999 as "99." Few programmers thought **it** would be a problem.

Alan Greenspan, once the head of the U.S. Federal Reserve Bank, used to write programs.

30 He told the United States Senate, "**It never entered our minds** that those programs would have lasted for more than a few years."

Some experts foresaw[2] Y2K as early as the 1980s. They proposed that software companies

35 make "patches": small programs that could fix larger software programs. With patches, computer users could avoid replacing entire programs. ▪ Software companies began acting on this advice as the 1990s wore on. ▪ The

40 strategy probably worked. No large-scale computer problems occurred. ▪ To the average computer user, New Year's Day in 2000 was just a normal day. ▪

Some changes made for Y2K had

45 unexpected benefits. Companies in the United States ran short of programmers to make patches so they began hiring Indian programmers. This jump-started[3] partnerships between U.S. and Indian computer companies.

[1.] *data = information*

[2.] *foresaw = saw in advance* [3.] *jump-started = applied a lot of power to set (something) in motion*

C Notice the Grammar Underline all the noun clauses.

Choose the best answer.

D Look for Main Ideas

1. What is the main topic of paragraph 3?
   - (A) fixing the Y2K problem
   - (B) discovering the Y2K problem
   - (C) the causes of the Y2K problem
   - (D) the dangers posed by the Y2K problem

E Look for Details

2. Many people thought that on January 1, 2000, computers might _____ .
   - (A) state the year in four digits instead of two
   - (B) state the year in two digits instead of four
   - (C) be unable to determine what year it was
   - (D) break down due to electrical problems

3. The reading mentions all of the following as possible consequences of the Y2K problem EXCEPT _____ .
   - (A) confusion in banking
   - (B) utility failures
   - (C) the fall of governments
   - (D) the disappearance of information

4. Why does the author mention India in paragraph 5?
   - (A) to show the damage done by software that wasn't patched
   - (B) to describe how to patch software
   - (C) to explain why Y2K was not a problem in some places
   - (D) to illustrate a benefit of efforts to fix Y2K

Questions on drawing conclusions are similar to inference questions because the answer is inferred but not directly stated in the passage. To draw conclusions, look at the information and ask yourself what the logical answer would be.

F Draw Conclusions

5. We can conclude from paragraph 5 that _____ .
   - (A) experts ignored the Y2K problem
   - (B) Indian and American computer companies are still working together
   - (C) programmers in the 1960s were not smart
   - (D) experts expected Y2K to be easy

G Look for Vocabulary

6. The phrase *it never entered our minds* in the reading is closest in meaning to _____ .
   - (A) we didn't care
   - (C) we weren't sure
   - (B) we didn't think
   - (D) we didn't want

H Look for References

7. The word *it* in the reading refers to _____ .
   - (A) stating years in two digits
   - (B) expressing 1999 as "99"
   - (C) saving space
   - (D) the year

I Sentence Addition

8. Look at the four squares ∎ that indicate where the following sentence could be added to the passage. **By then, Internet access was common, and the patches could be distributed that way.**
   Where would the sentence best fit?
   - (A) at the first square
   - (C) at the third square
   - (B) at the second square
   - (D) at the fourth square

Writing: Write a Fable or a Legend

All cultures have stories. A story that teaches a lesson, or a moral, is called a fable. The moral is usually stated at the end of the fable. In many fables, animals speak and act as humans do. A legend is another kind of story usually about famous people or events, that is handed down from generation to generation. It may be based in historical reality.

STEP 1   Think of a legend or fable that you know. Tell it to your partner. Discuss its meaning to the culture it comes from.

STEP 2   Write the events in your legend or fable in order.

STEP 3   Write the legend or fable. Include quoted and reported speech from the characters. Write a title for your story. Here is an example of a fable.

The Fox and the Crow

One day, a fox was walking through the forest when he noticed a crow up in a tree. The crow had a piece of cheese in its beak, and the fox was hungry. "That cheese looks delicious," the fox said to himself. He wondered how he could get the cheese. He thought, and then he said, "Good morning, beautiful bird. You are indeed beautiful, and I am sure that you have a beautiful voice. Let me hear you sing." The crow ruffled his feathers and looked proud. Then he opened his beak to sing. Immediately the cheese fell out. The fox snatched it up and ran away.

STEP 4   Evaluate your fable or legend.
          Checklist
          _____   Did you tell the events in the order in which they occurred?
          _____   Did you use quoted and reported speech?
          _____   Did you write a title for the story?
          _____   If you wrote a fable, did you write a moral at the end?

STEP 5   Work with a partner or a teacher to edit your essay. Check spelling, vocabulary, and grammar.

STEP 6   Write your final copy.

A Choose the best answer, A, B, C, or D, to complete the sentence. Darken the oval with the same letter.

1. I wondered where _____ .

   A. he came from Ⓐ Ⓑ Ⓒ Ⓓ
   B. did he came from
   C. came he from
   D. he did come from

2. My mother said, "Don't come in with your dirty shoes."
   My mother warned me _____ in with my dirty shoes.

   A. to come Ⓐ Ⓑ Ⓒ Ⓓ
   B. not come
   C. not came
   D. not to come

3. I don't know _____ the right place.

   A. is this Ⓐ Ⓑ Ⓒ Ⓓ
   B. if is this
   C. if this is
   D. this is

4. ED: Is Jim in his office?
   KATHY: _____ .

   A I think Jim is Ⓐ Ⓑ Ⓒ Ⓓ
   B. I think
   C. I think so
   D. Yes, Jim is

5. "I'll see you soon," she said. She said _____ .

   A. she will see me soon Ⓐ Ⓑ Ⓒ Ⓓ
   B. she would see me soon
   C. I would see her soon
   D. she see me soon

6. "Don't drive too fast."
   He told _____ drive fast.

   A. not to Ⓐ Ⓑ Ⓒ Ⓓ
   B. to
   C. us not to
   D. to us not to

7. He asked, "Where do you want to go?"
   He asked where _____ .

   A. did I want to go Ⓐ Ⓑ Ⓒ Ⓓ
   B. I want to go
   C. I wanted to go
   D. do I want to go

8. It is urgent that she _____ a decision right now.

   A. makes Ⓐ Ⓑ Ⓒ Ⓓ
   B. is able to make
   C. make
   D. to make

9. Can you tell me what time _____ ?

   A. the train arrives Ⓐ Ⓑ Ⓒ Ⓓ
   B. does the train arrive
   C. the train does it arrive
   D. arrives the train

10. "Have you finished your exams?" he asked.
    "Yes," I answered.
    He asked _____ my exams.

    A. whether I have finished Ⓐ Ⓑ Ⓒ Ⓓ
    B. whether did I finish
    C. if I had finished
    D. if I have finished

1. The teacher <u>warned</u> <u>us</u> <u>that</u> <u>not</u> to cheat
           A   **B** **C** **D**
   during the test.

   Ⓐ Ⓑ Ⓒ Ⓓ

2. The interviewer <u>asked</u> <u>to me</u> when <u>I wanted</u>
               A   **B**   **C**
   to start <u>working</u>.
          D

   Ⓐ Ⓑ Ⓒ Ⓓ

3. <u>Can you tell me</u> where <u>can I</u> get information
      A   **B**
   about trains and <u>where</u> <u>I can</u> buy tickets?
                 C   **D**

   Ⓐ Ⓑ Ⓒ Ⓓ

4. Paul asked if <u>did</u> they <u>told</u> <u>me</u> when they
             A   **B** **C**
   <u>were leaving</u>.
    D

   Ⓐ Ⓑ Ⓒ Ⓓ

5. <u>Do you know</u> <u>if or not</u> we <u>need</u> <u>to get</u> a visa to
     A   **B**   **C**   **D**
   enter the country?

   Ⓐ Ⓑ Ⓒ Ⓓ

6. Ted <u>said that</u> he <u>hadn't</u> <u>fill out</u> the application
        A   **B**   **C**
   form <u>yet</u>.
       D

   Ⓐ Ⓑ Ⓒ Ⓓ

7. <u>It is</u> <u>imperative that</u> <u>I fail not</u> any of my courses
    A   **B**   **C**
   this year <u>if</u> I want to apply to a university.
          D

   Ⓐ Ⓑ Ⓒ Ⓓ

8. Tony called from Boston <u>yesterday</u> and <u>told me</u>
                     A   **B**
   that <u>it was</u> extremely cold <u>here</u>.
       C   **D**

   Ⓐ Ⓑ Ⓒ Ⓓ

9. I <u>don't know</u> what <u>did happen</u> to <u>him</u> after I
     A   **B**   **C**
   <u>left</u> school.
   D

   Ⓐ Ⓑ Ⓒ Ⓓ

10. He <u>invited</u> <u>us</u> to <u>going</u> to the theater
        A   **B**   **C**
    next <u>Sunday</u>.
        D

    Ⓐ Ⓑ Ⓒ Ⓓ

Unit 12

Adjective Clauses

Where are the oranges **that you bought at the store?**

12A Adjective Clauses with Subject Relative Pronouns

Form/Function

A police officer is a person **who doesn't usually smile on the job**.

1. An adjective clause, like an adjective, describes or gives more information about a noun.
   We have **noisy** neighbors. (The adjective *noisy* describes the noun *neighbors*.)
   I have neighbors **that are very noisy**. (The adjective clause *that are very noisy* describes the noun *neighbors*.)

2. We introduce an adjective clause with the relative pronouns *who, whom, that,* or *which*. The relative pronoun refers to a noun in the main clause.

   I have a friend **who** lives in Mexico City.

3. When the relative pronoun comes before the verb in the adjective clause, the relative pronoun is the subject of the clause. It is a subject relative pronoun.

Main Clause	Adjective Clause	
	Subject Relative Pronoun	
I have a friend	**who**	lives in Mexico City.
I have neighbors	**that**	are very noisy.
I live in a building	**that/which**	has very thin walls.

4. We use *who* or *that* to refer to people.

5. We use *which* or *that* to refer to things. In careful writing, some people prefer *that*, not *which*, to refer to things.

   See pages 371–372 for information on when we must use *who* or *which*, not *that*.

6. A subject relative pronoun always has the same form. It does not change for singular, plural, feminine, or masculine words.

   That's the **man who** works in my office.

   That's the **woman who** works in my office.

   Those are the **people who** work in my office.

7. The verb in an adjective clause is singular if the subject relative pronoun refers to a singular noun. The verb is plural if it refers to a plural noun.

   Ken is a man **who works** in my office. (*Man* is third person singular, so the verb is also third person singular.)

   Tony and Fred are men **who work** in another department. (The noun *men* is plural, so the verb is plural.)

1 Practice

Read the paragraphs about inventors and their inventions. Then answer the questions using adjective clauses with subject relative pronouns. Then practice the conversation with a partner.

1. Mary Anderson invented the windshield wiper in 1903. She wanted to make streetcars safer in the rain. Her invention allowed the driver to control the wipers from inside the streetcar.

   a. Who was Mary Anderson?

   She was the person *who invented the windshield wiper*.

   _____

   b. What was the purpose of her invention?

   She wanted to invent something _____

   _____

2. Contact lenses were first made in 1887 by the German doctor Adolf Fick. His first lenses were for animals and were made from heavy brown glass. In 1889, August Muller made lenses to help people see things at a distance.

a. Who was Adolf Fick?

He was a German doctor _____

_____

b. What kind of lenses did August Muller make for people?

August Muller made lenses _____

_____

3. Levi Strauss and Jacob Davis were tailors. Many people went to California to look for gold in the 1890s. Strauss and Davis sold tents to them. Soon they developed the idea of making workpants from the tent material, and blue jeans were invented. The idea is still popular today.

a. Who were Strauss and Davis?

Strauss and Davis were tailors _____

_____

b. What kind of people bought the tents?

People _____

_____

bought the tents.

c. What kind of pants did they sell?

They sold pants _____

_____

2 Pair Up and Talk
A Practice the conversation with a partner.

A: I'm thinking of a black and white bird that can swim but can't fly.

B: Is it a penguin?

A: Yes, it is.

B Think of an interesting object, person, or animal. Describe it in a one-sentence definition using a relative clause. Ask your partner to guess what you are describing. If your partner can't guess, give more information with relative clauses.

Form/Function

These are oranges **that I picked** myself.

1. When the relative pronouns *who (whom), that,* or *which* come before a noun or pronoun, the relative pronoun takes the place of the object. It is an object relative pronoun.
2. When the relative pronoun comes before a noun or a pronoun, the relative pronoun is the object of the adjective clause.

Main Clause	Adjective Clause
Claudia is the woman	**that/who/whom we met yesterday.**
Where is the book	**that Tom put on the table?**

3. We use *that, who,* or *whom* to refer to people. We rarely use *whom* except in formal English.
4. We use *that* or *which* for things. See pages 371–372 for information on when to use *who* or *which*, not *that.*
5. The relative pronoun can be the object of a preposition. In conversational English, we usually put the preposition at the end of a clause and omit the relative pronoun. However, in formal English, we put the preposition at the beginning of the clause. When this is the case, we use *whom* and *which.* We do not use *who* or *that.*

	Main Clause	Adjective Clause
Informal	Where's the person	**who/that** I should speak **to?**
	That's the company	**that/which** we signed the agreement **with.**
Formal	Where is the person	**to whom** I should speak?
	That is the company	**with which** we signed the agreement.

6. We often omit object relative pronouns, especially when we speak.

On the street today, I ran into a man (**who/whom**) I knew a long time ago.

There's the set of keys (**that**) I lost yesterday!

Where's the person (**that**) I should speak to?

But we do not omit subject relative pronouns.

CORRECT: I have a friend **who** lives in Mexico City.

INCORRECT: I have a friend lives in Mexico City.

3 Practice
A Match the words with the correct definitions.

_h_ 1. We use this machine to keep food cold.	**a.** telescope
_____ 2. We eat this sauce with hamburgers and French fries.	**b.** dictionary
_____ 3. We speak on this machine over long distances.	**c.** telephone
_____ 4. We ask this person for help when we see a fire.	**d.** firefighter
_____ 5. We go to this place when we need to borrow a book.	**e.** ketchup
_____ 6. We ask this person for help when we are sick.	**f.** library
_____ 7. We look in this book to learn the meaning of a word.	**g.** doctor
_____ 8. We use this to see objects far away.	**h.** refrigerator

B Write a sentence using an adjective clause with an object relative pronoun for each item in part A on a separate sheet of paper.

Example

A refrigerator is a machine that we use to keep food cold.

4 Pair Up and Talk
A Practice the conversation with a partner.

A: What is a book that you especially like?

B: Well, *A China Journey* is a book that I always enjoy looking at. It has beautiful photos.

B Take turns asking and answering questions with *what* or *who* and the following prompts. Use adjective clauses with object relative pronouns.

a food you always think about
a job around your home that you hate doing

a person you look up to
a show on TV you always like to watch

5 Phrasal Verb Practice

A Complete the sentences with the correct form of the phrasal verbs. Use each verb only once.

break apart   bring in   come across   crush up   talk over   turn into

People in ancient Egypt used glass. For years, scientists _talked over_ the origin of
                                                        1
glass material. Most experts thought that the Egyptians had _____ the glass
                                                                     2
from Mesopotamia. Recently, researchers _____ evidence that the Egyptians
                                              3
made their own glass.

They think that the Egyptians made the glass by first _____ quartz pebbles
                                                            4
and plant ash, then heating this mixture at low temperatures in small clay jars until it

_____ a glass mass. Then they ground the mixture into a powder, colored it, and
        5
poured it into containers which they heated to high temperatures. After cooling, they

_____ the containers and removed solid discs of glass. Glassmakers heated the
        6
glass and shaped it into beautiful objects.

B Circle the correct definition of the phrasal verb.

1. crush up	**2.** bring in	**3.** come across
a. press with force	**a.** cause to happen	**a.** do what is needed
b. destroy	**b.** return to original form	**b.** meet or discover
c. fill a container	**c.** carry to a place	**c.** advance or improve

4. break apart	**5.** turn into	**6.** talk over
a. separate into smaller pieces	**a.** go in a different direction	**a.** discuss
b. force a way through	**b.** travel in a circle	**b.** take no notice of
c. remove a section	**c.** change from one thing to another	**c.** give great importance to

12c Adjective Clauses with *Whose*

Form/Function

Flamingoes are birds **whose feathers are pink** because of the food they eat.

1. We use the relative pronoun *whose* to show possession. We always use a noun after *whose*. We cannot omit *whose*.

   The English teacher **whose** course I'm taking is walking in front of us.

2. The noun after *whose* is the thing that the person or thing in the main clause possesses.

   That's the student **whose application** we just read.

3. Adjective clauses with *whose* usually show possession for people or animals, but sometimes they refer to things.

   I want to go to the university **whose engineering department** is the best.

4. Do not confuse *whose* with *who's*.

	Meaning	Example
Who's	who is	I know a man **who's** from Egypt.
Whose	shows possession	I know a man **whose** family is in Egypt.

Combine the sentences about famous Americans using *whose* in an adjective clause. Then listen and check your answers.

AUDIO
DOWNLOAD

CD3, 2

1. Martin Luther King, Jr., was a civil rights leader. His most famous speech contains the words "I have a dream."

   Martin Luther King, Jr., was a civil rights leader whose most famous speech contains the words "I have a dream."

2. Abraham Lincoln was a president of the United States. His most famous achievement was freeing African-Americans from slavery.

   _____

   _____

3. Benjamin Franklin was an American statesman and inventor. His most famous invention was the lightning rod.

   _____

   _____

4. Wilbur and Orville Wright were brothers. Their aircraft was the first wooden, piloted, heavier-than-air, self propelled machine to fly.

   _____

   _____

5. Dorothea Lange was a photographer. Her photos made people realize the poverty of workers during the Great Depression.

   _____

   _____

6. Alice Walker is an African-American writer. Her novel *The Color Purple* received the Pulitzer Prize in 1983.

   _____

   _____

7. Elizabeth Cady Stanton was a leader of the American women's rights movement. Her lifetime of work helped women gain the right to vote in the United States.

   _____

   _____

7 Pair Up and Talk

A Practice the conversation with a partner.

A: Who is a famous person that you know a lot about?

B: I'm a big fan of Selena. She was a Mexican-American singer whose music won a Grammy Award.

A: What do you admire about her?

B: She was someone whose songs inspired a lot of people.

B Think of three other famous people that you know about and admire. (They can be living or dead). Tell your partner about them and their biggest achievement. Ask and answer questions to get more information.

12D | *When, Where, Why,* and *That* as Relative Pronouns

Form/Function

The Netherlands is a place **where people wear clogs**.

1. We can use *when* and *where* to introduce an adjective clause.

Relative Pronoun	Function	Example
Where	refers to a place	That's the building **where** he works.
When	refers to a time	I remember the day **when** I met you.

Notice that the relative pronouns *where* and *when* can be replaced with *that* or *which* + a preposition.

That's the building **where** he works. =

That's the building (**that**) he works **in**. (OR **in which he works**.)

I remember the day **when** I met you. =

I remember the day (**that**) I met you **on**. (OR **on which I met you**.)

2. When we use *where* or *when*, we do not use a preposition in the adjective clause.

CORRECT: That's the building where he works. (no preposition)

INCORRECT: That's the building where he works ~~in~~.

3. After the word *reason*, we can use *why* or *that* in an adjective clause.

Is there a reason **why/that** you want to go to that university?

4. We can omit *when*, *why*, and *that* without changing the meaning.

I remember the day I first met you.

Is there a reason you want to go to that university?

We can also omit *where* if we use a preposition.

That's the building he works in.

8 Practice

Complete the sentences with the correct relative pronouns *that, who, where, when,* or *why*.

A

In 1666, there was a terrible plague in London. Isaac Newton went to stay in the country ____*where*____ his mother had a farm. While he was sitting under an apple tree
          1

one day, an apple fell on his head. Suddenly, Newton realized the reason _____
                                                                         2

objects on Earth fall downwards. It is because they are pulled toward Earth's center by

the force of gravity. Newton proposed that gravity was a universal force

_____ holds planets in their orbits. His universal law led to a principle
       3

_____ we now take for granted; the same physical laws are true anywhere in the
       4

universe. The day _____ an apple fell on Newton's head changed our view of the
                     5

world and the universe.

B

Louis Braille was the man _____ invented books for the blind. Louis became
        1

blind at the age of four. It was a time _____ there were very few schools for
        2

the blind. Blind people were not sent to school, but learned skills like weaving and

woodwork so they could earn a living. Louis was sent to a school in Paris _____
        3

there were very few books. The books were written with raised letters _____
        4

made them heavy and difficult to read. Louis invented a code of raised dots

_____ he arranged to represent each letter of the alphabet. The first Braille book
    5

was published in 1827.

9 Pair Up and Talk
A Practice the conversation with a partner.

A: What is a place where you feel peaceful?

B: A place where I feel peaceful is in my kitchen. It's also nice when my family helps me cook.

**B Use the prompts to ask questions and describe your feelings. Try to use at least
two relative pronouns (*when, where, why, or that*) in your response.**

a place where you feel peaceful
a reason why you feel anxious
a time when you feel happiest

12E Defining and Nondefining Adjective Clauses

Form/Function

> My grandmother, **who is 70**, has just started to drive. She likes driving on the highway, **which is always quite busy**.

1. There are two kinds of adjective clauses: defining clauses and nondefining clauses.* All of the types of adjective clauses in sections 12a to 12d in this unit have been defining adjective clauses.

2. We use a defining adjective clause to identify nouns. They tell us which person, thing, etc. the speaker means.

    I know the woman **who works at the registration office**.

    (The clause *who works at the registration office* tells us which woman.)

3. We use a nondefining adjective clause (sometimes known as an *appositive*, introduced on page 377) to add extra information about the noun it refers to. We can omit this information because it is not necessary to identify the noun. We begin a nondefining clause with the relative pronouns *who(m)*, *which*, or *whose*. The relative clause follows the noun in the main clause that it refers to.

    My grandmother, **who is 70**, has just passed her driving test.

    The adjective clause *who is 70* adds extra information about *my grandmother*. We already know which grandmother the speaker means without this information.

4. We use commas before and after a nondefining clause. If a nondefining clause ends a sentence, we do not use a comma after it. We use a period.

    My apartment, **which is in the center of town**, is very small.

    Jane Kendall, **who is one of my best friends**, has decided to live in New York.

    I'm very excited about my vacation, **which begins tomorrow**.

    In speech, we pause before and after a nondefining clause.

    My apartment [pause], **which is in the center of the town**, [pause] is very small.

---

*These clauses are also called restrictive and nonrestrictive clauses.

5. We use *who, whom, which,* and *whose* as relative pronouns in nondefining clauses. We do not use the relative pronoun *that* in a nondefining clause. We also do not omit the relative pronouns in a nondefining clause.

    CORRECT: He gave me the documents, which I put in my briefcase.

    INCORRECT: He gave me the documents, ~~that~~ I put in my briefcase.

    INCORRECT: He gave me the documents, I put in my briefcase.

6. As with defining adjective clauses, we use some forms of nondefining adjective clauses only in formal English.

Whom as Object

    FORMAL: The college president, **whom** I met last night, will attend our meeting.

    INFORMAL: The college president, **who** I met last night, will attend our meeting.

Preposition + Which or Whom

    FORMAL: My senator, **from whom** I expected support, has agreed to meet with me.

    INFORMAL: My senator, **who** I expected support **from**, has agreed to meet with me.

    FORMAL: This meeting, **for which** I will travel to Washington, will be next week.

    INFORMAL: This meeting, **which** I will travel to Washington **for**, will be next week.

7. We sometimes use expressions of quantity with *of* in an adjective clause. Examples are *some of, many of, much of, none of, all of, both of, each of, several of, a number of, a little of,* and *a few of*. These are more common in written English than in speech. Note the structure and the use of commas.

    A number of my friends, **some of whom you know**, will be coming tomorrow.

    She gave me a lot of advice, **most of which was not very useful**.

---

10   Practice

Underline the adjective clauses in this reading about fables. Mark defining adjective clauses as *D* and nondefining as *ND*. Add commas as necessary.

                   D

Fables are stories <u>that have animals in them</u>, but the animals behave as people do. The

                 ND

truth is that fables, <u>which seem to be about animals</u>, are really about people. The animal

characters do all the things that people do that can get us into trouble. At the end of the fable

there is a moral which is the lesson people should learn.

We have all heard of Aesop whose fables are world famous. However, we are not sure if

he was the person who wrote them. They say that Aesop who lived a long time ago in Greece was an African slave. Aesop's stories of which he wrote about 350 are short and entertaining.

These fables which give us lessons about life have been popular through the ages.

11 Practice

A worker is talking about a coworker. Complete the sentences with the words in parentheses and *of which* or *of whom*. Listen and check your answers.

CD3, 3

A: Let's go to lunch with Barbara.

B: Not with Barbara. I don't really like her.

A: Why not?

B: Well, she always tries to give advice, (most)_____*most of which*_____ is useless.
　　　　　　　　　　　　　　　　　　　　　　　　　　　1

A: That's not so bad.

B: And she talks about all the designer clothes she has, (none) _____
　　　　　　　　　　　　　　　　　　　　　　　　　　　　　　　　　　　　　2

we ever see on her. She tells everyone about how much money she spends on

things, (all) _____ can't be true because we all know how much
　　　　　　　　3

she makes.

A: I see.

B: She talks about her two "beautiful" children, (both) _____ look like
　　　　　　　　　　　　　　　　　　　　　　　　　　　　　4

her, and she is definitely not a beauty.

A: Uh-huh.

B: She always talks about choosing a medical school for her son and daughter,

(neither) _____ is doing very well in high school.
　　　　　　　　　　　　　　　5

She also talks about her wonderful husband and how good he is to her,

(a little) _____ must be true, because he has put up
　　　　　　　　　　　　　　6

with her for so long!

A: Uh-huh. Oh! Hi, Barbara. Would you like to go to lunch … with me?

Example

My teacher, whose name is Ms. Altchek, is a wonderful person.
The students in my class, most of whom are my age, find English difficult.
The biggest problem that most of us have in English grammar is articles.

12F   Using *Which* to Refer to an Entire Clause

Form/Function

Sarah is finished with her classes,
which makes her happy.

1. We can use a nondefining clause with *which* to refer to a whole clause. Look at
   these sentences.

   Example A: We had to wait for over an hour. **It** made us feel hungry and irritable.
   Example B: We had to wait for over an hour, **which** made us feel hungry and irritable.
   Example C: He gave me the money. **This** was very kind of him.
   Example D: He gave me the money, **which** was very kind of him.

   In examples A and C, the pronouns *it* and *this* refer to the entire sentence that comes before. We
   can use *which* in the same way, and it can refer to the whole main clause, as in examples B and D.
2. We usually use this form in spoken English and not often in formal writing.

13   Practice

A   Match each sentence on the left with the correct follow-up sentence on the right.

_____c_____ **1.** The teacher encouraged me.

_____ **2.** The teacher corrected my paper in red ink.

_____ **3.** She let us use the Internet to do our research.

_____ **4.** We didn't have tests every week in class.

_____ **5.** We wrote about the news of the day.

_____ **6.** We worked with other students in class.

_____ **7.** The teacher always paid a lot of attention to us.

_____ **8.** We lost points when we handed in homework late.

a. That was easier than finding books from the library.

b. This made us feel less pressure.

c. This motivated me to work harder.

d. That made us feel like she cared about us.

e. That helped me make new friends.

f. It made me read newspapers and listen to the news.

g. It meant I had to do my homework on time.

h. That helped me find my mistakes.

B   Now combine the pairs of ideas into one sentence with *which*. Listen to check your answers. Then take turns reading the sentences with a partner. Remember to pause before *which*.

AUDIO
DOWNLOAD
CD3, 4

1. *The teacher encouraged me, which motivated me to work harder.*

2. _____

3. _____

4. _____

5. _____

6. _____

7. _____

8. _____

14   Your Turn
Write a sentence that would naturally go with each of the following
sentences. Then combine the two using *which*.

1. *I heard the news about the principal of the school.*_____ This was a shock
    to me.

    I heard the news about the principal of the school, which was a shock
    to me.

2. _____ This was a nice surprise.
    _____

3. _____ This made it more difficult.
    _____

4. _____ This was very kind of her.
    _____

5. _____ This irritated me.
    _____

6. _____ This disappointed me.
    _____

12G Reduced Adjective Clauses

Form/Function

The boy **sitting on the bench**
looks sad. I saw his brother
running away from him. Maybe
they got into a fight.

1. We can reduce an adjective clause to an adjective phrase. An adjective phrase modifies a noun.
    An adjective phrase does not have a subject and a verb. Instead, it has a present participle (base
    verb + *-ing*) for the active voice or a past participle for the passive voice.

Adjective Clause:	The girl **who is waiting at the bus stop** is my sister.
Adjective Phrase:	The girl **waiting at the bus stop** is my sister.
Adjective Clause:	The information **that was found on that website** was incorrect.
Adjective Phrase:	The information **found on that website** was incorrect.

2. We can only reduce adjective clauses that have a subject relative pronoun.

   Remember that regular past participles end in -ed, but many past participles are irregular.

Adjective Clause:	The man **who is sitting in the corner** is well known.
Adjective Phrase:	The man **sitting in the corner** is well known.
Adjective Clause:	The man **who I sat next to** was well known.
Adjective Phrase:	(Not possible. *Who* is not a subject pronoun in this example.)

3. There are two ways to reduce an adjective clause.

   a. If the adjective clause has a form of *be*, we omit the subject relative pronoun and the form of *be*.

Adjective Clause:	Do you know the woman **who is standing by the window**?
Adjective Phrase:	Do you know the woman **standing by the window**?
Adjective Clause:	The words **that are underlined in red** have errors.
Adjective Phrase:	The words **underlined in red** have errors.

   b. If there is no form of *be* in the adjective clause, we can omit the subject pronoun and change the verb to the present participle (-*ing* form).

Adjective Clause:	Anyone **who wants to send a message** can use these computers to do so.
Adjective Phrase:	Anyone **wanting to send a message** can use these computers to do so.
Adjective Clause:	The Inuit have about 70 words **that describe different kinds of snow**.
Adjective Phrase:	The Inuit have about 70 words **describing different kinds of snow**.

4. If the adjective clause is defining, then the adjective phrase is also defining, and we don't put commas around it. But if the adjective clause is nondefining, the adjective phrase is also nondefining, and we must use commas.

Defining Clause:	Scientists **who were working before 1898** didn't know about the element radium.
Defining Clause:	Scientists **working before 1898** didn't know about the element radium.
Nondefining Clause:	Marie Curie, **who worked at the Sorbonne in Paris**, discovered the element radium in 1898.
Nondefining Clause:	Marie Curie, **working at the Sorbonne in Paris**, discovered the element radium in 1898.

5. If the adjective phrase follows a noun and starts with a noun, we call it an *appositive*. Use commas around an appositive if it is nondefining. Do not use commas if it is defining.

Adjective Clause:	Marie Curie, **who was a winner of the Nobel Prize**, discovered radium.
Appositive:	Marie Curie, **a winner of the Nobel Prize**, discovered radium.

Hans Christian Andersen

famous for his fairy tales

Hans Christian Andersen was a writer <u>who is famous for his fairy tales</u>. He wrote stories that are well known all over the world like *The Ugly Duckling*, *The Princess and the Pea*, and *The Little Mermaid*. Andersen, who was born in Denmark in 1805, is still a popular writer today.

As a boy who was growing up in poverty, Hans had a hard life. His father, who was a shoemaker, could not even afford to make leather shoes for him, so he wore wooden shoes. His mother, who was unable to read or write, never encouraged him. His father died when he was 11, so he went to work in a factory. Hans, who was dreaming of becoming an actor, could not work there for long. At age 14, he went to Copenhagen, which was the capital city of Denmark, to become an actor. Hans, who wanted his dream to come true, tried hard for three years, but he was not successful. The theater managers who saw him act said he was not a good actor, and they needed people with an education.

Hans, who was feeling very disappointed, decided to go back to school. At age 17, he went to school with much younger students. Hans was tall, with big hands and feet, and he had a very big nose. The other students laughed at him. The lessons were difficult, but Hans, who was studying hard, got good grades. However, he was shy and unhappy and wrote down his feelings. He later used these thoughts in his diary for his stories. *The Ugly Duckling,* which is a fairy tale about a baby duck with no friends, was really about himself.

Hans, who was like a child, was shy and sensitive, and he got hurt easily. He wanted to get married, but he was not successful. Andersen, who was becoming disappointed, decided he would not marry.

At age 30, he wrote his first fairy tales. The stories, which were thought to be too adult at first, were soon a great success.

16   Practice

Listen to statements about food products. You will hear sentences with adjective clauses. Write the past participle of the verb you hear to complete the sentences with reduced adjective clauses.

AUDIO
DOWNLOAD

CD3, 5

1. Most of the coffee ___*grown*___ in Brazil is exported.

2. The most popular hot beverage _____ by Americans is coffee.

3. Strawberries, bananas, tomatoes, and other fruits _____ in supermarkets are often unripe when they are picked.

4. Much of the fast food _____ by young people contains a lot of fat.

5. Hamburgers _____ on wheat buns are healthier.

6. Food _____ from the freezer must be defrosted before cooking.

7. Some people like potatoes _____ with butter; others prefer potatoes _____ in oil.

8. Roquefort is a French cheese _____ in caves.

17   Your Turn

Work with a partner, a group, or alone. Write a fairy tale that you know (you can make changes to it) using reduced relative clauses. Read the fairy tale to the class.

THE WARRIOR COMES BACK TO LIFE

One day, a warrior who was famous for his hunting achievements throughout the land did not return from a hunt. All his family thought he was dead, all except for his youngest child who each day asked, "Where is my father? Where is my father?"

The child's older brothers, who were magicians, finally went to look for him. They found their father's spear and a pile of bones. The first son put together the bones into a skeleton; the second son put flesh upon the bones; the third son breathed life into it.

The warrior who now breathed life then got up and walked into the village where there was great celebration. He said, "I will give a gift to the one who has brought me back to life."

Each one of his sons cried out, "Give it to me, for it is I whose magic has brought you back to life."

"I will give the gift to my youngest child," said the warrior. "Because it is this child who saved my life. A person is never really dead until he is forgotten!"

1. What was the warrior famous for?

   _____

2. Who was the only family member who asked about the warrior?

   _____

3. What were the child's older brothers?

   _____

4. Whose spear and bones did they find?

   _____

5. What happened to the warrior after his sons worked their magic on him?

   _____

6. Who(m) did he want to give a gift to?

   _____

7. What did each of his older sons say that they had done?

   _____

8. Why did he give the gift to his youngest son?

   _____

Listening Puzzle

AUDIO DOWNLOAD   CD3, 6

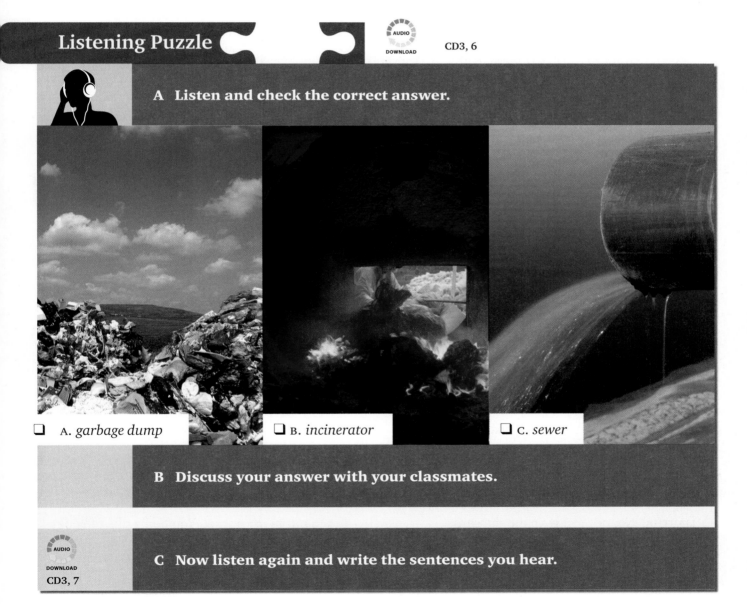

A Listen and check the correct answer.

❏ A. *garbage dump*   ❏ B. *incinerator*   ❏ C. *sewer*

B Discuss your answer with your classmates.

AUDIO DOWNLOAD CD3, 7

C Now listen again and write the sentences you hear.

1 Review (12a–12f)
Complete the sentences with the correct relative pronouns. Use informal English.

RICK: So this is the place ___where___ you come to read.
                          1

MARTHA: That's right. The public library is the only place _____ it's quiet.
                                                              2

RICK: My sister, _____ I introduced to you last week, told me you've been here every night
                   3
        for a week.

MARTHA: Yes, the author _____ book I'm reading now is going to give a lecture at my school. I
                        4
        want to finish the book before he comes.

RICK: Do you mean the man _____ sailed around the world twice?
                            5

MARTHA: Yes. He sailed a boat _____ was only 25 feet (7.6 meters) long, _____ is small
                              6   **7**
        for the open ocean. He actually had two boats. One boat, _____ turned over while he
                                                                 8
        was sailing around Cape Horn, sank.

RICK: I read about that. His boat sank in a violent storm, _____ must have been a terrible
                                                            9
        experience. The Horn is an area _____ waters are full of sunken ships. I know a
                                         10
        woman _____ rolled over twice in her sailboat, _____ she was
              11   **12**
        sailing there.

MARTHA: I'm fascinated by people _____ do adventurous things. My grandmother, _____
                                 13   **14**
        is 80 now, lived in Kenya for ten years.

RICK: Really? How interesting. Oh, no! Someone took the book _____ I put on this table. I
                                                               15
        need that book! My teacher, _____ I expect to get an A from, asked me to get it for her.
                                    16

MARTHA: The man _____ was standing here must have taken it.
                17

RICK: Oh, no! The library card _____ Ms. Amersbach gave me was in that book!
                                 18

MARTHA: No, no. You gave me the card, _____ I then put in my pocket. You had a pile of books
                                       19
        _____ you were about to drop.
        20

RICK: You're right. Oh, I see the man _____ took my book. He's the one _____
                                        21   **22**
        the librarian is speaking to.

On the morning of November 4, 1966, ~~that~~ *which* was a terrible day for art lovers, it was raining very hard in Italy. For many days, terrible rains had fallen on Italy which cities are filled with the world's greatest works of art. The Arno River, fill quickly, threatened to flood. Just before dawn, the Arno River that flows through Florence overflowed its banks, sending water into the countryside. The citizens of Florence which had been sleeping, awakened to find their city under water. Florence who is a famous art center was under 14 feet (4 meters) of water and mud in some places. Thousands of artworks many of whom were priceless masterpieces were also under water. Suddenly Florence was a city who was a graveyard of the world's finest art.

The Florentines that survived by climbing to their rooftops faced a terrible disaster. The city that they loved was flooded. The greatest artworks in the world many which had survived for hundreds of years were buried in water and mud. But Florence is a city in whom there are many art lovers.

On the morning after the flood, art students formed a human chain and pulled the artworks out of the water. Within 24 hours, people which restored paintings began arriving in the city. It was a time that many people came together for a common cause – to save the artwork. This disaster from who the Florentines never expected to recover caught the interest of people around the world. Donations came from everywhere. Experts worked tirelessly and much was saved. To be sure, many books and manuscripts who were very valuable were lost to the flood, but many were rescued. Perhaps most important, the flood of 1966 taught lessons will not be forgotten. Experts developed new methods whom protect artworks from natural disasters. People which worked on the art also developed new techniques will help keep art safe for future generations.

A Before You Read

1. Imagine that you are on a ship in the middle of an ocean. What are you likely to see?
2. Where does your household garbage go?

THE GARBAGE PATCH

DID YOU KNOW ... ?
The Garbage Patch—a section of the Pacific Ocean where floating trash collects—is bigger than the state of Texas.

B Read People who sail to the North Pacific Ocean are often surprised. ■ What they see on the surface
5 makes no sense in such a remote place. Garbage floats in the still water from one horizon to another. ■ It comes from every nation that has a North Pacific
10 shore, and many that don't. ■ Even in places where it is illegal to dump garbage in the ocean, some people still do. Other North Pacific junk got there by accident. ■
15 This area of the ocean has several names. "The Garbage Patch" is the one that best describes what sailors see. "The North Pacific Gyre" is what scientists call the system of currents that creates The Garbage Patch. The
20 gyre is a natural feature. It consists of ocean

currents that run south along the North American coast, westward south of Hawaii, then north along Asia's east coast. An eastward flow south of Siberia and Alaska completes
25 the circuit.

Objects that get caught in the gyre could be caught there for years. Most, however, typically exit the current when wind pushes them toward shore or toward the center of the system. This
30 center is a calm zone where The Garbage Patch floats. When an object enters, it is unlikely to go anywhere else. This is not harmful to the environment if the object is natural—driftwood, seaweed, or even a dead fish or bird. It will
35 biodegrade, a term which means that bacteria or some other animal will eventually eat it and break it down. The chemicals that make it up will return to nature. The same cannot be said of plastic. Plastic makes The Garbage Patch
40 a problem.

Plastic from grocery bags, toys, bottles, and even diapers can float for decades in The Garbage Patch. It does not biodegrade. Shipping accidents have occurred where items such as
45 30,000 plastic hockey gloves and 80,000 plastic sneakers, have fallen into the Pacific. All this plastic junk causes environmental damage. It keeps sunlight from reaching undersea organisms that need **it**. As some types of plastic
50 **deteriorate**, they may release poisons into the sea. Plastic trash kills seabirds, which think the plastic is food and swallow bits of it.

C Notice the Grammar Underline all the adjective clauses.

Choose the best answer.

D Look for Main Ideas

1. The reading's main point about The Garbage
    Patch is _____ .
    - Ⓐ why it is bad for birds and fish
    - Ⓑ how the area can be cleaned up
    - Ⓒ where it is located
    - Ⓓ what kind of garbage accumulates there

E Look for Details

2. A boat pulled into a current in the North
    Pacific Gyre would probably _____ .
    - Ⓐ keep circling the Pacific Ocean
    - Ⓑ eventually be blown outside the current
    - Ⓒ lose most of its cargo
    - Ⓓ be destroyed by the floating garbage

3. Natural materials _____ .
    - Ⓐ are not found in The Garbage Patch
    - Ⓑ help get the plastic out of the gyre
    - Ⓒ release poisons into the water
    - Ⓓ break down and return to nature

F Writer's Attitude

4. The author's attitude toward plastic items in
    the Pacific is _____ .
    - Ⓐ neutral   Ⓒ positive
    - Ⓑ negative   Ⓓ surprised

G Make Inferences

5. We can most strongly infer from the reading
    that _____ .
    - Ⓐ plastic is not natural
    - Ⓑ there was no gyre before plastic
         was introduced
    - Ⓒ the gyre is getting stronger
    - Ⓓ natural forces can break
         plastic down

H Look for Vocabulary

6. The word *deteriorate* in the reading is
    closest in meaning to _____ .
    - Ⓐ break down
    - Ⓑ get worse
    - Ⓒ open up
    - Ⓓ spread out

I Look for References

7. The word *it* in the reading refers to _____ .
    - Ⓐ plastic junk
    - Ⓑ environmental damage
    - Ⓒ sunlight
    - Ⓓ an undersea organism

J Sentence Addition

8. Look at the four squares ▪ that indicate
    where the following sentence could be
    added to the passage.
    **It is impossible to completely protect an
    entire ocean.**
    Where would the sentence best fit?
    - Ⓐ at the first square
    - Ⓑ at the second square
    - Ⓒ at the third square
    - Ⓓ at the fourth square

Writing: Write an Essay that Describes a Process

A process is a series of steps that leads to an end, for example, a set of instructions on how to set up a computer. Steps usually occur one after the other, but sometimes they happen at the same time. The order of the steps must be clear. If not, the process cannot be followed accurately. We can use time markers such as *first*, *then*, and *next* for the main steps.

STEP 1	**Discuss these process topics with a partner. Take notes on the important steps.**

        a. How courtship works in your country.   **c.** How you prepare for a New Year's celebration.

        b. How you prepare for a wedding.   **d.** How you prepare for a religious holiday.

STEP 2	**Choose one of the topics from Step 1, or use your own.**

STEP 3	**Write your essay.**

     1. Choose three or four of the main steps for your topic. Write a paragraph for each step. Give details and use some adjective clauses in your paragraphs. Look at the example in the box:

> Next, we prepare special food for this celebration. Dishes that are from an old tradition are prepared in a special way. For example, we always have a fish dish. The fish, which must be fresh, is boiled …

     2. Write an introduction to the essay. Include a thesis statement stating the number of steps and briefly summarize them.

     3. Write a conclusion. Your conclusion can summarize the information in the body and state why this process is important.

     4. Write a title for your essay.

STEP 4	**Evaluate your essay.**

Checklist

_____ Did you write an introduction, a paragraph for each step, and a conclusion?

_____ Did you write a title and put it in the right place?

_____ Did you present the order of the steps correctly and clearly?

_____ Would a reader who does not know the process understand it from your essay?

STEP 5	**Edit your essay with a partner or a teacher. Check spelling, vocabulary, and grammar.**

STEP 6	**Write your final copy.**

Self-Test

1. That's the doctor _____ husband is an attorney.

   A. she's
   B. who
   C. which
   D. whose

   Ⓐ Ⓑ Ⓒ Ⓓ

2. Tom, _____ was in our office yesterday, called me this morning.

   A. whose
   B. who
   C. that
   D. which

   Ⓐ Ⓑ Ⓒ Ⓓ

3. Where is the person _____ I should give this?

   A. who
   B. whom
   C. to whom
   D. to who

   Ⓐ Ⓑ Ⓒ Ⓓ

4. I remember the office _____ you worked when you first came to this city.

   A. which
   B. where
   C. whom
   D. that

   Ⓐ Ⓑ Ⓒ Ⓓ

5. Do you remember Jo Brown, _____ worked with last year?

   A. which I
   B. I
   C. who I
   D. who

   Ⓐ Ⓑ Ⓒ Ⓓ

6. Jack found the information _____ was looking for on the Internet.

   A. he
   B. who
   C. for which
   D. that

   Ⓐ Ⓑ Ⓒ Ⓓ

7. The person _____ the award was given will appear on television tonight.

   A. whom
   B. who
   C. to whom
   D. who to

   Ⓐ Ⓑ Ⓒ Ⓓ

8. I don't like the book _____ our teacher chose for us.

   A. –
   B. whom
   C. what
   D. who

   Ⓐ Ⓑ Ⓒ Ⓓ

9. I have applied to two universities, _____ are in this city.

   A. both which
   B. both of which
   C. of which
   D. both of whom

   Ⓐ Ⓑ Ⓒ Ⓓ

10. Prague, _____ capital of the Czech Republic, is a beautiful city.

    A. that is the
    B. the
    C. where
    D. is being

    Ⓐ Ⓑ Ⓒ Ⓓ

B Find the underlined word or phrase, A, B, C, or D, that is incorrect. Darken the oval with the same letter.

1. I went <u>to visit</u> a friend <u>his</u> father is the
         A   **B**
   <u>president</u> of <u>your brother's</u> college.
     C   **D**

   Ⓐ   Ⓑ   Ⓒ   Ⓓ

2. I remember <u>the hotel</u> <u>for which</u> we <u>stayed</u> at
            A   **B**   **C**
   <u>that</u> your friend owned.
     D

   Ⓐ   Ⓑ   Ⓒ   Ⓓ

3. We enjoyed <u>watching</u> the show <u>that</u> you <u>told us</u>
             A   **B**   **C**
   <u>about it</u>.
     D

   Ⓐ   Ⓑ   Ⓒ   Ⓓ

4. An <u>author</u> <u>who's</u> books <u>I like</u> a lot <u>is</u> Stephen
       A   **B**   **C**   **D**
   King.

   Ⓐ   Ⓑ   Ⓒ   Ⓓ

5. <u>His collection</u> of paintings, <u>most of them</u>
        A   **B**
   <u>are</u> from the 20th century, <u>is</u> famous.
     C   **D**

   Ⓐ   Ⓑ   Ⓒ   Ⓓ

6. My brother, <u>who his</u> company <u>makes</u> toys,
                 A   **B**
   <u>has moved</u> to <u>another city</u>.
     C   **D**

   Ⓐ   Ⓑ   Ⓒ   Ⓓ

7. <u>The organization</u>, <u>it</u> <u>having many members</u>,
         A   **B**   **C**
   <u>is</u> famous throughout the world.
     D

   Ⓐ   Ⓑ   Ⓒ   Ⓓ

8. <u>Do you</u> know <u>the name</u> of <u>the teacher is</u>
      A   **B**   **C**
   <u>standing</u> by the window?
     D

   Ⓐ   Ⓑ   Ⓒ   Ⓓ

9. All of the facts <u>what</u> <u>I have told</u> you <u>are</u> true
                A   **B**   **C**
   and <u>can be found</u> in this book.
          D

   Ⓐ   Ⓑ   Ⓒ   Ⓓ

10. <u>This course</u>, <u>which</u> I <u>had</u> to buy this book,
         A   **B** **C**
    <u>will be</u> very useful for me.
      D

   Ⓐ   Ⓑ   Ⓒ   Ⓓ

388 Unit 12

Unit 13

Adverb Clauses

Anne is angry **because Tony didn't wait for her after school**.

13A Adverb Clauses of Time

Form/Function

Ricky listens to music **while he does his homework**.

1. There are many kinds of adverb clauses. We recognize them by their special clause markers (conjunctions), for example, *when, as soon as, where, although,* and *because.*

2. Adverb clauses of time and place work like adverbs. They tell when and where something happens.

   I do my homework **as soon as I come home from school**.

   While I do my homework, I listen to music.

3. An adverb clause of time is a dependent clause. It must be used with a main clause. When an adverb clause comes at the beginning of a sentence, we put a comma after it. We do not use a comma when it comes at the end.

Clause Marker	Use	Examples
as while when whenever	To say that things happen at the same time. *Whenever* has the additional meaning of "every time."	**As** I was driving down the street, I saw Susan. I watch television **while** I'm having breakfast. They were hiking **when** they saw the bear. I order the fish **whenever** I go to that restaurant.
when* before after	To say that things happen one after another.	**When** he finished his test, he left the room. The show had begun **before** we arrived. **After** he finished his course, he found a job.

* We can use *when* instead of *while, as, before,* and *after* if the order of events is clear from other information in the sentence.

   When/While/As I was writing my essay, I had a brilliant idea.

   The movie had begun **when/before** we arrived.

   When/After he finished his degree, he quickly found a job.

Clause Marker	Use	Examples
as soon as once	To say that one thing happens quickly after another.	Please feed the dog **as soon as** you get home. **Once** he got home, he fed the dog.
the first time the next time the last time	To say which of several occurrences of something that we are talking about.	**The first time** I ate sushi, I hated it. **The next time** I ate it, I liked it a little bit. **The last time** I ate it, I ate all of it.
until	To say that something continues up to the time when something else happens.	You must stay in class **until** you finish your essay.
as long as*	To say that something continues to the end of something else.	I will dance **as long as** the band plays. (When the band stops playing, I will stop dancing.)
by the time	To say that something happens no later than the time when something else happens.	I will have finished my work **by the time** you come home.
since	To say that something happens between a point in the past and the present.	I've seen a lot of the city **since** I came here.

* We can also say *so long as*.

1 Practice
A Read about Helen Thayer's life.

Helen Thayer was the first woman to walk to the North Pole alone and unaided. She walked and skied for 27 days, pulling a 160-pound (72.5-kilogram) sled for 364 miles (586 kilometers). She had no help from aircraft, dog teams, or snowmobiles and only her dog for company. Helen was born in New Zealand. Turn the page to learn some facts about her life.

_____b_____ 1. She was attacked by polar bears.

a. She achieved her goal.

_____ 2. She was resting at night.

b. Her dog Charlie protected her.

_____ 3. She knew she would not give up.

c. She has traveled all over the world, giving talks about her experiences.

_____ 4. She returned home.

_____ 5. Her book was published.

d. She wrote a book, *Polar Dream*, about her amazing adventure.

e. She talked to Charlie about her plans.

C   Using the clause markers in parentheses, combine the pairs of sentences from Part B.

1.   <u>When she was attacked by polar bears, her dog Charlie protected her.</u>

2.   (while) _____

     _____

3.   (until) _____

     _____

4.   (as soon as) _____

     _____

5.   (since) _____

     _____

2 Pair Up and Talk

Practice the conversation with a partner. Then tell about a personal goal that you have achieved. What did you do before? What did you do after? How has your life changed since you achieved that goal?

A: I felt great when I got my driver's license.

B: Really? How has your life changed since you got it?

A: I used to depend on friends to drive me places. After I got my license, I could drive anywhere I wanted to go, anytime.

Form/Function

> Mona has a headache **because she has too much to do**.

1. There are several kinds of sentences that express a reason or a result. In these examples, notice that both the result and the reason can be in a main clause or an adverb clause.

Result (main clause)	Reason (adverb clause)
I felt tired in the morning	because I had gone to bed very late.

Reason (main clause)	Result (adverb clause)
I had gone to bed very late,	so I felt tired in the morning.

2. We use these clause markers to introduce clauses of reason: *as   because   since   so*
    Clauses with *because*, *as*, and *since* can go at the beginning or end of the sentence. We put a comma after the clause if it comes at the beginning. Result clauses with *so* must go at the end of the sentence. We put a comma in front of them.

    The children shouldn't have any ice cream now **because they're going to have dinner in half an hour**.

    As/Since the weather is bad, we shouldn't go out tonight.

    I got up very early, **so I needed another cup of coffee**.

    Do not confuse *because* with *because of*. Both show reasons, but *because of* is followed by a noun, not a subject and a verb.

    Because it was raining, we stayed home.
    Because of the rain, we stayed home.

Since and *as* mean about the same thing as *because*, but they suggest a meaning like "It is a fact that …" or "It's true that …"

Remember, *since* is also a time clause marker. See page 391.

3. We can use *so* + adjective/adverb + *that* or *such a/an* + adjective + noun + *that* to show a result. They have the same meaning.

> The sandwich was **so** tasty **that** I had another one.
>
> It was **such** a tasty sandwich **that** I had another one.

We can also use *such a/an* + noun with or without an adjective. In informal English, we can omit the *that* clause.

> It was **such a** terrible disaster (that it was on the evening news).
>
> It was **such a** disaster (that it was on the evening news).

When we speak, we often omit *that*.

> It was **such** tasty soup (that) I had another bowl.
>
> The movie was **so** good (that) I saw it three times.

4. There are other clause markers that introduce clauses of result. These markers introduce main clauses, not dependent clauses, so their punctuation is different. Clauses with these markers always go at the end of the sentence. Sometimes they can also be a separate sentence.

Main Clause (Reason)	Clause Marker	Main Clause (Result)
Our teacher was sick;	**as a result,**	our class was canceled.
I don't know much about computers;	**therefore,**	I can't help you.
The weather is very severe;	**consequently,**	all flights will be delayed.

We can punctuate the long clause markers *as a result, therefore,* and *consequently* in two ways. We can put a semicolon before the clause marker and a comma after it, or we can write two sentences with a comma after the clause marker.

> ONE SENTENCE: I don't know much about computers; **therefore,** I can't help you.
>
> TWO SENTENCES: I don't know much about computers. **Therefore,** I can't help you.

We can use *and* before these clause markers. In these cases, we use a comma between the two clauses.

> He was very qualified, **and so** he got the job.
>
> Our teacher was sick, **and as a result** our class was canceled.

3 Practice
Complete the sentences with *so* or *because*. Add commas where necessary.

1. On Monday, I got up early __*because*__ I had an important meeting.

2. I had gone to bed late, _____ I felt tired when I got up.

3. I needed more energy _____ I drank some coffee.

4. I took an umbrella _____ it was raining.

5. It was an important meeting _____ I wore my best suit.

6. I was feeling rather nervous _____ my boss was going to be there.

7. There was a lot of traffic _____ my bus was late.

8. My papers got mixed up _____ I dropped my briefcase.

9. My suit got mud on it _____ I was standing too near the cars, and it was raining.

10. I finally arrived in a complete mess. I was one hour late. The office was empty. I found a note which said, "Punctuality is very important to this company _____ you are fired."

4 Practice
Rewrite each of the sentences in two ways, once using *so ... that* and once using *such a/an ... that.*

Mia was lost in the forest. She wandered through the trees all day until she came to a small house.

1. The door to the house was very small. She had to stoop down to go in.
   The house was so small that she had to stoop down to go in.
   It was such a small house that she had to stoop down to go in.

2. The chairs and tables were very delicate. She was afraid to touch them.
   _____
   _____

3. A delicious cake was on the kitchen table. She ate three slices.
   _____
   _____

4. The house was very beautiful. She felt like she wanted to stay there forever.

_____

_____

5. The bed was very soft. She couldn't help lying down.

_____

_____

6. She heard some soft music. She fell asleep immediately.

_____

_____

7. She had a very peaceful dream. She didn't want to wake up.

_____

_____

8. She heard a loud noise. She woke up suddenly.

_____

_____

5 Your Turn

Finish the story. Use four adverb clauses of reason and result and correct punctuation.

6 Pair Up and Talk

A Practice the conversation with a partner.

A: I once saw a movie that was so good that I saw it three times!

B: Wow, it was that good? What was it about?

A: It was a true story about people in a small mountain village. They led a difficult life. It was such an inspiring story that it made me want to travel there and see it for myself.

B Tell a partner about something that was good, horrible, or difficult for you. Use an idea from the list or one of your own. Use *so … that* and *such a/an … that.*

a book	a movie	something in a store
a grammar point	a TV show	something to eat

Form/Function

Maria writes everything down **so that she can remember it**.

1. We use clauses of purpose to answer the questions *what for?* and *for what purpose?* We use the clause markers *so that* or *in order that** to introduce adverb clauses of purpose. In speech, we can omit *that* when we use *so that*.

   I'm saving money **so (that)** I can buy a car.

   We saved a lot of money **in order that** we could take a long vacation.

2. We can introduce a phrase (not a clause) of purpose with *in order to* + a base verb.

   I'm saving money **in order to buy** a car.

3. We often use *so that* with *can, can't, will,* or *won't* for the present or future, and *could, couldn't, would,* or *wouldn't* for the past. We sometimes, but not often, use *may* or *might* in place of *can* or *could*.

   He writes down everything **so (that)** he **can** remember it.

   She gets up early **so (that)** she **won't** be late.

   He wrote down everything **so (that)** he **could** remember it.

   She got up early **so (that)** she **wouldn't** be late.

   He wrote it down **so that** he **might** remember it.

   * *In order that* is rare.

7 Practice

Complete the sentences with *so that* to show purpose or *therefore* to show result. Listen to check your answers. Then add commas, semicolons, periods, and capital letters where necessary.

CD3, 8

Joanna wanted to go to the United States <u> so that </u> she could improve her
₁

English. She enrolled in an English program at a university ＿＿＿＿＿＿ she could
₂

learn quickly. She lived with her uncle and aunt, who wanted to speak their language

with her ＿＿＿＿＿＿ she couldn't practice English at home. At first, her English wasn't
₃

very good. ＿＿＿＿＿＿ she had to work hard. She learned to keep a notebook with
₄

her at all times ＿＿＿＿＿＿ she could write down new idioms and expressions that
₅

she heard. Also, she joined some clubs at the university. Many American students became

her friends ＿＿＿＿＿＿ she was able to practice with them.
₆

After six months, her English was very good. ＿＿＿＿＿＿ she decided to return
₇

home. She bought a computer ＿＿＿＿＿＿ she could stay in touch with her American
₈

friends. Now she is looking for a job in tourism ＿＿＿＿＿＿ she will be able to use her
₉

English at work.

8 Pair Up and Talk

A Practice the conversation with a partner.

A: It's important to me to have good English, so I study as much as possible.

B: That's great. What else do you do to improve your English?

A: I watch a lot of American movies so that I can improve my listening skills. I also read American newspapers every day so I can add to my vocabulary.

B Talk about things that are important to you. Use *so (that)* and *in order that* for purpose. Use ideas from the list or your own ideas.

be successful	get married	make friends	speak English well
find a job	improve my vocabulary	save money	travel a lot

Form/Function

Even though Tony apologized, Anne is still angry with him.

1. We use adverb clauses of contrast to show that two ideas differ, often in an unexpected or unusual way. We introduce them with the following clause markers:

   although   even though   though   whereas   while

   Although there was a snowstorm, all the trains were on time.

   Even though there was a snowstorm, all the trains were on time.

   Though there was a snowstorm, all the trains were on time.

2. *Even though* is more emphatic than *although*. *Though* is not as formal as *even though* or *although*.

3. In informal English, we can also use *though* to mean "however." In this case, it often comes at the end of a sentence. There is often a comma before it in writing.

   It is very cold outside. It's nice and warm in here, **though**.   (It's very cold outside; however, it's nice and warm in here).

4. We can also use *while* and *whereas* to introduce contrast between two ideas.

   Jim has dark hair, **while** his brother has light hair.

   Jim has dark hair, **whereas** his brother has light hair.

5. We can also show contrast between two ideas by using the transitional main clause markers *however* or *nevertheless*. Note the position and punctuation with *however* and *nevertheless*.

   I enjoy living in the city; **however**, the cost of living is quite high.

   I enjoy living in the city. **However**, the cost of living is quite high.

   I enjoy living in the city; **nevertheless**, I'm going to move to the suburbs soon.

   I enjoy living in the city. **Nevertheless**, I'm going to move to the suburbs soon.

9 Practice

Match the clauses and then combine them into sentences using *although*, *even though*, *while*, or *whereas*. Use correct punctuation.

<u> *f* </u> **1.** Samuel is rich

<u>   </u> **2.** Samuel has a lot of "friends"

<u>   </u> **3.** Samuel works very hard

<u>   </u> **4.** Samuel has a lot of money

<u>   </u> **5.** A lot of people want to meet him

<u>   </u> **6.** Samuel has several houses

a. he doesn't know what to spend it on

b. he doesn't like his job

c. none of them would help him if he were in trouble

d. none of them feels like home

e. he doesn't want to meet them

f. he isn't happy

1. <u>Although Samuel is rich, he isn't happy.</u>

2. _____

3. _____

4. _____

5. _____

6. _____

10 Practice

Rewrite the sentences from Practice 9 using *however* or *nevertheless*. Use correct punctuation.

1. <u>Samuel is rich; however, he is unhappy.</u>

2. _____

3. _____

4. _____

5. _____

6. _____

13E Adverb Clauses of Condition

Form/Function

Claudia's parents said they'd buy her a car **only if she graduated**.

1. Clauses of condition show that one thing depends on another. We use these markers to introduce clauses of condition: *even if, in case, unless, if, only if, whether or not.*

2. *If* clauses are adverb clauses of condition. The *if* clause contains the condition and the main clause contains the result. We use the simple present in the *if* clause, even if the main clause refers to the future.

    If I feel better tomorrow, I'll go to class.

    I'll stay in bed **if** I don't go to class.

3. We use *whether or not* to say that a situation will not be affected by one thing or another. *Even if* is close in meaning to *whether or not.* It means that no matter what the condition, the result will not change.

    Whether or not I feel well tomorrow, I'm going to school.

    OR **Whether** I feel well **or not** tomorrow, I'm going to school.

    Even if I am sick tomorrow, I'm going to school.

    (I don't care if I am sick. It doesn't matter. I'm going to school tomorrow.)

4. We use *unless* to mean "if … not."

    Unless I feel well, I won't go to school.

    (If I don't feel well, I won't go to school.)

    You can't see the doctor **unless** you have an appointment.

    (You can't see the doctor if you do not have an appointment.)

    We often use *unless* in threats and warnings.

    Unless you have an emergency, you must attend class.

5. We use *only if* to mean there is only one condition for a certain result.

   My parents will buy me a new computer **only if** I pass this class.

   (If I don't pass this class, they won't buy me a computer.)

   When we put *only if* at the beginning of a sentence, we must invert the subject and the verb.

   Only if I pass this class **will my parents buy** me a computer.

6. We use *in case* to talk about things we do because we think something else might happen.

   I'll make some extra food **in case** John wants to stay for dinner.

   (I will make some extra food now. Then if John wants to stay, there will be enough for him, too.)

   See Unit 14 for more information on clauses of condition.

---

11   Practice

Match the halves of the following sentences using adverbial clause markers from the list. Write the correct marker on the line in the first column. Then write the letter of the correct second half of the sentence on the shorter line. On a separate sheet of paper, write sentences that express rules for using computers in the library.

even if   if   in case   only if   unless   whether or not

_____unless_____ **1.** You may not use the computer _a._   **a.** you have signed up for it

_____ **2.** Children under six may _____   **b.** you can't log on to
                      use the computer   the Internet

_____ **3.** You need to get a new password _____   **c.** they are accompanied by an
                                                                     adult
_____ **4.** Ask a librarian for assistance _____
                                                                d. another student is waiting
_____ **5.** The maximum time per person is _____
                      one hour   **e.** other students are
                                                                     waiting or not
_____ **6.** You may use the computer _____
                      for the maximum time   **f.** you forget your old one

1.   *You may not use the computer unless you have signed up for it.*

---

12   Your Turn

On a separate sheet of paper, write a rule for each of the following situations, or use your own idea. Use adverb clauses of condition.

borrowing books from your library   **using your local sports center**

using the kitchen shared by several students   **using a cell phone at school**

13   Read

Read the story. Then write answers to the questions.

ONE GOOD MEAL DESERVES ANOTHER

The spider Anansi hated to share! When Turtle came to his house at lunchtime, he said, "I can't give you food until you've washed your dirty feet!"

Turtle saw the big plate of hot food in front of him. The food looked so tasty that his mouth watered, but he politely walked to the water's edge to wash. When he returned, the plate was empty. "Good meal," Anansi said, tapping his full stomach.

"One good meal deserves another!" said Turtle. "Come to my house for dinner tomorrow." Turtle made a fine dinner at the bottom of the river and waited for Anansi.

Anansi filled the pockets of his jacket with stones so he would be heavy enough to stay at the bottom of the river and eat. "It's impolite to wear a jacket to dinner!" Turtle said, "Take it off!"

However, as soon as greedy Anansi took off his jacket, he floated back to the surface of the water. Now Anansi, on an empty stomach, had to watch Turtle eat until he couldn't move any more.

1. When did Turtle go to Anansi's house? _____

2. What excuse did Anansi make not to give Turtle the food immediately? _____

3. Why did Turtle's mouth water? _____

4. Why couldn't Turtle eat any of the food? _____

5. Why did Anansi fill his pockets with stones? _____

6. Why did Turtle tell Anansi to take off his jacket? _____

7. What happened as soon as Anansi took off his jacket? _____

8. What did Anansi watch on an empty stomach? _____

13F Reduced Adverb Clauses

Form/Function

Since starting class, I have made a lot of friends.

1. We can reduce an adverb clause to a modifying adverb phrase in the same way we reduce adjective clauses to adjective phrases. An adverb phrase does not have a subject or a verb. It consists of a present or past participle and an adverb clause time marker. The present participle replaces verbs in the active voice, and the past participle replaces verbs in the passive voice.

    ADVERB CLAUSE: **Before I came** to the United States, I took some English classes.

    ADVERB PHRASE: **Before coming** to the United States, I took some English classes.

    ADVERB CLAUSE: The Internet was for the use of university and government scientists **when it was originally invented**.

    ADVERB PHRASE: **When originally invented**, the Internet was for the use of university and government scientists.

    We can use modifying adverb phrases with verbs of any form in the main clause.

    Before going to Korea, I **will take** some Korean classes. (main verb is future)

    When completed, these products **sell** around the world. (main verb is present)

2. The modifying adverb phrase can come before or after the main clause. We use a comma after the adverb phrase when it comes at the beginning of a sentence.

    Since starting this class, she has made a lot of friends.

    She has made a lot of friends **since starting** this class.

3. We can only change an adverb clause to an adverb phrase when the subject of the main clause and the adverb clause are the same.

    ADVERB CLAUSE: While I was traveling across Europe, I noticed the differences in architecture.

    ADVERB PHRASE: While traveling across Europe, I noticed the differences in architecture.

    ADVERB CLAUSE: While I was traveling across Europe, the differences in architecture became very clear.

    ADVERB PHRASE: (No reduction possible)

    We can sometimes omit *while* and still keep the meaning "at the same time."

    Traveling across Europe, I noticed the differences in architecture.

4. We do not use *because* in an adverb phrase. We omit *because* and use only the *-ing* phrase. This gives the same meaning as *because*.

Because he wanted to pass the class, he studied very hard.

Wanting to pass the class, he studied very hard.

5. We sometimes use *upon* or *on* in place of *when* in an adverb phrase. The meaning is the same.

ADVERB CLAUSE: **When we entered** the house, we took off our shoes.

ADVERB PHRASE: **Upon entering** the house, we took off our shoes.

ADVERB PHRASE: **On entering** the house, we took off our shoes.

---

14   Practice

Complete the sentences about Julia's routine with reduced adverb clauses. Some sentences require an adverb from the list; others do not. Some sentences require a present participle; some require a past participle.

after   before   once   since   when   while

Julia is a very organized person. She gets up at 6:00 every morning and goes running

for 30 minutes (begin) ___*before beginning*___ work. (run) _____
                                        1   2

_____ , she plans her schedule. (come back) _____
                                                                           3

from her run, she takes a shower and eats breakfast. Then she sets herself a goal for each

part of her day. (set) _____ her goals, she also estimates how
                                         4

long each one will take and which ones are most important. (complete) _____
                                                                                                      5

_____ , her goals are checked off on a calendar. This helps her to track her

progress. (hope) _____ to get high grades in her courses, she has
                                     6

set herself a strict schedule. She studies for four hours every morning. She sometimes

listens to music (study) _____ . (eat) _____
                                        7   8

lunch, she goes to classes or to the library. (start) _____ to use
                                                                            9

this schedule, her grades have improved, and she completes her work on time.

---

15   Practice

Listen to the sentences. Can they be reduced or not? Write *Y* (for *yes*) or *N* (for *no*) next to each one. If the sentence can be reduced, rewrite it.

___Y___ 1. *After finishing an assignment, Julia checks her work carefully.*

_____ 2. _____

	3. _____
	4. _____
	5. _____
	6. _____
	7. _____
	8. _____

16   Pair Up and Talk
A   Practice the conversation with a partner.

A: What do you do before starting school?

B: Well, I try to exercise. When exercising, I think about the day ahead. After exercising; I take a shower. While showering, I listen to loud music on the radio.

B   Tell a partner about your routines. Ask and answer questions like the following, or use your own ideas. Use at least three reduced adverb clauses.

What do you do after finishing work/school?   What do you do while exercising?

What do you do before starting work/school?   What do you do after finishing work/school?

17   Phrasal Verb Practice
A   Complete the sentences with the correct forms of the phrasal verbs. Use each verb only once.

browse through	crack down	set up
come along	deal with	turn out

While I was ___*browsing through*___ some books yesterday, I found one on
                                1
endangered animals. It _____ to be an interesting book that
                                          2
_____ many endangered animals such as the kakapo. The
                3
kakapo is a flightless parrot that lives in New Zealand. For centuries, it lived there safely.

Then humans _____ and brought cats, rats, possums, and other
                                4
animals. The poor kakapo didn't last too long after that. So in 1976, they were moved to

smaller and safer places. Conservationists _____ new programs

5

to save the kakapo and _____ on allowing animals such as cats

6

and rats in those places.

B   Match the phrasal verb with the correct definition.

_____ **1.** come along   **a.** become more strict about

_____ **2.** browse through   **b.** establish

_____ **3.** turn out   **c.** look at without a clear purpose

_____ **4.** set up   **d.** happen to be, in the end

_____ **5.** deal with   **e.** appear, arrive

_____ **6.** crack down   **f.** be about a subject or idea

Listening Puzzle

AUDIO DOWNLOAD   CD3, 10

A   Listen and check the correct answer.

❏ A. *typhoon*   ❏ B. *tornado*   ❏ C. *sandstorm*

B   Discuss your answer with your classmates.

AUDIO DOWNLOAD CD3, 11

C   Now listen again and write the sentences you hear.

Review

Paul Gauguin was born in Paris, (but/even though)¹ he spent part of his childhood in Peru before his family returned to France. (Even though/While)² a young man, he worked as a sailor; (whereas/however)³, he eventually settled down and got married. (While as/While)⁴ he was married, he worked as a stockbroker and had five children. (As/Although)⁵ time went by, Gauguin took up painting as a hobby. (After/Before)⁶ a few years, he realized that he wasn't happy (in case/unless)⁷ he was painting. (As/When)⁸ he was 35, he quit his job and started to paint full time; (although/however)⁹, he could not make enough money to support his family. (Even though/Because)¹⁰ his wife loved him, she felt she had to leave. She took the children to her family in Denmark (as/so)¹¹ they could have food and clothes. (Whereas/Although)¹² they had been happy for a time, Gauguin and his wife never lived together again.

(Because/While)¹³ Gauguin had a unique style of painting, he had difficulty selling his work; (nevertheless/consequently)¹⁴, he refused to give up. He was painting in large shapes and bright colors, (whereas/because)¹⁵ other artists were painting the old way, with small details and dark colors. There were a few other artists, such as Vincent Van Gogh, who were trying new things, (so that/but)¹⁶ they weren't selling their works either; (nevertheless/consequently)¹⁷, they were very poor.

Gauguin got tired of it all, (so/when)¹⁸ in 1891, he decided to go to the island of Tahiti in the South Pacific. (After/While)¹⁹ landing there, he moved into a grass hut and started to paint. Gauguin went back to France in 1893. He hoped to sell his paintings; (however/although)²⁰, the trip was not a success. Two years later, Gauguin went back to Tahiti—never to return home. In 1901, he went to the Marquesas Islands where he died penniless and alone. Like Van Gogh, he was considered a failure as an artist; (as a result/nevertheless)²¹, after their deaths they became famous. Today, their paintings sell for millions of dollars.

As
~~As soon as~~ more and more people try cross-country, or Nordic, skiing, it is becoming more popular than ever. There are several reasons why. In order ski downhill or snowboard, you must have deep snow where to do cross-country skiing you need only a few inches of snow on the ground. While you do downhill skiing you need to go to a special area and take lifts to the top of the mountain, nevertheless when do cross-country skiing, you can use any field or forest. You don't need to buy lift tickets to ski along forest trails because cross-country skiing doesn't cost very much to do.

Because of you're not rushing down a hill at a high speed Nordic skiing is safe and easy to learn. It's good for you, too. Since you're enjoying your winter surroundings, you're also getting a good physical workout. While you're ready to go cross-country skiing it's easy to find good cross-country routes. Even there's no snow where you live most mountain ski areas have miles and miles of trails.

Since it became a popular sport cross-country skiing was often the only way people could travel in snow country. In cold areas of the north, people couldn't go anywhere though they strapped on their skis. Because some people still cross-country ski out of necessity, most people do it for fun. Before go cross-country skiing, you probably should have a lesson. It may seem hard at first since most instructors say that people are usually gliding along after only a few hours.

A Before You Read

1. Food that contains a lot of chili peppers is considered "hot." How hot do you like your food?
2. Have you ever eaten a really hot pepper? Describe the experience.

Chili Peppers

DID YOU KNOW ... ?
The ribs inside a chili, to which the seeds are attached, are the hottest part.

B Read Wherever cooks pride themselves on spicy hot dishes, chili peppers are respected, but not loved.
5 Because they **routinely** burn people and bring them to tears, chilies are hard to love.

Although they share the name *pepper*, a chili is not related to the black pepper you
10 see on a dinner table. That is from the dried berries of Asian plants in the genus[1] *Piper*. Chili peppers belong to a different genus, *Capsicum*. They originally come from South America, probably from Bolivia. Over thousands of years,
15 they spread throughout the Americas and the Caribbean islands. Before Christopher Columbus brought some back in the 1490s, chili peppers were almost unknown in Europe and Asia. The Portuguese brought capsicum plants to their
20 settlements in India, China, and elsewhere in the 1500s. The chili-rich cuisines of India, Thailand, and other Asian countries are very young traditions.

Large green (or yellow or red) bell peppers
25 are mild, more like a salad vegetable than a spice. Others, such as the jalapeño or habañero, can be hot. The heat depends on the amount of a chemical called capsaicin. ▪ If this compound touches heat-sensing parts of the mouth, they tell
30 the brain that they are touching something hot. ▪ A bite into a hot chili releases so much capsaicin that the body reacts as if it were in danger. ▪ The skin sweats, the heart beats fast, and the brain produces painkillers called endorphins. ▪
35 Some people may like eating hot chilies because they like those endorphins. Chili-eaters may be willing to **go through** the pain in order to get the painkiller. Many athletes, after all, seek the endorphins of a "runner's high" by enduring
40 the pain of hard exercise. Or perhaps a chili-eater likes "controlled risk." Instead of encountering a truly dangerous situation, he or she deliberately does something that seems dangerous but really isn't. The relief at coming through it unharmed
45 may feel good. In any case, eating them is healthy. They contain vitamins C and A.

[1] *genus = a category of living things*

C Notice the Grammar Underline all the adverb clauses.

Choose the best answer.

D Look for Main Ideas

1. What is the main topic of paragraph 3?
   - (A) how endorphins work
   - (B) damage caused by chilies
   - (C) the body's reaction to chilies
   - (D) why people like chilies

E Look for Details

2. All of the following are mentioned in the reading as types of chilies EXCEPT _____ .
   - (A) bell pepper
   - (C) jalapeños
   - (B) black pepper
   - (D) habañeros

3. According to the reading, controlled risk involves a situation that _____ .
   - (A) is not truly dangerous
   - (B) may cause serious harm
   - (C) causes the production of endorphins
   - (D) feels comfortable and safe

F Make Inferences

4. We can most strongly infer from paragraph 2 that _____ .
   - (A) Columbus visited southeastern Bolivia
   - (B) Columbus ate food containing chilies
   - (C) capsicum grew where Columbus visited
   - (D) chilies cannot grow in Europe or Asia

G Look for Vocabulary

5. The word *routinely* in the reading is closest in meaning to _____ .
   - (A) often
   - (B) probably
   - (C) severely
   - (D) seldom

READING SKILL:
Organization Questions

Organization questions ask about the general organization of a passage. They may ask where information is located, how ideas are joined together, or what structure the author used (such as compare and contrast). To answer an organization question, look at the passage as a whole and find logical patterns or structures. Organization questions appear on many reading comprehension tests.

6. The term *go through* in the reading is closest in meaning to _____ .
   - (A) skip
   - (B) fear
   - (C) experience
   - (D) examine

H Sentence Addition

7. Look at the four squares ■ that indicate where the following sentence could be added to the passage.
   The body reacts in similar ways if capsaicin touches the eyes, nose, or other sensitive areas.
   Where would the sentence best fit?
   - (A) at the first square
   - (B) at the second square
   - (C) at the third square
   - (D) at the fourth square

I Organization

8. In which paragraph does the author describe the body's response to eating a hot pepper?
   - (A) paragraph 1
   - (B) paragraph 2
   - (C) paragraph 3
   - (D) paragraph 4

Writing: Write an Essay of Comparison or Contrast

When we compare, we look at the similarities between two things. When we contrast, we look at their differences.

STEP **1** **Choose a topic from the list. Take notes on the similarities or differences between the two things. Decide if you will write an essay of comparison or contrast.**

1. life in the country and life in the city
2. transportation now and transportation 20 years ago
3. owning a car or traveling by public transportation
4. studying in a foreign country or studying in your country

Transportation Now and 20 Years Ago

<u>Similarities</u>

most people drive cars

air travel for long distance

few areas have mass transit

<u>Differences</u>

some cars are more efficient now

air travel less comfortable then

some cars run on electricity now

STEP **2** **Choose two or three points of comparison or contrast.**

STEP **3** **Write your essay. Write a title for your essay. Organize your essay like this:**

1. Introduction: State your topic. Include a thesis statement that states what you will say.
2. Body: Write a paragraph on each of the points you chose in Step 2.
3. Conclusion: Summarize your points and restate your thesis statement.

STEP **4** **Evaluate your essay.**
Checklist

_____ Did you write an introduction with a thesis statement, one paragraph for each point of comparison or contrast, and a conclusion?

_____ Do your paragraphs support your thesis statement?

_____ Did you use some words and phrases of comparison or contrast?

STEP **5** **Edit your essay. With a partner or teacher. Check spelling, vocabulary, and grammar.**

STEP **6** **Write your final copy.**

Self-Test

1. _____ she arrives, she will check into a hotel.

   A. As soon as   Ⓐ   Ⓑ   Ⓒ   Ⓓ
   B. It is when
   C. Since
   D. As

2. _____ she was late, she didn't hurry.

   A. For   Ⓐ   Ⓑ   Ⓒ   Ⓓ
   B. Nevertheless
   C. However
   D. Although

3. The movie was so good _____ saw it three times.

   A. although I   Ⓐ   Ⓑ   Ⓒ   Ⓓ
   B. that I
   C. for I
   D. because I

4. We didn't go on a picnic _____ it was raining.

   A. although   Ⓐ   Ⓑ   Ⓒ   Ⓓ
   B. because of
   C. because
   D. as a result

5. She went to the library _____ return a book.

   A. in order to   Ⓐ   Ⓑ   Ⓒ   Ⓓ
   B. so to
   C. because
   D. so that to

6. It was _____ a difficult poem that nobody in class understood it.

   A. so   Ⓐ   Ⓑ   Ⓒ   Ⓓ
   B. too
   C. such
   D. that

7. Take some food with you _____ you get hungry on the way.

   A. in case   Ⓐ   Ⓑ   Ⓒ   Ⓓ
   B. unless
   C. even if
   D. while

8. You should see a doctor _____ you don't feel well.

   A. unless   Ⓐ   Ⓑ   Ⓒ   Ⓓ
   B. if
   C. in order to
   D. because of

9. _____ the best qualifications, she got the job.

   A. Because having   Ⓐ   Ⓑ   Ⓒ   Ⓓ
   B. Because she having
   C. Having
   D. Because having of

10. _____ sitting on a train, he had an idea.

   A. While   Ⓐ   Ⓑ   Ⓒ   Ⓓ
   B. While he
   C. He was
   D. While was

1. <u>Even</u> he has <u>a number of</u> relatives <u>who</u> live
     A   **B**   **C**
   close by, he never visits <u>them</u>.
                            D

   (A) (B) (C) (D)

2. She has <u>so</u> a good memory <u>that</u> she can
          A   **B**
   remember a <u>person's</u> exact words <u>even</u> a
             C   **D**
   week later.

   (A) (B) (C) (D)

3. He repeated <u>all</u> the new <u>vocabulary</u> <u>in order</u>
               A   **B**   **C**
   remember <u>it</u>.
          D

   (A) (B) (C) (D)

4. <u>Why don't we</u> close all the windows <u>case</u> <u>it</u>
     A   **B** **C**
   <u>rains while</u> we are not home?
     D

   (A) (B) (C) (D)

5. <u>She is</u> very <u>organized</u> at work; <u>therefore,</u> her
     A   **B**   **C**
   apartment is very <u>messy</u>.
                D

   (A) (B) (C) (D)

6. <u>Because working</u> from home, Ken <u>had</u> <u>little</u>
           A   **B** **C**
   <u>contact</u> with people.
     D

   (A) (B) (C) (D)

7. She called her mother <u>soon as</u> <u>she</u> heard <u>she</u>
                      A   **B**   **C**
   <u>had passed</u> the test.
     D

   (A) (B) (C) (D)

8. Whether <u>or not</u> <u>I pass</u> the test tomorrow, I
           A   **B**
   <u>will call</u> you <u>or not</u>.
     C   **D**

   (A) (B) (C) (D)

9. <u>I'll take</u> my umbrella with me now <u>if</u> it
    A   **B**
   <u>rains</u> <u>later</u>.
    C   **D**

   (A) (B) (C) (D)

10. Only if <u>I</u> <u>found</u> a job here <u>I would</u> <u>move</u> to
          A **B**   **C**   **D**
   this city.

   (A) (B) (C) (D)

Unit 14
Conditional Sentences

I feel **as if** I've been sitting in this traffic all day.

Real Conditional Sentences in the Present and Future

Form

If you **water** a plant, it **grows**.
A plant grows **if you water it.**

1. We use two clauses in a conditional sentence: a dependent *if* clause and a main clause. The *if* clause states a condition, and the main clause states a result.

2. The *if* clause can come before or after the main clause with no change in meaning. If the *if* clause comes first, we put a comma after it.

   If you water a plant, it grows. A plant grows **if you water it**.

3. A sentence that expresses a real condition has a present verb in the *if* clause, and a present or future verb in the main clause.

If Clause			Main Clause		
Subject	Present Verb		Subject	Present or Future Verb	
If you	water	a plant,	it	grows.	
If it	rains	tomorrow,	we	will go	to a movie.

Function

1. We use the present real conditional (present in the main clause) to say that something always happens in a specific situation.

   If I **eat** too much, I **don't feel** well.

2. We use the present real conditional to talk about a general fact that is always true.

   If you **heat** butter, it **melts**.

3. We use the future real conditional (future in the main clause) to talk about something that may possibly happen in the future.

   If it **rains**, we **will go** to a movie. (It may rain, or it may not. But if it does, we will go to a movie.)

   If my parents **come** to visit me this summer, I**'m going to take** them to New York.

4. We can also use *should* after *if* when we are less sure of something.

   If I **see** Tony, I'll tell him. (Perhaps I will see Tony.)

   If I **should see** Tony, I'll tell him. (I am less sure I will see Tony.)

5. We can also use the imperative in the main clause of a future conditional sentence.

   If you see Tony, **tell** him to wait.   If the phone rings, please **pick** it **up**.

1 Practice

With a partner, read the proverbs and decide what they mean. Then rewrite the proverbs using *if* sentences in the present. (Note: *He who …* is a way of starting a proverb. It means "a person who … ")

1. Don't cry over spilt milk. (spilt = spilled)

   If you make a mistake, there is no point in crying about it.

2. Look before you leap. (leap = jump)

_____

3. Many hands make light work. (light = easy)

_____

4. Where there's smoke, there's fire.

_____

5. An apple a day keeps the doctor away.

_____

6. It never rains, but it pours. (= Every time it rains, it pours.)

_____

7. Fish and guests smell after three days.

_____

8. First things first. (First things come first.)

_____

9. Nothing ventured, nothing gained. (ventured = risked, tried)

_____

2 Practice

Read the recipe. Then match the two halves of the sentences.

Chocolate Brownies

Ingredients	Directions
½ cup butter	Heat the butter and chocolate slowly
4 oz. chocolate	until they melt. Mix the eggs and add
4 eggs, at room temperature	the salt, sugar and vanilla gradually.
½ teaspoon salt	Add the butter and chocolate mixture
2 cups sugar	to the egg mixture and stir with a
1 teaspoon vanilla	spoon, not an electric mixer. Stir in the
1 cup sifted flour	flour and the nuts. Bake for 25 minutes
1 cup chopped nuts	in a 9 x 9-inch pan. Eat the brownies
	the same day or wrap them in foil.

____d____ 1. If you don't heat the butter
and chocolate slowly,

_____ 2. If you use an electric mixer,

_____ 3. If you don't sift the flour,

_____ 4. If you bake them for an hour,

_____ 5. If you wrap the brownies in foil,

a. the mixture will get lumpy.

b. they will burn.

c. they will stay fresh for several days.

d. the butter will burn.

e. the mixture will get too smooth.

3 Pair Up and Talk

A Practice the conversation with a partner.

A: Do you know any cooking tips?

B: Sure. I have a tip for boiling eggs. If you put a boiled egg in cold water, it will be easier to peel.

B Think of something you know how to cook or use an idea from the list. Share it with your partner using a real conditional sentence in the present or future.

boiling eggs   making rice

keeping bread fresh   ripening fruit quickly

making coffee or tea setting the table

Unreal Conditional Sentences in the Present or Future

Form

What **would** you do if you **saw** someone breaking into your house?

A sentence that expresses an unreal condition in the present or future has a past verb in the *if* clause and *would* or *could* + a base verb in the main clause.

If Clause			Main Clause		
Subject	**Past Verb**		**Subject**	**Would/Could + Base Verb**	
If I	had	a problem,	I	would tell	you.
If we	were	on vacation,	we	would be	on the beach.
If she	weren't	so busy,	she	could help	you.
If I	were*	you,	I	wouldn't accept	that offer.

*Careful speakers usually use *were* when the subject is *I, he, she, it,* or a singular noun. However, many people use *was*. In academic and formal business situations, it's better to use *were*.

Function

1. We use *if* + the simple past in the *if* clause and *would/could* + a base verb in the main clause to talk about an unreal, hypothetical, or contrary-to-fact situation in the present or future.

   If I **had** a lot of money, I **would** travel around the world. (But I don't have a lot of money.)

2. We often use *were* when giving advice. The *if* clause with *were* makes the sentence sound softer.

   A: Do you think that I can turn my paper in a few days late?

   B: If I **were** you, I'**d ask** the instructor.

3. We can use *could* instead of *would* in the main clause. *Could* means *would be able to*.

   If I **had** more time, I **could help** you.

4 Practice

On a separate sheet of paper, write what you would and wouldn't do in each situation. Give a reason for your advice.

1. If you found a wallet with $500 in it in a taxi, what would you do? Why?

   If I found a wallet with $500 in it, I would give it to the driver.
   Maybe the person who lost it would call the taxi company.
   OR If I found a wallet with $500 in it, I wouldn't keep it. I don't think
   that's honest.

2. If a burglar broke into your house, and you were alone, what would you do? Why?

3. If you saw someone stealing cans of soup in the supermarket, what would you do? Why?

4. If a car hit a cyclist, the driver didn't stop, and the cyclist were left lying injured in the road, what would you do? Why?

5. If a friend of yours were downloading music from a website without paying, and you knew it was illegal, what would you do? Why?

5 Pair Up and Talk

Think of a situation where you had to make a difficult decision. Describe the situation to a partner. Your partner will try to imagine what he or she would do in that same situation.

A: Once a clerk at a store gave me too much in change. I noticed it, but I didn't say anything. I just kept the money. I still feel bad about it. What would you do in that situation?

6 Phrasal Verb Practice

A Complete the sentences with the correct forms of the phrasal verbs. Use each verb only once.

allow for	miss out	stick to
load down	snap up	try on

MATT: Hi, John. Did you hear about the big sale at Sports City?

JOHN: Yes! I heard people have been leaving the store *loaded down* with great equipment.

1

MATT: Did you go?

JOHN: I went, but I got there too late. I got into a traffic jam on South Main Street.

MATT: You should have _____ the usual traffic and left earlier.

2

JOHN: Yes, you're right. I should have _____ my new resolution to get up earlier.

3

MATT: Well, I got there late, too. I _____ a pair of skis, but I didn't like them.

4

Everyone had already _____ all the best items.

5

JOHN: Well, it looks as if we both _____ on those great bargains. Oh, well.

6

B Underline the correct definition of the phrasal verb.

1. load down
a. give an unfair advantage
b. put a large amount on or in
c. take away a great weight

2. allow for
a. factor in
b. pass judgment on
c. give up

3. snap up
a. break apart
b. take or buy quickly
c. free oneself

4. stick to
a. carry out to the end
b. come or go after
c. listen carefully

5. try on
a. test something
b. complete
c. put on to see if it fits

6. miss out
a. reply to
b. not do something you would enjoy
c. encourage

Unreal Conditional Sentences in the Past; Mixed Conditional Sentences

Form

> If we **had left** earlier, we **wouldn't be** in this traffic.

UNREAL CONDITIONAL SENTENCES IN THE PAST

If Clause			Main Clause		
Subject	Past Perfect Verb		Subject	*Would/Could* + *Have* + Past Participle of Verb	
If I	**had worked**	harder,	I	**would have done**	better.
If she	**hadn't been**	so busy,	she	**might have helped**	you.
If we	**hadn't helped**	the man,	he	**could have died**.	

MIXED CONDITIONAL SENTENCES

If Clause			Main Clause		
Subject	Verb		Subject	Verb	
If we	**had left**	earlier,	we	**would be**	home now.
If they	**hadn't broken**	the DVD,	they	**could be watching**	a movie now.
If I	**were**	you,	I	**would have**	walked.

Function

UNREAL CONDITIONAL SENTENCES IN THE PAST

1. We use the past unreal conditional to talk about an unreal, hypothetical, or contrary-to-fact situation in the past. Both clauses refer to unreal conditions in the past.

> If she **had had** the opportunity, she **would have gone** to college.
>
> (But she didn't have the opportunity, and she didn't go to college.)
>
> If you **had seen** the movie, you **would have enjoyed** it.
>
> (But you didn't see the movie, so you didn't have the opportunity to enjoy it.)
>
> If it **hadn't rained** all morning, we **would have gone out**.
>
> (But it did rain all morning, and we didn't go out.)

2. We can use the modals *would*, *might*, and *could* in the main clause. We use *would have* + a past participle in the main clause if we think the past action was certain.

> If I **had seen** you yesterday, I **would have given** the money to you then.
>
> (I would definitely have given it to you.)

We use *might have* + a past participle in the main clause if we think the past action was possible.

> If you **had taken** the test, you **might have passed** it.
>
> (It's possible that you would have passed it.)

We use *could have* + a past participle to say that someone would have been able to do something in the past.

> We **could have eaten** in the park if we **had brought** some food with us.
>
> (We would have been able to eat in the park.)

In some parts of the United States, people use *would have* + a past participle in the *if* clause, as well as in the main clause.

> If you *would've* said something, I *wouldn't have* bought it.

This usage is not generally considered to be grammatically correct.

MIXED CONDITIONAL SENTENCES

3. Conditional sentences can have mixed sequences, but the form must make sense in the context.

> If he **had played** basketball in high school, he **would be** a great college player now.
>
> (He didn't play basketball in the past, and he isn't a great college player now.)

> If John **were** my child, I **would have encouraged** him to play basketball, not football.
>
> (John is not my child. I didn't encourage him to play basketball.)

7 Practice

A Read the story of Romeo and Juliet.

Romeo and Juliet are in love, but their families hate each other. The young couple know that they will never get permission to marry, so they decide to marry secretly. A friendly friar[1] agrees to perform the marriage ceremony. After the ceremony, Romeo finds his friends in a fight. Romeo kills Juliet's cousin because the cousin had killed his best friend. Romeo is then sent away from the city as a punishment. Juliet's father wants Juliet to marry another man, so Juliet goes to the friar for help. He gives her a sleeping potion[2] to make her appear dead, and he says that he will send a message to Romeo to come and take her away. However, Romeo never receives the message. When he hears of Juliet's death, he goes to the tomb to see her dead body. In despair, he drinks poison and he dies. At that moment, the friar's drink wears off, and Juliet wakes up to find Romeo dead beside her. When she realizes what has happened, Juliet takes Romeo's dagger[3] and kills herself.

[1.] friar = a man in a Roman Catholic order
[2.] sleeping potion = a liquid that makes you sleep
[3.] dagger = a kind of knife

B Answer the questions in complete sentences. For some questions, you must think of your own answer.

1. What would have happened if Romeo and Juliet hadn't fallen in love?
   If they hadn't fallen in love, this story wouldn't have happened.

2. What would Romeo and Juliet have done if the friar hadn't married them?

3. What would Juliet have done if the friar had not given her the sleeping potion?

4. What would Romeo have done if he had received the friar's message?

    _____

5. What would have happened if Romeo had not taken the poison?

    _____

6. What would have happened if Juliet had not killed herself?

    _____

C Complete the sentences about the story. Use *might have* or *could have* in your answers.

1. If Romeo had not met Juliet, he *might have married someone else.*

    _____

2. If Romeo and Juliet's families had not hated each other, _____

    _____

3. If Romeo's friends had not been in a fight, _____

    _____

4. If Juliet had not taken the sleeping potion, _____

    _____

5. If Juliet had not found Romeo's dagger, _____

    _____

6. If Juliet had woken up a little sooner, _____

    _____

8 Your Turn

Think of a past event in your life that could have been very different. Write three sentences about what would or would not have happened in your life if the event had been different.

Example

If I hadn't graduated from high school, I wouldn't have gotten into college.

14D Conditional Sentences with *As If* and *As Though*

It looks **as if** there is a lot of activity around here.

1. We use *as if* before a subject and a verb to say how someone or something seems. We can use *as though* instead of *as if*.

    He looks **as if** he's cold. OR He looks **as though** he's cold.
    (He looks cold, but I don't know if he really is cold).
    It looks **as if** it's going to snow. OR It looks **as though** it's going to snow.
    (The weather looks like it might snow, but I don't know if it really will snow.)

2. When we use *as if* or *as though* + a past verb to talk about the present, the situation is unreal or probably unreal.

    He's acting **as if** he **were** my father. (He definitely is not my father.)
    I felt **as though** I **had run** a marathon. (I definitely did not run a marathon.)
    Careful speakers use *were* instead of *was* in unreal situations.

3. In informal English, we often use *like* instead of *as if* or *as though*. However, we use *as if* and *as though* in formal writing.

    He looks **like** he's cold.
    It looks **like** it's going to snow.

9 Practice

Read the descriptions. What do you think is going to happen? Use *as if*, *as though*, and *like*.

1. There are big black clouds in the sky.
    It looks as if it is going to rain.

2. Stan has a headache and sore throat, and he keeps sneezing.

    He feels _____

3. My neighbors are shouting, and I can hear dishes breaking.

It sounds _____

4. My brother applied for a new job, and they invited him to go for an interview in Seoul.

It looks _____

5. My friend has just finished her exam, and she is smiling confidently.

She looks _____

6. There is a lot of cheering and clapping coming from the office next door.

It sounds _____

7. The classroom is empty. The tables are covered with paper plates and pieces of leftover sandwiches.

It looks _____

8. Ron looked very unhappy this morning, and I heard him crying earlier.

It sounds _____

10   Pair Up and Talk

A   Practice the conversation with a partner.

A: It looks as if the girl has taken too many books.

B: I agree. It looks as though she's going to drop them all soon.

B   Look at the photo. What do you think has happened? What do you think is going to happen? Share your ideas with a partner. Use *as if*, *as though*, and *like*.

Form/Function

Had we **known** it would rain so much, we would have stayed home.

1. We can sometimes omit *if* and invert the auxiliaries *had*, *were*, or *should* and the *if* clause. This form is more common with *had* than with *were* or *should*.

    If I had known you were coming, I would have prepared some food.

    Had I known you were coming, I would have prepared some food.

    If I were you, I wouldn't go.

    Were I you, I wouldn't go.

    If I should see him, I'll give him the message.

    Should I see him, I'll give him the message.

    Careful speakers use *were* instead of *was* in unreal situations.

2. We can sometimes imply (not say something directly) a real or unreal conditional. We use other words and phrases such as *if so*, *if not*, *otherwise*, *with*, or *without*.

	Implied Conditional	Conditional
otherwise	I didn't hear the phone; otherwise, I would have answered it.	If I heard the phone, I would have answered it.
if so	This sounds like a good opportunity. If so, you should take it.	If you think it is a good opportunity, you should take it.
if not	I think that the earliest flight is at 8:00 A.M. If not, wait for the next one.	If the earliest flight is not at 8:00 A.M., wait for the next one.
without	Without your help, I couldn't have done this.	If you hadn't helped me, I couldn't have done this.
with	With your help, I will be able to do this.	If you help me, I will be able to do this.

11 Practice

A Read Ms. Winters's letter of complaint about a product that she has bought.

Dear Mr. McMullen:

I am writing to complain about a kitchen mixer that I purchased in your store in December. It was a birthday present for my mother. The first time we tried to use it, it splashed tomato soup all over the kitchen!

(1) Had I known the mixer was faulty, I would never have bought it. (2) I'm sure that we would have enjoyed her birthday better without buying your mixer. (3) Had your mixer not been faulty, we would not have spent two hours that morning cleaning up the mess.

I would like a refund and compensation for the damage to my kitchen. (4) Otherwise, I will take the matter to my lawyer. (5) Were our home not so far away, I would bring the mixer back in person.

(6) Should I need any kitchen appliances in the future, you can be sure I will not purchase them at your store!

Yours sincerely,
Susan Winters

B Rewrite the numbered sentences from the letter in Part A as conditional sentences using *if*.

1. If I had known that the mixer was faulty, I would never have bought it.

2. _____

3. _____

4. _____

5. _____

6. _____

Good Buy Appliances
1105 N. 6th St.
Tulsa, OK 74103

December 20, 2009

Dear Ms. Winters:

I am writing to apologize for the faulty mixer that you purchased from our store in December.

(1) If we had known the mixer was faulty, we would never have sold this model in our store. (2) The sales assistant would have identified the fault if he had tried out the machine before selling it to you. (3) If we had not received this information from you, we would have continued selling faulty mixers to other customers. (4) If you wish to have a replacement mixer, we will send one out to you immediately. (5) If you do not wish to have a replacement, we can offer you a complete refund.

(6) If you were to have any further problems with the replacement mixer, please let us know immediately. (7) If you have any other questions, please do not hesitate to get in touch.

We hope you are satisfied with our service. Please shop with us again in the future.

Yours sincerely,

Andrew McMullen
Customer Service Manager

B Rewrite the sentences in Part A as conditional clauses without *if*. Start your sentences with words from the list.

had he   had we   should you   were you   without

1. *Had we known that the mixer was faulty, we would never have sold this model in our store.*

2. _____

3. _____

4. _____

5. _____

6. _____

7. _____

13 Your Turn

Work with a partner. Write three past conditional sentences with *if*. Give them to your partner. Your partner will rewrite them as sentences without *if*.

Example

If I'd known about downloading songs from the Internet for a dollar, I wouldn't have bought so many CDs.

Had I known ...

1. _____

2. _____

3. _____

Form

I **wish** I **had chosen** another day for the picnic.

WISHES ABOUT THE PRESENT AND FUTURE

Main Clause			Noun Clause		
Subject	***Wish***	**(*That*)**	**Subject**	**Verb**	
I	wish		I	had	a car.
He	wishes		he	were	here.
We	wish	(that)	you	could come.	
You	wish		she	would stop	complaining.
They	wish		you	would come	with me tomorrow.

1. For wishes referring to the present or the future, we use *wish* in the simple present + a noun clause with a simple past verb or *would/could* + a base verb.

    I wish you'd come with me. (I want you to come with me, but I don't think you will.)

    I wish I could leave now. (I can't leave now.)

2. The use of *that* in a wish clause is optional. We often omit it.

3. Careful speakers use *were* instead of *was* in unreal situations.

WISHES ABOUT THE PAST

Main Clause			Noun Clause		
Subject	***Wish***	**(*That*)**	**Subject**	**Past Perfect Verb**	
I	wish		I	had gone	with you.
He	wishes	(that)	we	had come	earlier.
She	wished		she	had booked	her flight earlier.

4. For wishes referring to the past, we use *wish* in the simple present + a noun clause with a past perfect verb or *would/could* + a past perfect verb.

Function

1. We use *wish* + the simple past or *would/could* + a base verb to say that we would like something to be different in the present and future.

    I **wish** I **had** a car. (I do not have a car.)

    He **wishes** he **could play** the guitar. (He cannot play the guitar.)

2. We use *would* after *wish* to express the future action that we want to happen.

    I **wish** you**'d come** with me to the doctor. I'm scared to go by myself.

3. We can also use *would* after *wish* when we want something to stop happening, or we want something to change, but it probably won't.

    I **wish** she **would stop** complaining!

    I **wish** people **wouldn't pick** the flowers.

4. We use *wish* + the past perfect to express regret that something happened or did not happen in the past.

    I **wish** I **hadn't gone** to bed so late. (I did go to bed late.)

5. We use *wish* to express a desire for an unreal situation, but we use *hope* to express a desire for a possible real situation. Note the different forms that follow.

    After *wish*, the simple past shows the unreal situation. After *hope*, the simple present or future shows that the situation is possible. We use the simple past to talk about hopes for the past.

    UNREAL SITUATION: I wish I **had** more time. (I don't have more time.)

    POSSIBLE SITUATION: I hope I **have** more time. OR I hope **I'll have** more time.

    (Maybe I will have more time. I hope so.)

14 Practice

A   For many reasons, Oscar isn't very happy. Write wishes for Oscar that will make him happy.

1.   Oscar isn't rich. *He wishes he were rich.* _____

2.   His life isn't exciting. _____

3.   His apartment is small. _____

4.   He feels tired. _____

5.   He doesn't have any friends. _____

6.   He can't play the guitar. _____

B Listen to what happened to Oscar last week. Write what happened, then write wishes for Oscar after each event.

AUDIO
DOWNLOAD

CD3, 12

1. *His car broke down. He wishes his car hadn't broken down.*

2. _____

3. _____

4. _____

5. _____

6. _____

---

15   Your Turn

Write five things you wish were different about your life right now. Write five things you wish you hadn't done last weekend.

Example

I wish I didn't have to do so much homework.

I wish I hadn't spent so much time at my computer.

14G Conditional Sentences with *If Only*

Form/Function

> **If only** I **were** bigger. Then I could cross the street by myself.

1. *If only* has the same meaning as *wish* or *hope,* but it is more emphatic. We use *if only* in conversation and informal writing.

---

2. When we use the simple present after *if only*, we hope that something may become real in the present or future.

   If only I **get** the news today. (I really hope that I get the news.)

   If only my boss **is not** in the office today! (I really hope that he won't be in the office.)

3. We use the simple past form after *if only* when we wish for something that is unreal in the present.

   If only he **trusted** me. (He doesn't trust me, and I wish he did.)

   If only I **were** ready for this test. (I'm not ready for it, and I wish I were.)

   If only we **knew** his address. (We don't know his address, but I wish we did.)

   Remember, careful speakers use *were* instead of *was* in unreal situations.

4. We use *if only* + past perfect when we wish something had happened differently in the past.

   If only I **had explained** the situation to him. (I wish I had explained the situation to him, but I didn't.)

16   Practice

Listen to Linda stating facts about herself. Write wishes for Linda using *if only*.

CD3, 13

1. She thinks, " *If only I were athletic.* "

2. She thinks, " _____ "

3. " _____ "

4. " _____ "

5. " _____ "

6. " _____ "

7. " _____ "

8. " _____ "

17   Pair Up and Talk

A   Practice the conversation with a partner.

A: If only I had learned to drive.

B: Is that because you wish you didn't have to take the bus every day?

A: Exactly.

B   Write three regrets you have about your life or the world. Write sentences starting with *if only*. Share each sentence with a partner. Your partner will try to guess why you regret these things.

If only I had a car.

18   Read
Read the story. Then write answers to the questions.

THE TRAVELER AND THE NUT TREE

One day, a traveler stopped to rest under a big nut tree. Soon, he noticed a huge pumpkin growing on a thin vine.

"The ways of nature are foolish," the traveler said to himself. "If things were as they should be, this big, strong tree would hold the large pumpkins, and the thin vine would hold the nuts. Now if I made the world, that is how I'd have done it!"

At that moment, from high up in the tree, a small nut fell and hit him right on the head. The traveler, who was startled, looked up into the branches and realized his mistake, "Forgive my arrogance! If it were a big pumpkin that had fallen out of the tree onto my head, it most certainly would have killed me!"

1. According to the traveler, if things were as they should be, what would the big tree hold?

   _____

   _____ .

2. What would the thin vine hold?

   _____ .

3. Under what circumstances would this happen?

   _____ .

4. What hit the traveler on the head?

   _____ .

5. If the nut hadn't fallen on his head, what wouldn't the traveler have realized?

   _____

   _____ .

6. What would have happened if a big pumpkin had fallen onto his head?

   _____ .

Listening Puzzle

AUDIO DOWNLOAD   CD3, 14

A Listen and check the correct answer.

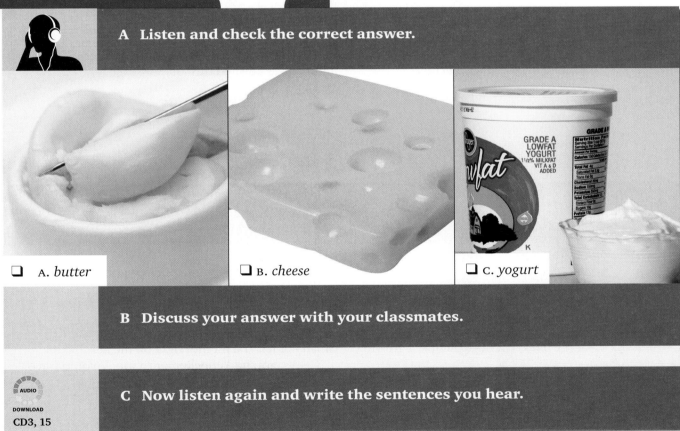

❏ A. *butter*   ❏ B. *cheese*   ❏ C. *yogurt*

GRADE A LOWFAT YOGURT 1½% MILKFAT VIT A & D ADDED

B Discuss your answer with your classmates.

AUDIO DOWNLOAD CD3, 15

C Now listen again and write the sentences you hear.

1 Review (14a–14c, 14e–14g)
Match the parts of the sentences.

_____ 1. If it snows,   a. otherwise, I would have told you it's sweet.

_____ 2. Had I known you were hungry,   b. I would put on a sweater.

_____ 3. Without your help,   c. I'd go to Australia.

_____ 4. If you need company,   d. leave a message.

_____ 5. I only wish   e. quit right now.

_____ 6. I didn't taste it;   f. we can go skiing.

_____ 7. If I don't answer the phone,   g. I would have made a sandwich.

_____ 8. If I had more vacation days,   h. I'll go with you.

_____ 9. If I were cold,   i. I hadn't bought those shoes.

_____ 10. I hate my job; I wish I could   j. I couldn't have finished this job.

Review

2 Review (14b–14d, 14f–g)
Complete the sentences with *if*, *as if*, *as though*, *if only*, or *wish*.

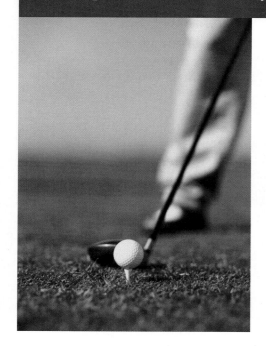

JIM: I'm in trouble! My boss saw me playing golf yesterday after I called the office to say I was sick. Now he's acting ____as if____ I were a criminal.
1

KELLEY: _____ you had checked with me, I would have
2
told you that he had a golf game yesterday.

JIM: When I saw him, I felt _____ a truck had hit me.
3
I _____ you'd come with me to his office.
4

KELLY: Oh no! _____ you gave me a million dollars, I still
5
wouldn't go into that office.

JIM: It's looks _____ things can't get worse. I
6

_____ I'd never called the office to say I was sick. I _____ I had a good excuse.
  7   8
I _____ I could change what happened. _____ I had gone to another golf
    9   10
course, he would never have seen me.

KELLY: You're acting _____ your choice of golf course was what you did wrong. _____
                          11   12
         you hadn't called to say you were sick and then gone golfing, you wouldn't be in trouble!

         _____ you play with fire, you get burned. _____ you took your work more
            13   14
         seriously, you wouldn't be in trouble.

JIM: I know.

KELLY: Anyway, _____ I were you. I'd tell the truth from now on.
                    15

JIM: Yes, it looks _____ I'll have to change my ways.
                          16

KELLY: You sound _____ that were a bad thing. You know that you need to change
                      17
         _____ you want to keep your job.
            18

JIM: I know. I know. I _____ you would stop talking about it. I've learned my lesson. But I
                              19
         still _____ I were rich so I wouldn't have to work at all!
                 20

A Before You Read

1. The sport called "soccer" in the U.S. and Canada is called "football" in most other English-speaking countries. What do you call it?

2. Why is soccer so popular?

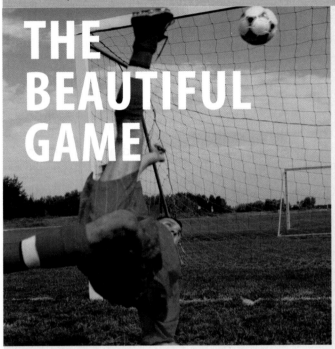

THE BEAUTIFUL GAME

DID YOU KNOW ... ?
Hungary scored the most goals of any team in a World Cup match. They beat El Salvador 10–1 in 1982.

B Read   You don't need much more to start a soccer game if you have a ball, an empty field, and four
5 rocks to mark goals. It has a small set of basic rules. But if simplicity were soccer's only virtue, **it** would not be the most popular sport on the planet. It's as if
10 it were a story with many levels. Simple action at the surface, deeper conflict underneath. The Brazilian soccer star Pelé once called it, "the beautiful game."

The sport is ancient. Archaeologists can
15 show that soccer-like games were played in Asia more than 3,000 years ago. But soccer and its cousins have always had a rough side. ▪ Sometimes, things got so far out of control that the game was made illegal. ▪ If you were caught
20 playing it in 14th-century England, you went to prison—as if that could kill the sport. ▪ It lived on among the English and others. ▪

If a war had not interrupted international soccer in the early 1900s, it might now be an
25 Olympic sport. European nations had formed a **governing** body for it (FIFA) in 1904. Then World War I came along. If soccer was to survive, it had to be on a nation-by-nation level. By the time international soccer became
30 possible again in the 1920s, professional leagues already existed in many countries. The Olympics at that time did not allow professionals to compete. So FIFA **founded** its own championship—the World Cup.

35 Today, the World Cup is the world's most-watched sporting event. More than one billion people watched the 2006 World Cup final on TV. That is about 15 percent of all the people on the planet at that time. If you're thinking about
40 the Super Bowl[1], the Wimbledon[2] final, or a World Series[3] game, forget it. In any year, you could add together the viewers[4] for all of them and not come close to one billion[5].

[1.] Super Bowl = the championship game in American football
[2.] Wimbledon = a tennis tournament held in England
[3.] World Series = the championship in North American baseball
[4.] viewer = someone who watches a TV show
[5.] billion = as used in North America, 1,000,000,000

C Notice the Grammar   Underline all the conditional sentences.

Choose the best answer.

D Look for Main Ideas

1. What is the main topic of paragraph 4?
    - Ⓐ the competition among sports for TV viewers
    - Ⓑ the popularity of the World Cup
    - Ⓒ winning the World Cup
    - Ⓓ the role of TV in soccer's success

E Look for Details

2. The reading mentions all of the following about soccer EXCEPT _____ .
    - Ⓐ it was once an Olympic sport
    - Ⓑ it was once illegal in England
    - Ⓒ it does not require much equipment
    - Ⓓ it is more complex than it appears to be

3. Why does the author mention the Super Bowl, Wimbledon, and the World Series in paragraph 4?
    - Ⓐ because they sometimes draw more viewers than the World Cup
    - Ⓑ because they are more international than the World Cup
    - Ⓒ because some readers might expect them to be bigger than the World Cup
    - Ⓓ because they are held every year, unlike the World Cup

F Make Inferences

4. We can most strongly infer from the reading that international soccer before World War I was _____ .
    - Ⓐ played by nonprofessionals
    - Ⓑ more popular than the Olympics
    - Ⓒ partly responsible for the war
    - Ⓓ one of the sports in the Olympics

G Look for Vocabulary

5. The word *founded* in the reading is closest in meaning to _____ .
    - Ⓐ completed
    - Ⓒ eliminated
    - Ⓑ discovered
    - Ⓓ established

6. The word *governing* in the reading is closest in meaning to _____ .
    - Ⓐ official
    - Ⓒ managing
    - Ⓑ professional
    - Ⓓ funding

H Look for References

7. The word *it* in the reading refers to _____ .
    - Ⓐ virtue
    - Ⓒ soccer
    - Ⓑ simplicity
    - Ⓓ set

I Sentence Addition

8. Look at the four squares ▪ that indicate where the following sentence could be added to the passage. **Soccer hooligans—fans who start fights and damage property—have been around for centuries.**
    Where would the sentence best fit?
    - Ⓐ at the first square
    - Ⓑ at the second square
    - Ⓒ at the third square
    - Ⓓ at the fourth square

Writing: Write a Persuasive Essay

When we write a persuasive essay, we try to make the reader agree with us. To do this, we give reasons for our point of view and support them with facts.

STEP 1   Write a persuasive essay about a global issue. Choose one of the following topics or one of your own. With a partner, think of two strong reasons for or against it.

1. eliminating nuclear weapons
2. reducing our dependence on oil
3. protecting endangered animals
4. the use of genetically modified foods

STEP 2   Think of or research facts to support your reasons.

STEP 3   Write your essay.

1. Write an introduction with a thesis statement. Your thesis statement should state your opinion and two reasons for it. Here is an example. The thesis statement is in bold.

2. Write the body of your essay. Write a paragraph for each of your two reasons. State the reasons and support them with facts.

> Every minute, over one hundred acres of the world's rain forests are destroyed to make land for farms and industries. The wood from the forests is made into paper, cardboard, and plywood. Rain forests cover only about two percent of the surface of Earth, but about half of the world's animals and plants live in them. **If we destroy our forests, we will not only destroy many of the world's animals and plants, but we will also threaten the livelihood of many of the people who depend on the forests.**

3. Write a conclusion that restates the thesis statement and your reasons.
4. Write a title for your essay.

STEP 4   Evaluate your essay.
Checklist

_____ Did you write an introduction that contains a thesis statement and a conclusion that restates your thesis statement and reasons?
_____ Did you present facts to support your reasons in the body?
_____ If you were another person reading your essay, would you be persuaded?

STEP 5   Edit your essay with a partner or teacher. Check spelling, vocabulary, and grammar.

STEP 6   Write your final copy.

Self-Test

1. You wouldn't be so hungry if you
   _____ breakfast.

   A. had eaten   Ⓐ Ⓑ Ⓒ Ⓓ
   B. have been eaten
   C. would have eaten
   D. eaten

2. I'll see her at the meeting if she _____ .

   A. came   Ⓐ Ⓑ Ⓒ Ⓓ
   B. come
   C. will come
   D. comes

3. I don't know what he _____ if he couldn't
   work there anymore.

   A. do   Ⓐ Ⓑ Ⓒ Ⓓ
   B. will do
   C. would do
   D. would have done

4. If you _____ warned us, we would have
   stayed at the hotel.

   A. wouldn't have   Ⓐ Ⓑ Ⓒ Ⓓ
   B. hadn't
   C. haven't
   D. didn't

5. If only I _____ his phone number, I would
   call him. Unfortunately, I never wrote it down.

   A. had known   Ⓐ Ⓑ Ⓒ Ⓓ
   B. know
   C. knew
   D. would have known

6. I don't know how to do this exercise. I wish I
   _____ the teacher about it.

   A. asked   Ⓐ Ⓑ Ⓒ Ⓓ
   B. had asked
   C. will ask
   D. would have asked

7. There are clouds in the sky. It looks _____
   it is going to rain.

   A. like if   Ⓐ Ⓑ Ⓒ Ⓓ
   B. as if
   C. though
   D. though if

8. If I _____ you, I wouldn't quit your job.

   A. were   Ⓐ Ⓑ Ⓒ Ⓓ
   B. was
   C. will be
   D. had been

9. I'm really tired. I wish I _____ on
   vacation now.

   A. could go   Ⓐ Ⓑ Ⓒ Ⓓ
   B. can go
   C. go
   D. would have gone

10. If you _____ tired, you should rest.

    A. would be   Ⓐ Ⓑ Ⓒ Ⓓ
    B. are
    C. had been
    D. were

B **Find the underlined word or phrase, A, B, C, or D, that is incorrect. Darken the oval with the same letter.**

1. Unless <u>I read</u> <u>the book</u>, I <u>will be</u> able <u>to answer</u>
        A   B   C   D
the questions about it.

      Ⓐ Ⓑ Ⓒ Ⓓ

2. I <u>could had</u> <u>finished</u> if I <u>had had</u> more time.
      A   B   C   D

      Ⓐ Ⓑ Ⓒ Ⓓ

3. I <u>would</u> <u>mail</u> the application now <u>if</u> I <u>am</u> you.
      A   B   C D

      Ⓐ Ⓑ Ⓒ Ⓓ

4. Tina <u>wishes</u> she <u>had</u> a better job and <u>can</u> <u>get</u> a
         A   B   C D
higher salary.

      Ⓐ Ⓑ Ⓒ Ⓓ

5. When should you go to New York? If you <u>don't</u>
                                               A
<u>like</u> hot weather, the best time <u>to go</u> <u>was</u> in
 B   C   D
May or June.

      Ⓐ Ⓑ Ⓒ Ⓓ

6. I <u>wish</u> I <u>could taken</u> guitar lessons <u>when</u> I
    A   B   C
<u>was</u> younger.
 D

      Ⓐ Ⓑ Ⓒ Ⓓ

7. If you <u>will</u> <u>mix</u> oil with water, the oil <u>sits</u>
  A   B   C   D
on top.

      Ⓐ Ⓑ Ⓒ Ⓓ

8. <u>If only</u> Tom <u>told</u> us earlier, we <u>wouldn't have</u>
   A   B   C
<u>gotten</u> an extra ticket for him.
 D

      Ⓐ Ⓑ Ⓒ Ⓓ

9. Where <u>you would</u> <u>go</u> <u>if</u> you <u>had</u> the opportunity?
         A   B C   D

      Ⓐ Ⓑ Ⓒ Ⓓ

10. I <u>could have</u> gone <u>for</u> a swim <u>if</u> I <u>brought</u> my
     A   B   C   D
swimsuit with me.

      Ⓐ Ⓑ Ⓒ Ⓓ

Audio Script

Unit 1, Practice 2, Page 5 (CD1, 2)

Karen: Hi, Dan! What are you doing these days?

Dan: Hi, Karen. I'm taking a course in computer programming. What about you?

Karen: Oh, I'm working at the library until July.

Dan: Do you like it?

Karen: Yes, I do. Right now, they're giving me a lot of training. Every morning, they train me for an hour. I work long hours, and I don't get home until seven. But that's OK because I'm learning a lot.

Dan: I'm looking for a job, too. It's becoming harder and harder to find a job. Companies are looking for people who are familiar with new software.

Karen: Are you learning about all the new software in your course?

Dan: Yes, I am.

Karen: How long does the course run?

Dan: It usually runs for eight weeks, but I'm doing it in six.

Karen: Do they give you a certificate at the end?

Dan: Yes, they do. They also give students a list of companies to contact about jobs.

Unit 1, Practice 3, Page 6 (CD1, 3)

1.

A: Where do your parents live?

B: They live in Mexico City.

2.

A: What's your brother doing these days?

B: He's looking for a new car.

3.

A: Look at that car! It's driving through a red light.

B: And now it's going faster. Where do you think it's going in such a hurry?

4.

A: How do you get to school every morning?

B: I usually walk. What about you?

5.

A: How are you doing in this class?

B: Not bad. My English compositions are getting better.

6.

A: Is the temperature cold enough to make ice?

B: Yes. Water freezes at 32 degrees Fahrenheit or 0 degrees celsius.

Unit 1, Practice 6, Page 10 (CD1, 4)

Ken: You have a nice apartment.

Maria: Thank you. It is small, but it has a nice view. You can see the lake from here.

Ken: Yes, I see it. Your apartment is very sunny, and I love your furniture.

Maria: Thank you. I know a very good furniture store that has great things, and they don't cost much. I'm going there today with a friend. You can come with us if you want.

Ken: That sounds great! I'm thinking about buying a new sofa, but I don't know where to go.

Unit 1, Practice 10, Page 16 (CD1, 5)

Barbara Bates is an actor who has made over 20 movies in her career. She started acting when she was 13 years old, and she has traveled to many parts of the world. She has finished a romantic comedy with the famous actor Jason James. Although she has done lots of comedies, she hasn't acted in a drama. But has she won an Oscar? Not yet, but she has not given up. She says that she has not had the right part that could win an Oscar for her.

Unit 1, Listening Puzzle, Page 21 (CD1, 6–7)

This is a grain from which many kinds of food are made. It is the world's number-one food crop, providing a greater volume of food than any other. The plants that produce it are kinds of grass and are annuals — meaning they grow for only one year. It probably originated somewhere in southwest or west-central Asia. Archaeologists have found remains of it in human settlements about 12,000 years old. It grows best in regions, like the grasslands of Asia, where rainfall is not very heavy and humidity is low. Unlike many other grains, it is not usually eaten whole. Most often, it is ground into flour for baking bread or making noodles. What is this?

Unit 2, Practice 1, Page 33 (CD1, 8)

A

Yushen: You won't believe what happened to me this morning.

Luke: What happened?

Yushen: I was waiting at the bus stop when I saw an accident, or almost an accident. A man was talking on his cell phone while he was driving. He wasn't paying attention to the road when suddenly the traffic light turned red. A woman was crossing the street at that moment.

Luke: Wow! Did he see her?

Yushen: Yes, he stopped the car just in time.

Luke: Was the woman hurt?

Yushen: No, she wasn't hurt, but she was lucky.

B

Sonia: Tell me about something scary that happened to you.

Jim: Well, let's see. A few months ago, I was sitting at home alone. I was watching a show on TV, and I was feeling tired. I was thinking about going to bed when I heard a noise.

Sonia: Where was the noise coming from?

Jim: It seemed to be coming from upstairs.

Sonia: Were you scared at that point?

Jim: Yes, I was. Very scared. I turned off the TV, took the cordless phone in my hand, and started to walk up the stairs. Then I heard the same noise again. I called the police.

Unit 2, Practice 5, Page 35 (CD1, 9)

Tiger Woods was born in California in 1975. His father taught Tiger to play golf when he was only nine months old, and Tiger played his first game when he was one and a half years old. At the age of eight, he won his first tournament. He has won many tournaments since then. He has also earned a lot of money! In recent years, Tiger has helped to make golf a popular sport. Tiger says the best advice he has ever gotten was from his father, who told him these words a long time ago, "Always be yourself."

Unit 2, Listening Puzzle, Page 49 (CD1, 10–11)

Work started on this canal in 1882. It was the idea of a Frenchman but after eight years he gave up because he had lost thousands of lives and millions of dollars. In fact, 20,000 had died because of the disease malaria. Mosquitos were spreading the disease. Before work began again on the canal, they had to solve the problem of the disease. They drained the swamps to kill the mosquitos. The Americans now started work on the canal in 1904. They used the largest and most modern machinery of the time. They completed the canal in 1914. It is the world's busiest ship canal and links the Pacific and Atlantic oceans. What is the name of this canal?

Unit 3, Practice 1, Page 60 (CD1, 12)

Tim: What are you going to do tonight?
Mike: I'm going to see the new Steven Spielberg movie with Melissa. How about you?
Tim: Oh, I think I'll stay home tonight.
Mike: Why don't you come with us? It'll be fun.
Tim: OK. I'll go with you.
Mike: We're going to leave at seven, and we'll probably get there by seven thirty.
Tim: OK. I'll see you in front of the movie theater at 7:30 then.

Unit 3, Practice 4A, Page 63 (CD1, 13)

I want to be a rich and famous rock star in the future. I will be a famous rock star before I am 25. When I'm 30, I'll have a lot of money. As soon as I become a millionaire, I'll retire.
After I retire early, I'll travel all over the world. As soon as I have enough time and money, I'll go to Africa. After I have seen the main cities, I'll go to Asia. When I go there, I'll visit my friend Hong in China. If he has time, he'll show me around. Before I come back home, I'll visit Japan.
When I come back home, I'll go back to my hometown and buy a big house. I'll help out my parents if they want me to.

Unit 3, Practice 12, Page 71 (CD1, 14)

Isabel is talking to her friend Susan about going on a vacation to Barcelona, Spain. Susan's family lives there, and Isabel is going to stay with them.

Susan: When you arrive at the airport in Barcelona, my sister will be waiting for you.
Isabel: How will we know each other? We've never met.
Susan: Don't worry. She has a photo of you. Anyway, you won't miss her. She looks like me, and she'll be wearing a red dress or jacket. She always wears red.
Isabel: OK. I won't worry. I still can't believe it. This time tomorrow, I'll be sitting on a plane on my way to Spain.
Susan: And at one o'clock the next day, you'll be eating lunch with my family, and then you'll be having a siesta, which is what we call an afternoon rest.

Unit 3, Listening Puzzle, Page 81 (CD1, 15–16)

This is a vehicle that orbits the Earth. They launch it from the surface on board a rocket. Then they drop the rocket, and the vehicle, now on its own, begins orbiting the planet. It completes two orbits of the Earth each day. It is part of a system run by the United States. The system is growing, and soon it will include 32 vehicles — or more. Controllers on Earth communicate with it by sending radio signals. In return, it sends radio signals back that help drivers, pilots, hikers, and explorers know where they are. All this is done automatically, because this vehicle carries no people. What is it?

Unit 4, Practice 6, Page 96 (CD1, 17)

Helen: Jack's sister and I went out to dinner last night. The food was wonderful, but I can't remember the name of the restaurant. It was something like Tony's Place.
Pete: Where was it?
Helen: I can't remember the name of the street, but it was on the opposite side of the street from Mike's Pizza. The freshness of the food was incredible, and you would like the size of the portions.
Pete: Was it expensive?
Helen: The price of the main courses was a little high, but if you have the specials of the day, you won't spend much.
Pete: Sounds good. Maybe I'll try it.

Unit 4, Practice 12, Page 103 (CD1, 18)

1.
A: May I have some water?
B: Of course. Help yourself. The glasses on this shelf are for water.
2.
A: How was your trip to Paris?
B: Amazing. Climbing the Eiffel Tower was an experience I will never forget.
3.
A: My mother's hair turned gray when she was only 30.
B: I hope that doesn't happen to me. I'm 25, and I already have two gray hairs.
4.
A: Do you have time to help me with my homework?
B: Sure. I can help you this afternoon.
5.
A: The company wanted someone with experience in marketing or sales.
B: That sounds perfect for you. You've worked in marketing before.
6.
A: Have you met the manager before?
B: Yes, we've met several times.
7.
A: What an unusual office building. What's it made of?
B: The outside is made of glass and wood.
8.
A: I like this desk.
B: Thanks. My brother made it. He used three different woods.

Unit 4, Practice 15, Page 105 (CD1, 19)

Maria: Could you go to the store for me? I want to make spaghetti tonight, and I need tomato sauce and some olive oil.
Carla: Sure! And are there any other things that you need?
Maria: Well, I don't have any cheese. Could you get some Parmesan cheese?
Carla: Of course, about half a pound? Oh, what kind of olive oil do you want?
Maria: Oh, any kind of olive oil will do ... as long as it's virgin olive oil.
Carla: Could you make some garlic bread to go with the spaghetti?
Maria: Good idea! Get some garlic, and get some more bread just in case we have some extra guests.
Carla: OK. I'm on my way. Oh, wait – I don't have any money!

Unit 4, Practice 22, Page 111 (CD1, 20)

A: We have breaking news from Miami, Florida, where firefighters are working hard to put out a fire. The fire started at seven this morning, at Andy's Restaurant on Palm Street. It then spread to Pat's Pizza Palace next door. The fire burned so fast that firefighters could not save either of these restaurants. The fire then spread to two other businesses nearby, a clothing store called Ocean Outfitters, and a photocopy shop called Cat's Copies. Firefighters are concerned that all of the other businesses on Ocean Street may be in danger if they can't get this fire under control very soon. The shops and restaurants on this street are very close to each other. However, the fire department warns worried business owners and shoppers to stay away from the area. A few minutes ago, we spoke with Fire Chief John Russell. Here's what he had to say:

B: We have great firefighters, and every one of them is working hard to get this situation under control. We think we can save many buildings, but unfortunately, it looks like almost all of them will have some smoke or water damage. Now, it's very important for everyone to stay out of their way and let them do their job. Also, there are only three streets that can take you to Ocean Street, and right now they are all blocked off by police cars. So if you need to travel near Ocean Street, please look for an alternative route.

Unit 4, Listening Puzzle, Page 113 (CD1, 21–22)

This is a baked food that we often eat for dessert. It often has round edges, like a circle. Most cooking traditions around the world include some form of it. It has pastry at the bottom. A layer of some other food, called the filling, comes next. It may also have a second layer of pastry on top of the filling. Without this second layer, people call it "open." There are recipes for it even in Roman writings that are two thousand years old. Until the 1900s, people usually made the filling out of meat or vegetables. Then fruit fillings became very popular.
What is it?

Unit 5, Practice 1, Page 125 (CD1, 23)

Ben is on a business trip. He is leaving a phone message for his wife, Rosie.

Hi Rosie, it's Ben. I left home in a big hurry this morning. Could you do a few things for me? The electricity bill is on the bookshelf. It is due tomorrow. Please pay it for me. Also, I left my glasses on the table. I'm afraid they might get broken. Can you put them on the desk for me? Oh, and I forgot it was Jenny's birthday. She will be upset. Would you mind getting her a card for me? What else … oh yes, remember to take Peter to his soccer game this afternoon. He will be waiting for you at school. Tell him I hope his team wins. Let me see … I fed the cat this morning – the poor girl seemed hungry! – but she didn't eat. Why don't you feed her a different kind of food tonight? Rosie, I'll be back tomorrow by 7 o'clock in the evening. I haven't forgotten it's your birthday. We both like Gino's restaurant, so I'll call and make a reservation for us. Miss you, and see you soon!

Unit 5, Practice 7, Page 131 (CD1, 24)

1.
Linda: Hello! Thanks for inviting us!
Mary: You're welcome. Please come in and make yourselves at home!
2.

Linda: Mary, this cake is delicious!
Mary: Thanks, I made it myself.
3.
Linda: Could I have some more cake?
Mary: Of course, Linda, please help yourself.
4.
Tony: Is this a photo of your twins when they were little?
Paul: Yes, they taught themselves to ride bikes when they were only four years old.
5.
Tony: Does Matthew still live at home?
Mary: No, he left home last year, and now he lives by himself.
6.
Tony: Is that an automatic light?
Paul: Yes, when you go into the room, it goes on by itself.
7.
Linda: What beautiful bookshelves!
Paul: Thank you, we couldn't make them ourselves, so a friend made them for us.

Unit 5, Practice 14, Page 138 (CD1, 25)

Customer: A loaf of bread, please.
Salesperson: Which kind?
Customer: I'm not sure. What's this one in front called?
Salesperson: It's called country farmhouse white.
Customer: And what's that one over there called?
Salesperson: The one on the top shelf? It's called German rye.
Customer: I'll take two of the white ones, please.
Salesperson: Would you like them sliced?
Customer: I'd like this one sliced, and that one unsliced, please.
Salesperson: Anything else?
Customer: Yes, I'd like four cupcakes.
Salesperson: I have cupcakes with orange or chocolate frosting. Which ones do you want?
Customer: The ones with the orange frosting.
Salesperson: Small or large?
Customer: The small ones, please. I don't like large ones.

Unit 5, Listening Puzzle, Page 143 (CD1, 26–27)

This is used at home by millions of people. The first models of it were invented in the late 1800s. However, it did not become common in homes until the 1920s. The earliest versions of it were very large and very dangerous. They contained poison gases that could leak out. After safer gases became available in the 1930s, this became more popular. It still contains gases, but they do not provide power to it. Electricity does. Instead, the gases carry heat away from food stored inside it. The food stays good a lot longer because this keeps it cool.
What is this?

Unit 6, Practice 1, Page 154 (CD1, 28)

1.
A: Stan is such a great swimmer!
B: I know. But he wasn't able to swim until he was 15 years old!
2.
A: So are we going to the concert this weekend?
B: I have to think about it. I can't make a decision right now.
3.
A: I regret that I won't be able to attend the meeting next Tuesday.
B: That's all right. Thank you for notifying me in advance.
4.
A: Anne broke her right arm last year.

B: You're kidding! She can use it very well now when she plays tennis.

5.
A: They weren't able to reach a decision at the meeting yesterday.
B: I can't believe it. The meeting lasted six hours!

6.
A: It's necessary to have a car in Los Angeles. Everything is so far apart.
B: Then I guess I'm at a big disadvantage there because I can't drive.

7.
A: Could you drive me home now?
B: Sure, I'd be happy to.

8.
A: The tech people are going to work on the server this afternoon.
B: Oh, no. We might not be able to get our email.

Unit 6, Practice 10, Page 163 (CD1, 29)

I'm having a lot of problems at work. My boss always gives me too much work, and I can never get it finished on time. Also, my desk area is much too small. I have so many papers and files that there's no room for them, and they end up all over the floor. And you wouldn't believe how hot it is in there. The heat is always on high, and it gives me a constant headache. But the worst thing is, I don't think any of my coworkers like me. They never ask me to eat lunch with them.

Unit 6, Practice 13, Page 166 (CD1, 30)

Gary: Julia and I decided to go to Spain for a vacation. We found a cheap hotel and flight package from a new discount travel agency.

Julia: I think that's where our troubles began. When we got to the airport, we found that the flight was overbooked. We didn't have seats. We had to wait six hours for the next flight.

Gary: Yeah. We didn't call ahead to confirm our seats. Anyway, we finally got to Spain, and to our hotel. After our flight problems, we couldn't wait to relax at the beach.

Julia: Yeah, but then we found out that the hotel was not near the beach, as the travel agent had said. It was at least two miles, 3.22 kilometers, away!

Gary: So we went out to eat at a nearby restaurant. But we couldn't speak any Spanish, and Julia had left her Spanish dictionary and phrasebook at home.

Julia: Yeah, we couldn't understand the menu at all. We both ordered meat, and we're both vegetarians!

Gary: It gets worse. When we got back to our hotel, we discovered my camera and cell phone were gone.

Unit 6, Listening Puzzle, Page 171 (CD1, 31–32)

This is a way of paying for things you buy. It became popular because it is light and easy to carry. It can be made of very cheap materials. No gold or other rare material has to be mined and processed when people use this. However, some people believe they had better not carry this. If it is stolen, it can easily be used by the thief. No one has to prove who he or she is in order to use it. Other people like to use this instead of other forms of payment. It is simple and easy to count. You don't have to do a lot of paperwork to keep track of your money when you use this. It comes in two forms - metal coins and paper bills.
What is it?

Unit 7, Practice 1, Page 181 (CD2, 2)

Rick and Olivia are having a cup of coffee between classes.

Rick: Shall we go to the movies tonight?
Olivia: Great idea! How about going to that new film at the Avon Cinema?
Rick: OK. Shall I pick you up at 5:30?
Olivia: Sure. Maybe we can go out to eat afterwards?
Rick: Great! Or we could eat at my place, if you like.
Olivia: Why don't we pick up some take-out Chinese food on the way to your house? Then you don't have to cook.
Rick: Perfect!

Unit 7, Practice 6A, Page 188 (CD2, 3)

1.
A: Could I leave work a little early today?
B: Certainly. That's fine.

2.
A: May I borrow your newspaper for a moment?
B: Of course.

3.
A: Could I have another cup of coffee?
B: Sure! Right away!

4.
A: Can Susan come to school early tomorrow? I want to help her with her math.
B: Of course. What time should she be there?

5.
A: May I hand in my paper a day late?
B: I'm sorry, but the date can't be changed.

6.
A: Can you give me five dollars, please?
B: Certainly not! I've already given you your allowance this week.

7.
A: Can I close the window?
B: Good idea. It's getting cold in here.

Unit 7, Practice 11A, Page 197 (CD2, 4)

Agatha Christie was a famous British author of mystery novels. But there was an incident in her own life that was mysterious — just like an incident from her novels. She married at the age of 24. Twelve years later, her husband Archie asked for a divorce because he had fallen in love with a younger woman. At this time, Agatha was upset by the death of her mother, and she suddenly disappeared. She was missing for three weeks. The police, newspaper reporters, and her husband searched for her everywhere. Finally, they found her. She was staying in a small hotel in Harrowgate, England, using the name Mrs. Neele. She told the police that she had lost her memory. No one knows why she went there or what she did during those three weeks. Soon after, she divorced her husband, and six months later she married again. She never talked about her mysterious disappearance incident again.

Unit 7, Practice 20, Page 207 (CD2, 5)

1.
A: What's happening next door? I heard people shouting this morning.
B: They must have been having an argument.

2.
A: I live in a five-story building. I heard a lot of noise on the stairs yesterday.
B: The new neighbor must have been moving in.

3.

A: The front door of the neighbor's house is open, and all the hall lights are on.
B: They must be expecting a lot of guests.
4.
A: I can hear a lot of loud music next door and people laughing and talking.
B: The neighbors must be having a party.
5.
A: There is smoke and the smell of delicious food coming from the backyard.
B: They must be cooking on the grill.
6.
A: They sent out invitations several weeks ago.
B: They must have been planning this party for some time.
7.
A: A delivery man from Christine's Bakery took a huge cake box into their house.
B: They must be celebrating a birthday.
8.
A: I called them to complain about the noise, but no one answered the phone.
B: They must be playing music too loud to hear anything.

Unit 7, Listening Puzzle, Page 211 (CD2, 6–7)

This island nation is longer (from north to south) than it is wide. It lies in one of the Earth's mild zones and has a pleasant climate. Only the highest parts of the country's main island get significant amounts of snow. The official head of state is a queen, and an elected legislature handles the day-to-day work of the government. Soccer and cricket are popular sports here, but no sport gets the nation as excited as rugby does. This land did not have a permanent human population until about AD 800. Its beautiful scenery is one reason why the Lord of the Rings movies were filmed here.
Which country is this?

Unit 8, Practice 3, Page 224 (CD2, 8)

1.
Many towns in the north have been cut off by snowstorms. The main highway to the north has been blocked by snow. The road is unable to be cleared because the snow is still coming down heavily.
2.
A total of two million dollars has been stolen from the National Bank in New York City. Two guards were taken to the hospital by Medical Emergency workers. Three men have been arrested in connection with the robbery. Another man is being questioned.
3.
Two teenage boys were found by the Coast Guard yesterday in a small boat far offshore. The boys and the boat had been missing since last Friday. The two boys were alive but weak. The boys were taken to the hospital. They are expected to recover soon.
4.
Two men are being sought in connection with a robbery at a gas station. The cashier was held up, but he wasn't injured. While the money was being stolen, the cashier was tied up by one of the men. The men escaped in a black truck which police think was used by the men in other robberies in the same area.

Unit 8, Practice 8A, Page 232 (CD2, 9)

1. Janice gets up at 8:00 A.M.
2. If she doesn't sleep enough, she gets tired by the end of the day.
3. She gets dressed before having her breakfast.
4. She gets her briefcase ready the night before.
5. She gets irritated when the bus is late.
6. She always gets her work done by the end of the day.
7. She doesn't like it when her boss gets angry.
8. She gets bored if she is not busy.
9. She would like to get another job next year.
10. She likes to go home before it gets dark.
11. She usually gets sleepy by 9:00 P.M.

Unit 8, Practice 15, Page 239 (CD2, 10)

1. He likes to wake up at 6:00 A.M. Please have the front desk call him at 6:00 A.M.
2. He likes to read three daily newspapers first thing in the morning. Please have the bellman deliver them.
3. He likes to have fresh fruit and coffee for breakfast at 7:00 A.M. Please have room service bring them at 7:00 A.M.
4. He doesn't like fresh flowers in his room. Don't have the florist put them in his room.
5. He needs three shirts to be washed every day. Please have the laundry wash them every day.
6. He needs a fax machine and a flat-screen TV installed in his room before he checks in. Please get the technical staff to install them.
7. He wants his shoes polished and left outside his door every morning. Please have the bellman polish them every morning.
8. He needs a limousine waiting for him in front of the hotel each day at 9:00 A.M. Please get a chauffeur to bring one each day at 9:00 A.M.

Unit 8, Practice 20A, Page 247 (CD2, 11)

I was born and brought up in Madrid. I was left alone a lot as a child and learned to look after myself. I did a lot of reading. One winter, while I was getting over the flu, I came across a book about Sherlock Holmes, the famous fictional detective. I loved it! And that's when I started thinking up mystery stories of my own and writing them down. I designed elaborate covers for the books and used up all the paper in the house. I gave them as presents to my family and challenged them to work out solutions to the crimes in my stories. My mother tried to get me to give up mystery stories and try some other form of fiction, but it was no good. Even now that I am older, I still read mysteries in my spare time. There's nothing like a good mystery to calm you down after a hectic day.

Unit 8, Listening Puzzle, Page 255 (CD2, 12–13)

This is an animal that lives most of its life in the water. It is a mammal. Whales and porpoises are its closest relatives. Water helps support its body weight, but it cannot float on the surface. Since it needs a breath of air every five minutes or so, it has to swim upward quite often. Instinct makes it do this automatically, even when it is asleep underwater. It eats only plants, but it is not gentle. It is believed to kill more people per year than any other animal. Despite its great weight, it can run twice as fast as a human. Even on land it has no trouble catching, biting, and crushing any human that annoys it. Its name comes from Greek words meaning "horse of the river."
What is it?

Unit 9, Practice 2, Page 266 (CD2, 14)

1.
A: The doctor said I could get heart disease.
B: Really? My doctor said I risk getting heart disease too!

2.
A: "It might be a good idea to go on a diet," she said.
B: My doctor also suggested going on a diet.

3.
A: I'm making other changes to improve my health. I decided not to drink coffee.
B: I decided to give up drinking coffee myself.

4.
A: It's difficult not to drink coffee when I'm tired.
B: For me, it's difficult to avoid drinking coffee in the mornings.

5.
A: I think that I shouldn't eat ice cream.
B: Me too. In fact, I want to stop eating ice cream and all other desserts.

6.
A: I sometimes buy a small bag of potato chips. They are so good!
B: I know. Sometimes I can't resist buying a bag of potato chips.

7.
A: I thought dieting would be hard. But it's OK to count calories at meals.
B: I don't mind counting calories at meals either.

8.
A: I used to cook a lot of rich food.
B: I used to enjoy cooking a lot of rich food, too.

9.
A: I have to learn to make new dishes with fewer calories.
B: I know what you mean. I have to practice making healthier meals.

10.
A: It's hard to make changes, but I want to take care of my health while I'm still young.
B: I feel the same way. I don't want to put off taking care of my health.

Unit 9, Practice 5, Page 270 (CD2, 15)

1. I can't type your report because I'm too busy typing my own report.
2. It's not worth watching movies in the theater because they come out on DVD very quickly.
3. There's no point in living in the city if you don't go out.
4. It's a waste of time complaining about your cell phone service.
5. The exam is over. It's no use worrying about it now.
6. I can't stand spending all of my money before the end of the month.

Unit 9, Practice 18, Page 285 (CD2, 16)

My first job was as a journalist for a local newspaper. Having spent four years in college earning a degree in English, I thought I would be able to do the job easily. I was pleased at having found the perfect job. After having made many corrections on my first article, my boss advised me to work harder. I tried hard, but I couldn't do better. After having been warned that I could lose my job, I started to worry. I think most people would get worried after having been told that they would lose their job. I felt like a complete failure. I felt angry at having been treated unfairly. I told my uncle that after having lost this job, I thought I would never find a job again. Having heard that, my uncle offered me a job as his personal assistant working for his magazine!

Unit 9, Practice 21, Page 288 (CD2, 17)

1. What would you do if you saw someone steal your car?
2. What would you do if you saw someone leave their car lights on?
3. What would you do if you heard someone breaking into your house at night?
4. What would you do if you heard someone scream and fall down the stairs?
5. What would you do if you noticed a mouse crawling towards your chair?
6. What would you do if you saw a spider sitting on your computer?

Unit 9, Listening Puzzle, Page 293 (CD2, 18–19)

This is a sport in which players kick a ball. Two teams compete on a grass-covered field. Several lines are marked on the field. At each end of the field is a goal line. A team can score points by making the ball go over a goal line. A structure called a "goal" marks the part of the line where points can be scored. A player called a goalkeeper tries to keep the ball from crossing the goal line. A net is attached to the goal structure. Touching the ball with one's hands is not allowed. Only the goalkeeper is allowed to do this. What is this sport?

Unit 10, Practice 3, Page 306 (CD2, 20)

There are 20 students in my daughter's class. Elena, along with all the other students, is taking a test right now. The subject of the test is mathematics. All of the children are allowed to use a calculator, which makes it easier. The instructions for the exam are on the board. There is a separate answer sheet for each section of the exam. The answers are written in pencil. My daughter, along with all the other students in the class, is trying hard to pass the exam. All of the children, except Elena, are having trouble with the questions. Elena is one of the few students who is able to finish all the questions on time.

Unit 10, Practice 11, Page 312 (CD2, 21)

1. In order to maintain youth and good health, we need to have a combination of exercise and proper nutrition.
2. Exercise is good for our physical health and psychology. Exercise is good for our physical and psychological health.
3. Regular exercise improves digestion, increases energy, burns fat, and lowers blood cholesterol.
4. It also reduces stress and anxiety, which are the main reasons for many illnesses and conditions.
5. Also, regular exercise elevates mood, increases feelings of well-being, and reduces anxiety and depression.
6. When you start an exercise program, remember to start out slowly, listen to your body, and gradually increase the difficulty and length of the exercise.
7. There are many different forms of moderate exercise including daily walking, bicycling, or even gardening.

Unit 10, Practice 17, Page 318 (CD2, 22)

1. Both vitamin C and calcium are important for good health.
2. Both your teeth and bones need calcium.
3. Either milk or products from milk contain a lot of calcium.
4. Both children and the elderly require calcium.
5. Neither chicken nor pork has much calcium.
6. Not only milk products but also green vegetables contain calcium.
7. Neither the liver nor the blood makes calcium.
8. Either food or drink gives the body the calcium it needs.

Unit 10, Listening Puzzle, Page 319 (CD2, 23–24)

This is a material used in making clothes. It can be produced in many different forms. Some are light and airy. Others are dense and heavy. It does not wrinkle very easily. This is good, because clothing made from it should not be ironed. Older forms of it could be uncomfortable to wear. Newer forms are more comfortable and less smelly. It is used in making clothing that will dry very quickly. It was first sold in the United States in 1951. If exposed to high heat, it will melt, not burn.
What is it?

Unit 11, Practice 4, Page 332 (CD2, 25)

1. How many people does your company employ?
2. When did the company first get started?
3. Where is the head office?
4. What are the job benefits?
5. How many vacation days do people get?
6. What is the salary?
7. Who will my manager be?
8. When does the job start?

Unit 11, Practice 8, Page 335 (CD2, 26)

Alice is thinking of having a birthday party at the Paradise Restaurant. She is asking her friend Todd about the restaurant.

Alice: Did we eat lunch there together last year, or didn't we?
Todd: I can't remember if we ate lunch there together last year.
Alice: Did we like the food?
Todd: I can't remember whether or not we liked the food.
Alice: Are they open for lunch on Saturday?
Todd: I don't know if they're open for lunch on Saturday.
Alice: Is there a fixed price lunch menu?
Todd: I don't know whether there's a fixed price lunch menu or not.
Alice: Are there enough tables for 50 guests?
Todd: I don't know if there are enough tables for 50 guests.
Alice: Do they have live music?
Todd: I can't say if they have live music.
Alice: Can they order a special birthday cake?
Todd: Good question. I wonder if they can order a special birthday cake.

Unit 11, Practice 14, Page 343 (CD2, 27)

Cindy: This is Cindy from the dentist's office. I'm calling to remind you that you have a dental appointment tomorrow at ten o'clock.
Janet: Hi, it's Janet. I just want to say hello. I'll call you later.
Ken: My name is Ken Stevens. I've been trying to reach you to talk about the new work schedule. My number is 678-555-9542. Please call me back. Thanks.
Tony: This is Tony from the Travel Shop. Your tickets will be ready tomorrow. If you'd like us to mail them to you, we can send them by regular mail or express mail. Let me know.
Jim: Hey, it's Jim. My boss gave me two tickets for the Wild Rockers concert next week. Do you want to go with me?
Mother: It's your mother, dear. I called you at work and you weren't there. I've been calling you at home, but there's no answer. Where are you? I'm worried. Please call me.

Unit 11, Practice 17, Page 347 (CD2, 28)

1. Listen carefully.
2. Don't talk.

3. Please put all your books and papers away.
4. Please do not try to copy your neighbor's work.
5. Cheating will be severely punished.
6. I will fail anyone who cheats.
7. Check the answers carefully before handing in your exam.
8. You will get a prize if you finish all the questions.
9. Would someone like to help me give out the papers?
10. Would you like me to repeat the instructions?

Unit 11, Practice 19, Page 349 (CD2, 29)

A 17-year-old boy was arrested for stealing CDs from a music store. He was sent to a youth correctional facility for a month. What were the opinions of the people involved in the case?

1. The judge recommended that he go to jail for two months.
2. The parents demanded that he get another trial.
3. The lawyer suggested that he do community service.
4. The police officer insisted that he repay the money to the store owner.
5. The store owner requested that he return the CDs.

Unit 11, Listening Puzzle, Page 351 (CD2, 30–31)

This is a way of recording information. It lets you go back to the information again and again. It also lets you find the specific information you need without going through all of it. It is easy to carry. It is also very sturdy. It usually will not break if it is dropped. There are special kinds of it that blind people can use. It can be made entirely by hand. However, almost all of them are now made by machine. They have been made this way since about the year 1450.
What is it?

Unit 12, Practice 6, Page 367 (CD3, 2)

1. Martin Luther King, Jr., was a civil rights leader whose most famous speech contains the words, "I have a dream."
2. Abraham Lincoln was a president of the United States whose most famous achievement was freeing African-Americans from slavery.
3. Benjamin Franklin was an American statesman and inventor whose most famous invention was the lightning rod.
4. Wilbur and Orville Wright were brothers whose aircraft was the first wooden, piloted, heavier-than-air, self-propelled machine to fly.
5. Dorothea Lange was a photographer whose photos made people realize the poverty of workers during the Great Depression.
6. Alice Walker is an African-American writer whose novel *The Color Purple* received the Pulitzer Prize in 1983.
7. Elizabeth Cady Stanton was a leader of the American women's rights movement whose lifetime of work helped women gain the right to vote in the United States.

Unit 12, Practice 11, Page 373 (CD3, 3)

A: Let's go to lunch with Barbara.
B: Not with Barbara. I don't really like her.
A: Why not?
B: Well, she always tries to give advice, most of which is useless.
A: That's not so bad.
B: And she talks about all the designer clothes she has, none of which we ever see on her. She tells everyone about how much money she spends on things, all of which can't be true because we all know how much she makes.
A: I see.

B: She talks about her two "beautiful" children, both of whom look like her, and she is definitely not a beauty.

A: Uh-huh.

B: She always talks about choosing a medical school for her son and daughter, neither of whom is doing very well in high school. She also talks about her wonderful husband and how good he is to her, a little of which must be true, because he has put up with her for so long!

A: Uh-huh. Oh! Hi, Barbara. Would you like to go to lunch ... with me?

Unit 12, Practice 13B, Page 375 (CD3, 4)

1. The teacher encouraged me, which motivated me to work harder.
2. The teacher corrected my paper in red ink, which helped me find my mistakes.
3. She let us use the Internet to do our research, which was easier than finding books from the library.
4. We didn't have tests every week in class, which made us feel less pressure.
5. We wrote about the news of the day, which made me read newspapers and listen to the news.
6. We worked with other students in class, which helped me make new friends.
7. The teacher always paid a lot of attention to us, which made us feel like she cared about us.
8. We lost points when we handed in homework late, which meant I had to do my homework on time.

Unit 12, Practice 16, Page 379 (CD3, 5)

1. Most of the coffee that is grown in Brazil is exported.
2. The most popular hot beverage that is drunk by Americans is coffee.
3. Strawberries, bananas, tomatoes, and other fruits that are sold in supermarkets are often unripe when they are picked.
4. Much of the fast food that is eaten by young people contains a lot of fat.
5. Hamburgers that are served on wheat buns are healthier.
6. Food that is taken from the freezer must be defrosted before cooking.
7. Some people like potatoes that are mashed with butter; others prefer potatoes that are fried in oil.
8. Roquefort is a French cheese that is stored in caves.

Unit 12, Listening Puzzle, Page 381 (CD3, 6–7)

This is a place to get rid of the waste produced in ordinary homes. Humans have used it for thousands of years. Most of the waste put here does not last very long. However, some things are not destroyed. These remaining items can tell us a lot about past civilizations. For example, bones or broken containers here can tell us about their eating habits. This waste system is sometimes criticized as bad for the environment. Waste can leak from it into underground streams. Also, it is criticized for using valuable land. As populations grow, even more land will be needed for this. What is it?

Unit 13, Practice 7, Page 398 (CD3, 8)

Joanna wanted to go to the United States so that she could improve her English. She enrolled in an English program at a university so that she could learn quickly. She lived with her uncle and aunt, who wanted to speak their language with her; therefore, she couldn't practice English at home. At first, her English wasn't very good. Therefore, she had to work hard. She learned to keep

a notebook with her at all times so that she could write down new idioms and expressions that she heard. Also, she joined some clubs at the university. Many American students became her friends; therefore, she was able to practice with them.

After six months, her English was very good. Therefore, she decided to return home. She bought a computer so that she could stay in touch with her American friends. Now she is looking for a job in tourism so that she will be able to use her English at work.

Unit 13, Practice 15, Page 405 (CD3, 9)

1. After she finishes an assignment, Julia checks her work carefully.
2. When her work is completed, Julia's friends can call her up on the phone.
3. Since she started her new schedule, Julia has been much happier.
4. When the instructor gives a new assignment, Julia starts work on it immediately.
5. While the instructor is handing out the grades, Julia feels very anxious.
6. Julia knows that she must stay healthy, so she runs every day and eats lots of fruit.
7. Before she returns home, she goes to the coffee shop with her friends.
8. When Julia gets a good grade, her parents are very pleased.

Unit 13, Listening Puzzle, Page 407 (CD3, 10–11)

This is a kind of storm. It can damage homes and other property. A very severe one may also kill people. The worst part of it is the strong wind. Scientists have measured winds as high as 318 miles, 512 kilometers, per hour in one of these storms. That is the highest wind speed ever recorded on Earth. Usually, it strikes a small area. It may destroy the homes on one side of a street but leave the other side untouched. This storm is far more common in the United States than anywhere else. On average, the state of Texas sees 126 of these storms each year.
What is it?

Unit 14, Practice 14B, Page 434 (CD3, 12)

1. My car broke down.
2. I ate all the food in my refrigerator.
3. I didn't pay my phone bill last month.
4. I spent all the money on my credit card.
5. I was late for work and got fired.
6. I couldn't find another job.

Unit 14, Practice 16, Page 435 (CD3, 13)

1. I'm not athletic.
2. I'm not rich.
3. I don't have much free time.
4. I have to work very hard.
5. I can't sing or dance.
6. I can't drive a car.
7. I don't have a boyfriend.
8. I worry about my life all the time.

Unit 14, Listening Puzzle, Page 437 (CD3, 14–15)

This is a dairy product. That means it is produced from the milk of an animal. Usually, the milk of cows is used. The origins of it are unknown. Most experts think it was first made somewhere in southwest Asia. A common guess is that it was made by accident. If warm milk was carried in a goatskin bag, this could form ... Most

kinds of it are solid at normal temperatures. Some modern types of it smell very bad. Some even contain lines of blue or green mold. Milder kinds are commonly used as pizza toppings.
What is it?

Index

Photo Credits

Page xii: © BananaStock/JupiterImages; xiii: © image 100 Ltd.; 1: © Jim Sugar/Corbis; 2: © Brand X Pictures/PunchStock; 7: © Ryan McVay/Getty Images; 8: © RubberBall Productions/Getty Images; 12: © The McGraw-Hill Companies, Inc./Lars A. Niki, photographer; 16: © liquidlibrary/PictureQuest; 18 (top): © Ryan McVay/Getty Images; 18 (bottom): © The McGraw-Hill Companies, Inc./Jill Braaten, photographer; 19 (top): © Simon Marcus/Corbis; 19 (bottom): © Mark Downey/Getty Images; 20: © Hyphen-Engineering Education (Thanos Tsilis); 21 (left to right): © Royalty-Free/Corbis, © Steven P. Lynch, © Getty Images; 22: © MedioImages/PictureQuest; 23 : © Jim Sugar/Corbis; 24: © Royalty-Free/Corbis; 29: © Reuters/Corbis; 30: © Digital Vision; 34: © Library of Congress; 35: © Reuters/Corbis; 36: © Liquidlibrary/Dynamic Graphics/Jupiterimages; 39: © Royalty-Free/Corbis; 40: © Hyphen-Engineering Education (Thanos Tsilis); 44: © Michael Ochs Archives/Corbis; 48: © Pixland/PunchStock; 49 (left to right): © Lee Snider/Photo Images/Corbis, © Royalty-Free/Corbis, © Purestock/Getty Images; 52: © Hyphen-Engineering Education; 57: © Image Source / JupiterImages; 58: © C Squared Studios/Getty Images; 62: © Digital Vision; 63: © Image Source/JupiterImages; 66: © Doug Menuez/Getty Images; 69: © Eric Audras/Photoalto/PictureQuest; 69 (inset): © Royalty-Free/Corbis; 70: © Hyphen-Engineering Education; 72: © Vicky Kasala/Getty Images; 75: © Digital Vision/Getty Images; 76: © Corbis/PunchStock; 79: © Hyphen-Engineering Education (Thanos Tsilis); 81 (left to right): © Brand X Pictures/PunchStock, © Brand X Pictures/PunchStock, © StockTrek/Getty Images; 82: © Courtesy NSSDC Goddard Space Flight Center; 84: © Jeremy Hoare/Life File/Getty Images; 89: © Royalty-Free/Corbis; 90: © Photo courtesy of USDA Natural Resources Conservation Service; 93: © Santokh Kochar/Getty Images; 95 (top): © Library of Congress Prints and Photographs Division [LC-USZ62-120430]; 95 (bottom): © Buccina Studios/Getty Images; 97 (left to right): © Jules Frazier/Getty Images, Jules Frazier/Getty Images, Royalty-Free/Corbis; 99: © Hyphen-Engineering Education; 100: © Christie's Images/Corbis; 101: © Patricia Brabant/Cole Group/Getty Images; 104: © Ryan McVay/Getty Images; 106: © Brand X Pictures; 109: © Royalty-Free/Corbis; 110 (left): Scott T. Baxter / Getty Images; 110 (right): Digital Vision/PunchStock; 111: © Comstock/Corbis; 112: © Hyphen-Engineering Education (Thanos Tsilis); 113 (left to right): © Ingram Publishing/Fotosearch, © Randy Allbritton/Getty Images, © Burke/Triolo Productions/Getty Images; 115: © Digital Vision/PunchStock; 116: © Burke/Triolo Productions/Getty Images; 121: © Brand X Pictures/PunchStock; 122: © Imagesource/Jupiterimages; 130: © Duncan Smith/Getty Images; 132: © Liquidlibrary/Dynamic Graphics/Jupiterimages; 134: © Brand X Pictures/PunchStock; 138: © PhotoLink/Getty Images; 139: © Brand X Pictures/PunchStock; 142: © Hyphen-Engineering Education (Thanos Tsilis); 143 (left to right): © Royalty-Free/Corbis, © Getty Images/Jonelle Weaver, © McGraw-Hill Companies/Jill Braaten, photographer; 146: © Library of Congress, Prints and Photographs Division [LC-USZ62-43603]; 151: © Frank Trapper/Corbis; 152: © Dex Image/PictureQuest; 153: © Big Cheese Photo/JupiterImages; 155: © Royalty-Free/Corbis; 156: © Royalty-Free/Corbis; 157: © Jack Hollingsworth/Getty Images; 159: © Dynamic Graphics/PictureQuest; 162: © Photodisc/Getty Images; 164: © PhotoDisc/Getty Images; 167: © Stockbyte/PunchStock; 169: © Hyphen-Engineering Education (Thanos Tsilis); 171 (left to right): © Don Farrall/Getty Images, : © Don Farrall/Getty Images, © C Squared Studios/Getty Images; 172: © Stockbyte/Punchstock Images; 174: © Frank Trapper/Corbis; 179: © Stockbyte/PunchStock; 180: © BananaStock/JupiterImages; 182: © Stockbyte/Punchstock; 186: © Stockbyte/PunchStock; 188: © Brand X Pictures/PunchStock; 190: © Punchstock; 193: © Scott T. Baxter/Getty Images; 194: © Keith Brofsky/Getty Images; 197: © Bettmann/Corbis; 198: © Brand X Pictures/PunchStock; 200: © trbfoto/Brand X Pictures/Jupiterimages; 202: © Brand X Pictures/PunchStock; 204: © Getty Images/Digital Vision; 208: © Royalty-Free/Corbis; 209: © Hyphen-Engineering Education (Thanos Tsilis); 211 (all): © Hyphen-Engineering Education; 213: © image100/PunchStock; 214: © Ryan Briscall/Design Pics/Corbis; 219: © C Squared Studios/Getty Images; 220: © Brand X Pictures/PunchStock; 226: © Brand X Pictures/PunchStock; 229: © Thinkstock Images/Jupiterimages; 231: © Corbis; 233: © C Squared Studios/Getty Images; 235: © Suza Scalora/Getty Images; 237: © Stockbyte/PunchStock; 240: © Skip Nall/Getty Images; 241: © David Buffington/Getty Images; 243: © Rubberball/Superstock; 248: © C. Borland/PhotoLink/Getty Images; 253: © Hyphen-Engineering Education (Thanos Tsilis); 255 (left to right): © Brand X Pictures/PunchStock, © Royalty-Free/Corbis, © Digital Vision/Getty Images; 256: © Creatas/PunchStock; 258: © StockTrek/Getty Images; 263: © Brand X Pictures/PunchStock; 264: © Digital Vision; 268: © Stockbyte/PunchStock; 271: © Getty Images/Digital Vision; 273: © Brand X Pictures/PunchStock; 276: © Stockbyte/PunchStock; 278: © Jules Frazier/Getty Images; 281: © C. Borland/PhotoLink/Getty Images; 283: © Jack Star/PhotoLink/Getty Images; 287: © Joshua Ets-Hokin/Getty Images; 288: © Stockbyte/PictureQuest; 290: © Hyphen-Engineering Education (Thanos Tsilis); 293 (left to right): © Brand X Pictures/PunchStock, © PhotoLink/Photodisc/Getty Images, © Jeff Maloney/Getty Images; 296: © Kim Kulish/Corbis; 301: © Getty Images/Digital Vision; 302: © Getty Images/Digital Vision; 305: © BananaStock/PictureQuest; 306: © Doug Menuez/Getty Images; 307: © The McGraw-Hill Companies, Inc.; 308: © Tanya Constantine/